ADVANCED TEXTBOOK ON TRADITIONAL CHINESE MEDICINE AND PHARMACOLOGY

Vol.IV

●Acupuncture and Moxibustion

NEW WORLD PRESS   BEIJING, CHINA

First Edition 1997

Written by Ming Shunpei, Yang Shunyi
Translated by Huang Jiexin, Lu Cheng
Edited by Bai Jin
Book design by Li Hui

Copyright by NEW WORLD PRESS, Beijing, China.
All rights reserved. No part of this book may be
reproduced in any form or by any means without
permission in writing from the publisher.

ISBN 7-80005-301-6

Published by
New World Press
24 Baiwanzhuang Road, Beijing 100037, China

Distributed by
China International Book Trading Corporation
35 Chegongzhuang Xilu, Beijing 100044, China
P.O.Box 399, Beijing, China

Printed in the People's Republic of China

Members of the Editorial Board

Cai Jingfeng	Jiang Jian	Yang Weiyi
Chao Guci	Li Anbang	Yu Xiaodan
Chen Daojin	Li Fei	Yu Yongjie
Chen Keji	Li Liangyu	Zeng Shouzeng
Chen Xianqing	Li Lixia	Zhang Dianpu
Cheng Xizhen	Li Yanwen	Zhang Guoliang
Dong Lianrong	Liu Darong	Zhang Haoliang
Fang Boying	Liu Yanchi	Zhang Kai
Fang Tingyu	Liu Xuehua	Zhang Ruifu
Fu Shiyuan	Luo Yikuan	Zhang Xinchun
Fu Weikang	Ou Ming	Zhou Jingping
Hou Can	Qian Chenghui	Zhou Xuesheng
Huang Yabei	Sun Meizhen	Zhen Zhiya
Huang Yuezhong	Wang Lufen	Zuo Yanfu
Hui Jiyuan	Xu Yizhi	

FOREWORD

In order to promote international exchange in the field of traditional Chinese medicine and to meet the needs of increasingly large numbers of foreign students studying traditional Chinese medicine, the Foreign Affairs Bureau of the State Education Commission and the Department of Traditional Chinese Medicine under the Ministry of Public Health (now the State Administration of Traditional Chinese Medicine and Pharmacy) held a meeting in Guangzhou in April 1986 to examine and approve textbooks of traditional Chinese medicine for foreign students. Eight textbooks for use by foreign students were examined during the meeting, including *Basic Theory of Traditional Chinese Medicine* and *The History of Traditional Chinese Medicine* compiled by the Beijing College of Traditional Chinese Medicine, *Traditional Chinese Internal Medicine* and *The Chinese Language* compiled by the Shanghai College of Traditional Chinese Medicine, *Chinese Pharmacy* and *The Science of Traditional Chinese Prescriptions* compiled by the Nanjing College of Traditional Chinese Medicine, and *Traditional Chinese Diagnosis* and *The Science of Acupuncture and Moxibustion* compiled by the Guangzhou College of Traditional Chinese Medicine.

The four colleges of traditional Chinese medicine involved in the compilation of the textbooks have been teaching foreign students for five to ten years, during which time they have accumulated a great deal of experience. Most of the editors have experience in compiling textbooks in the fields of study used nationwide by full-time colleges of traditional Chinese medicine. Many of these textbooks have long been used in teaching foreign students. As a result, they are both comprehensive and applicable.

This series of textbooks draws on the contents of the fourth and fifth editions of national textbooks used by full-time colleges of traditional Chinese medicine and takes into consideration the fact that foreign students have a relatively short time for classroom studies and that there are differences in cultures and traditions. Such aspects as the depth and range of the contents, and the scientific, ideological and advanced level of the textbooks have been carefully considered. Efforts have been made to shorten and simplify while preserving the essence of traditional Chinese medicine and its systematic theories.

The publication of these textbooks marks a great achievement in the dissemination of traditional Chinese medicine. Training foreign students is an important way of spreading traditional Chinese medicine throughout the world. We hope that teachers and students will comment on any shortcomings they discover in this series of textbooks so that we may alter and improve subsequent editions.

State Administration of Traditional
Chinese Medicine and Pharmacy
1991

ACUPUNCTURE AND MOXIBUSTION

CONTENTS

PART ONE MERIDIANS AND ACUPOINTS ... 1

Chapter One An Introduction to Acupoints ... 3
Section 1 Classification of Acupoints ... 3
Section 2 Therapeutic Effects of Acupoints ... 3
Section 3 Specific Points ... 5
Section 4 Method of Locating Acupoints ... 7

Chapter Two Meridians and Acupoints ... 10
Section 1 The Twelve Meridians ... 10
Section 2 The Eight Extra Meridians ... 100
Section 3 The Extra Acupoints ... 117

PART TWO MANIPULATION OF ACUPUNCTURE AND MOXIBUSTION ... 125

Chapter One Manipulation of Filiform Needle ... 127
Section 1 Structure, Specifications and Storage of Filiform Needle ... 127
Section 2 Needling Practice ... 128
Section 3 Preparations for Acupuncture Therapy ... 128
Section 4 Methods of Insertion ... 130
Section 5 Precautions and Emergency Handling ... 137
Section 6 Points for Attention ... 140

Chapter Two Manipulations of the Three-Edged and Dermal Needles ... 141
(Appendix: Manipulation of Intradermal Needle)
Section 1 Manipulation of Three-Edged Needle ... 141
Section 2 Manipulation of the Dermal Needle ... 143
Appendix: Manipulation of Intradermal Needle ... 144

Chapter Three Moxibustion (Appendix: Cupping) ... 146
Section 1 Effects of Moxibustion ... 146
Section 2 Classification and Application ... 146
Section 3 Points for Attention ... 151
Appendix: Cupping ... 151

Chapter Four Electroacupuncture, Acupoint Injection and Acupoint Magnetotherapy ... 154
Section 1 Electroacupuncture ... 154
Section 2 Acupoint Injection ... 156

Section 3 Acupoint Magnetotherapy ... 159

Chapter Five Ear and Scalp Acupuncture ... 163
Section 1 Ear Acupuncture ... 163
Section 2 Scalp Acupuncture ... 171

PART THREE THERAPEUTICS ... 177

Chapter One Introduction ... 179
Section 1 Principles of Syndrome Differentiation ... 179
Section 2 Therapeutic Effects ... 186
Section 3 The Principles of Treatment ... 187
Section 4 Acupoint Selection in Acupuncture and Moxibustion ... 189

Chapter Two Treatment of Various Kinds of Diseases ... 198
Section 1 Internal Diseases ... 198
Section 2 Gyniatrics and Pediatrics ... 245
Section 3 Surgical Diseases ... 260
Section 4 Diseases of Eyes, Ears, Nose and Throat ... 270
Section 5 Emergency Treatment ... 277

APPENDIX ... 291

Annex 1 Acupuncture Anesthesia ... 293
Annex 2 *Ziwuliuzhu* Acupuncture ... 297

PART ONE
MERIDIANS AND ACUPOINTS

PART ONE

MEMBRANES AND CYTOSOLS

Chapter One
AN INTRODUCTION TO ACUPOINTS

Acupoints are the sites where *qi* of *zang-fu* organs and meridians spreads to the body surface. They are used to give treatment in the form of acupuncture and moxibustion.

Section 1
CLASSIFICATION OF ACUPOINTS

Acupoints fall into three categories, namely, points along the fourteen meridians, extra points and *ashi* points.

1. Acupoints Along the Fourteen Meridians
Points along the fourteen meridians, "meridian points" for short, refer to the acupoints along the twelve regular meridians as well as *Ren* (Conception Vessel) and *Du* (Governor Vessel) meridians. These points total 361, accounting for the greatest part of the acupoints on the body. They share the function of treating diseases involving these meridians.

2. Extra Points
Extra points refer to the acupoints which have their names and locations but are not included in the fourteen meridians. They are extremely effective for certain diseases.

3. *Ashi* Points
Ashi points refer to the spots which respond to pressure easily and can be used as acupoints for acupuncture and moxibustion, though they have no specific names or locations. They are also called tender points or *tianying* points.

Section 2
THERAPEUTIC EFFECTS OF ACUPOINTS

1. The Effect on the Proximal Area
This effect is the general character of all acupoints. Every acupoint is able to treat disorders in the proximal area and nearby tissues and organs. For instance, acupoints on the eye such as *Jingming* (BL 1) and *Chengqi* (ST 1) can be used to treat disorders of eyes; *Zhongwan* (RN 12) and *Liangmen* (ST 21) are chosen to cure abdominal pain and stomachache.

2. The Effect on the Remote Area
The points along the fourteen meridians, especially those of the twelve points below the elbow and knee, have an effect on diseases in the remote area. They are also effective in treating disorders in the

remote tissues and *zang-fu* organs located along the fourteen meridians, and some of them can even influence the whole body. For example, *Hegu* (LI 4) can be used to treat the diseases of the mouth and face, and *Zusanli* (ST 36) can help adjust the function of digestive system and improve the immunologic function and defense mechanism.

3. Special Effect

Some acupoints have two regulatory functions. For example, to insert a needle into the *Neiguan* (PC 6) point can help alleviate both tachycardia and bradycardia. Besides, some acupoints are especially effective for certain ailments, such as *Dazhui* (DU 14) point for fever and *Zhiyin* (BL 67) for abnormal fetal position. For indications of acupoints along the fourteen meridians, see Table 1.

Table 1 Indications of Acupoints Along the Fourteen Meridians

Three *Yin* Meridians of Hand

Meridians	Indications		
	Indications of Individual Meridian	Indications of Two Meridians in Common	Indications of Three Meridians in Common
Lung Meridian of Hand-*Taiyin*	Lung and throat diseases		
Pericardium Meridian of Hand-*Jueyin*	Heart and stomach diseases	Mental disorders	Thoracopathy
Heart Meridian of Hand-*Shaoyin*	Heart diseases		

Three *Yang* Meridians of Hand

Meridians	Indications		
	Indications of Individual Meridian	Indications of Two Meridians in Common	Indications of Three Meridians in Common
Large Intestine Meridian of Hand-*Yangming*	Forehead, nose, mouth and tooth diseases		
Sanjiao Meridian of Hand-*Shaoyang*	Temporal and hypochondriac diseases	Eye and ear diseases	Throat and febrile diseases
Small Intestine Meridian of Hand-*Taiyang*	Occipital, scapular and mental diseases		

Three *Yang* Meridians of Foot

Meridians	Indications	
	Indications of Individual Meridian	Indications of Three Meridians in Common
Stomach Meridian of Foot-*Yangming*	Forehead, mouth, tooth, throat, stomach and intestinal diseases	
Gallbladder Meridian of Foot-*Shaoyang*	Temporal, ear and hypochondriac diseases	Eye diseases, mental disorders and febrile diseases
Bladder Meridian of Foot-*Taiyang*	Occipital, dorsolumbar diseases (*zang-fu* disorders)	

Three *Yin* Meridians of Foot

Meridians	Indications	
	Indications of Individual Meridian	Indications of Three Meridians in Common
Spleen Meridian of Foot-*Taiyin*	Spleen and stomach diseases	
Liver Meridian of Foot-*Jueyin*	Liver diseases	External genital and gynecological diseases
Kidney Meridian of Foot-*Shaoyin*	Kidney, lung and throat diseases	

Ren and *Du* Meridians

Meridians	Indications	
	Indications of Individual Meridian	Indications of Two Meridians in Common
Ren Meridian	Prolapse of *yang*, collapse, prostration syndromes (for general tonification)	Mental disorders, diseases of *zang-fu* organs, and gynecological diseases
Du Meridian	Apoplexy, coma, febrile diseases and disorders of the head and face	

SECTION 3
SPECIFIC POINTS

Specific points refer to those meridian acupoints with special effects. Since they have different functions, their names and meanings vary.

1. Five *Shu* Points

They refer to the five specific acupoints of the twelve regular meridians located below the elbow or knee joints, namely, *jiing** (well), *ying* (spring), *shu* (stream), *jing* (river) and *he* (sea) points. They are located from the tips of fingers and toes to the elbow and knee. Ancient physicians compared the flow of *qi* in the meridians to that of water, which explains its movement from the surface to the deep in a growing quantity.

Jiing points are the places where the *qi* of the meridians starts to flow, just like the water coming out of a well. *Ying* points are where the *qi* of the meridians starts to flourish, like the water in a spring. *Shu* points are the places where the *qi* of the meridians flourishes and rushes out, just like the water flowing in a stream. *Jing* points are where the *qi* of the meridians flows like the water in a river. *He* points are where the *qi* of the meridians accumulates like the confluence of rivers into a sea.

2. *Yuan* and *Luo* Points

Yuan refers to the origin and primordial *qi*, and each of the twelve regular meridians has a source point. The *yuan* points are of great significance for the diagnosis and treatment of diseases in the meridians and *zang-fu* organs.

Luo means connecting. Each of the twelve meridians as well as the *Ren* and *Du* meridians has a collateral branching out from a meridian, and the place where the collateral stems from is called a *luo* point. There are altogether 15 *luo* points including the *Dabao* (SP 21) point which is the major collateral of the spleen. There is another statement which says that there are 16 *luo* points, because in ancient

---

* In Chinese phonetic alphabet, "well" and "river" spell in the same way. In order to distinguish them, we add an "i" to "jing" which represents the third tone in Chinese pronunciation, meaning the well.

times there was a point called *xuli*, which is the great collateral of the stomach. The *luo* points can be used to treat diseases along the superficial and deep meridians and the areas they run through.

3. Back *Shu* Points and Front *Mu* Points

Back *shu* points refer to the acupoints where the *qi* of *zang-fu* organs flows to the back and lumbar region, while the front *mu* points on the chest and abdomen are where the *qi* of *zang-fu* organs accumulates. If any *zang-fu* organ is diseased, its corresponding back *shu* point or the front *mu* point would show abnormal reactions such as pain on pressure. For instance, if the lung is diseased, an abnormal sign will appear at the *Feishu* (BL 13) and *Zhongfu* (LU 1) points, with the former belonging to the back *shu* points and the latter the front *mu* points.

4. Eight Influential Points

Eight influential points refer to the eight acupoints where the essence of *zang*, *fu*, *qi*, blood, tendons, vessels, bones and marrow meet together. They are

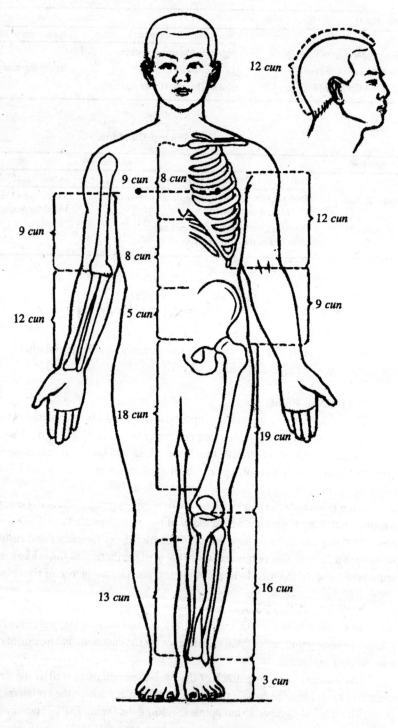

Fig. 1-1 Bone-Length Measurement

Zhangmen (LR 13) corresponding to *zang* organs, *Zhongwan* (RN 12) to *fu* organs, *Danzhong* (RN 17) to *qi*, *Geshu* (BL 17) to blood, *Yanglingquan* (GB 34) to tendons, *Taiyuan* (LU 9) to vessels, *Dazhu* (BL 11) to bones and *Xuanzhong* (GB 39) to the marrow.

5. Eight Confluent Points

Eight confluent points, spreading below the elbows and knees, are where the *qi* of the eight extra meridians meets that of the twelve regular meridians. The *Gongsun* (SP 4) point enters the abdomen through the Spleen Meridian of Foot-*Taiyin* and meets *Guanyuan* (RN 4) point before linking with the *Chong* Meridian (Thoroughfare Vessel). *Neiguan* (PC 6) emerges in the chest through the Pericardium Meridian of Hand-*Jueyin* and connects the *Yinwei* Meridian (*Yin* Link Vessel). *Waiguan* (SJ 5) enters the shoulder through the *Sanjiao* Meridian of Hand-*Shaoyang* and connects the *Yangwei* Meridian (*Yang* Link Vessel). *Linqi* (GB 41) travels along the hypochondrium through the Gallbladder Meridian of Foot-*Shaoyang* and connects the *Dai* Meridian (Belt Vessel). *Shenmai* (BL 62) communicates with the *Yangqiao* Meridian (*Yang* Heel Vessel) through the Bladder Meridian of Foot-*Taiyang*. *Houxi* (SI 3) communicates with the *Du* Meridian (Governor Vessel) through the Small Intestine Meridian of Hand-*Taiyang* and meets the *Dazhui* (DU 14) point. *Zhaohai* (KI 6) enters the abdomen and then the chest through the Kidney Meridian of Foot-*Shaoyin*, and communicates with the *Yinqiao* Meridian (*Yin* Heel Vessel). *Lieque* (LU 7) travels along the throat and communicates with the *Ren* Meridian (Conception Vessel) through the Lung Meridian of Hand-*Taiyin*.

6. Xi (Cleft) Points

Cleft points refer to the sites where the *qi* of the meridians accumulates deep. There are 16 cleft points located at the twelve meridians as well as *Yangqiao*, *Yinqiao*, *Yangwei* and *Yinwei* meridians.

7. Lower Confluent Points

Lower confluent points refer to the six acupoints where the *qi* of six *fu* organs runs downward to the three *yang* meridians of the foot. They are *Shangjuxu* (ST 37) corresponding to the large intestine, *Xiajuxu* (ST 39) to the small intestine, *Weiyang* (BL 39) to *sanjiao*, *Weizhong* (BL 40) to the urinary bladder, *Zusanli* (ST 36) to the stomach and *Yanglingquan* (GB 34) to the gallbladder.

Section 4
METHOD OF LOCATING ACUPOINTS

Bone-length measurement, anatomical location, identical body unit and simple measurement are frequently-used methods of locating acupoints.

1. Bone-Length Measurement

A certain part of the human body is divided into portions of equal length, with each portion being one *cun*. This method applies to all patients, whether they are male or female, old or young, tall or short (See Fig. 1-1). For commonly used standards of bone-length measurement, see Table 2.

Table 2 Commonly Used Standards of Bone-Length Measurement

Body Part	Distance	Bone-Length	Method	Explanations
Head	From the anterior hairline to the posterior hairline	12 *cun*	Longitudinal measurement	If the anterior and posterior hair lines are indistinguishable, take the distance from the glabella to *Dazhui* (DU 14) as 18 *cun*, the distance from the glabella to the anterior hairline as 3 *cun* and the distance from *Dazhui* (DU 14) to the posterior hairline as 3 *cun*.
	Between the two mastoid processes	9 *cun*	Transverse measurement	For the transverse measurement of the head.
Chest and abdomen	From *Tiantu* (RN 22) to the seventh costosternal juncture	9 *cun*	Longitudinal measurement	1) The longitudinal measurement of the chest and hypochondriac region is generally based on the intercostal space. The space between each two ribs is equivalent to 1.6 *cun*. 2) *Tiantu* refers to the place where the acupoint locates.
	From the seventh costosternal juncture to the center of the umbilicus	8 *cun*		
	From the center of the umbilicus to the upper border of symphysis pubis	5 *cun*		
	Between the two nipples	8 *cun*	Transverse measurement	The transverse measurement of the abdomen is based on the distance between the two nipples; for females, the distance between *Quepen* (ST 12) on both sides is used as a substitute for the transverse measurement of the two nipples.
Back and Lower Back	From *Dazhui* (DU 14) to the sacrococcygeal region	21 vertebrae	Longitudinal measurement	The longitudinal measurement for acupoints on the back is based on the spinal column. Clinically, the lower angle of the scapula is at the same level of the seventh thoracic vertebra, and the iliac spine is at the same level of the fourth lumbar vertebra.
	Between the vertebral margin of the two scapular	6 *cun*	Transverse measurement	
Upper Limbs	Between the end of the axillary fold and the transverse cubital crease	9 *cun*	Longitudinal measurement	For measurement of the three *yang* and three *yin* meridians of hand.
	From the elbow band to the wrist band	12 *cun*		
Lateral Side of the Chest	Between the end of the axilla and the end of the 11th rib	12 *cun*	Longitudinal measurement	
Lateral Side of the Abdomen	Between the end of the 11th rib and the greater trochanter	9 *cun*	Longitudinal measurement	
Lower Limbs	From the level of the upper border of symphysis pubis to the medial epicondyle of femur	18 *cun*	Longitudinal measurement	For measurement of the three *yin* meridians of foot.
	From the lower border of the medial condyle of tibia to the tip of medial malleolus	13 *cun*		
	From the greater trochanter to the center of patella	19 *cun*	Longitudinal measurement	1) For measurement of the three *yang* meridians of foot. 2) The anterior level of patella center is about at the same level of *Dubi* (ST 35), and the posterior level is at about the same level of *Weizhong* (BL 40).
	From the gluteal crease to the center of patella	14 *cun*		
	Between the center of patella and the tip of lateral malleolus	16 *cun*		
	From the tip of the lateral malleolus to the heel	3 *cun*		

2. Anatomical Location

Various anatomical landmarks on the surface of the body, such as the five sense organs, nails, hairlines, nipples, prominences and depressions of the bones, tendons and muscles, can be used to locate acupoints. For example, *Tianshu* (ST 25) is 2 *cun* lateral to the umbilicus and *Shaoshang* (LU 11) on the radial side of the thumb is about 0.1 *cun* lateral to the corner of the nail.

3. Identical Body Unit

This method refers to the use of the patient's finger as a criterion for locating acupoints.

Middle finger *cun*: When the patient's middle finger is flexed, the distance between the creases of the second segment is taken as one *cun*. It can be used to locate the acupoints on the limbs with longitudinal measurement and on the back with transverse measurement. (Fig. 1-2)

Thumb *cun*: The width of the interphalangeal joint of the patient's thumb is taken as one *cun*. It is also used to locate acupoints on the limbs with longitudinal measurement. (Fig. 1-3)

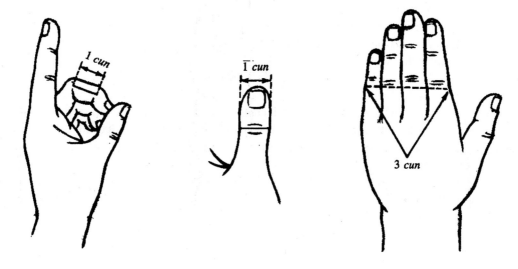

Fig. 1-2 Middle Finger *Cun*   Fig. 1-3 Thumb *Cun*   Fig. 1-4 Four Fingers *Cun*

Four fingers *cun*: When the index, middle, ring and small fingers are held together with the hand open, the width of the four fingers at the level of the middle interphalangeal crease of the middle finger is taken as three *cun*. (Fig. 1-4)

4. Simple Measurement

It is a simple way to locate acupoints in clinical practice. For instance, *Fengshi* (GB 31) is at the place where the patient's middle finger tip touches when he stands with hands down, and *Lieque* (LU 7) locates at the place where the index finger tip reaches when both hands are crossed with the index finger of one hand placed on the styloid process of the radius of the other.

Chapter Two
MERIDIANS AND ACUPOINTS

Section 1
THE TWELVE MERIDIANS

1. The Lung Meridian of Hand-*Taiyin* (LU)
(Fig. 2-1 and Fig. 2-2)
1) Traveling route
a) The meridian starts from the middle *jiao* (1) and runs downward to connect with the large intestine. Then it ascends along the upper orifice of the stomach (2) and crosses the diaphragm (3) before pertaining to the lung (4).

b) It exits the lung system (*Zhongfu*, LU 1) (5) and runs down along the medial side of the upper arm and the front of the Heart Meridian of Hand-*Shaoyin* and the Pericardium Meridian of Hand-*Jueyin* (6). Then it goes through the cubital fossa (7) and enters *cunkou* (9) (on the wrist over the radial artery where pulse is felt) along the anterior border of medial side of the forearm (8). It continues to run along the thenar eminence (10) and the thenar border (11) and arrives at the medial side of the thumb tip (*Shaoshang*, LU 11) (12).

c) A branch starts from *Lieque* (LU 7) (13) and runs along the radial side to the tip of the index finger. (Fig. 2-1)

2) Symptoms
Cough, asthma, shortness of breath, hemoptysis, common cold, fullness in the chest, sore throat and pain along the meridian.

3) Acupoints
Zhongfu (a front *mu* point, LU 1)
Location: Six *cun* lateral to the anterior midline and at the same level of the first intercostal space. (Fig. 2-3)
Indications: Cough, asthma, sore throat, fullness in the chest and pain in the shoulders and back.
Method: Insert the needle obliquely into the lateral side of the chest, 0.5-0.8 *cun* deep.
Notes: (1) Do not insert the needle too deep lest the lung should be injured. (2) Vasculature: Axillary artery and vein and thoracoacromial artery and vein. Innervation: Intermediate supraclavicular nerve, the branches of thoracic nerves and the lateral cord of the brachial plexus.

Yunmen (LU 2)
Location: Six *cun* lateral to the anterior midline and in the depression of the infraclavicular fossa. (Fig. 2-3)
Indications: Cough, asthma, sore throat, a hot sensation in the chest and pain in the chest.
Method: Insert the needle obliquely into the lateral side of the chest, 0.5-0.8 *cun* deep.
Notes: (1) Do not insert the needle too deep lest the lung should be injured. (2) Vasculature: Cephalic vein, thoracoacromial artery and vein, and axillary artery. Innervation: Intermediate and posterior supraclavicular nerves, the branches of thoracic nerves and brachial plexus.

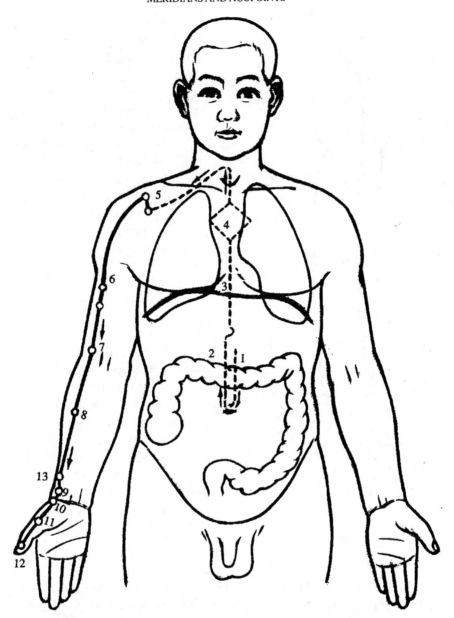

Fig. 2-1 Lung Meridian of Hand-*Taiyin*

Tianfu (LU 3)

Location: On the medial side of the upper arm, 3 *cun* below the anterior end of the axillary fold and on the radial side of biceps muscle of arm. (Fig. 2-4)

Indications: Cough, asthma, epistaxis and pain in the shoulders and medial side of the upper arm.

Method: Insert the needle perpendicularly, 0.5-1 *cun* deep.

Notes: (1) Simple measurement: Raise the arm horizontally forward and bend neck towards the arm. The place on the medial side where the tip of nose touches is the *Tianfu* acupoint. (2) According to *Verses for Hundred Symptoms*, *Tianfu* (LU 3) and *Hegu* (LI 4) are effective in treating epistaxis. (3) Vasculature: Cephalic vein and the branches of brachial artery and vein. Innervation: Lateral cutaneous nerve of arm and musculocutaneous nerve.

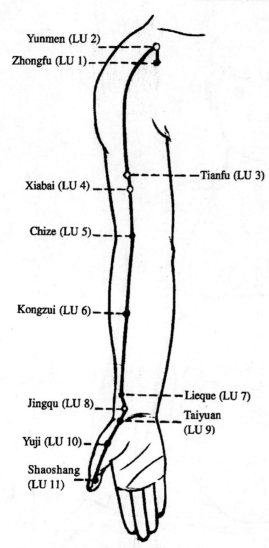

Fig. 2-2

Xiabai (LU 4)

Location: One *cun* below *Tianfu* (LU 3), 5 *cun* above the cubital crease and on the radial border of biceps muscle of arm. (Fig. 2-4)

Indications: Cough, shortness of breath, pain and fullness in the chest, pain in the medial side of the upper arm and retching.

Method: Insert the needle perpendicularly, 0.5-1 *cun* deep.

Notes: Vasculature and innervation are the same as those of *Tianfu* (LU 3).

Chize (a *he* point, LU 5)

Location: Above the cubital crease and on the radial border of the tendon of the biceps. (Fig. 2-4)

Indications: Cough, asthma, afternoon fever, hemoptysis, epistaxis, sore throat, pain and fullness in the chest, pain in the elbow and arm, infantile convulsion and acute mastitis.

Method: Insert the needle perpendicularly, 0.5-0.8 *cun* deep.

Notes: (1) *Chize* is a *he* point of the meridian, belonging to water of the Five Elements. According to the principle of treating excess syndrome by purgation and reduction, this acupoint is indicated for lung diseases of the excess type. (2) Use the point together with *Zhongfu* (LU 1), *Danzhong* (RN 17), *Feishu* (BL 13) and *Dingchuan* (EX-B 1) to cure cough and asthma, and in cooperation with *Jianyu* (LI 15) and *Quchi* (LI 11) to cure pain in the elbow and arm (3). According to *Tongxuan Verses for Acupoints*, *Chize* (LU 5) can be used to relieve spasmodic pain in the elbow. (4) Vasculature: Branches of the radial recurrent artery and vein and cephalic vein. Innervation: Antebrachial lateral cutaneous nerve and radial nerve.

Kongzui (a *xi* point, LU 6)

Location: On the medial side of the forearm and the line joining *Chize* (LU 5) and *Taiyuan* (LU 9), and 7 *cun* above the transverse crease of the wrist. (Fig. 2-5)

Indications: Cough, asthma, hemoptysis, sore throat, aphonia and spasmodic pain in the elbow and arm.

Method: Insert the needle perpendicularly, 0.5-1 *cun* deep.

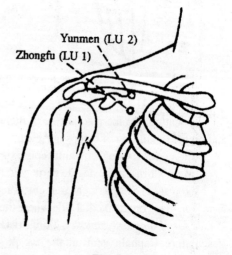

Fig. 2-3

MERIDIANS AND ACUPOINTS

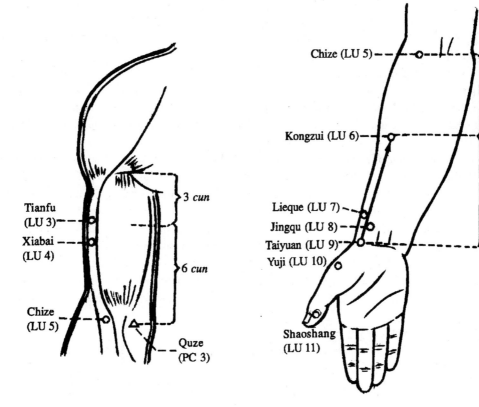

Fig. 2-4   Fig. 2-5

Notes: (1) Use the point together with *Hegu* (LI 4) to treat fever without sweating. (2) Vasculature: Cephalic vein and radial artery and vein. Innervation: Antebrachial lateral cutaneous nerve and the superficial ramus of radial nerve.

Lieque (a *luo* point and one of the eight confluent points, LU 7)

Location: On the radial side of the forearm, superior to the styloid process of the radius and 1.5 *cun* above the transverse crease of the wrist. (Fig. 2-6)

Indications: Cough, asthma, sore throat, pain in the wrist, rigidity of nape with headache, facial paralysis and toothache.

Method: Insert the needle obliquely upward, 0.3-0.5 *cun* deep.

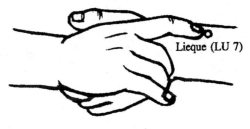

Fig.2-6

Notes: (1) Simple measurement: Cross the interspace between the index finger and thumb of both hands, with the index finger of one hand on the styloid process of the radius of the other, and the point is at the depression under the tip of the index finger. (2) Since this acupoint is one of the eight confluent points, it can be used together with *Zhaohai* (KI 6) to treat sore throat. (3) *Lieque* (LU 7) and *Wangu* (GB 12) are indicated for facial paralysis. (4) Vasculature: Cephalic vein and the branches of radial artery and vein. Innervation: Antebrachial lateral cutaneous nerve and the superficial ramus of radial nerve.

Jingqu (a *jing* point, LU 8)

Location: On the palmar side of the forearm, 1 *cun* above the transverse crease of the wrist and on the radial side of artery. (Fig. 2-5)

Indications: Cough, asthma, sore throat, chest pain and pain in the wrist.

Method: Keep away from radial artery and insert the needle perpendicularly, 0.3-0.5 *cun* deep. Moxibustion is contraindicated.

Notes: Vasculature: Radial artery and vein. Innervation: Antebrachial lateral cutaneous nerve and the superficial ramus of radial nerve.

Taiyuan (a *shu* point, a *yuan* point and one of the eight influential points, LU 9)

Location: On the transverse crease of the wrist and in the depression on the side of radial artery. (Fig. 2-5)

Indications: Cough, asthma, hemoptysis, sore throat, chest pain, acrotism and pain in the wrist.

Method: Keep away from artery and insert the needle perpendicularly, 0.3-0.5 *cun* deep.

Notes: (1) It is a *shu* point of the meridian, belonging to earth of the Five Elements. According to the principle of adopting the reinforcing and replenishing method for a deficiency syndrome, this acupoint is indicated for lung diseases of the deficiency type. (2) Use the point together with *Neiguan* (PC 6) and *Shenmen* (HT 7) to treat chest pain and palpitation. (3) According to *Jade Dragon Verses*, it is advisable to puncture *Taiyuan* (LU 9) and *Lieque* (LU 7) in treating cough and wind-phelgm syndrome. (4) It is said that *Taiyuan* and *Renying* (ST 9) can be used as the main acupoints to cure acrotism. (5) Vasculature: Radial artery and vein. Innervation: Antebrachial lateral cutaneous nerve and the superficial ramus of radial nerve.

Yuji (a *ying* point, LU 10)

Location: On the radial side of the midpoint of the first metacarpal bone and the dorso-ventral boundary of the hand. (Fig. 2-5)

Indications: Cough, asthma, hemoptysis, sore throat, aphonia, fever and a hot sensation in the palm.

Method: Insert the needle perpendicularly, 0.5-0.8 *cun* deep.

Notes: (1) It is said that when treating bronchial asthma, needling *Yuji* together with *Dazhui* (DU 14), *Zusanli* (ST 36) and *Guanyuan* (RN 4) will help improve pulmonary function, relieve bronchial spasm, reduce airway resistance, promote ventilatory function and alleviate the wheezing sound. (2) Vasculature: Venules linking the thumb with cephalic vein. Innervation: Superficial ramus of radial nerve.

Shaoshang (a *jiing* point, LU 11)

Location: On the radial side of the thumb and about 0.1 *cun* posterior to the corner of the fingernail. (Fig. 2-5)

Indications: Cough, sore throat, epistaxis, fever and syncope.

Method: Insert the needle obliquely upward, 0.1-0.2 *cun* deep or induce bleeding by prompt prick.

Notes: (1) *Renzhong* (DU 26) and *Zusanli* (ST 36) may be used together to treat syncope and shock. (2) According to *Epitome of Acupuncture and Moxibustion, Shaoshang, Tiantu* (RN 22) and *Hegu* (LI 4) are indicated for treating sore throat. (3) Vasculature: The arterial and venous network formed by palmar and digital proprial arteries and veins. Innervation: Mixed branches of antebrachial lateral cutaneous nerve and the superficial ramus of radial nerve and the peripheral nerve network formed by the palmar and digital proprial nerve of the median nerve.

2. The Large Intestine Meridian of Hand-*Yangming* (LI)

(Fig. 2-7 and Fig. 2-8)

1) Traveling route

a) The meridian starts from the tip of the index finger (*Shangyang*, LI 1) (1). Then it runs upward along the radial side of the index finger, passing the interspace of the first and second metacarpal bones

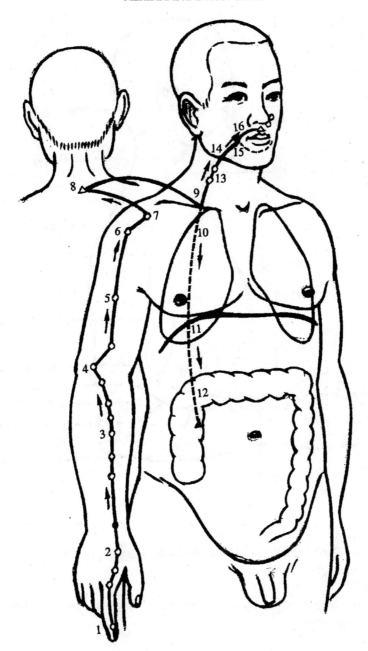

Fig. 2-7 Large Intestine Meridian of Hand-*Yangming*

and the tendons of long and short extensor muscle of the wrist (2). It continues to go further upward along the lateral side of the forearm (3), lateral side of the elbow (4), lateral side of the anterior aspect of the upper arm (5) and arrives at the shoulder (6). It runs along anterior border of the acromion (7), then meets *Dazhui* (DU 14) (8) and enters the supraclavicular fossa (9).

b) It runs down from the supraclavicular fossa to connect with the lung (10), crosses the diaphragm (11) and pertains to the large intestine (12).

c) It starts from the supraclavicular fossa, passes the neck (13), cheek (14), and the gums of the

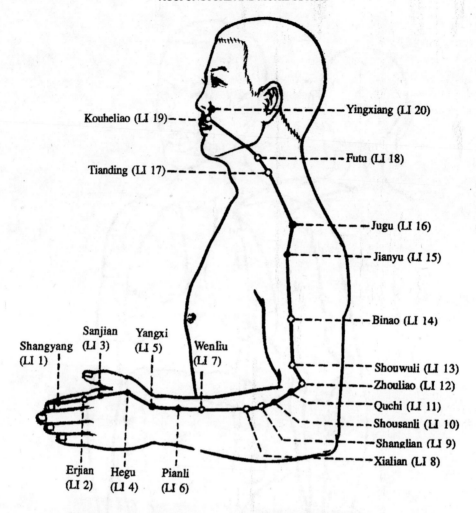

Fig. 2-8 Acupoints on the Large Intestine Meridian of Hand-*Yangming*

lower teeth (15), then exits the mouth cavity, runs around the upper lip, crosses at the philtrum and ends at the alae nasi (*Yingxiang*, LI 20) (16).

2) Symptoms

Abdominal pain, borborygmus, diarrhea, constipation, dysentery, toothache, sore throat, nasal stuffiness, pain along the meridian.

3) Acupoints

Shangyang (a *jiing* point, LI 1)

Location: On the radial side of the index finger and about 0.1 *cun* posterior to the corner of the fingernail. (Fig. 2-9)

Indications: Toothache, swollen cheek, sore throat, numb fingers, febrile disease without sweating, syncope.

Method: Insert the needle 0.1 *cun* deep into the skin, or prompt prick so that a little blood comes out.

Notes: Vasculature: The network of digit dorsal arteries and veins. Innervation: The proper palmar digital nerve and the intrinsic nerve derived from the median nerve.

Erjian (a *ying* point, LI 2)

Location: In the depression of the radial side and distal to the second metacarpophalangeal joint. (Fig. 2-9)

Indications: Toothache, wry mouth, sore throat, red and swollen eyes and pain in the interphalangeal joints.

Method: Insert the needle perpendicularly, 0.2-0.3 *cun* deep.

Notes: Vasculature: The dorsal digital and proper palmar digital arteries and veins. Innervation: The dorsal digital nerve of radial nerve and the proper palmar digital nerve of median nerve.

Sanjian (a *shu* point, LI 3)

Location: In the depression of the radial side and proximal to the second metacarpophalangeal joint. (Fig. 2-9)

Indications: Toothache, sore throat, red and swollen eyes and pain in the interphalangeal joints.

Method: Insert the needle perpendicularly, 0.3-0.5 *cun* deep.

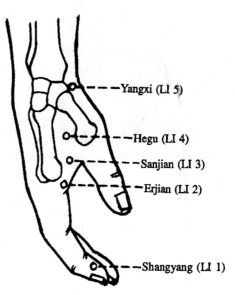

Fig. 2-9

Notes: Vasculature: The dorsal venous network of hand and the branch of the first dorsal metacarpal arteries. Innervation: The superficial ramus of radial nerve.

Hegu (a *yuan* point, LI 4)

Location: Between the first and second metacarpal bones and approximately on the radial side of the midpoint of the second metacarpal bone. (Fig. 2-9)

Indications: Toothache, trismus, facial paralysis, facial swelling, sore throat, red and swollen eyes, fever, anhidrosis and hyperhidrosis, cough, numbness and paralysis of the upper limbs, amenorrhea, prolonged labor, infantile convulsion and urticaria.

Method: Insert the needle perpendicularly, 0.5-0.8 *cun* deep. Acupuncture and moxibustion are contraindicated for pregnant women.

Notes: (1) Simple measurement: Place the transverse crease of the interphalangeal joint of the thumb on the web-space between the thumb and index finger of the other hand, the acupoint locates at the place where the tip of the thumb touches. (2) According to *Epitome of Acupuncture and Moxibustion*, insert the needle at *Hegu* first, using the reinforcing method, and then at *Fuliu* (KI 7), using the reducing method for hypohidrosis; insert the needle at *Hegu* first, using the reducing method, and then at *Fuliu* (KI 7), using the reinforcing method for hyperhidrosis. (3) According to *Illustrated Manual on the Points for Acupuncture and Moxibustion as Found on the Bronze Figure*, it is contraindicated to needle at *Hegu* for pregnant women lest it should harm the fetus. (4) Vasculature: Dorsal venous network of hand. Innervation: The superficial ramus of radial nerve.

Yangxi (a *jing* point, LI 5)

Location: On the radial side of the wrist crease and in the depression between the tendons of the long and short extensor muscles of the thumb. (Fig. 2-9)

Indications: Red and swollen eyes, sore throat, headache, tinnitus and pain in the wrist.

Method: Insert the needle perpendicularly, 0.3-0.5 *cun* deep.

Notes: Vasculature: Cephalic vein, radial artery and its dorsal carpal branch. Innervation: The superficial ramus of radial nerve.

Pianli (a *luo* point, LI 6)

Location: On the radial side of the dorsal surface of the forearm and 3 *cun* above the crease of the wrist. (Fig. 2-10)

Indications: Facial paralysis, red and swollen eyes, sore throat and pain in the arm.

Method: Insert the needle perpendicularly, 0.3-0.5 *cun* deep.

Notes: Vasculature: Cephalic vein. Innervation: Lateral cutaneous nerve of forearm, and the superficial ramus of radial nerve on the radial side, dorsal cutaneous nerve and dorsal interosseous nerve of forearm on the ulnar side.

Wenliu (a *xi* point, LI 7)

Location: On the radial side of the dorsal surface of the forearm and 5 *cun* above the crease of the wrist. (Fig. 2-10)

Indications: Facial paralysis, facial swelling, sore throat, headache, swollen mouth and tongue, and pain in the arm.

Method: Insert the needle perpendicularly, 0.5-0.8 *cun* deep.

Notes: Vasculature: The muscular branch of the radial artery, the cephalic vein. Innervation: The dorsal cutaneous nerve of forearm and the deep ramus of radial nerve.

Xialian (LI 8)

Location: On the radial side of the dorsal surface of the forearm and 4 *cun* below the cubital crease. (Fig. 2-10)

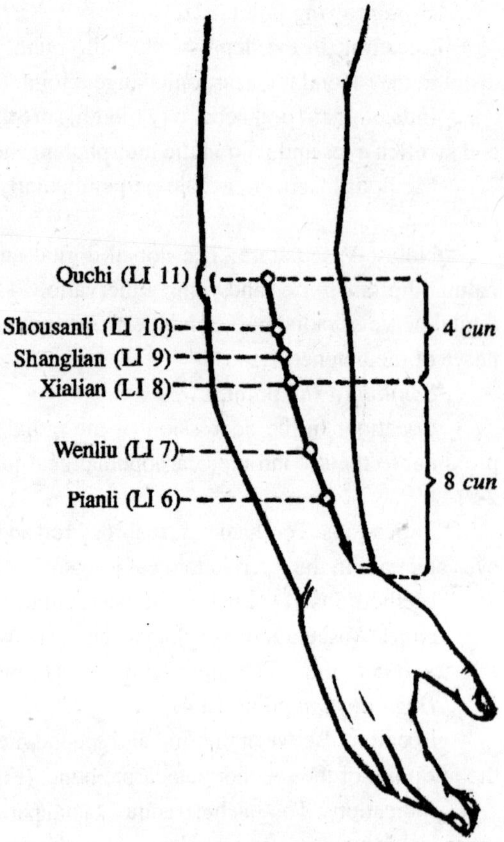

Fig. 2-10

Indications: Red and swollen eyes, headache, vertigo and pain in the elbow and arm.

Method: Insert the needle perpendicularly, 0.5-1 *cun* deep.

Notes: Vasculature and innervation are the same as those of *Wenliu* (LI 7).

Shanglian (LI 9)

Location: On the radial side of the dorsal surface of the forearm and 3 *cun* below the cubital crease. (Fig. 2-10)

Indications: Hemiplegia, headache, numbness and pain in the arm.

Method: Insert the needle perpendicularly, 0.5-1 *cun* deep.

Notes: Vasculature and innervation are the same as those of *Wenliu* (LI 7).

Shousanli (LI 10)

Location: On the radial side of the dorsal surface of the forearm and 2 *cun* below the cubital crease. (Fig. 2-10)

Indications: Toothache, swollen cheek, aphonia, numbness and motor impairment of the upper limbs, and pain in the shoulder and arm.

Method: Insert the needle perpendicularly, 0.5-1 *cun* deep.

Notes: (1) According to *Tongxuan Verses for Acupoints*, *Shousanli* in the anterior cubital region is indicated for pains in shoulder and back. This acupoint may be used together with *Jianyu* (LI 15) and *Waiguan* (SJ 5) to treat motor impairment of the upper limbs and pain in the shoulder. (2) Vasculature: The branches of radial recurrent artery and vein. Innervation: The same as that of *Wenliu* (LI 7).

Quchi (a *he* point, LI 11)

Location: At the lateral end of the cubital crease with the elbow flexed. (Fig. 2-10)

Indications: Toothache, red and swollen eyes, sore throat, motor impairment of the upper limbs, febrile diseases, scrofula, urticaria and vertigo.

Method: Insert the needle perpendicularly, 1-1.5 *cun* deep.

Notes: (1) It is a *he* point and belongs to earth of the Five Elements. It is indicated for febrile diseases and mania. (2) It can be used together with *Dazhui* (DU 14) and *Fengchi* (GB 20) to treat fever, with *Dazhui* and *Xuehai* (SP 10) to treat urticaria and with *Zusanli* (ST 36) and *Renying* (ST 9) to treat vertigo. (3) Studies show that it is also effective for simple appendicitis. (4) Vasculature: The branches of radial recurrent artery and vein. Innervation: The dorsal cutaneous nerve of forearm and radial nerve.

Zhouliao (LI 12)

Location: On the lateral side of the upper arm, 1 *cun* above *Quchi* (LI 11) and on the medial border of the humerus. (Fig. 2-11)

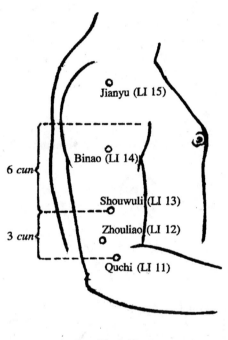

Fig.2-11

Indications: Numbness and pain in the arm, elbow and shoulder.

Method: Insert the needle perpendicularly, 0.5-0.8 *cun* deep.

Notes: Vasculature: Radial collateral artery and vein. Innervation: The dorsal cutaneous nerve of forearm and radial nerve.

Shouwuli (LI 13)

Location: On the lateral side of the upper arm and 3 *cun* above *Quchi*. (Fig. 2-11)

Indications: Spasmodic pain in the elbow and arm, and scrofula.

Method: Insert the needle perpendicularly, 0.5-0.8 *cun* deep.

Notes: Vasculature: Radial collateral artery and vein. Innervation: The dorsal cutaneous nerve of forearm and radial nerve.

Binao (LI 14)

Location: On the lateral side of the arm, at the insertion of the deltoid muscle and 7 *cun* above *Quchi* (LI 11). (Fig. 2-11)

Indications: Eye diseases, pain in the shoulder and arm, and scrofula.

Method: Insert the needle perpendicularly or obliquely upward, 0.8-1 *cun* deep.

Notes: (1) It is often used together with *Jianyu* (LI 15) for acupuncture anesthesia in pneumonectomy. (2) Vasculature: The branches of posterior humeral circumflex artery and vein, deep brachial artery and vein. Innervation: The dorsal cutaneous nerve of arm and radial nerve.

Jianyu (LI 15)

Location: On the shoulder and in the depression anterior and inferior to the acromion when the arm is abducted. (Fig. 2-11)

Indications: Toothache, motor impairment of the upper limbs, and pain in the shoulder and arm.

Method: Insert the needle perpendicularly or obliquely, 0.8-1.5 *cun* deep.

Notes: (1) According to *Basic Questions*, *Yunmen* (LU 2), *Jianyu* (LI 15), *Weizhong* (BL 40) and *Yaoshu* (DU 2) can be used to reduce heat in the limbs. (2) Vasculature: Posterior humeral circumflex

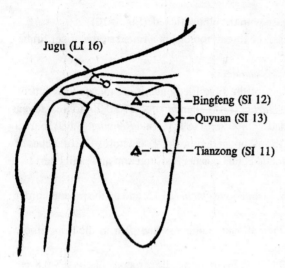

Fig. 2-12

artery and vein. Innervation: Supraclavicular nerve and axillary nerve.

Jugu (LI 16)

Location: In the depression between the acromial extremity of the clavicle and the scapular spine. (Fig. 2-12)

Indications: Pain in the shoulder, arm and back, scrofula and goiter.

Method: Insert the needle perpendicularly, 0.5-0.8 *cun* deep.

Notes: (1) Do not insert the needle too deep lest the lung should be harmed. (2) Vasculature: Suprascapular artery and vein. Innervation: Posterior supraclavicular nerve, the branch of accessory nerve, and suprascapular nerve.

Tianding (LI 17)

Location: On the posterior border of sternocleidomastoid muscle, 3 *cun* lateral to and 1 *cun* below the tip of Adam's apple. (Fig. 2-13)

Indications: Sore throat, sudden loss of voice, scrofula and goiter.

Method: Insert the needle perpendicularly, 0.5-0.8 *cun* deep.

Notes: Vasculature: External jugular vein. Innervation: Supraclavicular nerves and phrenic nerve at the posterior border of sternocleidomastoid muscle where cutaneous nerve of neck just emerges.

Futu (LI 18)

Location: 3 *cun* lateral to the tip of Adam's apple and between the sternal head and clavicular head of sternocleidomastoid muscle. (Fig. 2-13)

Indications: Cough, asthma, sore throat, sudden loss of voice, scrofula and goiter.

Method: Insert the needle perpendicularly, 0.5-0.8 *cun* deep.

Notes: Vasculature: Ascending cervical artery and vein. Innervation: Great auricular nerve, cutaneous nerve of neck, lesser occipital nerve and accessory nerve.

Kouheliao (LI 19)

Location: 0.5 *cun* lateral to *Shuigou* (DU 26). (Fig. 2-14)

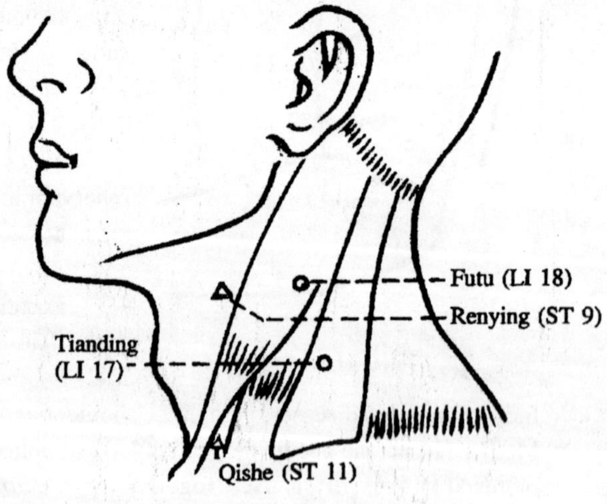

Fig. 2-13

Indications: Facial paralysis, trismus, nasal stuffiness and epistaxis.

Method: Insert the needle perpendicularly, 0.3-0.5 *cun* deep. Moxibustion is contraindicated.

Notes: Vasculature: The superior labial branches of facial artery and vein. Innervation: The anastomotic branch of facial nerve and infraorbital nerve.

Yingxiang (LI 20)

Location: In the nasolabial groove and beside the midpoint of the lateral border of ala nasi. (Fig. 2-14)

Indications: Nasal stuffiness, epistaxis, rhinorrhea with turbid discharge, facial paralysis and itching.

Method: Insert the needle perpendicularly, 0.1-0.2 *cun* deep; or insert obliquely upward, 0.5-0.8 *cun* deep. Moxibustion is contraindicated.

Notes: (1) According to *Verses for Hundred Symptoms*, if there is a feeling of a worm wriggling on the face, the acupoint *Yingxiang* (LI 20) can be used for the treatment. (2) According to *Tongxuan Verses for Acupoints*, *Yingxiang* (LI 20) can also be used to cure nasal stuffiness and anosmia. (3) Vasculature: Facial artery and vein, and infraorbital artery and vein. Innervation: The anastomotic branch of facial and infraorbital nerves.

3. The Stomach Meridian of Foot-*Yangming* (ST)

(Fig. 2-15 and Fig. 2-16)

1) Traveling route

a) The meridian starts at the lateral side of ala nasi (1), runs up to the root of the nose and meets the Bladder Meridian of Foot-*Taiyang* (2). Then it descends along the lateral side of the nose (*Chengqi*, ST 1) (3), enters the upper gum (4), curves around the lips (5), goes down to meet *Chengjiang* (RN 24) at the mentolabial groove (6), then runs along the posterior and lower part of the cheek to the acupoint *Daying* (ST 5) (7). It continues to travel along the angle of the mandible (8), passing the front of the ear (*Xiaguan*, ST 7) (9), ascends to the anterior hairline (10) and finally reaches the forehead (11).

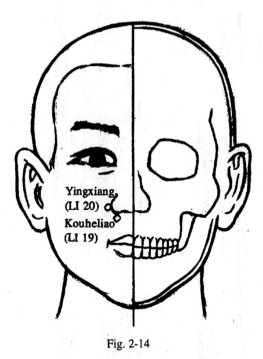

Fig. 2-14

b) One of its branches descends from *Daying* (ST 5) to *Renying* (ST 9) (12) and then running along the throat, reaches *Quepen* (ST 12), at the center of the supraclavicular fossa (13). It continues to go downward, through the diaphragm (14) and then connects with the stomach and spleen (15).

c) A straight branch starts from the supraclavicular fossa, crosses the nipple (16) and reaches *Qichong* (ST 30), at the lateral side of the abdomen (17).

d) Another branch starts from the lower orifice of the stomach, through the abdomen (18), and descends to *Qichong* (ST 30) where it joins the straight branch. Then it passes *Biguan* (ST 31) (19), running along the anterior border of the thigh, *Futu* (ST 32) (20), and then descends to the lateral side of the knee (21). It continues to travel along the lateral side of the crural tibia (22), reaches the dorsum of the foot (23) and then enters the lateral side of the tip of the second toe (24).

e) The tibial branch starts from *Zusanli* (ST 36), 3 *cun* below the knee (25) and goes down to the lateral side of the tip of the middle toe (26).

f) The dorsal foot branch starts from the dorsum of the foot (27) and ends at the medial side of the tip of the great toe.

2) Symptoms

Borborygmus, abdominal distention, edema, stomachache, vomiting, polyorexia, facial paralysis, sore throat, febrile diseases, mania, pain in the chest and along the meridian.

3) Acupoints

Chengqi (ST 1)

Location: On the face, directly below the pupil and between the eyeball and the inferior border of

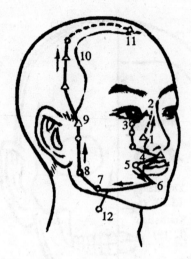

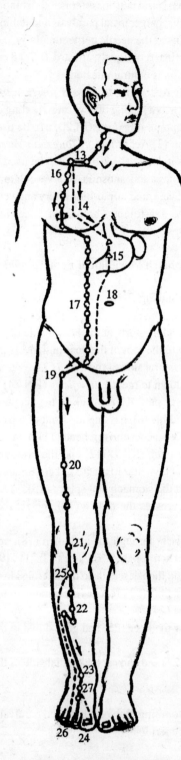

Fig. 2-15 Stomach Meridian of Foot-*Yangming*

the orbit. (Fig. 2-17)

Indications: Red and swollen eyes, night blindness, lacrimation induced by irritation of the wind, twitching eyelids, facial paralysis and myopia.

Method: When the eyeball is fixed, insert the needle perpendicularly and slowly along the infraorbital ridge, 0.5-0.8 *cun* deep. Do not use lifting and thrusting methods lest the blood vessel should be injured, resulting in edema due to blood stasis.

Notes: Vasculature: The branches of infraorbital and ophthalmic arteries and veins. Innervation: The branch of infraorbital nerve, the inferior branch of oculomotor nerve and the muscular branch of facial nerve.

Sibai (ST 2)

Location: On the face, directly below the pupil and in the depression of the infraorbital foramen. (Fig. 2-17)

Indications: Red and swollen eyes, corneal nebula, twitching eyelids, facial paralysis, headache and vertigo.

Method: Insert the needle perpendicularly, 0.3-0.5 *cun* deep. Take care not to puncture the eyeball.

Notes: Vasculature: The branches of facial artery and vein, the infraorbital artery and vein. Innervation: The branches of facial nerve and infraorbital nerve.

Juliao (ST 3)

Location: On the face, directly below the pupil and at the level of the lower border of ala nasi. (Fig. 2-17)

Indications: Facial paralysis, twitching eyelids and epistaxis, toothache.

Method: Insert the needle perpendicularly, 0.3-0.5 *cun* deep.

Notes: Vasculature: The branches of facial and

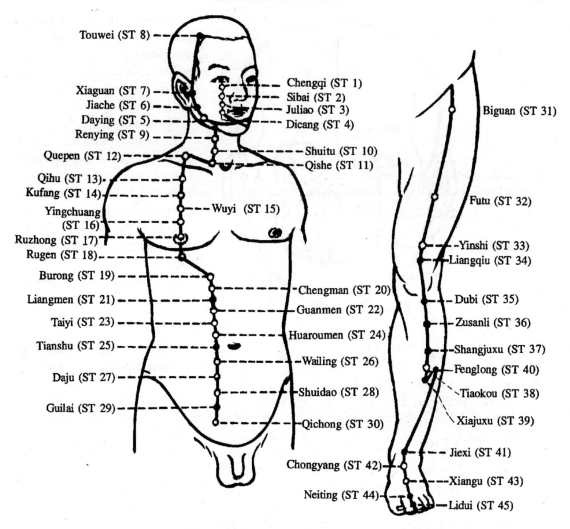

Fig. 2-16 Acupoints on the Stomach Meridian of Foot-*Yangming*

infraorbital arteries and veins. Innervation: The facial and infraorbital nerves.

Dicang (ST 4)

Location: 0.4 *cun* lateral to the corner of the mouth. (Fig. 2-17)

Indications: Facial paralysis, salivation, toothache and swollen cheek.

Method: Insert the needle perpendicularly, 0.2 *cun* deep or horizontally towards *Jiache* (ST 6), 0.8-1 *cun* deep.

Notes: (1) According to *Jade Dragon Verses*, *Dicang* (ST 4) is effective in treating facial paralysis when used together with *Jiache* (ST 6). When needled together with *Yingxiang* (LI 20), *Quanliao* (SI 18), *Qianzheng* (EX-HN), and *Hegu* (LI 4), it can treat facial paralysis and prosopalgia. (2) Vasculature: Facial artery and vein. Innervation: The branches of facial and infraorbital nerves and the terminal branch of buccal nerve.

Daying (ST 5)

Location: 1.3 *cun* anterior to the mandibular angle and on the anterior border of the masseter muscle where the pulsation of facial artery is palpable. (Fig. 2-18)

Indications: Facial paralysis, trismus, toothache and swollen cheek.

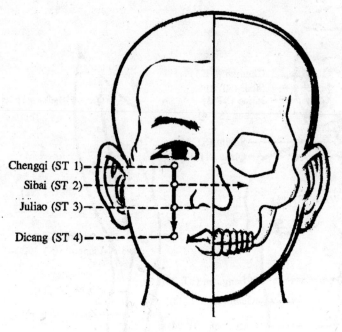

Fig. 2-17

Method: Insert the needle perpendicularly or horizontally, 0.2-0.5 *cun* deep.

Notes: Vasculature: Facial artery and vein. Innervation: Facial and buccal nerves.

Jiache (ST 6)

Location: On the cheek, one finger-breadth anterior and superior to the mandibular angle and at the prominence of the masseter muscle when the jaw is clenched. (Fig. 2-18)

Indications: Facial paralysis, trismus, toothache, swollen face and cheek.

Method: Insert the needle perpendicularly, 0.3-0.5 *cun* deep or insert the needle horizontally, 0.5-1 *cun* deep.

Notes: Vasculature: Masseteric artery. Innervation: Great auricular nerve, facial nerve and masseteric nerve.

Xiaguan (ST 7)

Location: In the depression below the zygomatic arch and anterior to the mandibular condyloid process. (Fig. 2-18)

Indications: Toothache, trismus, facial paralysis, deafness and tinnitus.

Method: Insert the needle perpendicularly, 0.5-1 *cun* deep.

Notes: Vasculature: Trans-verse facial artery and vein and maxillary artery and vein. Inner-vation: The zygoatic branch of facial nerve and the branches of auriculotemporal nerve.

Touwei (ST 8)

Location: On the lateral side of the head and 0.5 *cun* above the anterior hairline at the corner of the forehead. (Fig. 2-18)

Indications: Red and swollen eyes, twitching eyelids, headache and dizziness.

Method: Insert the needle horizontally, 0.5-1 *cun* deep. Moxibustion is contraindicated.

Notes: (1) According to *Essentially Treasured Prescriptions*, *Touwei* and *Daling* (PC 7) can be needled to treat severe headache and ophthalmalgia.

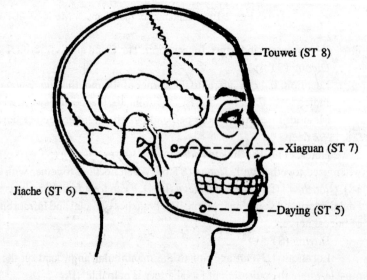

Fig. 2-18

This acupoint is also effective in treating migraine when used together with *Shuaigu* (GB 8) and *Fengchi* (GB 20). (2) Vasculature: The frontal branches of superficial temporal artery and vein. Innervation: The branch of auriculotemporal nerve and the temporal branch of facial nerve.

Renying (ST 9)

Location: 1.5 *cun* lateral to the tip of Adam's apple and on the anterior border of sternocleidomastoid muscle. (Fig. 2-19)

Indications: Sore throat, fullness in the chest, dyspnea, scrofula, goiter, headache, vertigo and hemiplegia.

Method: Insert the needle perpendicularly, 0.3-0.5 *cun* deep. Do not harm the artery. Moxibustion is contraindicated.

Notes: (1) It is effective in treating hypertension when used together with *Zusanli* (ST 36) and *Quchi* (LI 11); when needled together with *Neiguan* (PC 6), *Zusanli*, *Shemen* (HT 7) and *Sanyinjiao* (SP 6), it can treat hyperthyroidism. (2) Vasculature: Superior thyroid artery, internal and external carotid artery. Innervation: Cutaneous nerve of neck, the cervical branch of facial nerve, sympathetic trunk and the descending branch of hypoglossal nerve and the vagus nerve.

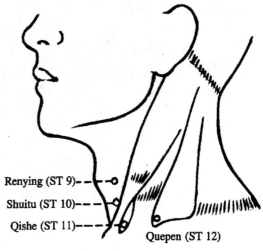

Fig. 2-19

Shuitu (ST 10)

Location: At the midpoint of the line connecting *Renying* (ST 9) and *Qishe* (ST 11) and on the anterior border of sternocleidomastoid muscle. (Fig. 2-19)

Indications: Sore throat, cough, asthma and goiter.

Method: Insert the needle perpendicularly, 0.3-0.5 *cun* deep.

Notes: Vasculature: Common carotid artery. Innervation: Cutaneous nerve of neck, the superior cardiac nerve stemming from sympathetic nerve and sympathetic trunk.

Qishe (ST 11)

Location: Directly below *Renying* (ST 9) and on the upper border of the medial end of the clavicle. (Fig. 2-19)

Indications: Sore throat, asthma, rigid neck and goiter.

Method: Insert the needle perpendicularly, 0.3-0.5 *cun* deep. Do not insert the needle too deep.

Notes: Vasculature: Anterior jugular vein and common carotid artery. Innervation: Anterior branch of the supraclavicular nerve and the muscular branch of ansa hypoglossi.

Quepen (ST 12)

Location: At the center of the supraclavicular fossa and 4 *cun* lateral to the anterior midline. (Fig. 2-19)

Indications: Cough, asthma, sore throat, pain in the supraclavicular fossa and scrofula.

Method: Insert the needle perpendicularly, 0.3-0.5 *cun* deep. Acupuncture is contraindicated for pregnant women.

Notes: Transverse cervical artery. Innervation: Intermediate supraclavicular nerve and the supraclavicular portion of brachial plexus.

Qihu (ST 13)

Location: At the lower border of the clavicle and 4 *cun* lateral to the anterior midline. (Fig. 2-20)

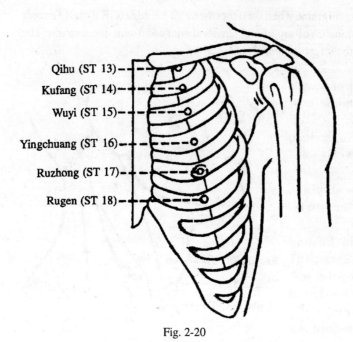

Fig. 2-20

Indications: Cough, asthma, fullness and pain in the chest.

Method: Insert the needle perpendicularly, 0.2-0.5 *cun* deep.

Notes: Vasculature: The branches of thoracoacromial artery and vein and sub-clavicular vein. Innervation: The branches of supraclavian nerve and anterior thoracic nerve.

Kufang (ST 14)

Location: In the first intercostal space and 4 *cun* lateral to the anterior midline. (Fig. 2-20)

Indications: Cough, asthma, and distending pain in the chest and hypochondriac region.

Method: Insert the needle obliquely, 0.5-0.8 *cun* deep.

Notes: Vasculature: Thoracoacromial artery and vein, and the branches of the lateral thoracic artery and vein. Innervation: The branch of the anterior thoracic nerve.

Wuyi (ST 15)

Location: In the second intercostal space and 4 *cun* lateral to the anterior midline. (Fig. 2-20)

Indications: Cough, asthma, distending pain in the chest and hypochondriac region and mastitis.

Method: Insert the needle obliquely or horizontally, 0.5-0.8 *cun* deep.

Notes: Vasculature: The same as that of *Kufang* (ST 14). Innervation: The branch of greater pectoral muscle stemming from the anterior thoracic nerve.

Yingchuang (ST 16)

Location: In the third intercostal space and 4 *cun* lateral to the anterior midline. (Fig. 2-20)

Indications: Cough, asthma, distending pain in the chest and hypochondriac region and mastitis.

Method: Insert the needle obliquely or horizontally, 0.5-0.8 *cun* deep.

Notes: Vasculature: Lateral thoracic artery and vein. Innervation: The branches of the anterior thoracic nerve.

Ruzhong (ST 17)

Location: At the center of the nipple. (Fig. 2-20)

Notes: This point is not for acupuncture or moxibustion but rather serves as a mark for locating the other acupoints. The distance between two nipples is 8 *cun*.

Rugen (ST 18)

Location: In the fifth intercostal space and 4 *cun* lateral to the anterior midline. (Fig. 2-20)

Indications: Cough, asthma, chest pain, mastitis and hypogalactia.

Method: Insert the needle obliquely or horizontally, 0.5-0.8 *cun* deep.

Notes: Vasculature: The branches of intercostal artery and vein. Innervation: The fifth intercostal nerve.

Burong (ST 19)

Location: 6 *cun* above the umbilicus and 2 *cun* lateral to the anterior midline. (Fig. 2-21)

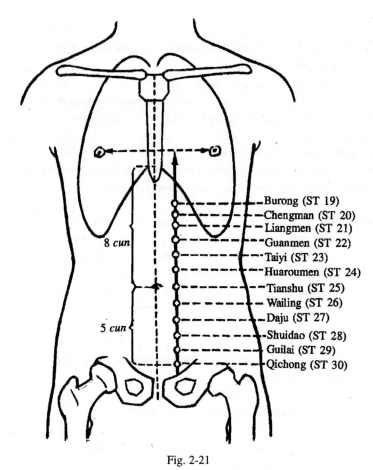

Fig. 2-21

Indications: Stomachache, vomiting, abdominal distention and pain, and anorexia.

Method: Insert the needle perpendicularly, 0.5-0.8 *cun* deep.

Notes: Vasculature: The branches of the seventh intercostal artery and vein, and the branches of superior epigastric artery and vein. Innervation: The branches of the seventh intercostal nerve.

Chengman (ST 20)

Location: 5 *cun* above the umbilicus and 2 *cun* lateral to the anterior midline. (Fig. 2-21)

Indications: Stomachache, vomiting, abdominal distention, borborygmus and pain in the hypochondriac region.

Method: Insert the needle perpendicularly, 0.5-0.8 *cun* deep.

Notes: Vasculature and innervation: The same as those of *Burong* (ST 19).

Liangmen (ST 21)

Location: 4 *cun* above the umbilicus and 2 *cun* lateral to the anterior midline. (Fig. 2-21)

Indications: Stomachache, vomiting, abdominal distention, diarrhea and anorexia.

Method: Insert the needle perpendicularly, 0.5-1 *cun* deep.

Notes: Vasculature: The branches of the eighth intercostal arteries and veins, and the branches of the superior epigastric arteries and veins. Innervation: The branch of the eighth intercostal nerve.

Guanmen (ST 22)

Location: 3 *cun* above the umbilicus and 2 *cun* lateral to the anterior midline. (Fig. 2-21)

Indications: Abdominal distention and pain, borborygmus, diarrhea and edema.

Method: Insert the needle perpendicularly, 0.5-1 *cun* deep.

Notes: Vasculature and innervation: The same as those of *Liangmen* (ST 21).

Taiyi (ST 23)

Location: 2 *cun* above the umbilicus and 2 *cun* lateral to the anterior midline. (Fig. 2-21)

Indications: Stomachache, abdominal pain, indigestion, irritability, and mania.

Method: Insert the needle perpendicularly, 0.5-1 *cun* deep.

Notes: Vasculature: The branches of the eighth and ninth intercostal arteries and veins, and the branches of the inferior epigastric arteries and veins. Innervation: The branches of the eighth and ninth intercostal nerves.

Huaroumen (ST 24)

Location: 1 *cun* above the umbilicus and 2 *cun* lateral to the anterior midline. (Fig. 2-21)

Indications: Stomachache, vomiting and mania.

Method: Insert the needle perpendicularly, 0.8-1.2 *cun* deep.

Notes: Vasculature: The branches of the ninth intercostal arteries and veins, and the branches of inferior epigastric arteries and veins. Innervation: The branch of the ninth intercostal nerve.

Tianshu (a front *mu* point of the large intestine, ST 25)

Location: 2 *cun* lateral to the center of the umbilicus. (Fig. 2-21)

Indications: Pain around the umbilicus, abdominal distention, borborygmus, diarrhea, constipation, dysentery, appendicitis, dysmenorrhea, irregular menstruation and abdominal mass.

Method: Insert the needle perpendicularly, 0.8-1.2 *cun* deep.

Notes: (1) It is a front *mu* point of the large intestine and usually used to treat abdominal distention and pain, diarrhea and constipation together with *Dachangshu* (BL 25). (2) It is also effective in treating irregular menstruation and dysmenorrhea when used together with *Sanyinjiao* (SP 6) and *Ciliao* (BL 32). (3) According to *Epitome of Acupuncture and Moxibustion*, this acupoint can be used to treat abdominal mass, blood stasis, metrorrhagia and irregular menstruation. (4) Vasculature: The branches of the tenth intercostal arteries and veins, and branches of the inferior epigastric arteries and veins. Innervation: The branches of the tenth intercostal nerve.

Wailing (ST 26)

Location: 1 *cun* below the umbilicus and 2 *cun* lateral to the anterior midline. (Fig. 2-21)

Indications: Abdominal pain, dysmenorrhea and hernia.

Method: Insert the needle perpendicularly, 0.8-1.2 *cun* deep.

Notes: Vasculature and innervation: The same as those of *Tianshu* (ST 25).

Daju (ST 27)

Location: 2 *cun* below the umbilicus and 2 *cun* lateral to the anterior midline. (Fig. 2-21)

Indications: Lower abdominal distention, dysuria, hernia, and seminal emission.

Method: Insert the needle perpendicularly, 0.8-1.2 *cun* deep.

Notes: Vasculature: The branches of the 11th intercostal arteries and veins, and inferior epigastric arteries and veins. Innervation: The 11th intercostal nerve.

Shuidao (ST 28)

Location: 3 *cun* below the umbilicus and 2 *cun* lateral to the anterior midline. (Fig. 2-21)

Indications: Lower abdominal distention, dysuria and dysmenorrhea.

Method: Insert the needle perpendicularly, 0.8-1.2 *cun* deep.

Notes: Vasculature: The branches of subcostal arteries and veins, and inferior epigastric arteries and veins. Innervation: The branches of subcostal nerve.

Guilai (ST 29)

Location: 4 *cun* below the umbilicus and 2 *cun* lateral to the anterior midline. (Fig. 2-21)

Indications: Lower abdominal distention, dysmenorrhea, irregular menstruation, impotence, seminal emission and hernia.

Method: Insert the needle perpendicularly, 0.8-1.2 *cun* deep.

Notes: (1) It is effective in treating hernia when used together with *Dadun* (LR 1); when used with *Sanyinjiao* (SP 6) and *Zusanli* (ST 36), it can treat irregular menstruation and dysmenorrhea. (2) According to *A Systematic Classic of Acupuncture*, *Guilai* (ST 29) is indicated for a feeling of gas rushing up from the lower abdomen, testis redux and pain in the penis. (3) Vasculature: Inferior epigastric artery and vein. Innervation: Iliohypogastric nerve.

Qichong (ST 30)

Location: 5 *cun* below the umbilicus and 2 *cun* lateral to the anterior midline. (Fig. 2-21)

Indications: Lower abdominal pain, hernia, irregular menstruation, dysmenorrhea, impotence and swollen vulva.

Method: Insert the needle perpendicularly, 0.5-1 *cun* deep.

Notes: Vasculature: The branches of superficial epigastric artery and vein, and inferior epigastric artery and vein. Innervation: Ilioinguinal nerve.

Biguan (ST 31)

Location: On the anterior side of the upper thigh, at the level of the inferior border of symphysis pubis and in the depression lateral to the sartorius muscle. (Fig. 2-22)

Indications: Abdominal pain, motor impairment of the lower limbs, numbness and pain in the lower limbs.

Method: Insert the needle perpendicularly, 1-1.5 *cun* deep.

Notes: Vasculature: The branches of lateral femoral circumflex artery and vein. Innervation: Lateral cutaneous nerve of thigh.

Futu (ST 32)

Location: On the line connecting the anterior superior iliac spine and lateral border of the patella and 6 *cun* above the superolateral corner of the patella. (Fig. 2-22)

Indications: Motor impairment and pain in the lower limbs, and pain in the knees and lumbar region.

Method: Insert the needle perpendicularly, 1-2 *cun* deep.

Notes: Vasculature: The branches of lateral femoral circumflex artery and vein. Innervation: Anterior and lateral cutaneous nerves of thigh.

Yinshi (ST 33)

Location: On the line connecting the anterior superior iliac spine and lateral border of the patella and 3 *cun* above the superolateral corner of the patella. (Fig. 2-22)

Indications: Motor impairment of the lower limbs, numbness and pain in the lower limbs, pain and stiffness in the knees, and hernia.

Method: Insert the needle perpendicularly, 0.8-1.5 *cun* deep.

Notes: Vasculature: The descending branch of the lateral femoral circumflex artery. Innervation: Anterior and lateral cutaneous nerves of thigh.

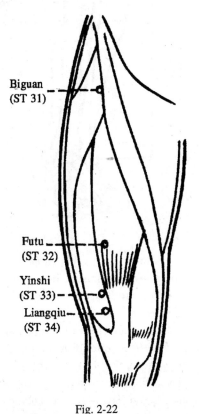

Fig. 2-22

Liangqiu (a *xi* point, ST 34)

Location: On the line connecting the anterior superior iliac spine and lateral border of the patella and 2 *cun* above the superolateral corner of the patella. (Fig. 2-22)

Indications: Stomachache, swollen knees, motor impairment of the lower limbs and mastitis.

Method: Insert the needle perpendicularly, 0.5-1 *cun* deep.

Notes: (1) As a *xi* point of the Stomach Meridian, this acupoint is effective in treating stomachache when used together with *Neiguan* (PC 6) and *Gongsun* (SP 4). (2) Vasculature and innervation: The same as those of *Yinshi* (ST 33).

Dubi (ST 35)

Location: On the knee, in the depression lateral to the patella and its ligament when the knee is

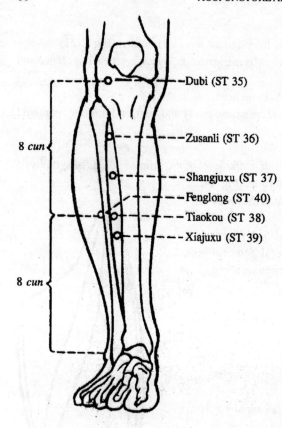

Fig. 2-23

flexed. (Fig. 2-23)

Indications: Pain in the knee joint.

Method: Insert the needle slightly towards the ligament, 0.8-1.2 *cun* deep.

Notes: (1) According to clinical reports, *Dubi* can be used for abdominal distention after the abdominal operation, dysentery and biliary ascariasis, and disorders along the Meridian of Foot-*Yangming* in particular. (2) Vasculature: The network of arteries and veins of the knee joint. Innervation: Lateral cutaneous nerve of calf and the articular branch of the common peroneal nerve.

Zusanli (a *he* point and a lower confluent point corresponding to the stomach, ST 36)

Location: 3 *cun* below *Dubi* (ST 35) and one finger-breadth from the anterior crest of the tibia. (Fig. 2-23)

Indications: Stomachache, abdominal distention, vomiting, diarrhea, dysentery, indigestion, edema, appendicitis, mastitis, mania, epilepsy, flaccidity and numbness of the lower limbs, dyspneic cough, vertigo, palpitation and emaciation due to consumptive disease.

Method: Insert the needle perpendicularly, 1-1.5 *cun* deep.

Notes: (1) It is both a *he* point and a lower confluent point of the meridian. According to *Basic Questions*, *he* points are indicated for diarrhea caused by the unhealthy *qi*. *Miraculous Pivot* says that *he* points are indicated for disorders in the *fu* organs. Therefore, this acupoint is often used to treat diarrhea and dysentery together with *Sanyinjiao* (SP 6), *Tianshu* (ST 25), and *Guanyuan* (RN 4). (2) It is also indicated for various abdominal diseases. *A Systematic Classic of Acupuncture* says that *Zusanli* proves effective for distention in the *zang-fu* organs. (3) This acupoint can be used to strengthen the body. According to clinical reports, moxibustion on *Zusanli* can prevent cerebral thrombosis and reduce plasma fibrinogen and fibrin degradation product. (4) According to reports, needling the acupoints *Zusanli* and *Dazhui* (DU 14) of the rabbit can improve its immunocompetence. (5) Vasculature: Anterior tibial artery and vein. Innervation: Branches of the lateral cutaneous nerve of calf and the saphenous nerve, and deep peroneal nerve.

Shangjuxu (a lower confluent point corresponding to the large intestine, ST 37)

Location: 3 *cun* below *Zusanli* (ST 36). (Fig. 2-23)

Indications: Abdominal pain, borborygmus, diarrhea, dysentery, appendicitis and motor impairment of the lower limbs.

Method: Insert the needle perpendicularly, 1-1.5 *cun* deep.

Notes: Vasculature and innervation: The same as those of *Zusanli* (ST 36).

Tiaokou (ST 38)

Location: 8 *cun* below *Dubi* (ST 35) and one finger-breadth from the anterior crest of the tibia. (Fig. 2-23)

Indications: Motor impairment, numbness and spasmodic pain in the lower limbs and pain in the shoulder.

Method: Insert the needle perpendicularly, 1-1.5 *cun* deep.

Notes: (1) It is usually indicated for scapulohumeral periarthritis. (2) Vasculature and innervation: The same as those of *Zusanli* (ST 36).

Xiajuxu (a lower confluent point corresponding to the small intestine, ST 39)

Location: 9 *cun* below *Dubi* (ST 35) and one finger-breadth from the anterior crest of the tibia. (Fig. 2-23)

Indications: Lower abdominal distention and pain, diarrhea, dysentery, motor impairment of the lower limbs and testalgia.

Method: Insert the needle perpendicularly, 1-1.5 *cun* deep.

Notes: Vasculature: Anterior tibial artery and vein. Innervation: The branches of the superficial peroneal nerve and deep peroneal nerve.

Fenglong (a *luo* point, ST 40)

Location: One finger-breadth from *Tiaokou* (ST 38). (Fig. 2-23)

Indications: Cough, asthma, mania, epilepsy, headache, vertigo and motor impairment of the lower limbs.

Method: Insert the needle perpendicularly, 1-1.5 *cun* deep.

Notes: (1) According to *Jade Dragon Verses*, *Fenglong* is effective in treating profuse expectoration. In clinical practice, it is often used for the diseases caused by phlegm-dampness, such as headache, vertigo and dyspneic cough. (2) Vasculature: Anterior tibial artery and vein. Innervation: Superficial peroneal nerve.

Jiexi (a *jing* point, ST 41)

Location: On the dorsum of the foot, at the midpoint of the transverse crease of the ankle joint, and between the tendons of long extensor muscle of thumb and long extensor muscle of toe. (Fig. 2-24)

Indications: Abdominal distention, constipation, mania, motor impairment, numbness and pain in the lower limbs, headache and vertigo.

Method: Insert the needle perpendicularly, 0.5-0.8 *cun* deep.

Notes: Vasculature: Anterior tibial artery and vein. Innervation: Superficial and deep peroneal nerves.

Chongyang (a *yuan* point, ST 42)

Location: At the prominence of the instep, where the pulsation of the dorsal artery of the foot is palpable, and 3 *cun* above *Xiangu* (ST 43). (Fig. 2-24)

Indications: Stomachache, abdominal distention, facial paralysis, facial swelling, toothache, and swollen instep.

Method: Keep the needle away from the artery and insert it perpendicularly, 0.3-0.5 *cun* deep.

Notes: Vasculature: Dorsal artery and vein of foot and dorsal venous network of foot. Innervation: Medial dorsal cutaneous nerve of foot stemming from the superficial peroneal nerve.

Xiangu (a *shu* point, ST 43)

Location: In the depression distal to the commissure of the second and third metatarsal bones.

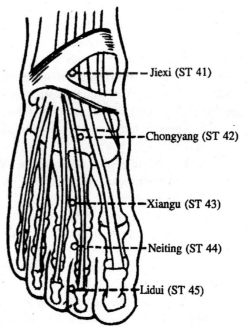

Fig. 2-24

(Fig. 2-24)

Indications: Abdominal pain, borborygmus, swollen face, general edema and swollen instep.

Method: Insert the needle perpendicularly, 0.3-0.5 *cun* deep.

Notes: Vasculature: Dorsal venous network of foot. Innervation: Medial dorsal cutaneous nerve of foot.

Neiting (a *ying* point, ST 44)

Location: On the instep and at the proximal end of the skin crease of the web between the second and third toes. (Fig. 2-24)

Indications: Abdominal distention, stomachache, diarrhea, dysentery, toothache, facial paralysis, sore throat and swollen instep.

Method: Insert the needle obliquely upward, 0.3-0.5 *cun* deep.

Notes: (1) It is a *ying* point and belongs to water of the Five Elements. It is indicated for heat and excess syndromes of the stomach. (2) Vasculature: Dorsal venous network of foot. Innervation: Dorsal digital nerves, and the lateral branch of medial dorsal cutaneous nerve of foot.

Lidui (a *jiing* point, ST 45)

Location: On the lateral side of the second toe and about 0.1 *cun* posterior to the corner of the toenail. (Fig. 2-24)

Indications: Abdominal distention, swollen face, facial paralysis, toothache, sore throat, epistaxis, mania, cold legs and feet.

Notes: Vasculature: Arterial and venous network formed by dorsal digital arteries and veins of foot. Innervation: Dorsal digital nerves of foot stemming from the superficial peroneal nerve.

4. The Spleen Meridian of Foot-*Taiyin* (SP)
(Fig. 2-25 and Fig. 2-26)

1) Traveling route

a) The meridian starts from the medial side of the great toe, along the dorso-ventral boundary of the foot (1) and passing the first phalanx and metatarsal joint (2), then reaches the anterior border of medial malleolus (3). It continues to ascend along the posterior border of the medial side of the tibia (4), emerges from the place 8 *cun* above the medial malleolus, and runs in front of the Liver Meridian of Foot-*Jueyin* (5). Then passing through the knee (6) and the inner side of the thigh (7) it enters the abdomen (8), connecting with the spleen and stomach (9). Finally, it goes through the diaphragm (10) and the pharynx (11), reaches the root of the tongue and further spreads under the tongue (12).

b) A branch starts from the stomach (13), passes the diaphragm and enters the heart (14).

2) Symptoms

Abdominal distention, stomachache, diarrhea, dysentery, edema, jaundice, dysuria, lassitude, stiffness and pain in the tongue, pain in the inner side of the thigh and irritability.

3) Acupoints

Yinbai (a *jiing* point, SP 1)

Location: On the medial side of the great toe and about 0.1 *cun* lateral to the corner of the toenail. (Fig. 2-27)

Indications: Abdominal distention, diarrhea, vomiting, menorrhagia, metrorrhagia, hematuria, irritability and mania.

Method: Insert the needle 0.1 *cun* into the skin, or prick so that a little blood comes out.

Notes: (1) This acupoint can be used together with *Sanyinjiao* (SP 6), *Xuehai* (SP 10), *Guanyuan* (RN 4) and *Tianshu* (ST 25) to treat irregular menstruation and metrorrhagia, and moxibustion is often

MERIDIANS AND ACUPOINTS 33

applied to this acupoint. (2) Vasculature: Dorsal digital arteries of foot. Innervation: Dorsal digital nerve of foot stemming from the superficial peroneal nerve, and the proper digital plantar nerve.

Dadu (a *ying* point, SP 2)

Location: On the medial side of the great toe and in the depression just distal to the metatarsophalangeal joint. (Fig. 2-27)

Indications: Stomachache, vomiting, abdominal distention, diarrhea, constipation and irritability.

Method: Insert the needle perpendicularly, 0.3-0.5 *cun* deep.

Notes: Vasculature: The branches of the medial plantar artery and vein. Innervation: Proper digital plantar nerve stemming from medial plantar nerve.

Taibai (a *shu* point and also *yuan* point, SP 3)

Location: On the medial border of the foot and in the depression on the medial side of the distal end of the first metatarsal. (Fig. 2-27)

Indications: Stomachache, abdominal distention and pain, diarrhea, dysentery, constipation, lassitude and heavy sensation in the limbs, and cardiodynia.

Method: Insert the needle perpendicularly, 0.3-0.5 *cun* deep.

Notes: Vasculature: Dorsal venous network of foot, medial plantar artery and the branches of the medial tarsal artery. Innervation: The branches of saphenous nerve and superficial peroneal nerve.

Gongsun (a *luo* point and also one of the eight confluent points, SP 4)

Location: On the medial border of the foot, anterior and inferior to the proximal end of the first metatarsal. (Fig. 2-27)

Indications: Stomachache, vomiting, abdominal pain, diarrhea, dysentery, irritability and insomnia.

Method: Insert the needle perpendicularly, 0.5-1 *cun* deep.

Notes: (1) As one of the eight confluent points communicating with the *Chong* Meridian (Thoroughfare Vessel), the point can be used together with *Neiguan* (PC 6) to treat disorders of the stomach, heart and chest. (2) According to *Shengyu Verses*, *Gongsun* is indicated for pain in the spleen and heart. (3) It is one of the acupoints frequently used for acupuncture anesthesia. (4) Vasculature: Medial tarsal artery and dorsal venous network of foot. Innervation: Saphenous nerve and the branch of the superficial peroneal nerve.

Shangqiu (a *jing* point, SP 5)

Location: On the medial side of the ankle and in the depression anterior and inferior to the medial malleolus. (Fig. 2-27)

Indications: Abdominal distention, diarrhea, constipation, indigestion, jaundice and pain in the foot and ankle.

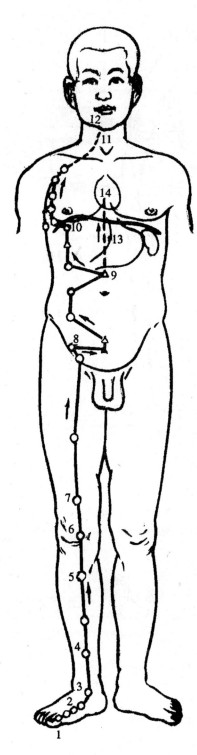

Fig. 2-25 Spleen Meridian of Foot-*Taiyin*

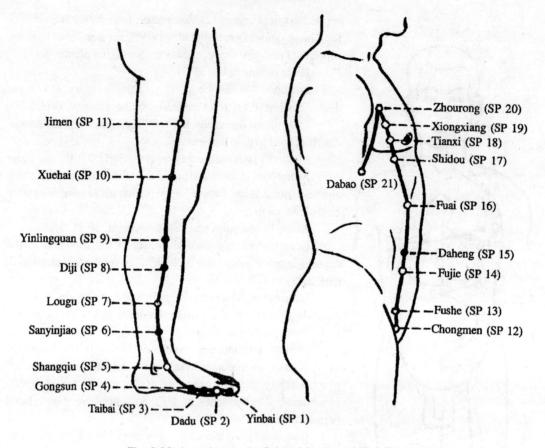

Fig. 2-26 Acupoints on the Spleen Meridian of Foot-*Taiyin*

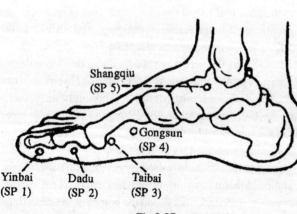

Fig.2-27

Method: Insert the needle perpendicularly, 0.3-0.5 *cun* deep.

Notes: Vasculature: Medial tarsal artery and great saphenous vein. Innervation: Medial cutaneous nerve of leg and the branch of the superficial peroneal nerve.

Sanyinjiao (SP 6)

Location: On the medial side of the leg, 3 *cun* above the tip of the medial malleolus and just posterior to the tibia. (Fig. 2-28)

Indications: Abdominal distention, borborygmus, diarrhea, dysentery, irregular menstruation, dysmenorrhea, metrorrhagia, difficult labor, sterility, leukorrhagia, impotence, seminal emission, dysuria, enuresis, edema, insomnia, motor impairment, numbness and pain in the lower limbs.

Method: Insert the needle perpendicularly, 0.5-1 *cun* deep.

Notes: This is the confluent point of three foot *yin* meridians, which has been confirmed by researches. (2) According to *Tongxuan Verses for Acupoints*, dead fetus can be delivered by needling at

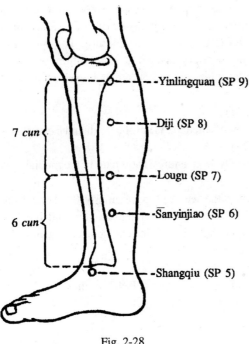

Fig. 2-28

Sanyinjiao. In addition, *Shengyu Verses* says that retained placenta can be removed by needling at *Sanyinjiao*. (3) It can treat enuresis when used together with *Guanyuan* (RN 4). With *Neiguan* (PC 6), *Guanyuan*, *Zusanli* (ST 36) and *Zhongwan* (RN 12), it can treat abdominal distention and pain and diarrhea. (4) Vasculature: Great saphenous vein, and posterior tibial artery and vein. Innervation: Medial cutaneous nerve of leg and tibial nerve.

Lougu (SP 7)

Location: On the medial side of the leg, 6 *cun* above the tip of the medial malleolus and just posterior to the tibia. (Fig. 2-28)

Indications: Abdominal distention, borborygmus, dysuria, enuresis and numbness in the lower limbs.

Method: Insert the needle perpendicularly, 0.5-1 *cun* deep.

Notes: Vasculature and innervation: The same as those of *Sanyinjiao* (SP 6).

Diji (a *xi* point, SP 8)

Location: On the medial side of the leg and 3 *cun* below *Yinlingquan* (SP 9). (Fig. 2-28)

Indications: Abdominal distention, abdominal pain, diarrhea, dysentery, irregular menstruation, dysmenorrhea and dysuria.

Method: Insert the needle perpendicularly, 0.5-1 *cun* deep.

Notes: Vasculature: Great saphenous vein, the branch of the supreme genicular artery and posterior tibial artery and vein. Innervation: The same as those of *Sanyinjiao* (SP 6).

Yinlingquan (a *he* point, SP 9)

Location: On the medial side of the leg and in the depression posterior and inferior to the medial condyle of the tibia. (Fig. 2-28)

Indications: Abdominal distention, diarrhea, dysentery, edema, jaundice, dysuria, dyspnea, and pain in the medial side of the knee and thigh.

Method: Insert the needle perpendicularly, 1-1.5 *cun* deep.

Notes: (1) It is a *he* point of the meridian. According to *The Classic of Questions*, *he* points are indicated for diarrhea caused by the unhealthy *qi*. It can treat diarrhea, dysentery and asthma. (2) Vasculature: Great saphenous vein, supreme genicular artery and posterior tibial artery and vein. Innervation: Medial cutaneous nerve of leg and tibial nerve.

Xuehai (SP 10)

Location: On the medial side of the thigh, 2 *cun* above the superior medial corner of the patella and on the prominence of the medial head of the quadriceps muscle. (Fig. 2-29)

Indications: Irregular menstruation, dysmenorrhea, metrorrhagia, pain in the medial side of the knee and thigh, urticaria, eczema and pruritus.

Method: Insert the needle perpendicularly, 1-1.2 *cun* deep.

Notes: (1) Simple measurement: First, the patient flexes his knee. Then the doctor places his left palm on the upper border of the patient's right knee-cap, with his four fingers extending upward and the thumb held at an angle of 45 degrees. The acupoint is right under the tip of the thumb. The other acupoint

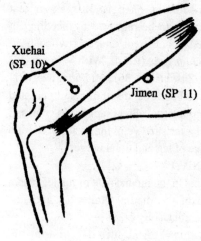

Fig. 2-29

on the other leg can be located in the same way. (2) It can treat urticaria and pruritus together with *Quchi* (LI 11), *Sanyinjiao* (SP 6) and *Geshu* (BL 17). (3) Vasculature: The muscular branches of femoral artery and vein. Innervation: Anterior cutaneous nerve of thigh and the muscular branch of femoral nerve.

Jimen (SP 11)

Location: On the medial side of the thigh and 6 *cun* above *Xuehai*. (Fig. 2-29)

Indications: Dysuria, enuresis and pain in the medial side of the thigh.

Method: Insert the needle perpendicularly, 0.5-1 *cun* deep.

Notes: Vasculature: Great saphenous vein and femoral artery and vein. Innervation: Anterior cutaneous nerve of thigh and saphenous nerve.

Chongmen (SP 12)

Location: In the inguinal region, 3.5 *cun* lateral to the midpoint (*Qugu*, RN 2) of the upper border of the symphysis pubis and lateral to the pulsating external iliac artery. (Fig. 2-30)

Indications: Abdominal pain, diarrhea, leukorrhagia and hernia.

Method: Insert the needle perpendicularly, 0.5-1 *cun* deep.

Note: Vasculature: Femoral artery and vein. Innervation: Femoral nerve.

Fushe (SP 13)

Location: On the lower abdomen, 4 *cun* below the center of the umbilicus and 4 *cun* lateral to the anterior midline. (Fig. 2-30)

Indications: Abdominal pain and masses, and hernia.

Method: Insert the needle perpendicularly, 0.5-1 *cun* deep.

Notes: Vasculature: Superficial epigastric artery, and intercostal artery and vein. Innervation: Ilioinguinal nerve.

Fujie (SP 14)

Location: On the lower abdomen, 4 *cun* lateral to the anterior midline and 3 *cun* above *Fushe* (SP 13). (Fig. 2-30)

Indications: Pain around the umbilicus, diarrhea and hernia.

Method: Insert the needle

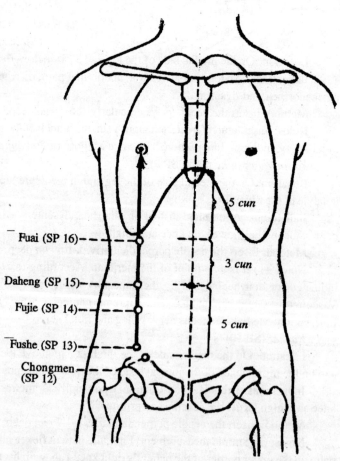

Fig. 2-30

perpendicularly, 1-1.2 *cun* deep.

Notes: Vasculature: The 11th intercostal artery and vein. Innervation: The 11th intercostal nerve.

Daheng (SP 15)

Location: On the middle abdomen and 4 *cun* lateral to the center of the umbilicus. (Fig. 2-30)

Indications: Abdominal pain, diarrhea and constipation.

Method: Insert the needle perpendicularly, 1-1.2 *cun* deep.

Notes: Vasculature: The tenth intercostal artery and vein. Innervation: The tenth intercostal nerve.

Fuai (SP 16)

Location: On the upper abdomen, 3 *cun* above the umbilicus and 4 *cun* lateral to the anterior midline. (Fig. 2-30)

Indications: Abdominal pain, diarrhea and constipation.

Method: Insert the needle perpendicularly, 0.5-1 *cun* deep.

Notes: Vasculature: The eighth intercostal artery and vein. Innervation: The eighth intercostal nerve.

Shidou (SP 17)

Location: On the lateral side of the chest, in the fifth intercostal space and 6 *cun* lateral to the anterior midline. (Fig. 2-31)

Indications: Fullness and pain in the chest and hypochondriac region, and edema.

Method: Insert the needle obliquely, 0.5-0.8 *cun* deep.

Notes: Vasculature: Thoraco-epigastric vein. Innervation: The lateral cutaneous branch of the fifth intercostal nerve.

Tianxi (SP 18)

Location: On the lateral side of the chest, in the fourth intercostal space and 6 *cun* lateral to the anterior midline. (Fig. 2-31)

Indications: Chest pain, cough and mastitis.

Method: Insert the needle obliquely, 0.5-0.8 *cun* deep.

Notes: Vasculature: The branches of lateral thoracic artery and vein, thoraco-epigastric artery and vein, the fourth intercostal artery and vein. Innervation: The lateral cutaneous branch of the fourth intercostal nerve.

Xiongxiang (SP 19)

Location: On the lateral side of the chest, in the third intercostal space and 6 *cun* lateral to the anterior midline. (Fig. 2-31)

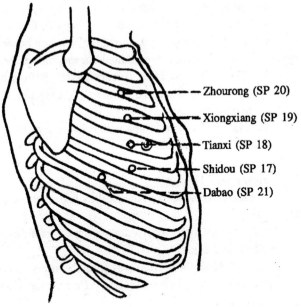

Fig. 2-31

Indications: Fullness and pain in the chest and hypochondriac region.

Method: Insert the needle obliquely, 0.5-0.8 *cun* deep.

Notes: Vasculature: Lateral thoracic artery and vein, and the third intercostal artery and vein. Innervation: The lateral cutaneous branch of the third intercostal nerve.

Zhourong (SP 20)

Location: On the lateral side of the chest, in the second intercostal space and 6 *cun* lateral to the anterior midline. (Fig. 2-31)

Indications: Fullness and pain in the chest and hypochondriac region, cough with dyspnea.

Method: Insert the needle obliquely, 0.5-0.8 *cun* deep.

Notes: Vasculature: Lateral thoracic artery and vein, the second intercostal artery and vein. Innervation: The muscular branch of the anterior thoracic nerve, and the lateral cutaneous branch of the second intercostal nerve.

Dabao (a *luo* point of the spleen, SP 21)

Location: On the lateral side of the chest, in the sixth intercostal space and on the middle axillary line. (Fig. 2-31)

Indications: Fullness and pain in the chest and hypochondriac region, cough and asthma.

Method: Insert the needle obliquely, 0.5-0.8 *cun* deep.

Notes: Vasculature: Thoracodorsal artery and vein, and the sixth intercostal artery and vein. Innervation: The sixth intercostal nerve and the terminal branch of the long thoracic nerve.

5. The Heart Meridian of Hand-*Shaoyin* (HT)

(Fig. 2-32)

1) Traveling route

a) The meridian originates in the heart, spreading over the cardiac system (1). It descends internally past the diaphragm and connects with the small intestine (2).

b) The cardiac branch starts from the cardiac system (3), running along the esophagus (4) and terminates in the ocular system (5).

c) The main branch traverses the lung (6), then runs downward and emerges in the midaxilla (*Jiquan*, HT 1) (7). Then it goes along the posterior border of the medial side of the upper arm (behind the meridians of Hand-*Taiyin* and Hand-*Jueyin*) and reaches the elbow (8). It then runs along the posterior border of the medial side of the forearm to the pisiform bone proximal to the palm (9), and enters the palm (10). It descends along the radial side of the palm, terminating at *Shaochong* (HT 9) (11).

2) Symptoms

Cardialgia, dry throat, thirst with a desire to drink, yellowish eyeballs, pain in the hypochondriac region and along the meridian.

3) Acupoints

Jiquan (HT 1)

Location: At the apex of the axillary fossa, where the pulsation of the axillary artery is palpable. (Fig. 2-33)

Indications: Palpitation, cardialgia, dry throat, fullness in the chest, cold-pain or motor impairment of the elbow and arm.

Method: Keep the needle away from the artery and insert it perpendicularly, 0.3-0.5 *cun* deep.

Notes: Vasculature: Axillary artery. Innervation: Ulnar nerve, median nerve and medial cutaneous nerve of arm.

Qingling (HT 2)

Location: On the medial side of the arm, 3 *cun* above the cubital crease and in the groove medial to the biceps muscle. (Fig. 2-34)

Indications: Yellowish eyeballs, pain in the hypochondriac region, pain in the elbow and arm, and headache.

Method: Insert the needle perpendicularly, 0.5-0.8 *cun* deep.

Notes: Vasculature: Basilic vein and superior ulnar collateral artery. Innervation: Medial cutaneous nerve of forearm, medial cutaneous nerve of arm and ulnar nerve.

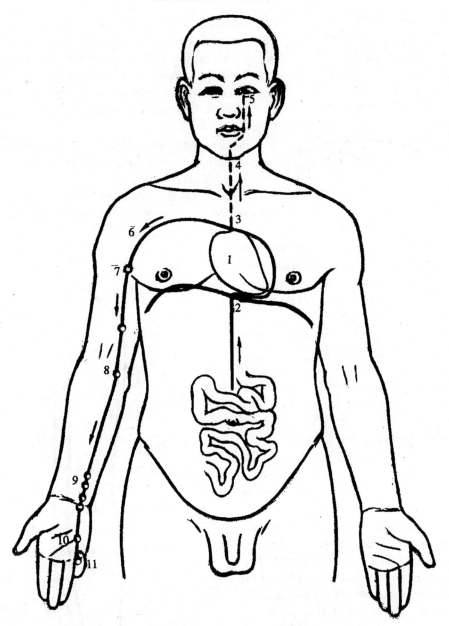

Fig. 2-32 Heart Meridian of Hand-*Shaoyin*

Shaohai (a *he* point, HT 3)

Location: At the midpoint of the line connecting the medial end of the cubital crease and the medial epicondyle of the humerus when the elbow is flexed. (Fig. 2-34)

Indications: Cardialgia, pain in the hypochondriac region, pain in the elbow and arm, headache and scrofula.

Method: Insert the needle perpendicularly, 0.5-0.8 *cun* deep.

Notes: Vasculature: Basilic vein, inferior ulnar collateral artery, and ulnar recurrent artery and vein. Innervation: Medial cutaneous nerve of forearm.

Lingdao (a *jing* point, HT 4)

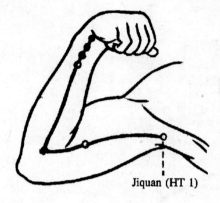

Jiquan (HT 1)

Fig. 2-33

Indications: Palpitation, cardialgia, sore throat, sudden loss of voice, aphasia with stiff tongue, and pain in the wrist and arm.

Method: Insert the needle perpendicularly, 0.3-0.5 *cun* deep.

Notes: Vasculature and innervation: The same as those of *Lingdao* (HT 4).

Yinxi (a *xi* point, HT 6)

Location: On the palmar side of the forearm and on the radial side of the tendon of the ulnar flexor muscle of the wrist, and 0.5 *cun* proximal to the crease of the wrist. (Fig. 2-34)

Indications: Cardialgia, palpitation, night sweat and aphasia.

Method: Insert the needle perpendicularly, 0.3-0.5 *cun* deep.

Notes: Vasculature and innervation: The same as those of *Lingdao* (HT 4).

Shenmen (a *shu* and *yuan* point, HT 7)

Location: On the transverse crease of the wrist and at the radial side of the tendon of the ulnar flexor muscle of the wrist. (Fig. 2-34)

Indications: Cardialgia, palpitation, insomnia, mania, epilepsy, aphonia and pain in the wrist and forearm.

Method: Insert the needle perpendicularly, 0.3-0.5 *cun* deep.

Notes: (1) According to *Tongxuan Verses for Acupoints*, *Shenmen* is effective for dementia. It is also effective for cardialgia when used together with *Neiguan* (PC 6) and *Xinshu* (BL 15). It can treat insomnia when used together with *Fengchi* (GB 20), *Neiguan* and *Sanyinjiao* (SP 6). (2)

Location: On the palmar side of the forearm and on the radial side of the tendon of the ulnar flexor muscle of the wrist, and 1.5 *cun* proximal to the crease of the wrist. (Fig. 2-34)

Indications: Palpitation, cardialgia, aphasia with stiff tongue, sudden loss of voice, and pain in the elbow and arm.

Method: Insert the needle perpendicularly, 0.3-0.5 *cun* deep.

Notes: Vasculature: Ulnar artery. Innervation: Medial cutaneous nerve of forearm and ulnar nerve.

Tongli (a *luo* point, HT 5)

Location: On the palmar side of the forearm and on the radial side of the tendon of the ulnar flexor muscle of the wrist, and 1 *cun* proximal to the crease of the wrist. (Fig. 2-34)

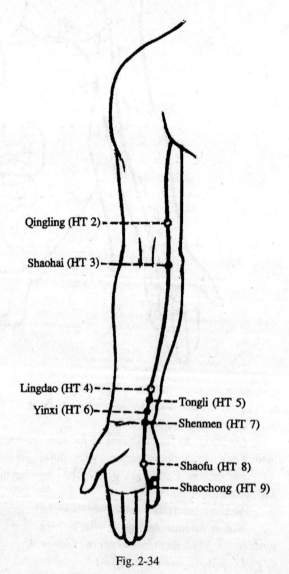

Fig. 2-34

Vasculature and innervation: The same as those of *Lingdao* (HT 4).

Shaofu (a *ying* point, HT 8)

Location: On the palmar surface, between the fourth and fifth metacarpal bones, and in the depression proximal to the metacarpophalangeal joint. (Fig. 2-34)

Indications: Palpitation, chest pain, feverish sensation in the palm and spasmodic pain in the little finger.

Method: Insert the needle perpendicularly, 0.3-0.5 *cun* deep.

Notes: Vasculature: Common palmar digital arteries and veins. Innervation: The fourth common palmar digital nerve stemming from the ulnar nerve.

Shaochong (a *jiing* point, HT 9)

Location: On the radial side of the little finger and 0.1 *cun* proximal to the corner of the nail. (Fig. 2-34)

Indications: Coma, palpitation, cardialgia, pain in the finger joint and febrile diseases.

Method: Insert the needle 0.1 *cun* into the skin, or prick so that a little blood comes out.

Notes: Vasculature: Arterial and venous network formed by the proper palmar digital artery and vein. Innervation: Proper palmar digital nerve stemming from the ulnar nerve.

6. The Small Intestine Meridian of Hand-*Taiyang* (SI)

(Fig. 2-35 and Fig. 2-36)

1) Traveling route

a) The meridian starts at the ulnar side of the little finger (*Shaoze*, SI 1) (1), running along the lateral side of the dorsum of hand, then enters the wrist. Passing the styloid process of ulna (2), it ascends along the posterior border of lateral side of the forearm and emerges from between the olecranon and the medial epicondyle of humerus (3). It continues to travel along the lateral side of the upper arm (4), comes out from the shoulder joint (5), circles around the scapular region (6), and then meets the *Du* Meridian on the shoulder (7). After that, it enters the supraclavicular fossa (*Quepen*, ST 12) (8), connects with the heart (9), descends along the esophagus (10), passes the diaphragm (11), reaches the stomach (12) and finally connects with the small intestine (13).

b) Another branch starts from the supraclavicular fossa (*Quepen*, ST 12) (14), running along the neck (15) and past the cheek (16), and reaches the outer canthus (17). It terminates in the ear (*Tinggong*, SI 19) (18).

c) The third branch starts at the cheek, ascends to the infraorbital region (19), passes the lateral side of the nose, and finally enters the medial canthus of the eye (20).

2) Symptoms

Sore throat, deafness, yellowish eyeballs, swollen cheek and pain in the neck, shoulder, arm and elbow.

3) Acupoints

Shaoze (a *jiing* point, SI 1)

Location: On the ulnar side of the little finger and about 0.1 *cun* lateral to the corner of the nail. (Fig. 2-37)

Indications: Tinnitus, ophthalmalgia, headache, sore throat, pain in the lateral side of the shoulder and arm, hypogalactia, mastitis, apoplexy and coma.

Method: Insert the needle 0.1 *cun* into the skin, or prick so that a little blood comes out.

Notes: (1) According to *Epitome of Acupuncture and Moxibustion*, *Shaoze*, *Hegu* (LI 4) and *Danzhong* (RN 17) can be used for hypogalactia. (2) Vasculature: Arterial and venous network formed by proper palmar digital artery and vein and dorsal digital artery and vein. Innervation: Proper palmar

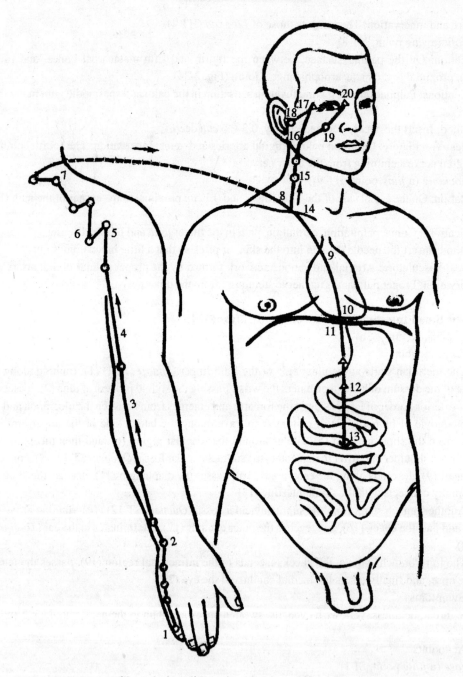

Fig. 2-35 Small Intestine Meridian of Hand-*Taiyang*

digital nerve and dorsal digital nerve stemming from the ulnar nerve.

Qiangu (a *ying* point, SI 2)

Location: At the intersection of the dorso-ventral border of the hand and the ulnar end of the crease of the fifth metacarpophalangeal joint. (Fig. 2-37)

Indications: Headache, tinnitus, deafness, sore throat, ophthalmalgia, malaria, mania, and pain in the elbow, wrist and arm.

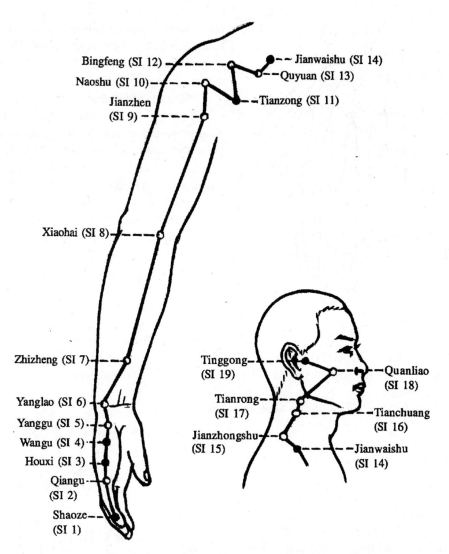

Fig. 2-36 Acupoints on the Small Intestine Meridian of Hand-*Taiyang*

Method: Insert the needle perpendicularly, 0.3-0.5 *cun* deep.
Notes: Vasculature: Dorsal digital artery and vein stemming from the ulnar artery and vein. Innervation: Dorsal digital nerve and proper palmar digital nerve stemming from the ulnar nerve.

Houxi (a *shu* point and one of the eight confluent points, SI 3)
Location: At the intersection of the dorso-ventral border of the hand and the ulnar end of the distal palmar crease. (Fig. 2-37)
Indications: Rigid nape with headache, conjunctival congestion, corneal nebula, deafness, tinnitus, sore throat, pain in the wrist, elbow and arm, malaria, mania and febrile diseases.
Method: Insert the needle perpendicularly, 0.5-1 *cun* deep.
Notes: (1) This is one of the eight confluent points communicating with the *Du* Meridian. It can treat rigid nape with headache when combined with *Fengchi* (GB 20) and *Jianjing* (GB 21). If used together with *Hegu* (LI 4), *Jianshi* (PC 5) and *Dazhui* (DU 14), it can treat malaria. When combined with *Shenmen* (HT 7), *Neiguan* (PC 6), *Dazhui* and *Fengfu* (DU 16), it can treat mania and epilepsy.

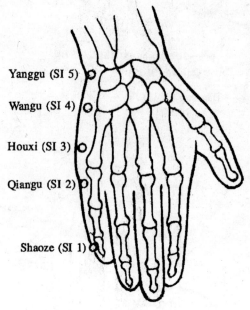

Fig. 2-37

Clinical practice shows that needling at *Houxi* and *Huantiao* (GB 30) may help relieve pain in the legs. (2) Vasculature: Dorsal digital artery and vein, and dorsal venous network of hand. Innervation: The dorsal branch stemming from the ulnar nerve.

Wangu (a *yuan* point, SI 4)

Location: On the ulnar border of the hand and in the depression between the proximal end of the fifth metacarpal bone and hamate bone. (Fig. 2-37)

Indications: Rigid nape with headache, tinnitus, corneal nebula, jaundice, pain in the shoulder, arm and wrist, febrile diseases with anhidrosis.

Method: Insert the needle perpendicularly, 0.3-0.5 *cun* deep.

Notes: Vasculature: Dorsal carpal artery (branch of the ulnar artery) and dorsal venous network of hand. Innervation: The dorsal branch of the ulnar nerve.

Yanggu (a *jing* point, SI 5)

Location: On the ulnar border of the wrist and in the depression between the styloid process of the ulna and triangular bone. (Fig. 2-37)

Indications: Rigid nape with headache, deafness, tinnitus, ophthalmalgia, swollen jaw and pain in the arm and wrist.

Method: Insert the needle perpendicularly, 0.3-0.5 *cun* deep.

Notes: Vasculature: Dorsal carpal artery. Innervation: The dorsal branch of the ulnar nerve.

Yanglao (a *xi* point, SI 6)

Location: On the ulnar side of the posterior surface of the forearm, and in the depression proximal to and on the radial side of the head of the ulna. (Fig. 2-38)

Indications: Blurred vision, and pain in the shoulder, arm and lumbar region.

Method: Insert the needle obliquely upward, 0.5-0.8 *cun* deep.

Notes: Vasculature: The terminal branches of interosseous dorsal artery and vein of forearm and the venous network of the wrist. Innervation: The anastomotic branches of dorsal cutaneous nerve of forearm and the dorsal branch of the ulnar nerve.

Zhizheng (a *luo* point, SI 7)

Location: On the ulnar side of the posterior surface of the forearm and 5 *cun* proximal to the dorsal crease of the wrist. (Fig. 2-38)

Indications: Rigid nape with headache, pain in the elbow, forearm and fingers, febrile diseases and mania.

Method: Insert the needle perpendicularly, 0.5-0.8 *cun*

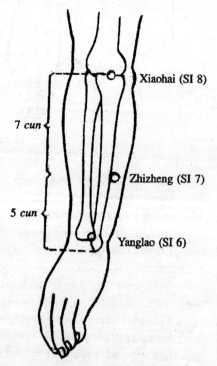

Fig. 2-38

deep.

Notes: Vasculature: The terminal branches of interosseous dorsal artery and vein of forearm. Innervation: The branch of the medial cutaneous nerve of forearm and interosseous dorsal nerve of forearm at the radial side.

Xiaohai (a *he* point, SI 8)

Location: On the medial side of the elbow and in the depression between the olecranon of the ulna and the medial epicondyle of the humerus. (Fig. 2-38)

Indications: Headache, pain in the neck, swollen jaw, spasmodic pain and motor impairment of the elbow and arm.

Method: Insert the needle perpendicularly, 0.3-0.5 *cun* deep.

Notes: Vasculature: Superior and inferior ulnar collateral arteries and veins, and ulnar recurrent artery and vein. Innervation: The branches of medial cutaneous nerve of forearm, and the ulnar nerve.

Jianzhen (SI 9)

Location: Posterior and inferior to the shoulder joint and 1 *cun* above the posterior end of the axillary fold when the arm is adducted. (Fig. 2-39)

Indications: Tinnitus, deafness, pain and motor impairment of the shoulder and arm.

Method: Insert the needle perpendicularly, 0.5-1 *cun* deep.

Notes: Vasculature: Circumflex artery and vein of scapula. Innervation: The branch of axillary nerve, and radial nerve.

Naoshu (SI 10)

Location: On the shoulder, above the posterior end of the axillary fold and in the depression below the lower border of the scapular spine. (Fig. 2-39)

Indications: Pain in the shoulder and arm, and scrofula.

Method: Insert the needle perpendicularly or obliquely outward, 0.5-1 *cun* deep.

Notes: Vasculature: Posterior humeral circumflex artery and vein, and suprascapular artery and vein. Innervation: Axillary nerve and suprascapular nerve.

Tianzong (SI 11)

Location: In the depression of the center of the subscapular fossa. (Fig. 2-39)

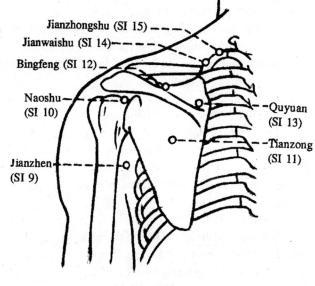

Fig. 2-39

Indications: Pain in the scapular region and the latero-posterior side of the elbow and arm.

Method: Insert the needle perpendicularly, 0.5-1 *cun* deep.

Notes: Vasculature: The muscular branches of circumflex artery and vein of scapula. Innervation: Suprascapular nerve.

Bingfeng (SI 12)

Location: Directly above *Tianzong* (SI 11) and in the center of the suprascapular fossa. (Fig. 2-39)

Indications: Pain in the scapular region and aching in the shoulder and arm.

Method: Insert the needle perpendicularly, 0.5-0.8 *cun* deep.

Notes: Vasculature: Suprascapular artery and vein. Innervation: Posterior branch of the supraclavicular nerve and accessory nerve, and suprascapular nerve.

Quyuan (SI 13)

Location: In the depression at the medial side of the suprascapular fossa. (Fig. 2-39)

Indications: Spasmodic pain in the shoulder and scapular region.

Method: Insert the needle perpendicularly, 0.5-0.8 *cun* deep.

Notes: Vasculature: The descending branch of the transverse cervical artery and vein, and the muscular branch of the suprascapular artery and vein. Innervation: The lateral branch of the second rami posteriores nervorum thoracalium and accessory nerve, and the muscular branch of the suprascapular nerve.

Jianwaishu (SI 14)

Location: 3 *cun* lateral to the lower border of the spinous process of the first thoracic vertebrae. (Fig. 2-39)

Indications: Stiffness of nape and back, pain in the shoulder and back, and cold-pain in the upper limbs.

Method: Insert the needle perpendicularly, 0.5-0.8 *cun* deep.

Notes: Vasculature: Transverse cervical artery and vein. Innervation: The medial cutaneous branch of the first rami posteriores nervorum thoracalium and accessory nerve, and dorsal nerve of scapula.

Jianzhongshu (SI 15)

Location: On the back and 2 *cun* lateral to the lower border of the spinous process of the seventh cervical vertebrae (*Dazhui*, DU 14). (Fig. 2-39)

Indications: Pain in the shoulder and back, cough, dyspnea, chills and fever.

Method: Insert the needle perpendicularly, 0.5-0.8 *cun* deep.

Notes: Vasculature and innervation: The same as those of *Jianwaishu* (SI 14).

Tianchuang (SI 16)

Location: On the lateral side of the neck, 3.5 *cun* lateral to the tip of Adam's apple, and on the posterior border of the sternocleidomastoid muscle. (Fig. 2-40)

Indications: Tinnitus, deafness, sore throat, swollen cheek and sudden loss of voice.

Method: Insert the needle perpendicularly, 0.5-0.8 *cun* deep.

Notes: Vasculature: Ascending cervical artery. Innervation: Cutaneous nerve of neck at the place where the great auricular nerve plexus generates.

Tianrong (SI 17)

Location: On the lateral side of the neck, posterior to the mandibular angle and in the depression of the anterior border of the sternocleidomastoid muscle. (Fig. 2-40)

Indications: Tinnitus, deafness, sore throat, swollen neck and nape, and goiter.

Method: Insert the needle perpendicularly, 0.5-0.8 *cun* deep.

Notes: Vasculature: External jugular vein, internal carotid artery and internal jugular vein. Innervation: The anterior branch of the great auricular nerve, the cervical branch of the facial nerve and the sympathetic nerve.

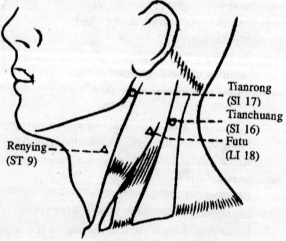

Fig. 2-40

Quanliao (SI 18)

Location: On the face, directly below the outer canthus and in the depression below the zygomatic bone. (Fig. 2-41)

Indications: Facial paralysis, twitching eyelids and toothache.

Method: Insert the needle perpendicularly, 0.3-0.5 *cun* deep.

Notes: Vasculature: The branches of transverse facial artery and vein. Innervation: Facial and infraorbital nerves.

Tinggong (SI 19)

Location: On the face, anterior to the tragus and posterior to the mandibular condyloid process and in the depression found when the mouth is open. (Fig. 2-41)

Indications: Deafness, tinnitus, otorrhea, toothache and pain in the mandibular joint.

Method: Insert the needle perpendicularly, 1-1.2 *cun* deep.

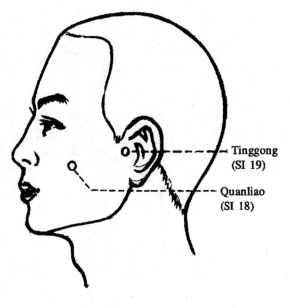

Fig. 2-41

Notes: Vasculature: Rami auriculares anteriores of the superficial temporal artery and vein. Innervation: The branch of the facial nerve, and auriculotemporal nerve.

7. The Bladder Meridian of Foot-*Taiyang* (BL)

(Fig. 2-42 and Fig. 2-43)

1) Traveling route

a) The meridian starts at the medial canthus of the eye (*Jingming*, BL 1) (1), ascends to the forehead (2) and then arrives at the vertex (3).

b) The cephalic branch descends from the vertex to the upper corner of the ear (4).

c) The straight cephalic branch descends from the vertex to the brain (5), exits along the nape (6) and the medial side of the scapula, runs down along the spine (7), and then reaches the lumbar region (8). It enters the abdomen (9) and connects with the kidney (10) and the urinary bladder (11).

d) The lumbar branch starts at the lumbar and gluteal region (12) and runs to the popliteal fossa (13).

e) Another branch starts at the medial side of the scapula, running along the spine (14), and reaches the greater trochanter of femur in the gluteal region (15). Then it descends along the latero-posterior side of the thigh (16) and meets the lumbar branch at the popliteal fossa (17). It continues to descend along the posterior side of the calf (18) and emerges from the posterior side of the external malleolus (19). After passing the tuberosity of the fifth metatarsal bone (20), it reaches the lateral side of the tip of the little toe (*Zhiyin*, BL 67) (21).

2) Symptoms

Dysuria, enuresis, yellowish eyeballs, epistaxis, headache, mania, pain in the nape, back, lumbar region and along the meridian.

3) Acupoints

Jingming (BL 1)

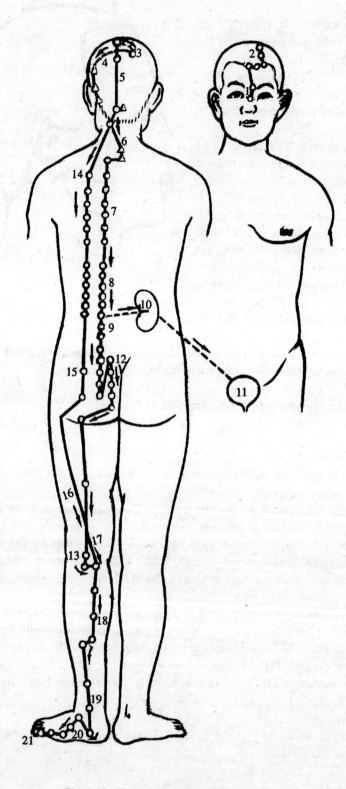

Fig. 2-42 Bladder Meridian of Foot-*Taiyang*

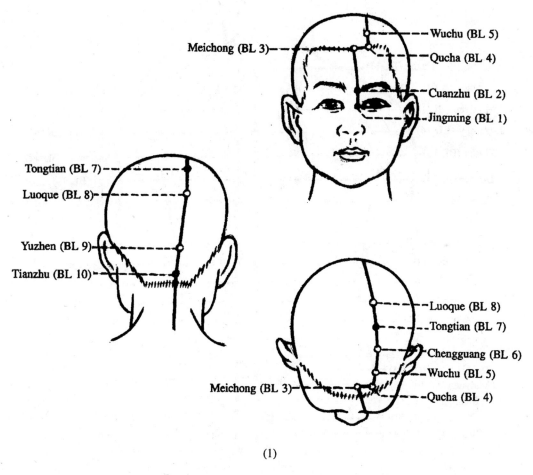

Fig. 2-43 Acupoints on the Bladder Meridian of Foot-*Taiyang*

Location: On the face and in the depression slightly medial to the inner canthus. (Fig. 2-44)

Indications: Eye disorders (red and swollen eyes, corneal nebula and blurred vision), and the inability of eyelids to close completely.

Method: With the patient's eyes closed and eyeballs fixed on the lateral side of the orbit, insert the needle slowly along the orbit, 0.5-1 *cun* deep. Do not twirl, lift or thrust the needle forcefully. Withdraw the needle slowly at the end of the treatment and press the point for a while to avoid bleeding. In addition, moxibustion is contraindicated.

Notes: Vasculature: Angular artery and vein, and ophthalmic artery and vein. Innervation: Supratrochlear and infratrochlear nerves, oculomotor nerve, and ophthalmic nerve.

Cuanzhu (BL 2)

Location: On the face, in the depression of the medial end of the eyebrow and at the supraorbital notch. (Fig. 2-44)

Indications: Frontal headache, pain in the supraorbital region, red and swollen eyes, blurred vision and twitching eyelids.

Method: Insert the needle horizontally toward *Yuyao* (EX-HN 4, on the forehead and in the eyebrow, directly above the pupil), 0.3-0.5 *cun* deep. Moxibustion is contraindicated.

Notes: Vasculature: Frontal artery and vein. Innervation: The medial branch of the frontal nerve.

Meichong (BL 3)

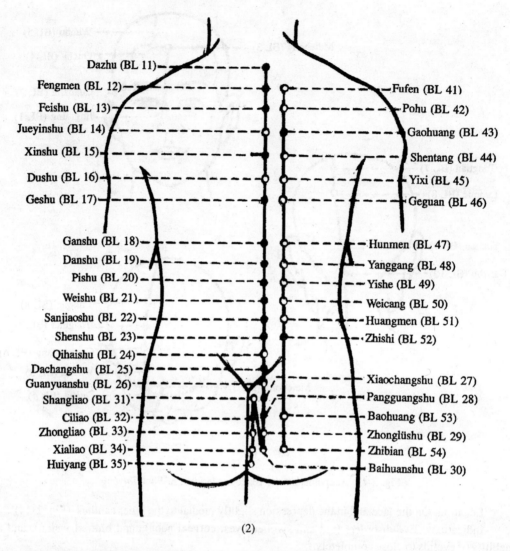

(2)

Fig. 2-43 Acupoints on the Bladder Meridian of Foot-*Taiyang*

Location: On the head, directly above the medial end of the eyebrow and 0.5 *cun* above the anterior hairline. (Fig. 2-45)

Indications: Headache, nasal stuffiness, vertigo and epilepsy.

Method: Insert the needle horizontally, 0.3-0.5 *cun* deep. Moxibustion is contraindicated.

Notes: Vasculature and innervation: The same as those of *Cuanzhu* (BL 2).

Qucha (BL 4)

Location: On the head, 1.5 *cun* lateral to the anterior midline, 0.5 *cun* above the anterior hairline and 1.5 *cun* lateral to *Shenting* (DU 24). (Fig. 2-45)

Indications: Headache, nasal stuffiness, epistaxis and blurred vision.

Method: Insert the needle horizontally, 0.3-0.5 *cun* deep.

Notes: Vasculature: Frontal artery and vein. Innervation: The lateral branch of the frontal nerve.

Wuchu (BL 5)

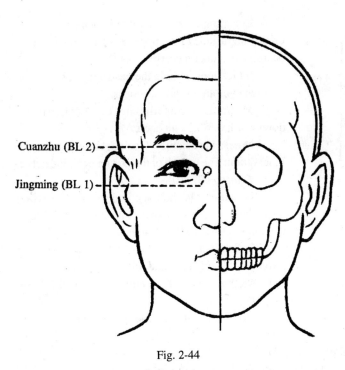

Fig. 2-44

Location: On the head, 0.5 *cun* above *Qucha* (BL 4) and 1.5 *cun* lateral to *Shangxing* (DU 23). (Fig. 2-45)

Indications: Headache, dizziness and epilepsy.

Method: Insert the needle horizontally, 0.3-0.5 *cun* deep.

Notes: Vasculature and innervation: The same as those of *Qucha* (BL 4).

Chengguang (BL 6)

Location: 1.5 *cun* above *Wuchu* (BL 5). (Fig. 2-45)

Indications: Headache, dizziness, nasal stuffiness and febrile diseases with anhidrosis.

Method: Insert the needle horizontally, 0.3-0.5 *cun* deep.

Notes: Vasculature: The anastomotic network of the frontal artery and vein, temporal artery and vein, and occipital artery and vein. Innervation: The lateral branch of the frontal nerve, and the anastomotic branch of the greater occipital nerve.

Tongtian (BL 7)

Location: 1.5 *cun* above *Chengguang* (BL 6). (Fig. 2-45)

Indications: Headache, dizziness, nasal stuffiness and epistaxis.

Method: Insert the needle horizontally, 0.3-0.5 *cun* deep.

Notes: Vasculature: The anastomotic network of the superficial temporal artery and vein and occipital artery and vein. Innervation: The branch of the greater occipital nerve.

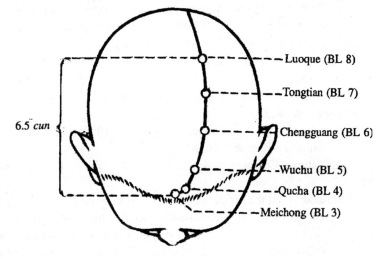

Fig. 2-45

Luoque (BL 8)

Location: 1.5 *cun* posterior to *Tongtian* (BL 7). (Fig. 2-45)

Indications: Vertigo, tinnitus, blurred vision, swollen nape, mania and epilepsy.

Method: Insert the needle horizontally, 0.3-0.5 *cun* deep.

Notes: Vasculature: The branches of the occipital artery and vein. Innervation: The branch of the greater occipital nerve.

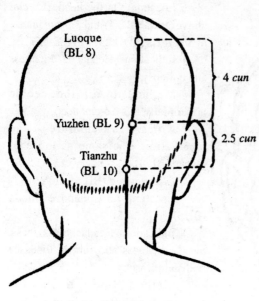

Fig. 2-46

Yuzhen (BL 9)

Location: 1.3 *cun* lateral to *Naohu* (DU 17) and on the lateral side of the upper border of the external occipital protuberance. (Fig. 2-46)

Indications: Pain in the head and nape, red and swollen eyes and nasal stuffiness.

Method: Insert the needle horizontally downward, 0.3-0.5 *cun* deep.

Notes: Vasculature: Occipital artery and vein. Innervation: The branch of the greater occipital nerve.

Tianzhu (BL 10)

Location: On the nape and in the depression on the lateral side of trapezius muscle, 1.3 *cun* lateral to *Yamen* (DU 15). (Fig. 2-46)

Indications: Rigid nape with headache, sore throat, nasal stuffiness and mania.

Method: Insert the needle obliquely, 0.5-1 *cun* deep. Do not insert deep.

Notes: Vasculature: Occipital artery and vein. Innervation: Greater occipital nerve.

Dazhu (one of the eight influential points, BL 11)

Location: On the back, 1.5 *cun* lateral to the midpoint between the spinous processes of the first and second thoracic vertebrae. (Fig. 2-47)

Indications: Rigid nape with headache, back rigidity, fever, nasal stuffiness and cough.

Method: Insert the needle perpendicularly, 0.5-0.8 *cun* deep. Do not insert deep.

Notes: (1) This is one of the eight influential points and where the essence of bones meets together. It can help relieve exterior syndromes and reduce heat. *Basic Questions* points out that *Dazhu*, *Zhongfu* (LU 1), *Quepen* (ST 12) and *Fengmen* (BL 12) can disperse heat in the chest. (2) Vasculature: The medial branches of the posterior intercostal artery and vein. Innervation: The medial cutaneous branches of the first rami posteriores nervorum thoracalium and its lateral branches.

Fengmen (BL 12)

Location: On the back, 1.5 *cun* lateral to the midpoint between the spinous processes of the second and third thoracic vertebrae. (Fig. 2-47)

Indications: Common cold, cough, fever, rigid nape with headache, and pain in the chest and back.

Method: Insert the needle obliquely, 0.5-0.8 *cun* deep.

Notes: (1) Known as "heat house" in ancient times, the point can help disperse wind-cold, and eliminate heat in the *yang* meridians. It is often used to treat fever and cough together with *Waiguan* (SJ 5), *Dazhui* (DU 14), *Hegu* (LI 4), and *Lieque* (LU 7). (2) Vasculature: The same as that of *Dazhu* (BL 11). Innervation: The medial cutaneous branches of the second and third rami posteriores nervorum thoracalium, and their lateral branches.

Feishu (a back *shu* point corresponding to the lung, BL 13)

Location: On the back and 1.5 *cun* lateral to the midpoint between the spinous processes of the third and fourth thoracic vertebrae. (Fig. 2-47)

Indications: cough, asthma, afternoon fever, night sweat, haematemesis and pain in the chest and back.

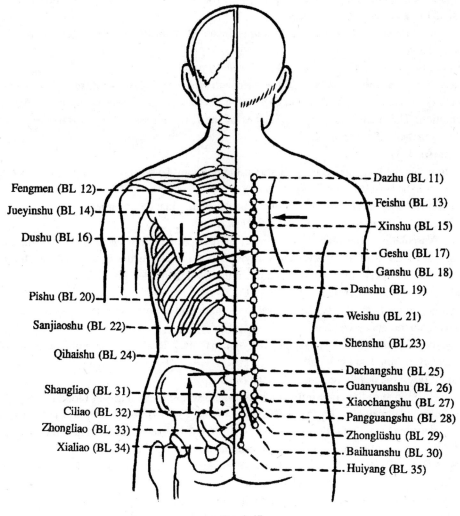

Fig. 2-47

Method: Insert the needle obliquely, 0.5-0.8 *cun* deep.

Notes: (1) According to *Verses for Acupuncture Manipulations*, moxibustion should be used on *Feishu* and *Fengmen* (BL 12) for cough. Clinical report shows that needling at *Feishu* is more effective in treating asthma than at *Dazhui* (DU 14) and *Fengmen*. (2) Vasculature: The same as that of *Dazhu* (BL 11). Innervation: The medial cutaneous branches of the third and fourth rami posteriores nervorum thoracalium, and their lateral branches.

Jueyinshu (a back *shu* point corresponding to the pericardium, BL 14)

Location: On the back and 1.5 *cun* lateral to the midpoint between the spinous processes of the fourth and fifth thoracic vertebrae. (Fig. 2-47)

Indications: Cough, palpitation, cardialgia, oppressed feeling and pain in the chest.

Method: Insert the needle obliquely, 0.5-0.8 *cun* deep.

Notes: Vasculature: The same as that of *Dazhu* (BL 11). Innervation: The medial cutaneous branches of the fourth and fifth rami posteriores nervorum thoracalium and their lateral branches.

Xinshu (a back *shu* point corresponding to the heart, BL 15)

Location: On the back and 1.5 *cun* lateral to the midpoint between the spinous processes of the fifth and sixth thoracic vertebrae. (Fig. 2-47)

Indications: Palpitation, cardialgia, irritability, insomnia, pain and oppressed feeling in the chest, mania and epilepsy.

Method: Insert the needle obliquely, 0.5-0.8 *cun* deep.

Notes: (1) The acupoint can be used together with *Neiguan* (PC 6) and *Zusanli* (ST 36) to treat angina pectoris, coronary heart disease and arrhythmia. (2) Vasculature: The same as that of *Dazhu* (BL 11). Innervation: The medial cutaneous branches of the fifth and sixth rami posteriores nervorum thoracalium, and their lateral branches.

Dushu (BL 16)

Location: On the back and 1.5 *cun* lateral to the midpoint between the spinous processes of the sixth and seventh thoracic vertebrae. (Fig. 2-47)

Indications: Fever, chills, cardialgia, stomachache, abdominal pain, borborygmus and hiccup.

Method: Insert the needle obliquely, 0.5-0.8 *cun* deep.

Notes: Vasculature: The medial branches of the posterior intercostal artery and vein, and the descending branch of the transverse cervical artery. Innervation: The medial cutaneous branches of the sixth and seventh rami posteriores nervorum thoracalium, and their lateral branches.

Geshu (one of the eight influential points, BL 17)

Location: On the back and 1.5 *cun* lateral to the midpoint between the spinous processes of the seventh and eighth thoracic vertebrae. (Fig. 2-47)

Indications: Vomiting, hiccup, dysphagia, cough, asthma, afternoon fever, night sweat, dizziness due to deficiency of blood and palpitation.

Method: Insert the needle obliquely, 0.5-0.8 *cun* deep.

Notes: (1) As one of the eight influential points and where the essence of blood meets together *Geshu* is often used together with *Pishu* (BL 20), *Xuehai* (SP 10) and *Sanyinjiao* (SP 6) to treat thrombocytopenic purpura. (2) *Geshu* and *Danshu* (BL 19) can be used together to treat deficiency of *qi* and blood, night sweat, afternoon fever, cough, asthma and obstinate disorders. (3) Vasculature: The same as that of *Dazhu* (BL 11). Innervation: The medial branches of the seventh and eighth rami posteriores nervorum thoracalium and their lateral branches.

Ganshu (a back *shu* point corresponding to the liver, BL 18)

Location: On the back and 1.5 cun lateral to the midpoint between the spinous processes of the ninth and tenth thoracic vertebrae. (Fig. 2-47)

Indications: Pain in the hypochondriac region, jaundice, hematemesis, eye diseases and mania.

Method: Insert the needle obliquely, 0.5-0.8 *cun* deep.

Notes: Vasculature: The same as that of *Dazhu* (BL 11). Innervation: The medial cutaneous branches of the ninth and tenth rami posteriores nervorum thoracalium, and their lateral branches.

Danshu (a back *shu* point corresponding to the gallbladder, BL 19)

Location: On the back and 1.5 *cun* lateral to the midpoint between the spinous processes of the tenth and 11th thoracic vertebrae. (Fig. 2-47)

Indications: Pain in the hypochondriac region, jaundice, bitter taste and afternoon fever.

Method: Insert the needle obliquely, 0.5-0.8 *cun* deep.

Notes: Vasculature: The same as that of *Dazhu* (BL 11). Innervation: The medial cutaneous branches of the tenth and 11th rami posteriores nervorum thoracalium, and their lateral branches.

Pishu (a back *shu* point corresponding to the spleen, BL 20)

Location: On the back and 1.5 *cun* lateral to the midpoint between the spinous processes of the 11th and 12th thoracic vertebrae. (Fig. 2-47)

Indications: Abdominal distention, diarrhea, jaundice, dysentery, edema, vomiting, hematochezia, and weak spleen and stomach.

Method: Insert the needle obliquely, 0.5-0.8 *cun* deep.

Notes: Vasculature: The same as that of *Dazhu* (BL 11). Innervation: The medial cutaneous branches of the 11th and 12th rami posteriores nervorum thoracalium, and their lateral branches.

Weishu (a back *shu* point corresponding to the stomach, BL 21)

Location: On the back and 1.5 *cun* lateral to the midpoint between the spinous processes of the 12th and the first lumbar vertebrae. (Fig. 2-47)

Indications: Stomachache, abdominal distention, borborygmus, vomiting, weak spleen and stomach.

Method: Insert the needle obliquely, 0.5-0.8 *cun* deep.

Notes: Vasculature: The medial rami of the posterior branches of subcostal artery and vein. Innervation: The medial cutaneous branch of the 12th rami posteriores nervorum thoracalium, and its lateral branches.

Sanjiaoshu (a back *shu* point corresponding to *sanjiao*, BL 22)

Location: On the lower back and 1.5 *cun* lateral to the midpoint between the spinous processes of the first and second lumbar vertebrae. (Fig. 2-47)

Indications: Abdominal distention, borborygmus, diarrhea, dysentery, dysuria, edema, lumbago and back pain.

Method: Insert the needle perpendicularly, 0.5-1 *cun* deep.

Notes: Vasculature: The posterior rami of the first lumbar artery and vein. Innervation: The lateral cutaneous branch of the tenth rami posteriores nervorum thoracalium, and the lateral ramus of the posterior branch of the first lumbar nerve.

Shenshu (a back *shu* point corresponding to the kidney, BL 23)

Location: On the lower back and 1.5 *cun* lateral to the midpoint between the spinous processes of the second and third lumbar vertebrae. (Fig. 2-47)

Indications: Impotence, seminal emission, irregular menstruation, leukorrhagia, sterility, dysuria, enuresis, edema, tinnitus, deafness, and pain in the knee and lumbar region.

Method: Insert the needle perpendicularly, 0.5-1 *cun* deep.

Notes: Vasculature: The posterior rami of the second lumbar artery and vein. Innervation: The lateral cutaneous branch of the posterior ramus of the first lumbar nerve, and its lateral branch.

Qihaishu (BL 24)

Location: On the lower back and 1.5 *cun* lateral to the midpoint between the spinous processes of the third and fourth lumbar vertebrae. (Fig. 2-47)

Indications: Pain in the back and lumbar region, dysmenorrhea, hemorrhoid, and pain and flaccidity of the lower limbs.

Method: Insert the needle perpendicularly, 0.5-1 *cun* deep.

Notes: Vasculature: The posterior rami of the third lumbar artery and vein. Innervation: The lateral cutaneous branch of the posterior ramus of the second lumbar nerve.

Dachangshu (a back *shu* point corresponding to the large intestine, BL 25)

Location: On the lower back and 1.5 *cun* lateral to the midpoint between the spinous processes of the fourth and fifth lumbar vertebrae. (Fig. 2-47)

Indications: Abdominal distention, borborygmus, diarrhea, dysentery, lumbago, numbness and pain in the lower limbs, and hemorrhoid.

Method: Insert the needle perpendicularly, 1-1.2 *cun* deep.

Notes: (1) It is often used together with *Tianshu* (ST 25) to treat borborygmus, diarrhea and dysentery. (2) Vasculature: The posterior rami of the fourth lumbar artery and vein. Innervation: The posterior ramus of the third lumbar nerve.

Guanyuanshu (BL 26)

Location: On the lower back and 1.5 *cun* lateral to the midpoint between the spinous processes of the fifth lumbar and first sacral vertebrae. (Fig. 2-47)

Indications: Abdominal distention, diarrhea, dysuria and lumbago.

Method: Insert the needle perpendicularly, 1-1.2 *cun* deep.

Notes: Vasculature: The posterior rami of the lowest lumbar artery and vein. Innervation: The posterior ramus of the fifth lumbar nerve.

Xiaochangshu (a back *shu* point corresponding to the small intestine, BL 27)

Location: On the sacrum, at the level of the first posterior sacral foramen and 1.5 *cun* lateral to the medial sacral crest. (Fig. 2-47)

Indications: Distention and pain in the lower abdomen, dysuria, enuresis, seminal emission, leukorrhagia and lumbago.

Method: Insert the needle perpendicularly, 1-1.2 *cun* deep.

Notes: Vasculature: The posterior branches of the lateral sacral artery and vein. Innervation: The lateral ramus of the posterior branch of the first sacral nerve.

Pangguangshu (a back *shu* point corresponding to the urinary bladder, BL 28)

Location: On the sacrum, at the level of the second posterior sacral foramen and 1.5 *cun* lateral to the medial sacral crest. (Fig. 2-47)

Indications: Stranguria, retention of urine, enuresis, seminal emission, stiffness and pain along the spinal column, and numbness pain in the lower limbs.

Method: Insert the needle perpendicularly, 1-1.2 *cun* deep.

Notes: Vasculature: The posterior branches of the lateral sacral artery and vein. Innervation: The lateral rami of the posterior branches of the first and second sacral nerves.

Zhonglüshu (BL 29)

Location: On the sacrum, at the level of the third posterior sacral foramen and 1.5 *cun* lateral to the medial sacral crest. (Fig. 2-47)

Indications: Dysentery, hernia, stiffness and pain along the spinal column, and diabetes.

Method: Insert the needle perpendicularly, 1-1.2 *cun* deep.

Notes: Vasculature: The posterior branches of the lateral sacral artery and vein, and the branches of the inferior gluteal artery and vein. Innervation: The lateral rami of the posterior branches of the third and fourth sacral nerves.

Baihuanshu (BL 30)

Location: On the sacrum, at the level of the fourth posterior sacral foramen and 1.5 *cun* lateral to the medial sacral crest. (Fig. 2-47)

Indications: Enuresis, hernia, leukorrhagia and irregular menstruation.

Method: Insert the needle perpendicularly, 1-1.2 *cun* deep.

Notes: Vasculature: Inferior gluteal artery and vein, and internal pudendal artery and vein. Innervation: Inferior clunial nerve, the lateral rami of the posterior branches of the third and fourth sacral nerves, and inferior gluteal nerve.

Shangliao (BL 31)

Location: On the sacrum, at the midpoint between the posterosuperior iliac spine and the posterior midline, just at the first posterior sacral foramen. (Fig. 2-47)

Indications: Lumbosacral pain, irregular menstruation, leukorrhagia, seminal emission and dysuria,

Method: Insert the needle perpendicularly, 1-1.2 *cun* deep.

Ciliao (BL 32)

Location: On the sacrum, medial and inferior to the posterosuperior iliac spine, just at the second posterior sacral foramen. (Fig. 2-47)

Indications: Lumbosacral pain, irregular menstruation, leukorrhagia, impotence, seminal emission, hernia, numbness and pain in the lower limbs.

Method: Insert the needle perpendicularly, 1-1.2 *cun* deep.

Notes: Vasculature: The same as that of *Shangliao* (BL 31). Innervation: The posterior ramus of the second sacral nerve.

Zhongliao (BL 33)

Location: On the sacrum, medial and inferior to *Ciliao*, just at the third posterior sacral foramen. (Fig. 2-47)

Indications: Lumbosacral pain, irregular menstruation, leukorrhagia, and dysuria.

Method: Insert the needle perpendicularly, 1-1.2 *cun* deep.

Notes: Vasculature: The same as that of *Shangliao* (BL 31). Innervation: The posterior ramus of the third sacral nerve.

Xialiao (BL 34)

Location: On the sacrum, medial and inferior to *Zhongliao*, just at the fourth posterior sacral foramen. (Fig. 2-47)

Indications: Lumbago, abdominal pain, borborygmus, diarrhea and dysuria.

Method: Insert the needle perpendicularly, 1-1.2 *cun* deep.

Notes: Vasculature: The branches of the inferior gluteal artery and vein. Innervation: The posterior ramus of the fourth sacral nerve.

Huiyang (BL 35)

Location: On the sacrum and 0.5 *cun* lateral to the tip of the coccyx. (Fig. 2-47)

Indications: Dysentery, diarrhea, hemafecia, hemorrhoids and impotence.

Method: Insert the needle perpendicularly, 1-1.2 *cun* deep.

Notes: Vasculature: The branches of the inferior gluteal artery and vein. Innervation: Coccygeal nerve.

Chengfu (BL 36)

Location: On the posterior side of the thigh and at the midpoint of the inferior gluteal crease. (Fig. 2-48)

Indications: Lumbago, numbness and pain in the lower limbs and hemorrhoids.

Method: Insert the needle perpendicularly, 1-2.5 *cun* deep.

Notes: Vasculature: Companion artery and vein of sciatic nerve. Innervation: Cutaneous nerve of thigh, and sciatic nerve.

Yinmen (BL 37)

Location: On the posterior side of the thigh and on the line connecting *Chengfu* (BL 36) and *Weizhong* (BL 40), and 6 *cun* below *Chengfu* (BL 36). (Fig. 2-48)

Indications: Stiffness and pain along the spinal column, numbness and pain in the lower limbs.

Method: Insert the needle perpendicularly, 1-2 *cun* deep.

Notes: Vasculature: The third perforating branch of the deep femoral artery and vein. Innervation: Posterior cutaneous nerve of thigh and sciatic nerve.

Fuxi (BL 38)

Location: At the lateral end of the popliteal crease, 1 *cun* above *Weiyang* (BL 39) and medial to the

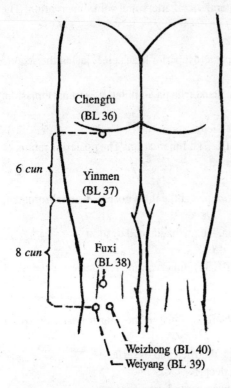

Fig. 2-48

tendon of the biceps muscle of the thigh. (Fig. 2-48)

Indications: Numbness and pain in the gluteal and femoral region, and pain in the popliteal fossa.

Method: Insert the needle perpendicularly, 1-1.2 cun deep.

Notes: Vasculature: Superolateral genicular artery and vein. Innervation: Posterior cutaneous nerve of thigh and common peroneal nerve.

Weiyang (a lower confluent point corresponding to *sanjiao*, BL 39)

Location: At the lateral end of the popliteal crease and medial to the tendon of the biceps muscle of the thigh. (Fig. 2-48)

Indications: Dysuria, lower abdominal distention, stiffness and pain along the spinal column, and spasmodic pain in the lower limbs.

Method: Insert the needle perpendicularly, 1-1.2 cun deep.

Notes: Vasculature and innervation: The same as those of *Fuxi* (BL 38).

Weizhong (a *he* point, and a lower confluent point corresponding to the urinary bladder, BL 40)

Location: At the midpoint of the popliteal crease and between the tendon of the biceps muscle of the thigh and the semitendinous muscle. (Fig. 2-48)

Indications: Abdominal pain, vomiting, diarrhea, dysuria, pain in the leg, lumbar and popliteal regions, motor impairment of the lower limbs, and sunstroke.

Method: Insert the needle perpendicularly, 1-1.2 cun deep or prick the acupoint so that a little blood comes out. Moxibustion can be used except scar-producing moxibustion.

Notes: (1) As a *he* point of the meridian, it can help disperse heat, activate the circulation of *qi*, resolve stasis and stop vomiting. (2) According to *The Inner Canon of the Yellow Emperor*, acupoints on the popliteal region can be used to treat lumbar disorders. *Weizhong* is therefore often used together with *Shenshu* (BL 23) and *Huantiao* (GB 30) to treat pains in the lumbar region and legs. (3) Vasculature: Vena femoropoplitea, and popliteal vein and artery. Innervation: Posterior cutaneous nerve of thigh and tibial nerve.

Fufen (BL 41)

Location: On the back and 3 *cun* lateral to the midpoint between the spinous processes of the second and third thoracic vertebrae. (Fig. 2-49)

Indications: Spasmodic pain in the nape, shoulder and back, and numbness in the upper limbs.

Method: Insert the needle obliquely, 0.5-0.8 *cun* deep.

Notes: Vasculature: The descending branch of the transverse cervical artery, and the lateral rami of the posterior branches of the intercostal artery and vein. Innervation: The lateral cutaneous branches of the first and second rami posteriores nervorum thoracalium, and dorsal nerve of scapula.

Pohu (BL 42)

Location: On the back and 3 *cun* lateral to the midpoint between the spinous processes of the third and fourth thoracic vertebrae. (Fig. 2-49)

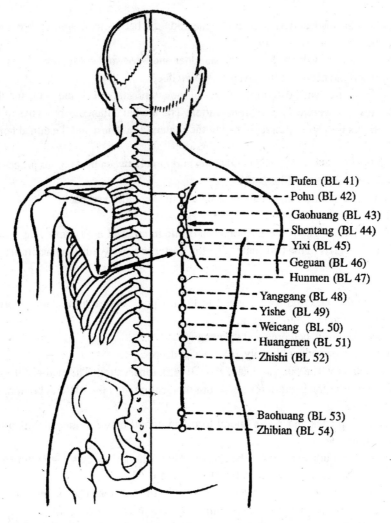

Fig. 2-49

Indications: Cough, asthma, stiffness and pain in the nape and back.

Method: Insert the needle obliquely, 0.5-0.8 *cun* deep.

Notes: Vasculature: The posterior branch of the intercostal artery, and the descending branch of the transverse cervical artery. Innervation: The medial cutaneous branches of the second and third rami posteriores nervorum thoracalium and their lateral branches, the dorsal nerve of scapula.

Gaohuang (BL 43)

Location: On the back and 3 *cun* lateral to the midpoint between the spinous processes of the fourth and fifth thoracic vertebrae. (Fig. 2-49)

Indications: Pulmonary tuberculosis, cough, asthma, seminal emission, night sweat, weak spleen and stomach, pain in the shoulder and back.

Method: Insert the needle obliquely, 0.5-0.8 *cun* deep.

Notes: Vasculature: The posterior branch of the intercostal artery, and the descending branch of the transverse cervical artery. Innervation: The medial cutaneous branches of the third and fourth rami posteriores nervorum thoracalium and their lateral branches, and the dorsal nerve of scapula.

Shentang (BL 44)

Location: On the back and 3 *cun* lateral to the midpoint between the spinous processes of the fifth and sixth thoracic vertebrae. (Fig. 2-49)

Indications: Cough, asthma, pain in the shoulder and back, and chest pain.

Method: Insert the needle obliquely, 0.5-0.8 *cun* deep.

Notes: Vasculature: The posterior branches of the intercostal artery and vein, and the descending branch of the transverse cervical artery. Innervation: The medial cutaneous branches of the fourth and fifth rami posteriores nervorum thoracalium and their lateral branches, and the dorsal nerve of scapula.

Yixi (BL 45)

Location: On the back and 3 *cun* lateral to the midpoint between the spinous processes of the sixth and seventh thoracic vertebrae. (Fig. 2-49)

Indications: Cough, asthma, malaria and pain in the shoulder and back.

Method: Insert the needle obliquely, 0.5-0.8 *cun* deep.

Notes: Vasculature: The posterior branches of the intercostal artery and vein. Innervation: The medial cutaneous branches of the fifth and sixth rami posteriores nervorum thoracalium and their lateral branches.

Geguan (BL 46)

Location: On the back and 3 *cun* lateral to the midpoint between the spinous processes of the seventh and eighth thoracic vertebrae. (Fig. 2-49)

Indications: Vomiting, belching and dysphagia.

Method: Insert the needle obliquely, 0.5-0.8 *cun* deep.

Notes: Vasculature: The same as that of *Yixi* (BL 45). Innervation: The medial cutaneous branches of the sixth and seventh rami posteriores nervorum thoracalium and their lateral branches.

Hunmen (BL 47)

Location: On the back and 3 *cun* lateral to the midpoint between the spinous processes of the ninth and tenth thoracic vertebrae. (Fig. 2-49)

Indications: Distention and pain in the chest and hypochondriac region, vomiting and dysphagia.

Method: Insert the needle obliquely, 0.5-0.8 *cun* deep.

Notes: Vasculature: The same as that of *Yixi* (BL 45). Innervation: The medial cutaneous branches of the eighth and ninth rami posteriores nervorum thoracalium.

Yanggang (BL 48)

Location: On the back and 3 *cun* lateral to the midpoint between the spinous processes of the tenth and 11th thoracic vertebrae. (Fig. 2-49)

Indications: Jaundice, abdominal pain, borborygmus, diarrhea and diabetes.

Method: Insert the needle obliquely, 0.5-0.8 *cun* deep.

Notes: Vasculature: The same as that of *Yixi* (BL 45). Innervation: The lateral branches of the ninth and tenth rami posteriores nervorum thoracalium.

Yishe (BL 49)

Location: On the back and 3 *cun* lateral to the midpoint between the spinous processes of the 11th and 12th thoracic vertebrae. (Fig. 2-49)

Indications: Abdominal distention, borborygmus, diarrhea, vomiting and dysphagia.

Method: Insert the needle obliquely, 0.5-0.8 *cun* deep.

Notes: Vasculature: The same as that of *Yixi* (BL 45). Innervation: The lateral branches of the tenth and 11th rami posteriores nervorum thoracalium.

Weicang (BL 50)

Location: On the back and 3 *cun* lateral to the midpoint between the spinous processes of the 12th thoracic and first lumbar vertebrae. (Fig. 2-49)

Indications: Abdominal distention, stomachache, edema and infantile indigestion with food retention.

Method: Insert the needle obliquely, 0.5-0.8 *cun* deep.

Notes: Vasculature: The posterior branches of the subcostal artery and vein. Innervation: The lateral branch of the 11th rami posteriores nervorum thoracalium.

Huangmen (BL 51)

Location: On the lower back and 3 *cun* lateral to the midpoint between the spinous processes of the first and second lumbar vertebrae. (Fig. 2-49)

Indications: Abdominal pain, mass in the abdomen, constipation and breast disorders of women.

Method: Insert the needle obliquely, 0.5-0.8 *cun* deep.

Notes: Vasculature: The posterior branches of the first lumbar artery and vein. Innervation: The lateral branch of the 12th rami posteriores nervorum thoracalium.

Zhishi (BL 52)

Location: On the lower back and 3 *cun* lateral to the midpoint between the spinous processes of the second and third lumbar vertebrae. (Fig. 2-49)

Indications: Seminal emission, impotence, dysuria, edema and lumbago.

Method: Insert the needle perpendicularly, 1-1.2 *cun* deep.

Notes: Vasculature: The posterior branches of the second lumbar artery and vein. Innervation: The lateral branch of the 12th and the lateral branch of the first lumbar nerve.

Baohuang (BL 53)

Location: On the buttock, at the level of the second posterior sacral foramen and 3 *cun* lateral to the median sacral crest. (Fig. 2-49)

Indications: Borborygmus, abdominal distention, dyschesia, dysuria, pain along the spinal column and swollen vulva.

Method: Insert the needle perpendicularly, 1-1.2 *cun* deep.

Notes: Vasculature: Superior gluteal artery and vein. Innervation: Superior clunial nerve, and superior gluteal nerve.

Zhibian (BL 54)

Location: On the buttock, at the level of the fourth posterior sacral foramen and 3 *cun* lateral to the median sacral crest. (Fig. 2-49)

Indications: Dysuria, dyschesia, pain in the lumbar and sacral region, numbness and pain with motor impairment of the lower limbs, and hemorrhoids.

Method: Insert the needle perpendicularly, 1-2 *cun* deep.

Notes: Vasculature: Inferior gluteal artery and vein. Innervation: Inferior gluteal nerve, posterior cutaneous nerve of thigh, and sciatic nerve.

Heyang (BL 55)

Location: On the posterior side of the leg and 2 cun below *Weizhong* (BL 40). (Fig. 2-50)

Indications: Stiffness and pain along the spinal column, numbness and pain in the lower limbs, hernia and metrorrhagia.

Method: Insert the needle perpendicularly, 1-1.5 *cun* deep.

Notes: Vasculature: Small saphenous vein, and popliteal artery and vein. Innervation: Medial cutaneous nerve of calf, and tibial nerve.

Chengjin (BL 56)

Location: On the posterior side of the leg and between *Heyang* (BL 55) and *Chengshan* (BL 57), at the center of the gastrocnemius muscle belly and 5 *cun* below *Weizhong* (BL 40). (Fig. 2-50)

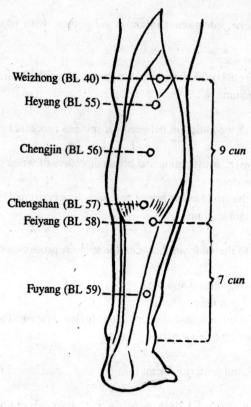

Fig. 2-50

Indications: Pain in the back and lumbar region, pain in the leg and spasm of gastrocnemius muscle, hemorrhoids.

Method: Insert the needle perpendicularly, 1-1.5 *cun* deep.

Notes: Vasculature: Small saphenous vein, and posterior tibial artery and vein. Innervation: Medial cutaneous nerve of calf, and tibial nerve.

Chengshan (BL 57)

Location: On the posterior midline of the leg, between *Weizhong* (BL 40) and *Kunlun* (BL 60), 8 *cun* below *Weizhong*, and in the depression formed below the gastrocnemius muscle belly when the leg is stretched or the heel is lifted. (Fig. 2-50)

Indications: Lumbago, pain in the leg and spasm of the gastrocnemius muscle, hemorrhoids and constipation.

Method: Insert the needle perpendicularly, 1-1.5 *cun* deep.

Notes: (1) Simple measurement: When the leg is stretched the acupoint is in the depression below the gastrocnemius muscle belly. (2) It is usually used together with *Changqiang* (DU 1), *Erbai* (EX-UE 2) and *Dachangshu* (BL 25) in treating hemorrhoids. (3) Vasculature and innervation: The same as those of *Chengjin* (BL 56).

Feiyang (a *luo* point, BL 58)

Location: On the posterior side of the leg, 7 *cun* directly above *Kunlun* (BL 60) and 1 *cun* lateral and inferior to *Chengshan* (BL 57). (Fig. 2-50)

Indications: Pain in the back and lumbar region, weakness and numbness of the lower limbs, headache, dizziness and hemorrhoids.

Method: Insert the needle perpendicularly, 1-1.5 *cun* deep.

Notes: Vasculature: Posterior tibial artery. Innervation: Lateral cutaneous nerve of calf.

Fuyang (a *xi* point of the *Yangqiao* Meridian, BL 59)

Location: On the posterior side of the leg, posterior to the lateral malleolus and 3 *cun* directly above *Kunlun* (BL 60). (Fig. 2-50)

Indications: Pain in the lower limbs and lumbar region, motor impairment of the lower limbs, pain and swelling in ankle, headache.

Method: Insert the needle perpendicularly, 0.5-1 *cun* deep.

Notes: Vasculature: Small saphenous vein and the terminal branch of the peroneal artery. Innervation: Sural nerve.

Kunlun (a *jing* point, BL 60)

Location: Posterior to the lateral malleolus and in the depression between the tip of the external malleolus and Achilles tendon. (Fig. 2-51)

Indications: Rigid nape with headache, dizziness, malaria, lumbago, swollen ankle, infantile epilepsy and difficult labor.

Method: Insert the needle perpendicularly, 0.5-1 *cun* deep.

Notes: (1) According to *Epitome of Acupuncture and Moxibustion*, needling at this acupoint may cause abortion. (2) Vasculature: Small saphenous vein and posterior artery and vein of lateral malleolus. Innervation: Sural nerve.

Pucan (BL 61)

Location: On the lateral side of the foot, in the depression posterior and inferior to the external malleolus and 1.5 *cun* directly below *Kunlun* (BL 60). (Fig. 2-51)

Indications: Weakness and numbness of the lower limbs, swollen heel and epilepsy.

Method: Insert the needle perpendicularly, 0.3-0.5 *cun* deep.

Notes: Vasculature: Lateral calcaneus branches of the peroneal artery and vein. Innervation: Lateral calcaneus branch of the sural nerve.

Shenmai (one of the eight confluent points, BL 62)

Location: On the lateral side of the foot and in the depression directly below the external malleolus. (Fig. 2-51)

Indications: Rigid nape with headache, vertigo, insomnia, epilepsy, numbness and pain in the lower limbs.

Method: Insert the needle perpendicularly, 0.3-0.5 *cun* deep.

Notes: (1) This is one of the eight confluent points communicating with the *Yangqiao* Meridian. It can treat inner canthus and disorders of the neck, nape, ear and shoulder when used together with *Houxi* (SI 3). (2) When used together with *Zhaohai* (KI 6), it can treat insomnia. (3) Vasculature: Lateral malleolar arterial network. Innervation: Sural nerve.

Jinmen (a *xi* point, BL 63)

Location: On the lateral side of the foot, directly below the anterior border of the external malleolus and in the depression lateral to the cuboid bone. (Fig. 2-51)

Indications: Lumbago, stranguria, numbness and pain in the lower limbs, pain in the foot and ankle, epilepsy and infantile convulsion.

Method: Insert the needle perpendicularly, 0.3-0.5 *cun* deep.

Notes: (1) As a *xi* point of the meridian, it is especially effective for lumbago and stranguria. (2) Vasculature: Lateral plantar artery and vein. Innervation: Lateral dorsal cutaneous nerve of foot and lateral plantar nerve.

Jinggu (a *yuan* point, BL 64)

Location: On the lateral side of the foot and in the depression below the tuberosity of the fifth metatarsal bone. (Fig. 2-51)

Indications: Epilepsy, headache, rigid nape, corneal nebula and pain in the legs and lumbar region.

Method: Insert the needle perpendicularly, 0.3-0.5 *cun* deep.

Notes:

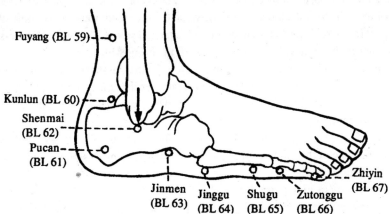

Fig 2-51

Vasculature and innervation: The same as those of *Jinmen* (BL 63).

Shugu (a *shu* point, BL 65)

Location: On the lateral side of the foot and in the depression posterior to the fifth metatarsophalangeal joint. (Fig. 2-51)

Indications: Epilepsy, rigid nape with headache, dizziness and pain in the legs and lumbar region.

Method: Insert the needle perpendicularly, 0.3-0.5 *cun* deep.

Notes: Vasculature: The fourth common plantar digital artery and vein. Innervation: The fourth common digital plantar nerve and lateral dorsal cutaneous nerve of foot.

Zutonggu (a *ying* point, BL 66)

Location: On the lateral side of the foot and in the depression anterior to the fifth metatarsophalangeal joint. (Fig. 2-51)

Indications: Rigid nape with headache, dizziness, mania and epilepsy.

Method: Insert the needle perpendicularly, 0.3-0.5 *cun* deep.

Notes: Vasculature: Plantar digital artery and vein. Innervation: Proper digital plantar nerve and lateral dorsal cutaneous nerve of foot.

Zhiyin (a *jiing* point, BL 67)

Location: On the lateral side of the small toe, about 0.1 *cun* to the corner of the toe nail. (Fig. 2-51)

Indications: Headache, nasal stuffiness, ophthalmalgia, abnormal fetal position, difficult labor and retention of placenta.

Method: Insert the needle 0.1 *cun* into the skin.

Notes: (1) *Zhiyin* is often used for abnormal fetal position, either with acupuncture or moxibustion. Clinical reports show that using laser onto *Zhiyin* can help treat abnormal fetal position with a success rate of 76.26%. Some scholars believe that acupuncture and moxibustion promote uterine and fetal activities and relax abdominal muscle, which help the fetal position becomes normal. (2) Vasculature: The arterial network formed by dorsal digital artery of foot and proper digital plantar artery. Innervation: Proper digital plantar nerve and lateral dorsal cutaneous nerve of foot.

8. The Kidney Meridian of Foot-*Shaoyin* (KI)

(Fig. 2-52 and Fig. 2-53)

1) Traveling route

a) The meridian starts at the plantar tip of the small toe and runs obliquely towards *Yongquan* (KI 1) (1) in the center of the sole. Passing *Rangu* (KI 2) which locates in front of the medial malleolus (2), it circles the posterior medial malleolus (3) and runs in the heel (4). Then it ascends along the medial side of the calf (5), and emerges from between the semitendinous and semimembranous muscles in the popliteal fossa (6). It further ascends along the medial side of the thigh (7), enters the spinal column and terminates in the kidneys (8), connecting with the urinary bladder (9).

b) The kidney branch starts from the kidney (10), passes the liver and diaphragm (11), enters the lung (12), runs through the throat (13) and finally reaches the root of the tongue (14).

c) Another branch starts from the lung, links with the heart and enters the chest (15).

2) Symptoms

Hemoptysis, asthma, dry tongue and swollen pharynx, pain in the lumbar region, spinal column and medial side of the thigh, diarrhea, palpitation, and feverish sensation in the center of the sole.

3) Acupoints

Yongquan (a *jiing* point, KI 1)

Location: On the sole, in the depression which appears on the anterior part of the sole when the foot is in the plantar flexion and approximately at the junction of the anterior third and posterior two-

MERIDIANS AND ACUPOINTS

thirds of the line connecting the base of the second and third toes and the heel. (Fig. 2-54)

Indications: Coma, headache, vertigo, dry tongue, swollen pharynx, aphonia, dysuria, infantile convulsion and epilepsy.

Method: Insert the needle perpendicularly, 0.5-0.8 *cun* deep.

Notes: (1) This acupoint is often used for coma together with *Shuigou* (DU 26), *Zusanli* (ST 36) and *Shixuan* (EX-UE 11). According to *Verses for Hundred Symptoms*, *Yongquan* can help relieve coma caused by cold or heat. (2) Vasculature: The plantar arch of the anterior tibial artery. Innervation: The second common plantar digital nerve.

Rangu (a *ying* point, KI 2)

Location: On the medial border of the foot and in the depression below the tuberosity of the navicular bone. (Fig. 2-55)

Indications: Seminal emission, diabetes, jaundice, irregular menstruation, pruritus vulvae, prolapse of uterus and swollen instep.

Method: Insert the needle perpendicularly, 0.5-1 *cun* deep.

Notes: Vasculature: The branches of the medial plantar artery and medial tarsal arteries. Innervation: The terminal branch of the medial cutaneous nerve of leg and medial plantar nerve.

Taixi (a *shu* point and a *yuan* point, KI 3)

Location: On the medial side of the foot, posterior to the medial malleolus and in the depression between the tip of the medial malleolus and Achilles tendon. (Fig. 2-55)

Indications: Impotence, seminal emission, frequent micturition, diabetes, irregular menstruation, headache, vertigo, insomnia, deafness, asthma, sore throat, lumbago, toothache and swollen ankle.

Method: Insert the needle perpendicularly, 0.5-0.8 *cun* deep.

Notes: (1) As a *shu* and *yuan* point of the meridian, this acupiont can help replenish the kidney and strengthen the loins and knees. It is effective for lumbago, impotence, seminal emission and irregular menstruation when used together with *Shenshu* (BL 23), *Guanyuan* (RN 4) and *Sanyinjiao* (SP 6). If used together with *Shenmen* (HT 7) and *Sanyinjiao* it can treat insomnia. (2) As *Jade Dragon Verses* points out, *Taixi*, *Kunlun* (BL 60) and *Shenmai* (BL 62) are the first choices in treating swollen foot. (3) Vasculature: Posterior tibial artery and vein. Innervation: Medial cutaneous nerve of leg and tibial nerve.

Dazhong (a *luo* point, KI 4)

Location: On the medial side of the foot, posterior and inferior to the medial malleolus and in the depression medial to the attachment of the Achilles tendon. (Fig. 2-55)

Indications: Hemoptysis, asthma, dysuria, lumbago,

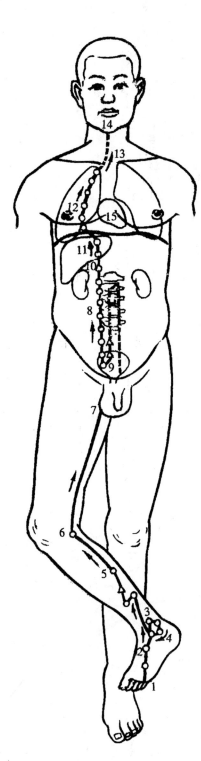

Fig. 2-52 Kidney Meridian of Foot-*Shaoyin*

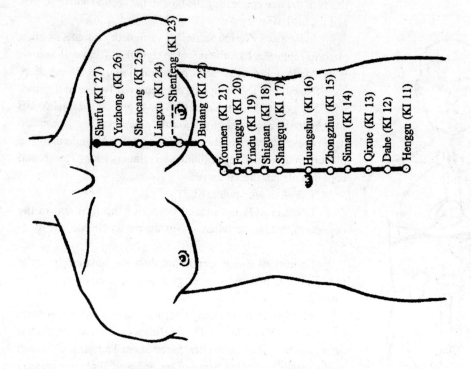

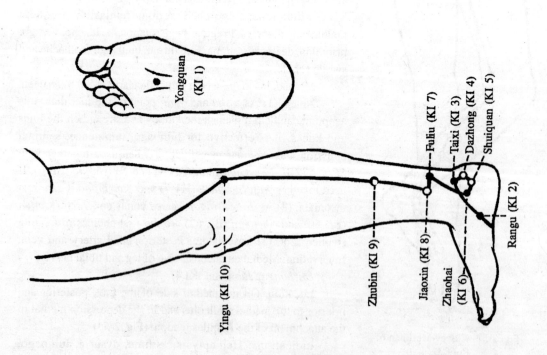

Fig. 2-53

MERIDIANS AND ACUPOINTS 67

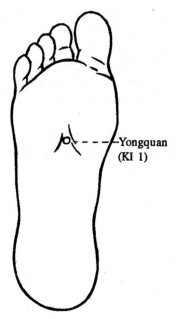

Fig. 2-54

dementia, irregular menstruation and swollen ankle.

Method: Insert the needle perpendicularly, 0.3-0.5 *cun* deep.

Notes: Vasculature: The medial calcaneal branch of posterior tibial artery. Innervation: Medial cutaneous nerve of leg, and the medial calcaneal ramus stemming from the tibial nerve.

Shuiquan (a *xi* point, KI 5)

Location: On the medial side of the foot, 1 *cun* directly below *Taixi* (KI 3) and in the depression of the medial side of the tuberosity of the calcaneum. (Fig. 2-55)

Indications: Dysuria, amenorrhea, dysmenorrhea, irregular menstruation, prolapse of uterus, blurred vision.

Method: Insert the needle perpendicularly, 0.3-0.5 *cun* deep.

Notes: Vasculature and innervation: The same as those of *Dazhong* (KI 4).

Zhaohai (one of the eight confluent points, KI 6)

Location: On the medial side of the foot and in the depression below the tip of the medial malleolus. (Fig. 2-55)

Indications: Sore throat, insomnia, irregular menstruation, dysmenorrhea, leukorrhagia, frequent micturition, dysuria, red and swollen eyes, and epilepsy.

Method: Insert the needle perpendicularly, 0.5-1 *cun* deep.

Notes: (1) As one of the eight confluent points communicating with the *Yinqiao* Meridian (*Yin* Heel Vessel), it is often used to treat disorders of the lung, throat, chest and diaphragm together with *Lieque* (LU 7). (2) The point is effective for constipation when used together with *Zhigou* (SJ 6), and effective for insomnia when used together with *Shenmai* (BL 62). According to *Jade Dragon Verses*, *Zhaohai* and *Zhigou* are indicated for constipation. (3) Vasculature: Posterior tibial artery and vein. Innervation: Medial cutaneous nerve of leg and tibial nerve.

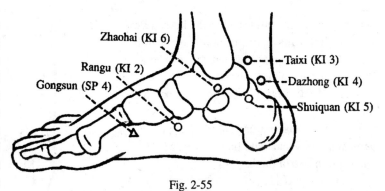

Fig. 2-55

Fuliu (a *jing* point, KI 7)

Location: On the medial side of the leg, 2 *cun* directly above *Taixi* (KI 3) and anterior to the Achilles tendon. (Fig. 2-56)

Indications: Abdominal distention, diarrhea, edema, swollen foot, night sweat, febrile diseases with anhidrosis or hyperhidrosis.

Method: Insert the needle perpendicularly, 0.5-1 *cun* deep.

Notes: (1) It is often used together with *Hegu* (LI 4) to treat anhidrosis and hyperhidrosis. (2) Vasculature: Posterior tibial artery and vein. Innervation: Medial cutaneous nerve of calf and medial cutaneous ramus of leg, and tibial nerve.

Jiaoxin (KI 8)

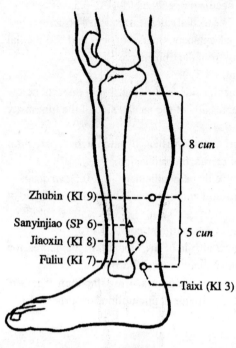

Fig. 2-56

Location: On the medial side of the leg, 2 *cun* above *Taixi* (KI 3), 0.5 *cun* anterior to *Fuliu* (KI 7) and posterior to the medial border of the tibia. (Fig. 2-56)

Indications: Irregular menstruation, metrorrhagia, prolapse of uterus, diarrhea, hernia and swollen testis.

Method: Insert the needle perpendicularly, 0.5-1 *cun* deep.

Notes: Vasculature: Posterior tibial artery and vein. Innervation: Medial cutaneous nerve of leg and tibial nerve.

Zhubin (KI 9)

Location: On the medial side of the leg and 5 *cun* above *Taixi* (KI 3). (Fig. 2-56)

Indications: Mania, epilepsy, hernia and pain in the calf.

Method: Insert the needle perpendicularly, 0.5-1 *cun* deep.

Notes: Vasculature: Posterior tibial artery and vein. Innervation: Medial cutaneous nerve of calf, medial cutaneous nerve of leg and tibial nerve.

Yingu (a *he* point, KI 10)

Location: On the medial side of the popliteal fossa and between the tendons of semitendinous and semimembranous muscles when the knee is flexed. (Fig. 2-57)

Indications: Impotence, seminal emission, irregular menstruation, metrorrhagia, dysuria and pain in the knee and popliteal fossa.

Method: Insert the needle perpendicularly, 1-1.2 *cun* deep.

Notes: Vasculature: Medial superior genicular artery and vein. Innervation: Medial cutaneous nerve of thigh.

Henggu (KI 11)

Location: On the lower abdomen, 5 *cun* below the center of the umbilicus and 0.5 *cun* lateral to the anterior midline. (Fig. 2-58)

Indications: Distensive pain in the lower abdomen, impotence, seminal emission, dysuria, enuresis and hernia.

Method: Insert the needle perpendicularly, 1-1.2 *cun* deep.

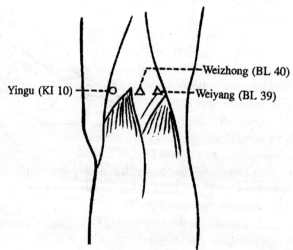

Fig. 2-57

Notes: Vasculature: Inferior epigastric artery and vein, and external pudendal artery. Innervation: The branch of iliohypogastric nerve.

Dahe (KI 12)

Location: On the lower abdomen, 4 *cun* below the center of the umbilicus and 0.5 *cun* lateral to the anterior midline. (Fig. 2-58)

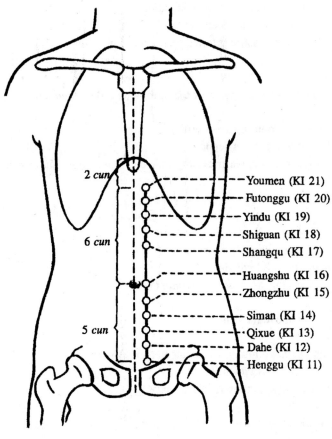

Fig. 2-58

Indications: Seminal emission, impotence, irregular menstruation, leukorrhagia, pain in the pudendal region, hysteroptosis and diarrhea.

Method: Insert the needle perpendicularly, 1-1.2 *cun* deep.

Notes: Vasculature: The muscular branches of the inferior epigastric artery and vein. Innervation: The intercostal nerve and iliohypogastric nerve.

Qixue (KI 13)

Location: On the lower abdomen, 3 *cun* below the center of the umbilicus and 0.5 *cun* lateral to the anterior midline. (Fig. 2-58)

Indications: Amenorrhea, irregular menstruation, leukorrhagia, dysuria, diarrhea and impotence.

Method: Insert the needle perpendicularly, 1-1.2 *cun* deep.

Notes: Vasculature: The same as that of *Dahe* (KI 12). Innervation: The 12th intercostal nerve.

Siman (KI 14)

Location: On the lower abdomen, 2 *cun* below the center of the umbilicus and 0.5 *cun* lateral to the anterior midline. (Fig. 2-58)

Indications: Abdominal pain, diarrhea, edema, hernia, irregular menstruation and seminal emission.

Method: Insert the needle perpendicularly, 1-1.2 *cun* deep.

Notes: Vasculature: The same as that of *Dahe* (KI 12). Innervation: The 11th intercostal nerve.

Zhongzhu (KI 15)

Location: On the lower abdomen, 1 *cun* below the center of the umbilicus and 0.5 *cun* lateral to the anterior midline. (Fig. 2-58)

Indications: Abdominal pain, diarrhea, constipation and irregular menstruation.

Method: Insert the needle perpendicularly, 1-1.2 *cun* deep.

Notes: Vasculature: The same as that of *Dahe* (KI 12). Innervation: The tenth intercostal nerve.

Huangshu (KI 16)

Location: On the middle abdomen and 0.5 *cun* lateral to the center of the umbilicus. (Fig. 2-58)

Indications: Abdominal pain and distention, constipation, diarrhea, hernia and irregular menstruation.

Method: Insert the needle perpendicularly, 1-1.2 *cun* deep.

Notes: Vasculature and innervation: The same as those of *Zhongzhu* (KI 15).

Shangqu (KI 17)

Location: On the upper abdomen, 2 *cun* above the center of the umbilicus and 0.5 *cun* lateral to the anterior midline. (Fig. 2-58)

Indications: Abdominal pain and distention, diarrhea and constipation.

Method: Insert the needle perpendicularly, 1-1.2 *cun* deep.

Notes: Vasculature: Superior and inferior epigastric arteries and veins. Innervation: The ninth intercostal nerve.

Shiguan (KI 18)

Location: On the upper abdomen, 3 *cun* above the center of the umbilicus and 0.5 *cun* lateral to the anterior midline. (Fig. 2-58)

Indications: Abdominal pain, constipation, vomiting and sterility.

Method: Insert the needle perpendicularly, 1-1.2 *cun* deep.

Notes: Vasculature: The branches of the superior epigastric artery and vein. Innervation: The eighth intercostal nerve.

Yindu (KI 19)

Location: On the upper abdomen, 4 *cun* above the center of the umbilicus and 0.5 *cun* lateral to the anterior midline. (Fig. 2-58)

Indications: Abdominal distention and pain, diarrhea, constipation and sterility.

Method: Insert the needle perpendicularly, 1-1.2 *cun* deep.

Notes: Vasculature and innervation: The same as those of *Shiguan* (KI 18).

Futonggu (KI 20)

Location: On the upper abdomen, 5 *cun* above the center of the umbilicus and 0.5 *cun* lateral to the anterior midline. (Fig. 2-58)

Indications: Abdominal distention and pain, vomiting, weak spleen and stomach.

Method: Insert the needle perpendicularly, 0.5-1 *cun* deep.

Notes: Vasculature and innervation: The same as those of *Shiguan* (KI 18).

Youmen (KI 21)

Location: On the upper abdomen, 6 *cun* above the center of the umbilicus and 0.5 *cun* lateral to the anterior midline. (Fig. 2-58)

Indications: Abdominal pain, vomiting, diarrhea, dysentery, pain in the chest and hypochondriac region and irritability.

Method: Insert the needle perpendicularly, 0.5-0.8 *cun* deep.

Notes: Vasculature: The same as that of *Shiguan* (KI 18). Innervation: The seventh intercostal nerve.

Bulang (KI 22)

Location: On the chest, in the fifth intercostal space and 2 *cun* lateral to the anterior midline. (Fig. 2-59)

Indications: Chest pain, cough, asthma and vomiting.

Method: Insert the needle obliquely or horizontally, 0.5-0.8 *cun* deep.

Notes: Vasculature: The fifth intercostal artery and vein. Innervation: The anterior cutaneous branch of the fifth intercostal nerve, and the fifth intercostal nerve.

Shenfeng (KI 23)

Location: On the chest, in the fourth intercostal space and 2 *cun* lateral to the anterior midline. (Fig. 2-59)

Indications: Cough, chest pain, asthma, vomiting and mastitis.

Method: Insert the needle obliquely or horizontally, 0.5-0.8 *cun* deep.

Notes: Vasculature: The fourth intercostal artery and vein. Innervation: The anterior cutaneous branch of the fourth intercostal nerve, and the fourth intercostal nerve.

Lingxu (KI 24)

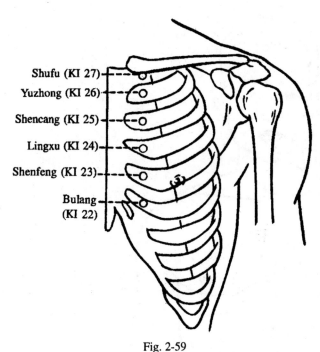

Fig. 2-59

Location: On the chest, in the third intercostal space and 2 *cun* lateral to the anterior midline. (Fig. 2-59)

Indications: Cough, asthma, chest pain and mastitis.

Method: Insert the needle obliquely or horizontally, 0.5-0.8 *cun* deep.

Notes: Vasculature: The third intercostal artery and vein. Innervation: The anterior cutaneous branch of the third intercostal nerve, and the third intercostal nerve.

Shencang (KI 25)

Location: On the chest, in the second intercostal space and 2 *cun* lateral to the anterior midline. (Fig. 2-59)

Indications: Cough, asthma, chest pain and irritability.

Method: Insert the needle obliquely or horizontally, 0.5-0.8 *cun* deep.

Notes: Vasculature: The second intercostal artery and vein. Innervation: The anterior cutaneous branch of the second intercostal nerve, and the second intercostal nerve.

Yuzhong (KI 26)

Location: On the chest, in the first intercostal space and 2 *cun* lateral to the anterior midline. (Fig. 2-59)

Indications: Cough, asthma, distensive pain in the chest and anorexia.

Method: Insert the needle obliquely or horizontally, 0.5-0.8 *cun* deep.

Notes: Vasculature: The first intercostal artery and vein. Innervation: The anterior cutaneous branch of the first intercostal nerve, the anterior branch of the supraclavicular nerve and the first intercostal nerve.

Shufu (KI 27)

Location: On the chest, below the lower border of the clavicle and 2 *cun* lateral to the midline. (Fig. 2-59)

Indications: Cough, asthma, chest pain and anorexia.

Method: Insert the needle obliquely or horizontally, 0.5-0.8 *cun* deep.

Notes: Vasculature: The anterior perforating branches of the internal mammary artery and vein. Innervation: The anterior branch of the supraclavicular nerve.

9. The Pericardium Meridian of Hand-*Jueyin* (PC)

(Fig. 2-60 and Fig. 2-61)

1) Traveling route

a) The meridian starts from the chest and connects with the pericardium (1). Then it passes through the diaphragm (2) and connects with *sanjiao* (3).

b) The thoracic branch starts from the chest and hypochondriac region (4) and exits at *Tianchi* (PC 1), 3 *cun* below the axilla (5). Then it ascends to the axillary fossa (6), runs along the medial side of

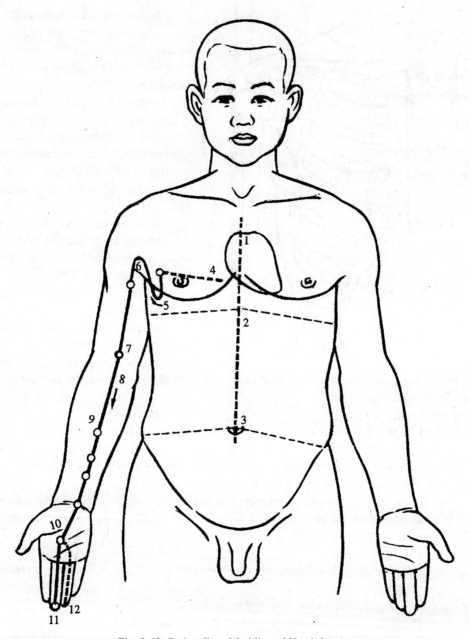

Fig. 2-60 Pericardium Meridian of Hand-*Jueyin*

the upper arm and between the Hand-*Taiyin* and Hand-*Shaoyin* meridians (7), and enters the cubital fossa (8). Finally, it goes between the tendons of the long palmar muscle and radial flexor muscle (9), enters the palm (10) and terminates at the tip of the middle finger (*Zhongchong*, PC 9) (11).

c) The palmar branch originates from the palm and runs to the tip of the ring finger (12).

2) Symptoms

Cardialgia, palpitation, irritability, mania, epilepsy, fullness in the chest and hypochondriac region, swollen axilla, spasmodic pain in the elbow and arm, and feverish sensation in the palm.

3) Acupoints

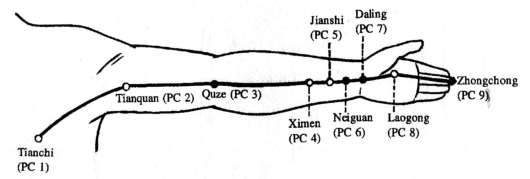

Fig. 2-61 Acupoints on the Pericardium Meridian of Hand-*Jueyin*

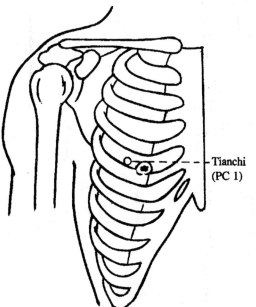

Fig. 2-62

Tianchi (PC 1)

Location: On the chest, in the fourth intercostal space and 1 *cun* lateral to the nipple. (Fig. 2-62)

Indications: Irritability, swollen axilla, distensive pain in the chest and hypochondriac region, cough, asthma and scrofula.

Method: Insert the needle obliquely or horizontally, 0.5-0.8 *cun* deep.

Notes: Vasculature: Thoraco-epigastric vein and the branches of the lateral thoracic artery and vein. Innervation: The muscular branch of the anterior thoracic nerve and the fourth intercostal nerve.

Tianquan (PC 2)

Location: On the medial side of the arm, 2 *cun* below the anterior end of the axillary fold and between the long and short heads of the biceps muscle of the arm. (Fig. 2-63)

Indications: Cardialgia, distensive pain in the chest and hypochondriac region, pain in the elbow and arm, and cough.

Method: Insert the needle perpendicularly, 0.5-1 *cun* deep.

Notes: Vasculature: The muscular branches of brachial artery and vein. Innervation: Medial cutaneous nerve of arm and musculocutaneous nerve.

Quze (a *he* point, PC 3)

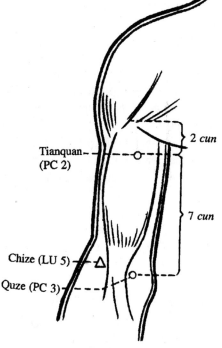

Fig. 2-63

Location: At the midpoint of the cubital crease and on the ulnar side of the tendon of the biceps muscle of the arm. (Fig. 2-63)

Indications: Palpitation, cardialgia, irritability, pain in the elbow and arm, febrile diseases and vomiting.

Method: Insert the needle perpendicularly, 0.8-1 *cun* deep. Or prick the acupoint so that a little blood comes out.

Notes: Vasculature: Brachial artery and vein. Innervation: Median nerve.

Ximen (a *xi* point, PC 4)

Location: On the palmar side of the forearm and on the line connecting *Quze* (PC 3) and *Daling* (PC 7), and 5 *cun* above the crease of the wrist. (Fig. 2-64)

Indications: Cardialgia, palpitation, irritability, epilepsy and epistaxis.

Method: Insert the needle perpendicularly, 0.5-1 *cun* deep.

Notes: (1) As a *xi* point of the meridian, *Ximen* can be used to relieve acute pain. It can be needled together with *Geshu* (BL 17) and *Neiguan* (PC 6) to relieve pain in the heart and chest. (2) *Ximen* is frequently used for acupuncture anesthesia in pulmonary operation. (3) Vasculature: Median antebrachial artery and vein, and the palmar interosseous artery and vein of forearm. Innervation: Medial cutaneous nerve of forearm, median nerve and palmar interosseous nerve of forearm.

Jianshi (a *jing* point, PC 5)

Location: On the palmar side of the forearm, 3 *cun* above the crease of the wrist and between the tendons of the long palmar muscle and radial flexor muscle of the wrist. (Fig. 2-64)

Indications: Palpitation, cardialgia, mania, epilepsy, pain in the chest and hypochondriac region, stomachache and malaria.

Method: Insert the needle perpendicularly, 0.5-1 *cun* deep.

Notes: Vasculature: The same as that of *Ximen* (PC 4). Innervation: Medial and lateral cutaneous nerves of forearm, the palmar cutaneous branch of median nerve, and the palmar interosseous nerve of forearm.

Neiguan (a *luo* point and one of the eight confluent points, PC 6)

Location: On the palmar side of the forearm, 2 *cun* above the crease of the wrist and between the tendons of the long palmar muscle and radial flexor muscle of the wrist. (Fig. 2-64)

Indications: Cardialgia, palpitation, epilepsy, insomnia, pain in the elbow and arm, pain in the chest and hypochondriac region, stomachache and vomiting.

Method: Insert the needle perpendicularly, 0.5-1 *cun* deep.

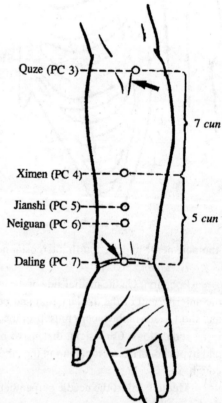

Fig. 2-64

Notes: (1) As one of the eight confluent points communicating with the *Yinwei* Meridian (*Yin* Link Vessel), it is indicated for disorders of the stomach, heart and chest. Used together with *Zusanli* (ST 36) and *Gongsun* (SP 4), it can treat stomachache; with *Ximen* (PC 4), *Xinshu* (BL 15) and *Geshu* (BL 17), it can treat cardialgia. (2) Clinical reports show that *Neiguan, Shuigou* (DU 26) and *Sanyinjiao* (SP 6) can be used to treat apoplexy. (3) Researches show that *Neiguan* can help improve the cardiac function of those suffering from myocardiac infarction, manifesting in the shortening ST_1 in ECG, decreasing ε ST segment and lowering oxygen consumption of myocardium, and cholesterol, triglyceride and ß-lipoprotein decrease in varying degrees. (4) Vasculature and innervation: The same as those of *Jianshi* (PC 5).

Daling (a *shu* point and a *yuan* point, PC 7)

Location: At the midpoint of the crease of the wrist and between the tendons of the long palmar muscle and radial flexor muscle of the wrist. (Fig. 2-64)

Indications: Cardialgia, palpitation, mania, epilepsy, pain in the chest and hypochondriac region, and stomachache.

Method: Insert the needle perpendicularly, 0.3-0.5 *cun* deep.

Notes: Vasculature: Palmar carpometacarpal arterial and venous network. Innervation: Median nerve.

Laogong (a *ying* point, PC 8)

Location: At the center of the palm, between the second and third metacarpal bones but close to the latter, and where the tip of the middle finger touches when the hand is clenched. (Fig. 2-65)

Indications: Cardialgia, apoplexy, coma, sunstroke, mania, epilepsy, stomatitis and foul breath.

Method: Insert the needle perpendicularly, 0.3-0.5 *cun* deep.

Notes: (1) Simple measurement: Clench the hand, the acupoint locates at the place where the tip of the middle finger touches. (2) Vasculature: Common palmar digital artery. Innervation: The second common palmar digital nerve of median nerve.

Zhongchong (a *jiing* point, PC 9)

Location: At the center of the middle fingertip. (Fig. 2-65)

Indications: Coma, sunstroke, cardialgia, irritability, dysphasia and sublingual pain and swelling.

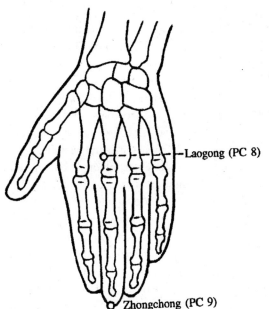

Fig. 2-65

Method: Insert the needle 0.1 *cun* into the skin, or prick so that a little blood comes out.

Notes: Vasculature: The arterial and venous network formed by the proper palmar digital artery and vein. Innervation: The proper palmar digital nerve of median nerve.

10. The *Sanjiao* (Triple Energizer) Meridian of Hand-*Shaoyang* (SJ)

(Fig. 2-66 and Fig. 2-67)

1) Traveling route

a) The meridian starts at the end on the ulnar side of the ring finger (*Guanchong*, SJ 1) (1), goes along the ulnar side of the ring finger (2) and reaches the wrist through the dorsum of the hand (3). Then it ascends along the lateral side of the forearm and between the ulna and radius (4). Passing through the posterior cubitus (5) and the lateral side of the upper arm (6), it arrives at the shoulder (7). Traveling

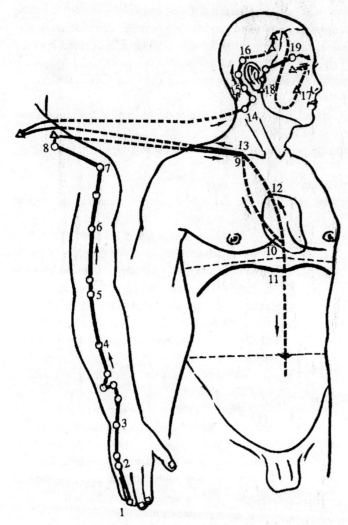

Fig. 2-66 *Sanjiao* (Triple Energizer) Meridian of Hand-*Shaoyang*

behind the Gallbladder Meridian (8), it then enters the supraclavicular fossa (9) and spreads in the chest to connect with the pericardium (10). Finally, it crosses the diaphragm and links with *sanjiao* (11).

b) One branch starts from the chest (12) and comes out of the supraclavicular fossa (13). Then it goes along the nape (14) and reaches the back of the ear (15). Passing the upper corner of the ear (16) and the cheek, it terminates at the infraorbital region (17).

c) The other branch enters the ear from behind. Passing the front of the ear (*Shangguan*, GB 3), it meets the above branch on the cheek (18) and terminates at lateral canthus (*Sizhukong*, SJ 23) (19).

2) Symptoms

Deafness, sweating, sore throat and pain in the lateral canthus, cheek, retroauricular region, shoulder, arm, elbow and fingers.

3) Acupoints

Guanchong (a *jiing* point, SJ 1)

Location: On the ulnar side of the ring finger and about 0.1 *cun* lateral to the corner of the nail. (Fig. 2-68)

Indications: Headache, red and swollen eyes, deafness, tinnitus, sore throat, irritability and stiff tongue.

Method: Insert the needle 0.1 *cun* into the skin. Or prick the acupoint so that a little blood comes out.

Notes: Vasculature: Arterial and venous network formed by proper palmar digital artery and vein. Innervation: Proper palmar digital nerve stemming from ulnar nerve.

Yemen (a *ying* point, SJ 2)

Location: On the dorsum of the hand, between the ring and little fingers and 0.5 *cun* proximal to the margin of the web. (Fig. 2-68)

Indications: headache, red and swollen eyes, tinnitus, deafness, sore throat, malaria and pain in the finger joints.

Method: Insert the needle perpendicularly, 0.3-0.5 *cun* deep.

Notes: Vasculature: Dorsal digital artery of ulnar artery. Innervation: The dorsal branch of ulnar nerve.

Zhongzhu (a *shu* point, SJ 3)

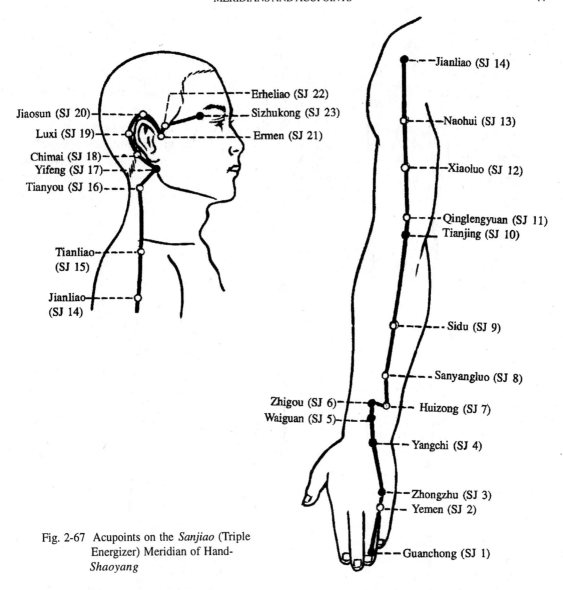

Fig. 2-67 Acupoints on the *Sanjiao* (Triple Energizer) Meridian of Hand-*Shaoyang*

Location: On the dorsum of the hand, proximal to the fourth metacarpophalangeal joint and in the depression between the fourth and fifth metacarpal bones. (Fig. 2-68)

Indications: Headache, red and swollen eyes, tinnitus, deafness, sore throat, malaria and pain in the arm, wrist and finger joints.

Method: Insert the needle perpendicularly, 0.5-0.8 *cun* deep.

Notes: Vasculature: Dorsal venous network of hand and the fourth dorsal metacarpal artery. Innervation: The dorsal branch of ulnar nerve.

Yangchi (a *yuan* point, SJ 4)

Location: At the midpoint of the dorsal crease of the wrist and in the depression on the ulnar side of the tendon of the common extensor muscle of the fingers. (Fig. 2-68)

Indications: Deafness, malaria, sore throat, and pain in the arm and wrist.

Method: Insert the needle perpendicularly, 0.3-0.5 *cun* deep.

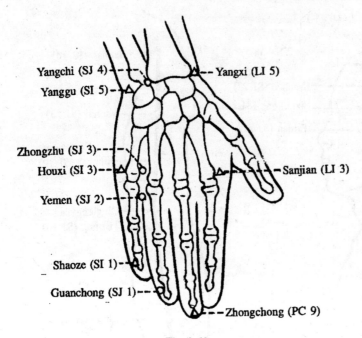

Fig. 2-68

Notes: Vasculature: Dorsal venous network of wrist and dorsal carpal artery. Innervation: The dorsal branch of ulnar nerve and the terminal branch of the dorsal cutaneous nerve of forearm.

Waiguan (a *luo* point and one of the eight confluent points, SJ 5)

Location: On the dorsal side of the forearm, 2 *cun* proximal to the dorsal crease of the wrist and between the radius and ulna. (Fig. 2-69)

Indications: Headache, red and swollen eyes, tinnitus, deafness, pain in the hypochondriac region, pain in the shoulder and back, febrile diseases and scrofula.

Method: Insert the needle perpendicularly, 0.5-1 *cun* deep.

Notes: (1) As one of the eight confluent points communicating with the *Yangwei* Meridian (*Yang* Link Vessel), *Waiguan* can help disperse wind-heat. If used together with *Hegu* (LI 4) and *Dazhui* (DU 14), it can treat fever with swollen eyes caused by exogenous affection. (2) Vasculature: Dorsal and palmar interosseous arteries and veins of forearm. Innervation: Dorsal cutaneous nerve of forearm, dorsal interosseous nerve of forearm of the radial nerve and volar interosseous nerve of median nerve.

Zhigou (a *jing* point, SJ 6)

Location: On the dorsal side of the forearm, 3 *cun* proximal to the dorsal crease of the wrist and between the radius and ulna. (Fig. 2-69)

Indications: Tinnitus, deafness, sudden loss of voice, pain in the hypochondriac region, pain in the shoulder and back, febrile diseases and constipation.

Method: Insert the needle perpendicularly, 0.5-1 *cun* deep.

Notes: (1) According to *Illustrated Supplementary to the Classified Canon*, *Zhigou* can be needled with reductive method

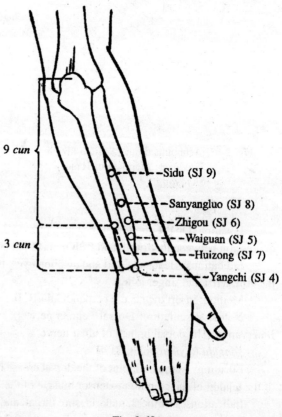

Fig. 2-69

to treat hyperactive ministerial fire in *sanjiao*, constipation and pain in the hypochondriac region. Needled together with *Yanglingquan* (GB 34), it can treat pain in the hypochondriac region; with *Zhaohai* (KI 6) or *Tianshu* (ST 25) and *Daheng* (SP 15), it can treat constipation. (2) Vasculature and innervation: The same as those of *Waiguan* (SJ 5).

Huizong (a *xi* point, SJ 7)

Location: On the dorsal side of the forearm, 3 *cun* proximal to the dorsal crease of the wrist, and on the ulnar side of *Zhigou* (SJ 6) and on the radial side of the ulna. (Fig. 2-69)

Indications: Deafness, tinnitus, pain in the arm and epilepsy.

Method: Insert the needle perpendicularly, 0.5-1 *cun* deep.

Notes: Vasculature: Dorsal interosseous artery and vein of the forearm. Innervation: Dorsal cutaneous nerve and dorsal interosseous nerve of the forearm and volar interosseous nerve.

Sanyangluo (SJ 8)

Location: On the dorsal side of the forearm, 4 *cun* proximal to the dorsal crease of the wrist and between the radius and ulna. (Fig. 2-69)

Indications: Sudden deafness, toothache, sudden loss of voice, and pain in the arm.

Method: Insert the needle perpendicularly, 0.5-1 *cun* deep.

Notes: Vasculature and innervation: The same as those of *Huizong* (SJ 7).

Sidu (SJ 9)

Location: On the dorsal side of the forearm, 5 *cun* distal to the tip of the olecranon and between the radius and ulna. (Fig. 2-69)

Indications: Tinnitus, deafness, sore throat, sudden loss of voice and pain in the arm.

Method: Insert the needle perpendicularly, 0.5-1 *cun* deep.

Notes: Vasculature and innervation: The same as those of *Huizong* (SJ 7).

Tianjing (a *he* point, SJ 10)

Location: On the lateral side of the upper arm and in the depression 1 *cun* proximal to the tip of the olecranon. (Fig. 2-70)

Indications: Tinnitus, deafness, migraine, and pain in the hypochondriac region, nape, shoulder and arm.

Method: Insert the needle perpendicularly, 0.5-1 *cun* deep.

Notes: Vasculature: Arterial and venous network of elbow. Innervation: Dorsal cutaneous nerve of the arm and the muscular branch of the radial nerve.

Qinglengyuan (SJ 11)

Location: On the lateral side of the upper arm, 2 *cun* above the tip of the olecranon and 1 *cun* above *Tianjing* (SJ 10). (Fig. 2-70)

Indications: Headache, yellowish eyeballs, pain and motor impairment of the shoulder and arm.

Method: Insert the needle perpendicularly, 0.5-1 *cun* deep.

Notes: Vasculature: The terminal branches of the median accessory artery and vein. Innervation: Dorsal cutaneous nerve of arm and the muscular

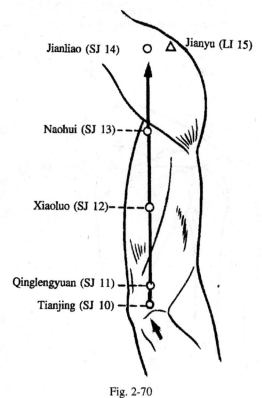

Fig. 2-70

branch of radial nerve.

Xiaoluo (SJ 12)

Location: On the lateral side of the upper arm and at the midpoint of the line connecting *Qinglengyuan* (SJ 11) and *Naohui* (SJ 13). (Fig. 2-70)

Indications: Headache, rigid nape, toothache, and pain in the shoulder, back and arm.

Method: Insert the needle perpendicularly, 1-1.2 *cun* deep.

Notes: Vasculature and innervation: The same as those of *Qinglengyuan* (SJ 11).

Naohui (SJ 13)

Location: On the lateral side of the upper arm and on the line connecting the tip of the olecranon and *Jianliao* (SJ 14), and on the posteroinferior border of the deltoid muscle. (Fig. 2-70)

Indications: Pain in the shoulder and arm, goiter and scrofula.

Method: Insert the needle perpendicularly, 0.5-1.2 *cun* deep.

Notes: Vasculature: The same as those of *Qinglengyuan* (SJ 11). Innervation: The dorsal cutaneous nerve of the arm and the muscular branch of radial nerve and radial nerve.

Jianliao (SJ 14)

Location: On the shoulder, posterior to *Jianyu* (LI 15) and in the depression inferior and posterior to the acromion when the arm is abducted. (Fig. 2-70)

Indications: Pain and motor impairment of the shoulder and arm.

Method: Insert the needle into the shoulder joint perpendicularly, 1-1.5 *cun* deep.

Notes: Vasculature: The muscular branch of the posterior humeral circumflex artery. Innervation: The muscular branch of axillary nerve.

Tianliao (SJ 15)

Location: On the scapula, at the midpoint between *Jianjing* (GB 21) and *Quyuan* (SI 13) and at the superior angle of the scapula. (Fig. 2-71)

Indications: Pain in the shoulder and arm, stiffness and pain in the nape and back.

Method: Insert the needle perpendicularly, 0.5-0.8 *cun* deep.

Notes: Vasculature: The descending branch of the transverse cervical artery, and the muscular branch of suprascapular artery. Innervation: Accessory nerve and the branch of suprascapular nerve.

Tianyou (SJ 16)

Location: On the lateral side of the neck, directly below the posterior border of the mastoid process, on the level of the mandibular angle and on the posterior border of the sternocleidomastoid muscle. (Fig. 2-72)

Indications: Headache, stiff nape, sudden loss of voice, and vertigo.

Method: Insert the needle perpendicularly, 0.5-1 *cun* deep.

Notes: Vasculature: Posterior auricular artery. Innervation: Lesser occipital nerve.

Yifeng (SJ 17)

Location: Posterior to the ear lobe and in the depression between the mastoid process and mandibular angle. (Fig. 2-73)

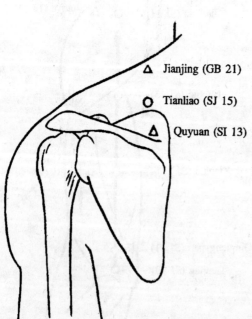

Fig. 2-71

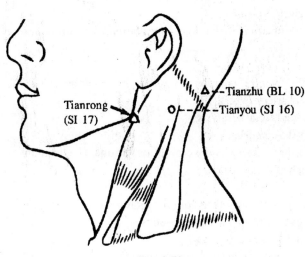

Fig. 2-72

Indications: Tinnitus, deafness, facial paralysis and swollen cheeks.

Method: Insert the needle perpendicularly, 0.8-1.2 *cun* deep.

Notes: Vasculature: Posterior auricular artery and vein. Innervation: Great auricular nerve and facial nerve perforating from stylomastoid foramen.

Chimai (SJ 18)

Location: On the head, at the center of the mastoid process and at the junction of the middle third and lower third of the line connecting *Yifeng* (SJ 17) and *Jiaosun* (SJ 20) along the curve of the ear helix. (Fig. 2-73)

Indications: Headache, tinnitus, deafness and epilepsy induced by fright.

Method: Insert the needle horizontally, 0.3-0.5 *cun* deep.

Notes: Vasculature: Posterior auricular artery and vein. Innervation: The posterior auricular branch of great auricular nerve.

Luxi (SJ 19)

Location: On the head and at the junction of the upper third and middle third of the line connecting *Yifeng* (SJ 17) and *Jiaosun* (SJ 20) along the curve of the ear helix. (Fig. 2-73)

Indications: Headache, tinnitus, earache, infantile convulsion.

Method: Insert the needle horizontally, 0.3-0.5 *cun* deep.

Notes: Vasculature: Posterior auricular artery and vein. Innervation: The anastomotic branch of great auricular nerve and lesser occipital nerve.

Jiaosun (SJ 20)

Location: On the head and directly above the ear apex just within the hairline. (Fig. 2-73)

Indications: Tinnitus, deafness, red and swollen eyes, corneal nebula, swollen gum and rigid nape.

Method: Insert the needle horizontally, 0.3-0.5 *cun* deep.

Notes: Vasculature: The branches of superficial temporal artery and vein. Innervation: The branches of auriculotemporal nerve.

Ermen (SJ 21)

Location: On the face, anterior to the supratragic notch and in the depression behind the posterior border of the condyloid process of the mandible. (Fig. 2-73)

Indications: Deafness, tinnitus, earache

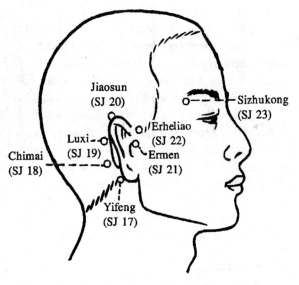

Fig. 2-73

and toothache.

Method: Insert the needle perpendicularly, 0.5-1 *cun* deep.

Notes: Vasculature: Superficial temporal artery and vein. Innervation: The branches of auriculotemporal nerve and facial nerve.

Erheliao (SJ 22)

Location: On the posterior margin of the temples, anterior to the root of the ear auricle at the hairline and posterior to the superficial temporal artery. (Fig. 2-73)

Indications: Headache, tinnitus, lockjaw and facial paralysis.

Method: Insert the needle obliquely, 0.3-0.5 *cun* deep.

Notes: Vasculature: Superficial temporal artery and vein. Innervation: The branch of auriculotemporal nerve and the temporal branch of facial nerve.

Sizhukong (SJ 23)

Location: On the face and in the depression at the lateral end of the eyebrow. (Fig. 2-73)

Indications: Headache, red and swollen eyes, vertigo, twitching eyelids.

Method: Insert the needle horizontally, 0.5-1 *cun* deep.

Notes: Vasculature: The frontal branches of superficial temporal artery and vein. Innervation: The zygomatic branch of facial nerve and the branch of auriculotemporal nerve.

11. The Gallbladder Meridian of Foot-*Shaoyang* (GB)

(Fig. 2-74 and Fig. 2-75)

1) Traveling route

a) The meridian starts at the outer canthus (*Tongziliao*, GB 1) (1), ascends to the corner of the forehead (2) and reaches the retroauricular region (3). Then it runs along the neck in front of the *Sanjiao* Meridian (4). After arriving at the shoulder, it runs behind the *Sanjiao* Meridian and enters the supraclavicular fossa (5).

b) The auricle branch arises from the retroauricular region, enters the ear (6), comes out in front of the ear (7) and arrives at the posterior side of the outer canthus (8).

c) The canthus branch starts at the outer canthus (9) and runs downward to the area near *Daying* (ST 5) (10). After meeting the Hand-*Shaoyang* Meridian, it goes upward to the infraorbital region (11). Passing *Jiache* (ST 6) (12) in its downward movement, it reaches the neck (13) and meets the auricle branch in the supraclavicular fossa. Then it further descends into the chest, crosses the diaphragm (14), and connects with the liver (15) and gallbladder (16). Running through the hypochondriac region (17), it comes out from both sides of the lower abdomen (*Qichong*, ST 30) (18) and runs along the margin of the pubic hair (19). Finally, it reaches *Huantiao* (GB 30) (20).

d) The vertical branch starts at the supraclavicular fossa (21), passes the axilla (22), the lateral side of the chest (23) and the hypochondriac region (24), and meets the canthus branch at *Huantiao* (GB 30) (25). Then it travels along the lateral side of the thigh (26) and the knee (27), passes the anterior side of the fibula (28) and runs directly downward to the lower end of the fibula and above the external malleolus (29). Finally, it goes along the anterior border of the external malleolus and the dorsum of the foot (30) and enters the lateral side of the tip of the fourth toe (31).

e) The dorsal branch starts from between the first and second metatarsal bones (32), enters the tip of the great toe, turns back and penetrates the nail, and terminates in the hairy region proximal to the nail.

2) Symptoms

Bitter taste, headache, malaria, dizziness, scrofula, swelling in the axillary region, pain in the outer canthus, mandible, supraclavicular fossa, chest, hypochondriac region, thigh and knee.

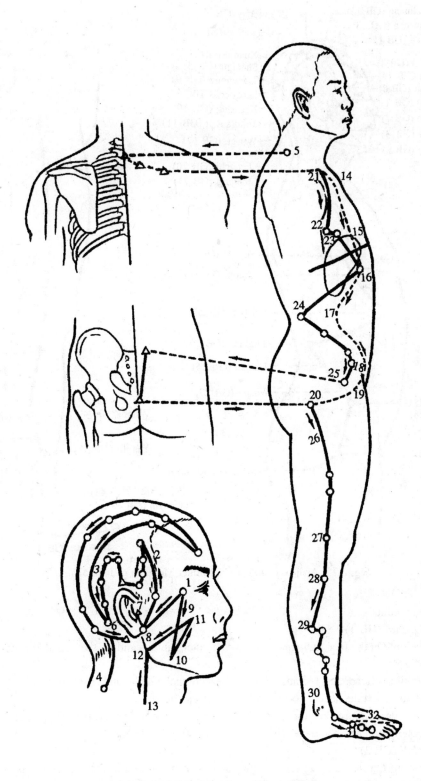

Fig. 2-74 Gallbladder Meridian of Foot-*Shaoyang*

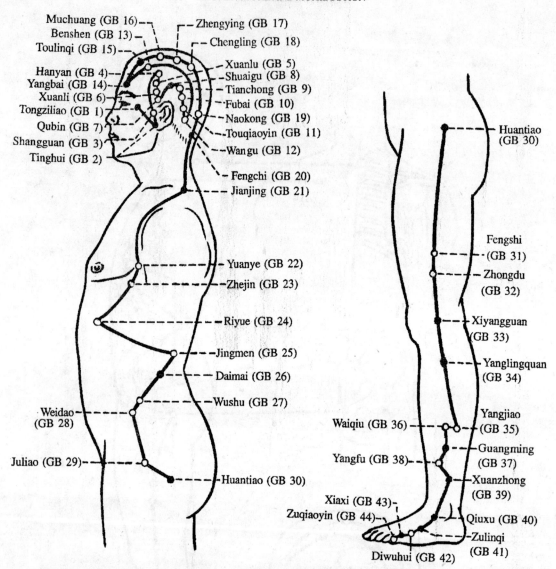

Fig. 2-75 Acupoints on the Gallbladder Meridian of Foot-*Shaoyang*

3) Acupoints

Tongziliao (GB 1)

Location: On the face, 0.5 *cun* lateral to the outer canthus and on the lateral border of the orbit. (Fig. 2-76)

Indications: Headache, red and swollen eyes, corneal nebula, and optic atrophy.

Method: Insert the needle horizontally, 0.3-0.5 *cun* deep.

Notes: Vasculature: Zygomaticoorbital artery and vein. Innervation: Zygomaticofacial and zygomaticotemporal nerve and the temporal branch of the facial nerve.

Tinghui (GB 2)

Location: On the face, anterior to the intertragic notch and in the depression posterior to the condyloid process of the mandible when the mouth is open. (Fig. 2-76)

Indications: Tinnitus, deafness, facial paralysis, headache and pain in the face.

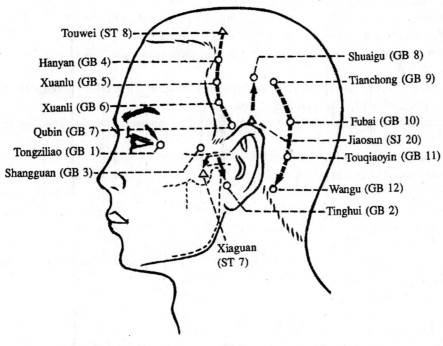

Fig. 2-76

Method: With the patient's mouth open, insert the needle perpendicularly, 0.5-1 *cun* deep.

Notes: Vasculature: Superficial temporal artery. Innervation: Great auricular nerve and facial nerve.

Shangguan (GB 3)

Location: Anterior to the ear, directly above *Xiaguan* (ST 7) and in the depression above the upper border of the zygomatic arch. (Fig. 2-76)

Indications: Headache, tinnitus, deafness, toothache, facial paralysis, pain in the face and epilepsy induced by terror.

Method: Insert the needle perpendicularly, 0.5-1 *cun* deep.

Notes: Vasculature: Zygomaticoorbital artery and vein. Innervation: The zygomatic branch of facial nerve.

Hanyan (GB 4)

Location: On head, in the hair above the temple and at the junction of the upper fourth and lower three-fourths of the curved line connecting *Touwei* (ST 8) and *Qubin* (GB 7). (Fig. 2-76)

Indications: Migraine, vertigo and toothache.

Method: Insert the needle horizontally, 0.5-0.8 *cun* deep.

Notes: Vasculature: The parietal branches of superficial temporal artery and vein. Innervation: The temporal branch of auriculotemporal nerve.

Xuanlu (GB 5)

Location: On the head, in the hair above the temple and at the midpoint of the curved line connecting *Touwei* (ST 8) and *Qubin* (GB 7). (Fig. 2-76)

Indications: Migraine, pain in the outer canthus and tinnitus.

Method: Insert the needle horizontally, 0.5-0.8 *cun* deep.

Notes: Vasculature and innervation: The same as those of *Hanyan* (GB 4).

Xuanli (GB 6)

Location: On the head, in the hair above the temple and at the junction of the upper three-fourths and lower fourth of the curved line connecting *Touwei* (ST 8) and *Qubin* (GB 7). (Fig. 2-76)

Indications: Migraine, pain in the outer canthus, tinnitus and toothache.

Method: Insert the needle horizontally, 0.5-0.8 *cun* deep.

Notes: Vasculature and innervation: The same as those of *Hanyan* (GB 4).

Qubin (GB 7)

Location: On the head and at the crossing point of the vertical posterior hairline of the temple and horizontal line through the ear apex. (Fig. 2-76)

Indications: Headache, red and swollen eyes, swelling and pain in the cheek and jaw, trismus and sudden loss of voice.

Method: Insert the needle horizontally, 0.5-0.8 *cun* deep.

Notes: Vasculature and innervation: The same as those of *Hanyan* (GB 4).

Shuaigu (GB 8)

Location: On the head, directly above the ear apex and 1.5 *cun* above the hairline. (Fig. 2-76)

Indications: Migraine, vertigo, vomiting and infantile convulsion.

Method: Insert the needle horizontally, 0.5-0.8 *cun* deep.

Notes: Vasculature: The parietal branches of superficial temporal artery and vein. Innervation: The anastomotic branch of auriculotemporal nerve and great occipital nerve.

Tianchong (GB 9)

Location: On the head, directly above the posterior border of the ear root and 2 *cun* above the hairline. (Fig. 2-76)

Indications: Headache, tinnitus, deafness, convulsion, palpitation and epilepsy.

Method: Insert the needle horizontally, 0.5-0.8 *cun* deep.

Notes: Vasculature: Posterior auricular artery and vein. Innervation: The branch of great occipital nerve.

Fubai (GB 10)

Location: On the head, posterior and superior to the mastoid process and at the junction of the middle third and upper third of the curved line connecting *Tianchong* (GB 9) and *Wangu* (GB 12). (Fig. 2-76)

Indications: Headache, tinnitus, deafness, rigid nape, scrofula and goiter.

Method: Insert the needle horizontally, 0.5-0.8 *cun* deep.

Notes: Vasculature and innervation: The same as those of *Tianchong* (GB 9).

Touqiaoyin (GB 11)

Location: On the head, posterior and superior to the mastoid process and at the junction of the middle third and lower third of the curved line connecting *Tianchong* (GB 9) and *Wangu* (GB 12). (Fig. 2-76)

Indications: Headache, vertigo, tinnitus and deafness.

Method: Insert the needle horizontally, 0.5-0.8 *cun* deep.

Notes: Vasculature: The branches of posterior auricular artery and vein. Innervation: The anastomotic branch of great and lesser occipital nerves.

Wangu (GB 12)

Location: On the head and in the depression posterior and inferior to the mastoid process. (Fig. 2-76)

Indications: Headache, rigid nape, deafness, facial paralysis and swollen cheeks.

Method: Insert the needle obliquely, 0.5-0.8 *cun* deep.

Notes: Vasculature: Posterior auricular artery and vein. Innervation: Lesser occipital nerve.

Benshen (GB 13)

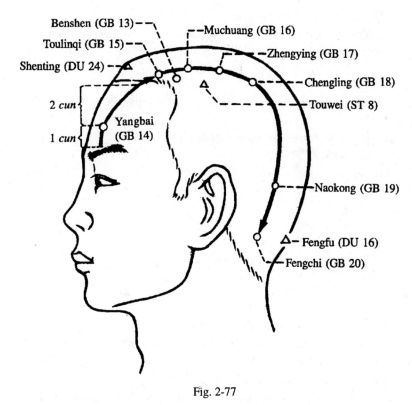

Fig. 2-77

Location: On the head, 3 *cun* lateral to *Shenting* (DU 24), 0.5 *cun* above the anterior hairline and 3 *cun* lateral to the anterior midline. (Fig. 2-77)

Indications: Headache, dizziness, epilepsy and infantile convulsion.

Method: Insert the needle horizontally, 0.5-0.8 *cun* deep.

Notes: Vasculature: The frontal branches of the superficial temporal artery and vein, and the lateral branches of the frontal artery and vein. Innervation: The lateral branch of the frontal nerve.

Yangbai (GB 14)

Location: On the forehead, directly above the pupil and 1 *cun* above the eyebrow. (Fig. 2-77)

Indications: Headache, dizziness, pain in the orbital ridge, facial paralysis and twitching eyelids.

Method: Insert the needle horizontally downward, 0.5-0.8 *cun* deep.

Notes: Vasculature: The lateral branches of frontal artery and vein. Innervation: The lateral branch of frontal nerve.

Toulinqi (GB 15)

Location: On the head, directly above the pupil and 0.5 *cun* above the anterior hairline. (Fig. 2-77)

Indications: Headache, dizziness, red and swollen eyes, nasal obstruction and infantile convulsion.

Method: Insert the needle horizontally, 0.5-0.8 *cun* deep.

Notes: Vasculature: Frontal artery and vein. Innervation: The anastomotic branch of the medial and lateral branches of frontal nerve.

Muchuang (GB 16)

Location: On the head, 1.5 *cun* above the anterior hairline and on the line connecting *Toulinqi* (GB 15) and *Fengchi* (GB 20). (Fig. 2-77)

Indications: Headache, dizziness, optic atrophy, red and swollen eyes, swollen head and face.

Method: Insert the needle horizontally, 0.5-0.8 *cun* deep.

Notes: Vasculature: The frontal branches of superficial temporal artery and vein. Innervation: The anastomotic branch of the medial and lateral branches of frontal nerve.

Zhengying (GB 17)

Location: On the head, 2.5 *cun* above the anterior hairline and on the line connecting *Toulinqi* (GB 15) and *Fengchi* (GB 20). (Fig. 2-77)

Indications: Headache, vertigo and toothache.

Method: Insert the needle horizontally, 0.5-0.8 *cun* deep.

Notes: Vasculature: The anastomotic plexus formed by the parietal branches of superficial temporal artery and vein, and occipital artery and vein. Innervation: The anastomotic branch of the frontal and great occipital nerves.

Chengling (GB 18)

Location: On the head, 4 *cun* above the anterior hairline and on the line connecting *Toulinqi* (GB 15) and *Fengchi* (GB 20). (Fig. 2-77)

Indications: Headache, vertigo, nasal obstruction and ophthalmalgia.

Method: Insert the needle horizontally, 0.5-0.8 *cun* deep.

Notes: Vasculature: The branches of occipital artery and vein. Innervation: The branch of great occipital nerve.

Naokong (GB 19)

Location: On the head, directly above *Fengchi* (GB 20) and at the level of the upper border of the external occipital protuberance. (Fig. 2-77)

Indications: Headache, rigid nape, vertigo, red and swollen eyes and epilepsy.

Method: Insert the needle horizontally, 0.5-0.8 *cun* deep.

Notes: Vasculature and innervation: The same as those of *Chengling* (GB 18).

Fengchi (GB 20)

Location: On the nape, below the occipital bone, at the level of *Fengfu* (DU 16) and in the depression between the upper ends of the sternocleidomastoid and trapezius muscles. (Fig. 2-77)

Indications: Headache, vertigo, red and swollen eyes, rigidity and pain in the nape and back, apoplexy, facial paralysis, febrile diseases, common cold, malaria and goiter.

Method: Insert the needle obliquely towards the medial orbit of the opposite eye or the tip of the nose, 0.8-1 *cun* deep.

Notes: (1) According to *Tongxuan Verses for Acupoints*, *Fengchi* is effective for dizziness and vertigo. It can be used together with *Taichong* (LR 3), *Quchi* (LI 11) and *Neiguan* (PC 60) to treat vertigo. *Dazhui* (DU 14), *Hegu* (LI 4) and *Waiguan* (SJ 5) can be used together with *Fengchi* to treat fever due to exogenous affection and headache. (2) Vasculature: The branches of occipital artery and vein. Innervation: The branch of lesser occipital nerve.

Jianjing (GB 21)

Location: On the shoulder, at the midpoint of the line connecting *Dazhui* (DU 14) and the acromion. (Fig. 2-78)

Indications: Rigidity and pain in the nape and back, pain and motor impairment of the shoulder and arm, mastitis, lack of lactation, and scrofula.

Method: Insert the needle perpendicularly, 0.5-0.8 *cun* deep. Do not insert the needle too deep. Acupuncture is contraindicated for pregnant women.

Notes: Vasculature: Transverse cervical artery and vein. Innervation: The lateral branch of supraclavicular nerve, and accessory nerve.

Yuanye (GB 22)

Location: On the lateral side of the chest,

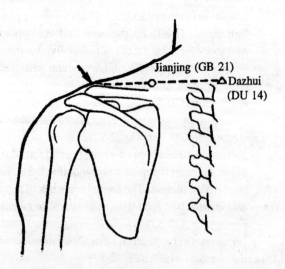

Fig. 2-78

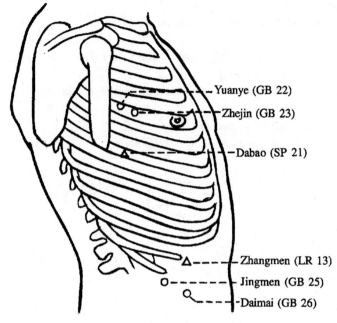

Fig. 2-79

on the mid-axillary line when the arm is raised, 3 *cun* below the axilla and in the fourth intercostal space. (Fig. 2-79)

Indications: Fullness and pain in the chest and hypochondriac region, swollen axillary region, pain and motor impairment of the upper limbs.

Method: Insert the needle obliquely, 0.5-0.8 *cun* deep.

Notes: Vasculature: Thoraco-epigastric vein, lateral thoracic artery and vein, and the fourth intercostal artery and vein. Innervation: The lateral cutaneous branch of the fourth intercostal nerve and the branch of long thoracic nerve.

Zhejin (GB 23)

Location: On the lateral side of the chest, 1 *cun* anterior to *Yuanye* (GB 22), at the level of the nipple and in the fourth intercostal space. (Fig. 2-79)

Indications: Pain in the chest and hypochondriac region, asthma, swollen axillary region, and pain in the shoulder and arm.

Method: Insert the needle obliquely, 0.5-0.8 *cun* deep.

Notes: Vasculature: Lateral thoracic artery and vein. Innervation: The lateral cutaneous branch of the fourth intercostal nerve.

Riyue (a front *mu* point of the gallbladder, GB 24)

Location: On the upper abdomen, directly below the nipple, in the seventh intercostal space and 4 *cun* lateral to the anterior midline. (Fig. 2-80)

Indications: Jaundice, vomiting, abdominal distention, and pain in the chest and hypochondriac region.

Method: Insert the needle obliquely, 0.5-0.8 *cun* deep.

Notes: Vasculature: The seventh intercostal artery and vein. Innervation: The seventh intercostal nerve.

Jingmen (a front *mu* point of the kidney, GB 25)

Location: On the lateral side of the waist and just below the free end of the 12th rib. (Fig. 2-79)

Indications: Abdominal distention, borborygmus, diarrhea, pain in the lumbar and hypochondriac regions, and dysuria.

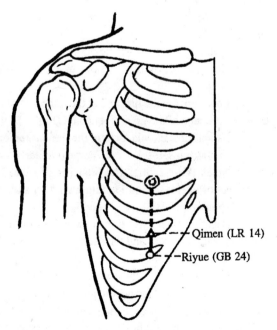

Fig. 2-80

Method: Insert the needle obliquely, 0.5-0.8 *cun* deep.

Notes: Vasculature: The 11th intercostal artery and vein. Innervation: The 11th intercostal nerve.

Daimai (GB 26)

Location: On the lateral side of the abdomen, at the crossing point of a vertical line through the free end of the 11th rib and a horizontal line through the umbilicus. (Fig. 2-79)

Indications: Irregular menstruation, amenorrhea, leukorrhagia, and pain in the lumbar and hypochondriac regions.

Method: Insert the needle perpendicularly, 0.5-1 *cun* deep.

Notes: Vasculature: Intercostal artery and vein. Innervation: Intercostal nerve.

Wushu (GB 27)

Location: On the lateral side of the abdomen, anterior to the anterosuperior iliac spine and 3 *cun* below the level of the umbilicus. (Fig. 2-81)

Indications: Metroptosis, leukorrhagia, hernia, and pain in the lower abdomen.

Method: Insert the needle perpendicularly, 0.5-1 *cun* deep.

Notes: Vasculature: Superficial and deep circumflex iliac arteries and veins. Innervation: Iliohypogastric nerve.

Weidao (GB 28)

Location: On the lateral side of the abdomen, anterior and inferior to the anterosuperior iliac spine and 0.5 *cun* anterior and inferior to *Wushu* (GB 27). (Fig. 2-81)

Indications: Pain in the lower abdomen, metroptosis, leukorrhagia and hernia.

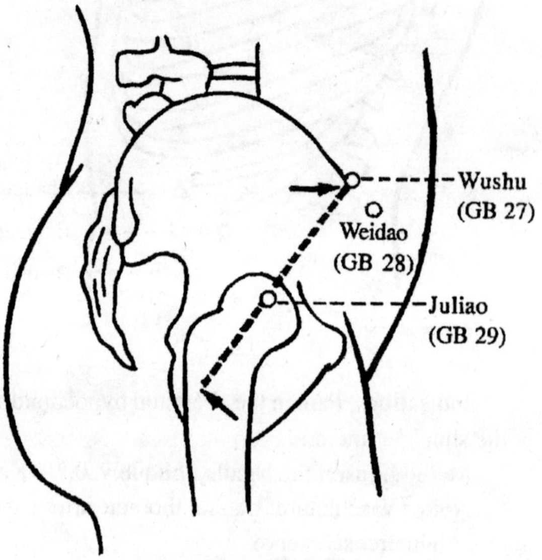

Fig. 2-81

Method: Insert the needle perpendicularly or obliquely anteroinferiorly, 1-1.5 *cun* deep.

Notes: Vasculature: The same as that of *Wushu* (GB 27). Innervation: Ilioinguinal nerve.

Juliao (GB 29)

Location: On the hip, and at the midpoint of the line connecting the anterosuperior iliac spine and the prominence of the great trochanter. (Fig. 2-81)

Indications: Hernia, pain in the lumbar region and lower limbs, weakness of the lower limbs.

Method: Insert the needle perpendicularly, 1-1.5 *cun* deep.

Notes: Vasculature: The branches of superficial circumflex iliac artery and vein; the ascending branches of lateral circumflex femoral artery and vein. Innervation: Lateral femoral cutaneous nerve.

Huantiao (GB 30)

Location: At the junction of the middle third and lateral third of the line connecting the prominence of the great trochanter and the sacral hiatus when the patient is in a lateral recumbent position with the thigh flexed. (Fig. 2-82)

Indications: Flaccidity, weakness and motor impairment of the lower limbs.

Method: Insert the needle perpendicularly, 2-3 *cun* deep.

Notes: (1) As a crossing point of the Foot-*Taiyang* and Foot-*Shaoyang* meridians, *Huantiao* is effective for pain, numbness and motor impairment of the lumbar region and lower limbs when used together with *Dachangshu* (BL 25), *Shenshu* (BL 23) and *Yanglingquan* (GB 34). (2) Vasculature: Inferior

MERIDIANS AND ACUPOINTS 91

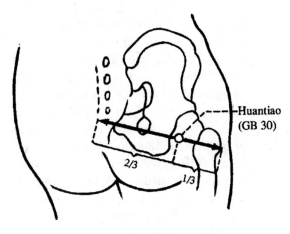

Fig. 2-82

gluteal artery and vein. Innervation: Inferior gluteal cutaneous nerve, inferior gluteal nerve and sciatic nerve.

Fengshi (GB 31)

Location: On the lateral midline of the thigh, 7 *cun* above the popliteal crease, or at the place touching the tip of the middle finger when the patient stands erect with the arms hanging down freely. (Fig. 2-83)

Indications: Flaccidity, weakness and motor impairment of the lower limbs, general pruritus and beriberi.

Method: Insert the needle perpendicularly, 1-2 *cun* deep.

Notes: Vasculature: The muscular branches of lateral circumflex femoral artery and vein. Innervation: Lateral femoral cutaneous nerve, and the muscular branch of femoral nerve.

Zhongdu (GB 32)

Location: On the lateral side of the thigh and 2 *cun* below *Fengshi* (GB 31). (Fig. 2-83)

Indications: Flaccidity, weakness and motor impairment of the lower limbs.

Method: Insert the needle perpendicularly, 1-1.5 *cun* deep.

Notes: Vasculature and innervation: The same as those of *Fengshi* (GB 31).

Xiyangguan (GB 33)

Location: On the lateral side of the knee, 3 *cun* above *Yanglingquan* (GB 34) and in the depression above the external epicondyle of the femur. (Fig. 2-83)

Indications: Pain in the knee, spasmodic pain in the popliteal fossa, pain and numbness in the lower limbs.

Method: Insert the needle perpendicularly, 0.8-1 *cun* deep.

Notes: Vasculature: Lateral superior genicular artery and vein. Innervation: The terminal branch of lateral femoral cutaneous nerve.

Yanglingquan (a *he* point and a lower *confluent* point corresponding to the gallbladder, and one of the eight influential points, GB 34)

Location: On the lateral side of the leg and in the depression anteroinferior to the capitulum of the fibula. (Fig. 2-84)

Indications: Jaundice, bitter taste, vomiting, pain in the chest, hypochondriac region and knee, weakness and flaccidity of the lower limbs.

Method: Insert the needle perpendicularly, 1-1.5 *cun* deep.

Notes: (1) *The Classic on Medical Problems* points out that *Yanglingquan* dominates the tendons, so it can be used to treat diseases of the tendons. It can be

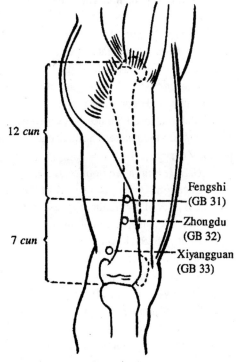

Fig. 2-83

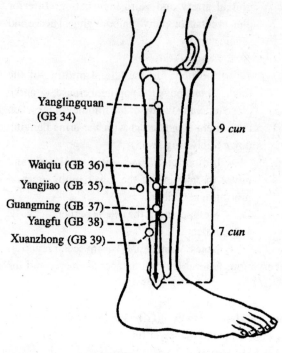

Fig. 2-84

punctured together with *Shenshu* (BL 23), *Huantiao* (GB 30) and *Kunlun* (BL 60) for pain and numbness in the lumbar region and lower limbs. (2) As a *he* point of the meridian and a lower confluent point, it is effective in treating disorders of gallbladder. Studies show that inserting the needle into *Yanglingquan* can promote the the movement and evacuation of the gallbladder. This effect begins when the patient feels punctured and becomes more apparent in ten minutes after the treatment. (3) Vasculature: Inferior lateral genicular artery and vein. Innervation: Common peroneal nerve bifurcating into superficial and deep peroneal nerves.

Yangjiao (GB 35)

Location: On the lateral side of the leg, 7 *cun* above the tip of the external malleolus and 1 *cun* posterior to *Waiqiu* (GB 36). (Fig. 2-84)

Indications: Distensive pain in the chest and hypochondriac region, weakness and flaccidity of the lower limbs, depression, and sore throat.

Method: Insert the needle perpendicularly, 0.5-1 *cun* deep.

Notes: Vasculature: The branches of peroneal artery and vein. Innervation: Lateral cutaneous nerve of calf.

Waiqiu (a *xi* point, GB 36)

Location: On the lateral side of the leg, 7 *cun* above the tip of the external malleolus and on the anterior border of the fibula. (Fig. 2-84)

Indications: Distensive pain in the chest and hypochondriac region, weakness and flaccidity of the lower limbs, and depression.

Method: Insert the needle perpendicularly, 0.5-1 *cun* deep.

Notes: Vasculature: The muscular branches of anterior tibial artery and vein. Innervation: Superficial peroneal nerve.

Guangming (a *luo* point, GB 37)

Location: On the lateral side of the leg, 5 *cun* above the tip of the external malleolus and on the anterior border of the fibula. (Fig. 2-84)

Indications: Ophthalmalgia, blurred vision, night blindness, distensive pain in the breast, weakness and flaccidity of the lower limbs.

Method: Insert the needle perpendicularly, 0.5-1 *cun* deep.

Notes: (1) *Shenying Classic* says, "*Guangming* and *Diwuhui* (GB 42) can be used for itching and pain in the eyes." Clinically, it is usually combined with *Ganshu* (BL 18), *Fengchi* (GB 20), *Taiyang* (EX-HN 5), *Jingming* (BL 1) and *Sizhukong* (SJ 23) for cataract in the early stage. (2) Vasculature and innervation: The same as those of *Waiqiu* (GB 36).

Yangfu (a *jing* point, GB 38)

Location: On the lateral side of the leg, 4 *cun* above the tip of the external malleolus and slightly anterior to the anterior border of the fibula. (Fig. 2-84)

Indications: Pain in the chest and hypochondriac region, swollen axillary region, pain in the outer canthus, weakness and flaccidity of the lower limbs.

Method: Insert the needle perpendicularly, 0.5-1 *cun* deep.

Notes: Vasculature and innervation: The same as those of *Waiqiu* (GB 36).

Xuanzhong (one of the eight influential points, GB 39)

Location: On the lateral side of the leg, 3 *cun* above the tip of the external malleolus and on the posterior border of the fibula. (Fig. 2-84)

Indications: Distensive pain in the chest, abdomen and hypochondriac region, weakness and motor impairment of the lower limbs, and bleeding due to hemorrhoids.

Method: Insert the needle perpendicularly, 0.5-1 *cun* deep.

Notes: (1) It is also known as *Juegu* (GB 39). *The Classic on Medical Problems* points out that *Juegu* dominates the marrow, and is therefore indicated for marrow disorders. To treat numbness and motor impairment of the lower limbs, use *Shenshu* (BL 23), *Huantiao* (GB 30) and *Zusanli* (ST 36) together with *Xuanzhong*. (2) Vasculature and innervation: The same as those of *Waiqiu* (GB 36).

Qiuxu (a *yuan* point, GB 40)

Location: Anteroinferior to the external malleolus and in the depression lateral to the tendon of the long extensor muscle of the toes. (Fig. 2-85)

Indications: Red and swollen eyes, malaria, distensive pain in the chest and hypochondriac region, swollen axillary region, pain and swelling in the malleolus and foot.

Method: Insert the needle perpendicularly, 0.5-0.8 *cun* deep.

Notes: Vasculature: The branches of anterolateral malleolar artery and vein. Innervation: The branches of intermediate dorsal cutaneous nerve and superficial peroneal nerve.

Zulinqi (a *shu* point and one of the eight confluent points, GB 41)

Location: On the lateral side of the instep of the foot, and in the depression lateral to the junction of the fourth and fifth metatarsal bones. (Fig. 2-85)

Indications: Migraine, malaria, dizziness, pain in the outer canthus, scrofula and swollen instep.

Method: Insert the needle perpendicularly, 0.3-0.5 *cun* deep.

Notes: Vasculature: Dorsal arterial and venous network of foot and the fourth dorsal metatarsal artery and vein. Innervation: The branch of intermediate dorsal cutaneous nerve of foot.

Diwuhui (GB 42)

Location: On the lateral side of the instep, between the fourth and fifth metatarsal bones and on the medial side of the tendon of the extensor muscle of the little toe. (Fig. 2-85)

Indications: Headache, tinnitus, deafness, swollen breast, fullness and pain in the chest and hypochondriac region, and swollen instep.

Method: Insert the needle perpendicularly, 0.3-0.5 *cun* deep.

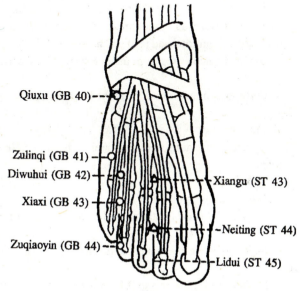

Fig. 2-85

Notes: (1) According to *A Systematic Classic of Acupuncture*, *Diwuhui* is contraindicated for moxibustion. (2) Vasculature and innervation: The same as those of *Zulinqi* (GB 41).

Xiaxi (a *ying* point, GB 43)

Location: On the lateral side of the instep, between the fourth and fifth toes and proximal to the margin of the web. (Fig. 2-85)

Indications: Headache, vertigo, tinnitus, deafness, pain in the outer canthus, distensive pain in the chest and hypochondriac region, and swollen instep.

Method: Insert the needle perpendicularly, 0.3-0.5 *cun* deep.

Notes: Vasculature: Dorsal digital artery and vein. Innervation: Dorsal digital nerve.

Zuqiaoyin (a *jiing* point, GB 44)

Location: On the lateral side of the fourth toe and about 0.1 *cun* lateral to the corner of the toe nail. (Fig. 2-85)

Indications: Headache, dizziness, red and swollen eyes, tinnitus, deafness, distensive pain in the chest and hypochondriac region and irritability.

Method: Insert the needle 0.1 *cun* into the skin.

Notes: Vasculature: Arterial and venous network formed by dorsal digital artery and vein and plantar digital artery and vein. Innervation: Dorsal digital nerve.

12. The Liver Meridian of Foot-*Jueyin* (LR)

(Fig. 2-86 and Fig. 2-87)

1) Traveling route

a) The meridian starts at the hairy region posterior to the nail of the great toe (*Dadun*, LR 1) (1), goes upward along the dorsum of foot (2) and passes through the area 1 *cun* in front of the medial malleolus (3). It ascends along the medial side of the leg and in front of the Lung Meridian of Hand-*Taiyin*. Then it emerges from behind the Foot-*Taiyin* Meridian at the level 8 *cun* above the medial malleolus (4). Passing the medial side of the knee (5) and the thigh (6), it enters the pubes (7) and curves around the external genitals (8) before arriving at the lower abdomen (9). It continues to run along the stomach on both sides, pertains to the liver and connects with the gallbladder (10). Still then it passes through the diaphragm (11) and spreads in the chest and hypochondriac region (12). Finally it ascends along the posterior side of the throat (13), enters the nasopharynx (14), connects with the eye system (15), emerges from forehead (16) and meets the *Du* Meridian at the vertex (17).

b) One branch arises from the eye system, descends to the cheek (18) and curves around the lips (19).

c) Another branch arises from the liver (20), goes through the diaphragm (21) and enters the lung (22).

2) Symptoms

Diarrhea, vomiting, hernia, enuresis, dysuria, fullness in the chest, swollen lower abdomen and lumbago.

3) Acupoints

Dadun (a *jiing* point, LR 1)

Location: On the lateral side of the great toe and 0.1 *cun* lateral to the corner of the toe nail. (Fig. 2-88)

Indications: Hernia, enuresis, dysuria, irregular menstruation, metrorrhagia, mania and swollen vulva.

Method: Insert the needle 0.1 *cun* into the skin.

Notes: (1) *Dadun* is effective for hernia when used together with *Zhaohai* (KI 6) and *Guanyuan*

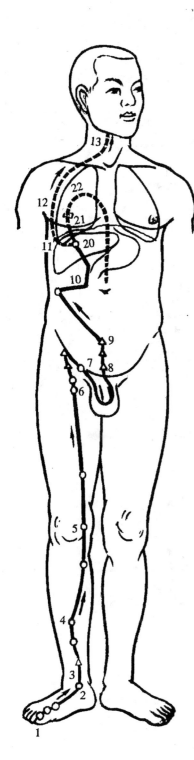

Fig. 2-86 Liver Meridian of Foot-*Jueyin*

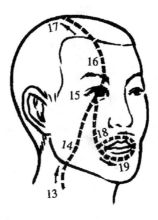

(RN 4). (2) According to *Illustrated Supplementary to the Classified Canon*, moxibustion is not suitable for pregnant and puerperal women. (3) Vasculature: Dorsal digital artery and vein. Innervation: Dorsal digital nerve stemming from the deep peroneal nerve.

Xingjian (a *ying* point, LR 2)

Location: On the instep and at the end of the web between the first and second toes. (Fig. 2-88)

Indications: Headache, vertigo, red and swollen eyes, optic atrophy, hernia, dysuria, irregular menstruation and epilepsy.

Method: Insert the needle obliquely upward, 0.5-0.8 *cun* deep.

Notes: (1) As a *ying* point of the meridian which belongs to fire in the Five Elements, *Xingjian* can help disperse liver-fire. *Fengchi* (GB 20), *Taiyang* (EX-HN 5) and *Hegu* (LI 4) can be used together with *Xingjian* to treat headache, vertigo, red and swollen eyes and optic atrophy. (2) Vasculature: Dorsal venous network of foot, and the first dorsal digital artery and vein. Innervation: Dorsal digital nerve stemming from the deep peroneal nerve.

Taichong (a *shu* point and a *yuan* point, LR 3)

Location: On the dorsum of foot and in the depression distal to the junction of the first and second metatarsal bones. (Fig. 2-88)

Indications: Headache, vertigo, hernia, irregular menstruation, jaundice, red and swollen eyes, optic atrophy, epilepsy, facial paralysis, pain in the chest and hypochondriac region, weakness and flaccidity of the lower limbs.

Method: Insert the needle perpendicularly, 0.5-1 *cun* deep.

Notes: (1) *Taichong* can be used together with *Fengchi* (GB 20), *Sanyinjiao* (SP 6) and *Zusanli* (ST 36) to treat vertigo (hypertension) in clinical practice. (2) It is one of the acupoints frequently used for acupuncture anesthesia. (3) According to reports, puncturing at *Taichong* can help alleviate the pressure of the biliary duct caused by acute biliary diseases. *Taichong* is more effective in relieving the Oddi's sphincterismus than *Zusanli* (ST 36) and *Yanglingquan* (GB 34). (4) Vasculature: Dorsal venous network of foot and the first dorsal metatarsal artery.

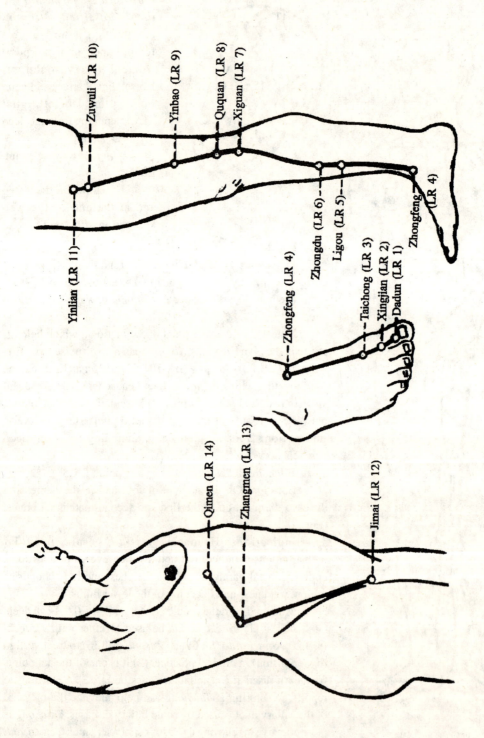

Fig. 2-87 Acupoints on the Liver Meridian of Foot-*Jueyin*

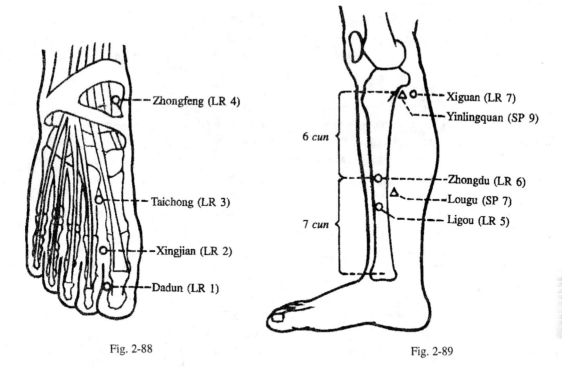

Fig. 2-88   Fig. 2-89

Innervation: The branch of the deep peroneal nerve.

Zhongfeng (a *jing* point, LR 4)

Location: On the instep, 1 *cun* anterior to the medial malleolus, in the depression on the medial side of the tendon of the anterior tibial muscle, and on the line connecting *Shangqiu* (SP 5) and *Jiexi* (ST 41). (Fig. 2-88)

Indications: Seminal emission, dysuria, hernia, jaundice, swollen lower abdomen, and pain in the chest and hypochondriac region.

Method: Insert the needle perpendicularly, 0.5-0.8 *cun* deep.

Notes: Vasculature: Dorsal venous network of foot and anterior medial malleolar artery. Innervation: The branch of medial dorsal cutaneous nerve of foot, and saphenous nerve.

Ligou (a *luo* point, LR 5)

Location: On the medial side of the leg, 5 *cun* above the tip of the medial malleolus and on the medial border of the tibia. (Fig. 2-89)

Indications: Irregular menstruation, leukorrhagia, hernia, dysuria and tibial pain.

Method: Insert the needle horizontally, 0.5-0.8 *cun* deep.

Notes: Vasculature: Great saphenous vein. Innervation: The branch of saphenous nerve.

Zhongdu (a *xi* point, LR 6)

Location: On the medial side of the leg, 7 *cun* above the tip of the medial malleolus and on the medial border of the tibia. (Fig. 2-89)

Indications: Diarrhea, abdominal distention, hernia, pain in the hypochondriac region, and metrorrhagia.

Notes: Vasculature: Great saphenous vein. Innervation: The branch of saphenous nerve.

Xiguan (LR 7)

Location: Posteroinferior to the medial condyle of the tibia and 1 *cun* posterior to *Yinlingquan* (SP

9). (Fig. 2-89)

Indications: Sore throat, weakness and flaccidity in the lower limbs, and swollen knee.

Method: Insert the needle perpendicularly, 0.8-1 *cun* deep.

Notes: Vasculature: Posterior tibial artery. Innervation: The branch of medial sural cutaneous nerve and the tibial nerve.

Ququan (a *he* point, LR 8)

Location: On the medial side of the knee, at the medial end of the popliteal crease when the knee is flexed, posterior to the medial epicondyle of the tibia and in the depression of the anterior border of the insertions of the semimembranous and semitendinous muscles. (Fig. 2-90)

Indications: Dysuria, pain in the lower abdomen, headache, vertigo, irregular menstruation, prolapse of uterus, and pain in the knee.

Method: Insert the needle perpendicularly, 0.8-1 *cun* deep.

Notes: Vasculature: Great saphenous vein and supreme genicular artery. Innervation: Saphenous nerve.

Yinbao (LR 9)

Location: On the medial side of the thigh, 4 *cun* above the medial epicondyle of the femur and between the medial vastus and sartorius muscles. (Fig. 2-90)

Indications: Dysuria, enuresis, irregular menstruation and pain in the lumbosacral region.

Method: Insert the needle perpendicularly, 0.8-1.5 *cun* deep.

Notes: Vasculature: Femoral artery and vein, and the superficial branch of medial circumflex femoral artery. Innervation: The anterior femoral cutaneous nerve on the pathway of the anterior branch of obturator nerve.

Zuwuli (LR 10)

Location: On the medial side of the thigh, 2 *cun* lateral to and 3 *cun* directly below *Qugu* (RN 2). (Fig. 2-91)

Indications: Dysuria, metroptosis, and distention and fullness in the lower abdomen.

Method: Insert the needle perpendicularly, 0.8-1.5 *cun* deep.

Notes: Vasculature: The superficial branches of medial circumflex femoral artery and vein.

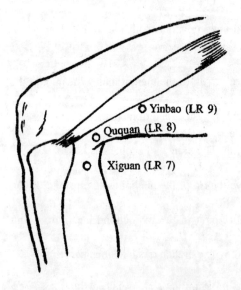

Fig. 2-90

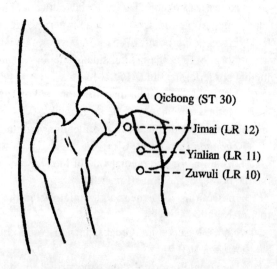

Fig. 2-91

Innervation: Genitofemoral nerve, anterior femoral cutaneous nerve and the anterior branch of obturator nerve.

Yinlian (LR 11)

Location: On the medial side of the thigh, and 2 *cun* lateral to and 2 *cun* directly below *Qugu* (RN 2). (Fig. 2-91)

Indications: Irregular menstruation, leukorrhagia, pain in the lower abdomen and medial side of the thigh.

Method: Insert the needle perpendicularly, 0.8-1.5 *cun* deep.

Notes: Vasculature: The branches of medial circumflex femoral artery and vein. Innervation: Genitofemoral nerve, the branch of medial femoral cutaneous nerve and the anterior branch of obturator nerve.

Jimai (LR 12)

Location: Lateral to the pubic tubercle, lateral and inferior to *Qichong* (ST 30) and 2.5 *cun* lateral to the anterior midline. (Fig. 2-91)

Indications: Hernia, metroptosis, and pain in the penis and lower abdomen.

Method: Insert the needle perpendicularly, 0.5-0.8 *cun* deep.

Notes: Vasculature: The branches of external pudendal artery and vein, the pubic branches of inferior epigastric artery and vein and femoral vein. Innervation: Ilioinguinal nerve and the anterior branch of obturator nerve.

Zhangmen (a front *mu* point of the spleen and one of the eight influential points, LR 13)

Location: Below the free end of the 11th rib. (Fig. 2-92)

Indications: Abdominal distention, diarrhea, jaundice, vomiting, abdominal mass, pain in the chest and hypochondriac region.

Method: Insert the needle obliquely, 0.5-0.8 *cun* deep.

Notes: Vasculature: The terminal branch of the tenth intercostal artery. Innervation: The tenth and 11th intercostal nerves.

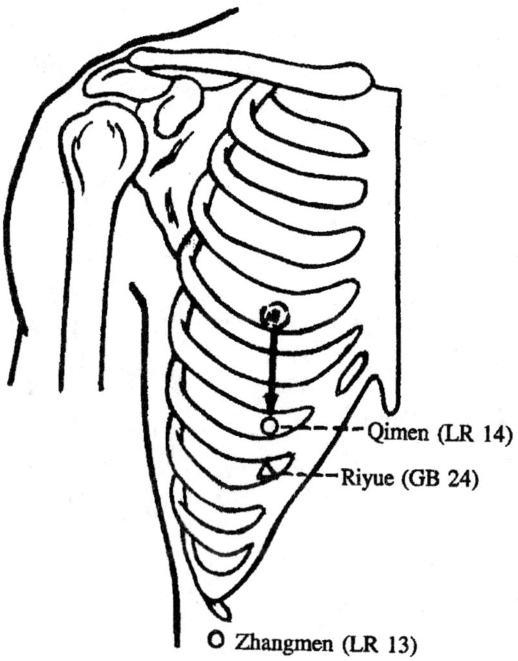

Fig. 2-92

Qimen (a front *mu* point of the liver, LR 14)

Location: On the chest, directly below the nipple and in the sixth intercostal space, 4 *cun* lateral to the anterior midline. (Fig. 2-92)

Indications: Abdominal distention, diarrhea, vomiting, abdominal mass, distensive pain in the chest and hypochondriac region.

Method: Insert the needle obliquely or horizontally, 0.5-0.8 *cun* deep.

Notes: Vasculature: The sixth intercostal artery and vein. Innervation: The sixth intercostal nerve.

Section 2
THE EIGHT EXTRA MERIDIANS

1. The *Ren* Meridian (Conception Vessel) (RN)
(Fig. 2-93 and Fig. 2-94)
1) Traveling route

The meridian starts at the lower abdomen and emerges from the perineum (*Huiyin*, RN 1) (1). Passing the pubes (2), it ascends along the midline of the abdomen and chest (3). Then it reaches the throat (4) and curves around the lips (5). After running through the face (6), it enters the infraorbital region (7).

2) Symptoms

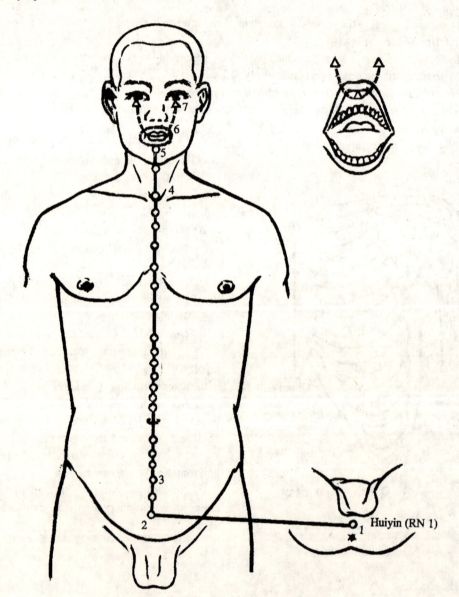

Fig. 2-93 *Ren* Meridian (Conception Vessel)

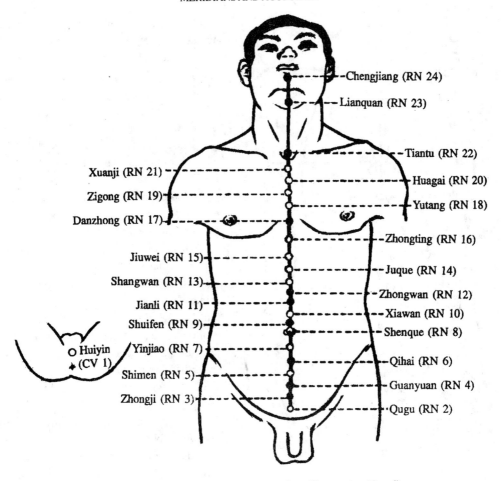

Fig. 2-94 Acupoints on the *Ren* Meridian (Conception Vessel)

Hernia, leukorrhagia and abdominal mass.

3) Acupoints

Huiyin (RN 1)

Location: On the perineum, at the midpoint between the posterior border of the scrotum and anus in male. (Fig. 2-93)

Indications: Dysuria, dyschesia, seminal emission, metroptosis, hemorrhoids, prolapse of anus, epilepsy and asphyxia due to drowning.

Method: Insert the needle perpendicularly, 0.5-1 *cun* deep. Be careful when needling at pregnant women.

Notes: Vasculature: The branches of perineal artery and vein. Innervation: The branch of perineal nerve.

Qugu (RN 2)

Location: On the anterior midline of the abdomen and at the midpoint of the upper border of the symphysis pubis. (Fig. 2-95)

Indications: Stranguria, enuresis, seminal emission, impotence, fullness of the lower abdomen, hernia, irregular menstruation and leukorrhagia.

Method: Insert the needle perpendicularly, 0.5-1 *cun* deep.

Notes: (1) Be careful when puncturing acupoints from *Qugu* (RN 2) to *Shangwan* (RN 13) along

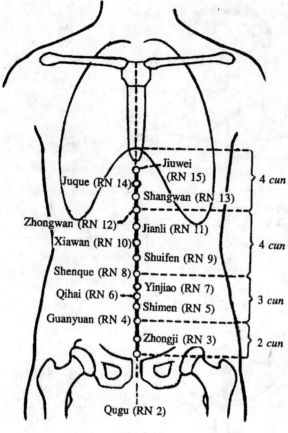

Fig. 2-95

the *Ren* Meridian of pregnant women. (2) Vasculature: The branches of inferior epigastric artery and obturator artery. Innervation: The branch of iliohypogastric nerve.

Zhongji (a front *mu* point of the urinary bladder, RN 3)

Location: On the anterior midline of the abdomen and 4 *cun* below the umbilicus. (Fig. 2-95)

Indications: Dysuria, enuresis, seminal emission, impotence, hernia, irregular menstruation and metroptosis.

Method: Insert the needle perpendicularly, 0.5-1 *cun* deep.

Notes: (1) As a front *mu* point of the urinary bladder, *Zhongji* can be used together with *Pangguangshu* (BL 28), a back *shu* point of the bladder, to treat enuresis and dysuria. (2) Vasculature: The branches of superficial epigastric and inferior epigastric arteries and veins. Innervation: The branch of iliohypogastric nerve.

Guanyuan (a front *mu* point of the small intestine, RN 4)

Location: On the anterior midline of the abdomen and 3 *cun* below the umbilicus. (Fig. 2-95)

Indications: Impotence, seminal emission, enuresis, irregular men-struation, leukorrhagia, metroptosis, apoplexy and prostration syndrome, general debility.

Method: Insert the needle perpendicularly, 0.8-1.2 *cun* deep.

Notes: (1) For disorders of urogenital system, *Shenshu* (BL 23), *Sanyinjiao* (SP 6) and *Zusanli* (ST 36) can be used together with *Guanyuan*. (2) It can be used to treat apoplexy and general debility. According to reports, apply moxibustion to *Guanyuan* may help strengthen the compensatory function, regulate blood flow and alleviate the condition of shock. (3) Vasculature: The same as that of *Zhongji* (RN 3). Innervation: The medial branch of the anterior cutaneous branch of the 12th intercostal nerve.

Shimen (a front *mu* point of *sanjiao*, RN 5)

Location: On the anterior midline of the abdomen and 2 *cun* below the umbilicus. (Fig. 2-95)

Indications: Dysuria, edema, diarrhea, abdominal pain, hernia, seminal emission and irregular menstruation.

Method: Insert the needle perpendicularly, 0.8-1.2 *cun* deep.

Notes: (1) According to *A Systematic Classic of Acupuncture*, acupuncture and moxibustion on this acupoint is contraindicated for females, otherwise infertility may occur. (2) Vasculature: The same as that of *Zhongji* (RN 3). Innervation: The anterior cutaneous branch of the 11th intercostal nerve.

Qihai (RN 6)

Location: On the anterior midline of the abdomen and 1.5 *cun* below the umbilicus. (Fig. 2-95)

Indications: Pain in the lower abdomen, enuresis, incontinence of urine, dysuria, diarrhea, impotence, seminal emission, hernia, irregular menstruation, metroptosis, apoplexy and general debility.

Method: Insert the needle perpendicularly, 0.8-1.2 *cun* deep.

Notes: (1) This acupoint can help replenish the body. According to *Verses for Acupuncture Manipulations*, *Qihai*, *Guanyuan* (RN 4) and *Weizhong* (BL 40) can be used to strengthen the body. (2) Vasculature and innervation: The same as those of *Shimen* (RN 5).

Yinjiao (RN 7)

Location: On the anterior midline of the abdomen and 1 *cun* below the umbilicus. (Fig. 2-95)

Indications: Pain and distention in the abdomen, dysuria, edema, diarrhea, amenorrhea and leukorrhagia.

Method: Insert the needle perpendicularly, 0.8-1.2 *cun* deep.

Notes: Vasculature: The same as that of *Zhongji* (RN 3). Innervation: The anterior cutaneous branch of the tenth intercostal nerve.

Shenque (RN 8)

Location: In the center of the umbilicus. (Fig. 2-95)

Indications: Apoplexy, abdominal pain with cold limbs, diarrhea and edema.

Method: Acupuncture is prohibited and moxibustion is applicable.

Notes: Vasculature: Inferior epigastric artery and vein. Innervation: The anterior cutaneous branch of the tenth intercostal nerve.

Shuifen (RN 9)

Location: On the anterior midline of the abdomen and 1 *cun* above the umbilicus. (Fig. 2-95)

Indications: Pain and distention of the abdomen, edema, diarrhea, regurgitation and vomiting.

Method: Insert the needle perpendicularly, 0.8-1.2 *cun* deep.

Notes: Vasculature: The same as that of *Shenque* (RN 8). Innervation: The anterior cutaneous branches of the eighth and ninth intercostal nerves.

Xiawan (RN 10)

Location: On the anterior midline of the upper abdomen, 2 *cun* above the umbilicus. (Fig. 2-95)

Indications: Stomachache, abdominal pain and distention, vomiting, regurgitation and hiccup.

Method: Insert the needle perpendicularly, 0.8-1.2 *cun* deep.

Notes: Vasculature: The same as that of *Shenque* (RN 8). Innervation: The anterior cutaneous branch of the eighth intercostal nerve.

Jianli (RN 11)

Location: On the anterior midline of the abdomen, 3 *cun* above the umbilicus. (Fig. 2-95)

Indications: Stomachache, abdominal pain and distention, diarrhea and vomiting.

Method: Insert the needle perpendicularly, 0.8-1.2 *cun* deep.

Notes: Vasculature: The branches of superior and inferior epigastric arteries and veins. Innervation: The anterior cutaneous branch of the eighth intercostal nerve.

Zhongwan (a front *mu* point of the stomach and one of the eight influential points, RN 12)

Location: On the anterior midline of the upper abdomen and 4 *cun* above the umbilicus. (Fig. 2-95)

Indications: Stomachache, abdominal pain and distention, vomiting, hiccup, diarrhea, jaundice, cough, asthma, excess sputum, and weak spleen and stomach.

Method: Insert the needle perpendicularly, 0.8-1.2 *cun* deep.

Notes: (1) As an acupoint dominating *fu* organs, *Zhongwan* is often used for disorders of spleen and stomach. For abdominal pain and stomachache, *Zusanli* (ST 36), *Neiguan* (PC 6) and *Weishu* (BL 21) could be used together with *Zhongwan*. (2) Vasculature: Superior epigastric artery and vein.

Innervation: The anterior cutaneous branch of the seventh intercostal nerve.

Shangwan (RN 13)

Location: On the anterior midline of the upper abdomen and 5 *cun* above the umbilicus. (Fig. 2-95)

Indications: Abdominal distention, stomachache, vomiting and epilepsy.

Method: Insert the needle perpendicularly, 0.8-1.2 *cun* deep.

Notes: Vasculature and innervation: The same as those of *Zhongwan* (RN 12).

Juque (a front *mu* point of the heart, RN 14)

Location: On the anterior midline of the upper abdomen and 6 *cun* above the umbilicus. (Fig. 2-95)

Indications: Cardialgia, palpitation, epilepsy, chest pain, stomachache and vomiting.

Method: Insert the needle obliquely downward, 0.5-1 *cun* deep.

Notes: Vasculature and innervation: See *Zhongwan* (RN 12).

Jiuwei (a *luo* point, RN 15)

Location: On the anterior midline of the upper abdomen and 7 *cun* above the umbilicus. (Fig. 2-95)

Indications: Cardialgia, palpitation, chest pain, mania and epilepsy.

Method: Insert the needle obliquely downward, 0.5-1 *cun* deep.

Notes: Vasculature and innervation: See *Zhongwan* (RN 12).

Zhongting (RN 16)

Location: On the anterior midline of the sternum and at the junction of the gladiolus and xiphoid process. (Fig. 2-96)

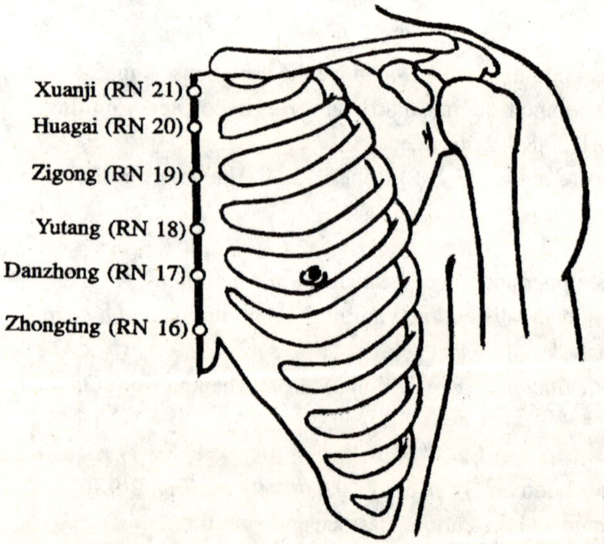

Indications: Fullness in the chest and hypochondriac region, vomiting, dysphagia anorexia and globus hystericus.

Method: Insert the needle horizontally, 0.3-0.5 *cun* deep.

Notes: Vasculature: The perforating branches of internal mammary artery and vein. Innervation: The anterior cutaneous branch of the fifth intercostal nerve.

Danzhong (a front *mu* point of the pericardium and one of the eight influential points, RN 17)

Location: On the mid-sternal line and at the level of the fourth intercostal space. (Fig. 2-96)

Fig. 2-96

Indications: Palpitation, chest pain, cough, asthma and lack of lactation.

Method: Insert the needle horizontally, 0.3-0.5 *cun* deep.

Notes: (1) As one of the eight influential points dominating *qi*, this acupoint is often used to treat *qi* disorders such as cough and asthma together with *Feishu* (BL 13), *Chize* (LU 5), and *Fenglong* (ST 40). (2) As *Essentially Treasured Prescriptions* puts it, *Danzhong* and *Huagai* (RN 20) are indicated for short breath, asthma and dysphasia. *Danzhong* and *Tianjing* (SJ 10) are indicated for pain in the chest and cardialgia. (3) Vasculature: The same as that of *Zhongting* (RN 16). Innervation: The anterior cutaneous branch of the fourth intercostal nerve.

Yutang (RN 18)

Location: On the mid-sternal line and at the level of the third intercostal space. (Fig. 2-96)

Indications: Cough, asthma, chest pain, sore throat and swollen breasts.

Method: Insert the needle horizontally, 0.3-0.5 *cun* deep.

Notes: Vasculature: The same as that of *Zhongting* (RN 16). Innervation: The anterior cutaneous branch of the third intercostal nerve.

Zigong (RN 19)

Location: On the mid-sternal line and at the level of the second intercostal space. (Fig. 2-96)

Indications: Cough, asthma, chest pain, sore throat and vomiting.

Method: Insert the needle horizontally, 0.3-0.5 *cun* deep.

Notes: Vasculature: The same as that of *Zhongting* (RN 16). Innervation: The anterior cutaneous branch of the second intercostal nerve.

Huagai (RN 20)

Location: On the mid-sternal line and at the level of the first intercostal space. (Fig. 2-96)

Indications: Cough, asthma, chest pain and sore throat.

Method: Insert the needle horizontally, 0.3-0.5 *cun* deep.

Notes: Vasculature: The same as that of *Zhongting* (RN 16). Innervation: The anterior cutaneous branch of the first intercostal nerve.

Xuanji (RN 21)

Location: On the mid-sternal line and at the midpoint of the sternal manubrium. (Fig. 2-96)

Indications: Cough, asthma and sore throat.

Method: Insert the needle horizontally, 0.3-0.5 *cun* deep.

Notes: Vasculature: The same as that of *Zhongting* (RN 16). Innervation: The anterior branch of the supraclavicular nerve and the anterior cutaneous branch of the first intercostal nerve.

Tiantu (RN 22)

Location: On the anterior midline of the neck and in the center of the suprasternal fossa. (Fig. 2-97)

Indications: Cough, asthma, sore throat, sudden loss of voice, goiter and globus hystericus.

Method: First, insert the needle perpendicularly, 0.2 *cun* deep. Then turn the needle tip downward and insert it between the posterior side of the sternum and the trachea slowly, 0.5-1 *cun* deep. Pay attention to the accuracy of insertion.

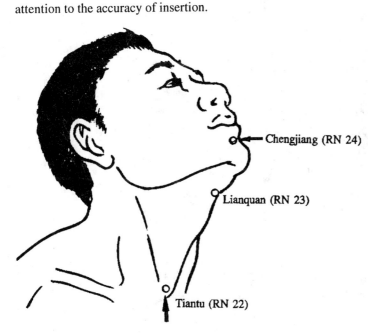

Fig. 2-97

Notes: Vasculature: Jugular venous arch and the branch of inferior thyroid artery, innominate vein and aortic arch. Innervation: The anterior branch of the supraclavicular nerve.

Lianquan (RN 23)

Location: On the anterior midline of the neck and at the midpoint of the upper border of the hyoid bone. (Fig. 2-97)

Indications: Swollen sublingual region, aphasia with stiff tongue, sudden loss of voice, dysphagia and sore throat.

Method: Insert the needle obliquely towards the root of the tongue, 0.5-1 *cun* deep.

Notes: Vasculature: Anterior jugular vein. Innervation: The branch of cutaneous cervical nerve, hypoglossal nerve, and the branch of glossopharyngeal nerve.

Chengjiang (RN 24)

Location: On the face and in the depression at the midpoint of the mentolabial sulcus. (Fig. 2-97)

Indications: Facial paralysis, swollen gums, sudden loss of voice, salivation, epilepsy and swollen face.

Method: Insert the needle obliquely, 0.3-0.5 *cun* deep.

Notes: Vasculature: The branches of inferior labial artery and vein. Innervation: The branch of facial nerve.

2. The *Du* Meridian (Governor Vessel) (DU)

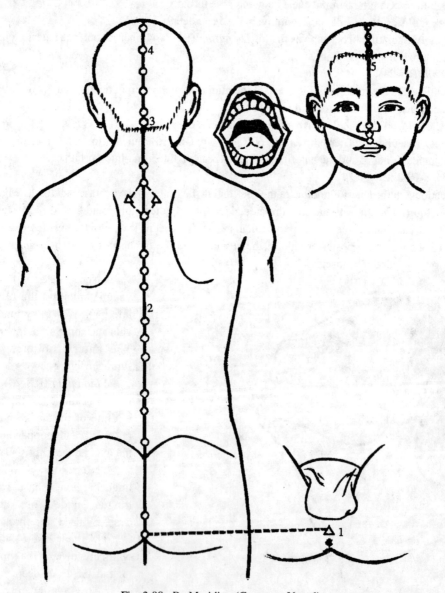

Fig. 2-98 *Du* Meridian (Governor Vessel)

(Fig. 2-98 and Fig. 2-99)

1) Traveling route

The meridian starts from the lower abdomen and emerges at the perineum (1). Then it ascends along the spinal column (2) and reaches *Fengfu* (DU 16) on the nape. (3) It then enters the brain and the vertex. (4) Finally, it winds along the forehead to the nose bridge (5).

2) Symptoms

Pain and stiffness in the spinal column, and opisthotonos.

3) Acupoints

Changqiang (a *luo* point, DU 1)

Location: 0.5 *cun* below the tip of the coccyx. (Fig. 2-100)

Indications: Hemorrhoids, prolapse of anus, mania, epilepsy, diarrhea and constipation.

Method: Insert the needle obliquely towards the anterior side of the coccyx, 0.5-0.8 *cun* deep.

Notes: Vasculature: The branches of anal artery and vein. Innervation: The posterior ramus of coccygeal nerve, and anal nerve.

Yaoshu (DU 2)

Location: At the hiatus of the sacrum. (Fig. 2-100)

Indications: Mania, epilepsy, hemorrhoids, irregular menstruation, weakness and pain in the lower limbs.

Method: Insert the needle slightly upwards, 0.5-0.8 *cun* deep.

Notes: Vasculature: The branches of middle sacral artery and vein. Innervation: The branch of coccygeal nerve.

Yaoyangguan (DU 3)

Location: Below the spinous process of the fourth lumbar vertebra. (Fig. 2-100)

Indications: Impotence, seminal emission, irregular menstruation, and pain in the lumbosacral region.

Method: Insert the needle perpendicularly, 0.5-1 *cun* deep.

Notes: Vasculature: The posterior branch of lumbar artery. Innervation: The medial branch of the posterior ramus of lumbar nerve.

Mingmen (DU 4)

Location: Below the spinous process of the second lumbar vertebra. (Fig. 2-100)

Indications: Impotence, seminal emission, irregular menstruation, leukorrhagia, sterility and lumbago.

Method: Insert the needle perpendicularly, 0.5-1 *cun* deep.

Notes: Vasculature and innervation: The same as those of *Yaoyangguan* (DU 3).

Xuanshu (DU 5)

Location: Below the spinous process of the first lumbar vertebra. (Fig. 2-100)

Indications: Lumbago, abdominal distention, diarrhea and dysentery.

Method: Insert the needle perpendicularly, 0.5-1 *cun* deep.

Notes: Vasculature and innervation: The same as those of *Yaoyangguan* (DU 3).

Jizhong (DU 6)

Location: Below the spinous process of the 11th thoracic vertebra. (Fig. 2-100)

Indications: Diarrhea, jaundice, hemorrhoids, epilepsy, and stiffness and pain in the spinal column.

Method: Insert the needle perpendicularly, 0.5-1 *cun* deep.

Notes: Vasculature: The posterior branch of the 11th intercostal artery. Innervation: The medial branch of the posterior ramus of the 11th thoracic nerve.

Zhongshu (DU 7)

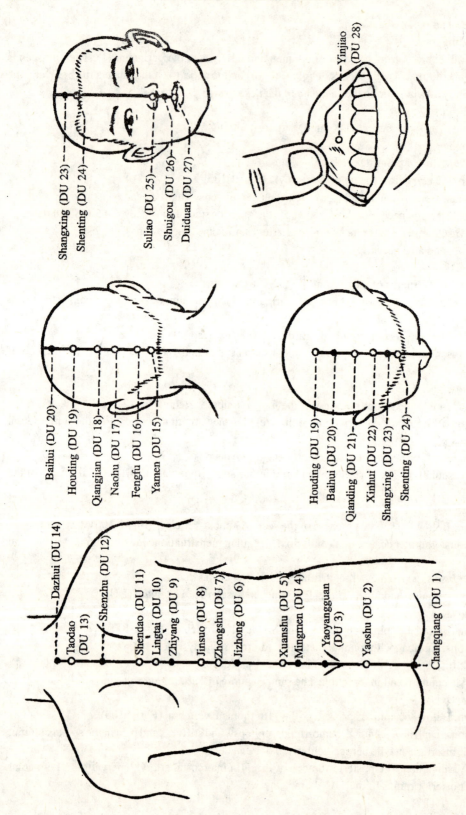

Fig. 2-99 Acupoints on the *Du* Meridian (Governor Vessel)

MERIDIANS AND ACUPOINTS 109

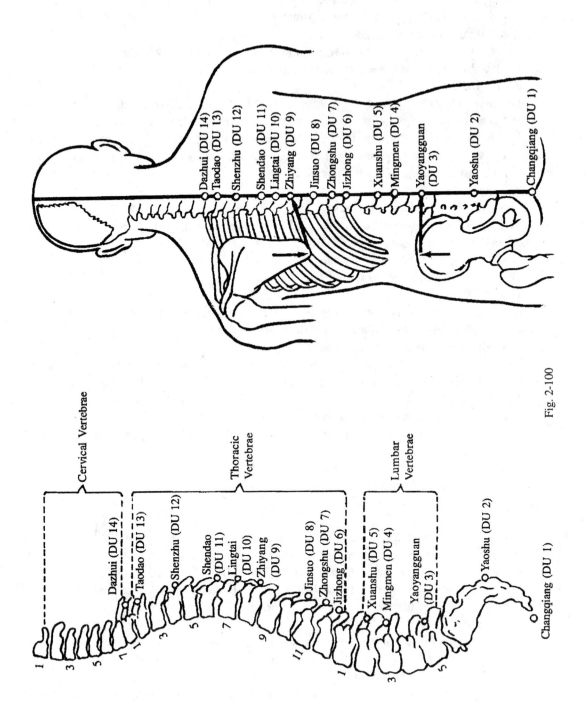

Fig. 2-100

Location: Below the spinous process of the tenth thoracic vertebra. (Fig. 2-100)

Indications: Fullness in the abdomen, jaundice and lumbago.

Method: Insert the needle perpendicularly, 0.5-1 *cun* deep.

Notes: Vasculature: The posterior branch of the tenth intercostal artery. Innervation: The medial branch of the posterior ramus of the tenth thoracic nerve.

Jinsuo (DU 8)

Location: Below the spinous process of the ninth thoracic vertebra. (Fig. 2-100)

Indications: Epilepsy, stomachache and stiff spine.

Method: Insert the needle perpendicularly, 0.5-1 *cun* deep.

Notes: Vasculature: The posterior branch of the ninth intercostal artery. Innervation: The medial branch of the posterior ramus of the ninth thoracic nerve.

Zhiyang (DU 9)

Location: Below the spinous process of the seventh thoracic vertebra. (Fig. 2-100)

Indications: Jaundice, cough, asthma, and distensive pain in the chest and hypochondriac region.

Method: Insert the needle perpendicularly, 0.5-1 *cun* deep.

Notes: Vasculature: The posterior branch of the seventh intercostal artery. Innervation: The medial branch of the posterior ramus of the seventh thoracic nerve.

Lingtai (DU 10)

Location: Below the spinous process of the sixth thoracic vertebra. (Fig. 2-100)

Indications: Cough, asthma, furuncles, stiffness and pain in the back.

Method: Insert the needle perpendicularly, 0.5-1 *cun* deep.

Notes: Vasculature: The posterior branch of the sixth intercostal artery. Innervation: The medial branch of the posterior ramus of the sixth thoracic nerve.

Shendao (DU 11)

Location: Below the spinous process of the fifth thoracic vertebra. (Fig. 2-100)

Indications: Palpitation, cardialgia, apoplexy with aphasia, epilepsy, cough, stiffness and pain in the back.

Method: Insert the needle perpendicularly, 0.5-1 *cun* deep.

Notes: Vasculature: The posterior branch of the fifth intercostal artery. Innervation: The medial branch of the posterior ramus of the fifth thoracic nerve.

Shenzhu (DU 12)

Location: Below the spinous process of the third thoracic vertebra. (Fig. 2-100)

Indications: Cough, asthma, epilepsy, stiffness and pain in the back.

Method: Insert the needle perpendicularly, 0.5-1 *cun* deep.

Notes: Vasculature: The posterior branch of the third intercostal artery. Innervation: The medial branch of the posterior ramus of the third thoracic nerve.

Taodao (DU 13)

Location: Below the spinous process of the first thoracic vertebra. (Fig. 2-100)

Indications: Headache, malaria, fever, stiffness and pain in the nape and back.

Method: Insert the needle perpendicularly, 0.5-1 *cun* deep.

Notes: Vasculature: The posterior branch of the first intercostal artery. Innervation: The medial branch of the posterior ramus of the first thoracic nerve.

Dazhui (DU 14)

Location: Below the spinous process of the seventh cervical vertebra. (Fig. 2-100)

Indications: Febrile diseases, common cold, malaria, cough, asthma, epilepsy, rubella, stiffness and pain in the nape and back.

Method: Insert the needle perpendicularly, 0.5-1 *cun* deep.

Notes: (1) It is usually used together with *Waiguan* (SJ 5), *Hegu* (LI 4) and *Fengchi* (GB 20) for common cold and fever in clinical practice. (2) According to reports, *Dazhui*, *Hegu* (LI 4) and *Zusanli* (ST 36) together are effective for leukopenia caused by radiotherapy or chemotherapy. (3) Vasculature: The branch of transverse cervical artery. Innervation: The posterior ramus of the eighth cervical nerve, and the medial branch of the posterior ramus of the first thoracic nerve.

Yamen (DU 15)

Location: On the nape and 0.5 *cun* directly above the midpoint of the posterior hairline. (Fig. 2-101)

Indications: Mutism, aphasia with stiff tongue, sudden loss of voice, mania and epilepsy.

Method: Insert the needle perpendicularly or obliquely downward, 0.5-1 *cun* deep.

Notes: (1) Do not insert too deep because *Yamen* is near the medullary bulb. *A Systematic Classic of Acupuncture* notes that moxibustion on this acupoint may cause aphonia, so it is contraindicated. (2) Vasculature: The branches of occipital artery and vein. Innervation: The third occipital nerve.

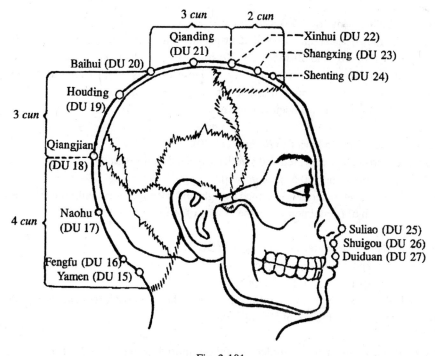

Fig. 2-101

Fengfu (DU 16)

Location: On the nape and 1 *cun* directly above the midpoint of the posterior hairline. (Fig. 2-101)

Indications: Apoplexy with aphasia, hemiplegia, rigid nape with headache, mania and epilepsy.

Method: Insert the needle perpendicularly or obliquely downward, 0.5-1 *cun* deep.

Notes: (1) *Verses for Acupuncture Manipulations* says that *Fengfu* and *Baihui* (DU 20) are the first choice when treating wind syndromes. (2) Vasculature: The branch of occipital artery. Innervation: The branches of the third occipital nerve and great occipital nerve.

Naohu (DU 17)

Location: On the head and 1.5 *cun* directly above *Fengfu* (DU 16). (Fig. 2-101)

Indications: Headache, vertigo, mutism, epilepsy and rigid nape.

Method: Insert the needle horizontally, 0.5-0.8 *cun* deep.

Notes: Vasculature: The branches of left and right occipital arteries and veins. Innervation: The branch of great occipital nerve.

Qiangjian (DU 18)

Location: On the head and 1.5 *cun* directly above *Naohu* (DU 17). (Fig. 2-101)

Indications: Headache, vertigo, rigidity and pain in the nape and back, insomnia and epilepsy.

Method: Insert the needle horizontally, 0.5-0.8 *cun* deep.

Notes: Vasculature and innervation: The same as those of *Naohu* (DU 17).

Houding (DU 19)

Location: On the head and 1.5 *cun* directly above *Qiangjian* (DU 18). (Fig. 2-101)

Indications: Headache, vertigo, rigid nape, insomnia and epilepsy.

Method: Insert the needle horizontally, 0.5-0.8 *cun* deep.

Notes: Vasculature and innervation: The same as those of *Naohu* (DU 17).

Baihui (DU 20)

Location: On the head and 7 *cun* directly above the midpoint of the posterior hairline. (Fig. 2-101)

Indications: Headache, vertigo, apoplexy with aphasia, mania, epilepsy, prolapse of anus, metroptosis and syncope.

Method: Insert the needle horizontally, 0.5-0.8 *cun* deep.

Notes: (1) This acupoint may help recuperate depleted *yang* and relieve prostration syndromes. It is used together with *Shuigou* (DU 26) and *Zusanli* (ST 36) for syncope. *Changqiang* (DU 1) and *Chengshan* (BL 57) can be used together with *Baihui* for prolapse of anus. (2) Vasculature: The anastomotic network formed by superficial temporal arteries and veins, and occipital arteries and veins on both sides. Innervation: The branch of great occipital nerve.

Qianding (DU 21)

Location: On the head and 1.5 *cun* anterior to *Baihui* (DU 20). (Fig. 2-101)

Indications: Headache, vertigo, epilepsy, red and swollen eyes and rhinorrhea.

Method: Insert the needle horizontally, 0.5-0.8 *cun* deep.

Notes: Vasculature: The anastomotic network formed by right and left superficial temporal arteries and veins. Innervation: The branch of frontal nerve and the branch of great occipital nerve.

Xinhui (DU 22)

Location: On the head and 1.5 *cun* anterior to *Qianding* (DU 21). (Fig. 2-101)

Indications: Headache, vertigo, epilepsy, infantile convulsion, rhinorrhea and epistaxis.

Method: Insert the needle horizontally, 0.5-0.8 *cun* deep.

Notes: Vasculature: The anastomotic network formed by superficial temporal artery and vein, and frontal artery and vein. Innervation: The branch of frontal nerve.

Shangxing (DU 23)

Location: On the head and 1 *cun* above the midpoint of the anterior hairline. (Fig. 2-101)

Indications: Headache, vertigo, red and swollen eyes, mania, rhinorrhea, epistaxis and febrile diseases.

Method: Insert the needle horizontally, 0.5-0.8 *cun* deep.

Notes: Vasculature: The branches of frontal artery and vein, and the branches of superficial temporal artery and vein. Innervation: The branch of frontal nerve.

Shenting (DU 24)

Location: On the head and 0.5 *cun* above the midpoint of the anterior hairline. (Fig. 2-101)

Indications: Headache, vertigo, mania, insomnia, epistaxis and rhinorrhea.

Method: Insert the needle horizontally, 0.5-0.8 *cun* deep.

Notes: Vasculature: The branches of frontal artery and vein. Innervation: The branch of frontal nerve.

Suliao (DU 25)

Location: On the face and at the center of the tip of the nose. (Fig. 2-101)

Indications: Nose disorders (such as nasal stuffiness, epistaxis and rhinorrhea) and syncope.

Method: Insert the needle obliquely upward, 0.3-0.5 *cun* deep. Or prick so that a little blood comes out. Moxibustion is contraindicated.

Notes: Vasculature: The dorsal nasal branches of facial artery and vein. Innervation: The lateral nasal branch of anterior ethmoidal nerve.

Shuigou (DU 26)

Location: On the face and at the junction of the upper third and middle third of the philtrum. (Fig. 2-101)

Indications: Coma, syncope, trismus, epilepsy, facial paralysis, swollen lips and face.

Method: Insert the needle obliquely upward, 0.3-0.5 *cun* deep. Moxibustion is contraindicated.

Notes: (1) The other name of *Shuigou* is *Renzhong*. (2) It is used together with *Yongquan* (KI 1) and *Zusanli* (ST 36) for shock. *Hegu* (LI 4) and *Shixuan* (EX-UE 11) could be punctured together with *Shuigou* to treat sunstroke. (3) Vasculature: Superior labial artery and vein. Innervation: The buccal branch of facial nerve, and the branch of infraorbital nerve.

Duiduan (DU 27)

Location: On the labial tubercle of the upper lip and at the junction of the philtrum and the upper lip. (Fig. 2-101)

Indications: Mania, facial paralysis, swollen lips and gums.

Method: Insert the needle obliquely upward, 0.2-0.3 *cun* deep. Moxibustion is contraindicated.

Notes: Vasculature and innervation: The same as those of *Shuigou* (DU 26).

Yinjiao (DU 28)

Location: At the junction of the upper gum and the frenulum of the upper lip. (Fig. 2-99)

Indications: Red and swollen gums, mania and rhinorrhea.

Method: Insert the needle obliquely upward, 0.2-0.3 *cun* deep. Moxibustion is contraindicated.

Notes: Vasculature: Superior labial artery and vein. Innervation: The branch of superior alveolar nerve.

3. The *Chong* Meridian (Thoroughfare Vessel)

(Fig. 2-102)

1) Traveling route

The meridian starts at the lower abdomen and emerges from the perineum (1). Then it goes up along the spine (2), meets the Foot-*Shaoyin* Meridian and runs on both sides of the abdomen. After passing the throat (4), it circles the lips (5).

2) Symptoms

Contracture due to unhealthy *qi* in the abdomen.

3) Acupoints to be met

The *Ren* meridian: *Huiyin* (RN 1) and *Yinjiao* (RN 7); the Stomach Meridian of Foot-*Yangming*: *Qichong* (ST 30); and the Kidney Meridian of Foot-*Shaoyin*: *Henggu* (KI 11), *Dahe* (KI 12), *Qixue* (KI 13), *Siman* (KI 14), *Zhongzhu* (KI 15), *Huangshu* (KI 16), *Shangqu* (KI 17), *Shiguan*

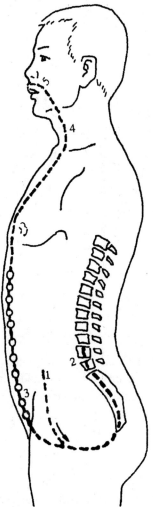

Fig. 2-102 *Chong* Meridian (Thoroughfare Vessel)

(KI 18), *Yindu* (KI 19), *Futonggu* (KI 20) and *Youmen* (KI 21).

4. The *Dai* Meridian (Belt Vessel)
(Fig. 2-103)
1) Traveling route

The meridian starts at the lower part of the hypochondria (1), runs downward along the *Daimai* (GB 26), *Wushu* (GB 27) and *Weidao* (GB 28) acupoints, and circles around the body (2).

2) Symptoms

Abdominal distention and cold sensation in the lumbar region.

3) Acupoints to be met

The Gallbladder Meridian of Foot-*Shaoyang*: *Daimai* (GB 26), *Wushu* (GB 27) and *Weidao* (GB 28).

5. The *Yinqiao* Meridian (*Yin* Heel Vessel)
(Fig. 2-104)
1) Traveling route

The meridian starts at the posterior side of the navicular bone (1) and runs along the medial side of the ankle (2). Then it ascends along the medial side of the thigh (3), passes the pudendum (4) and reaches both sides of the chest (5) and the supraclavicular fossa (6). Running before *Renying* (ST 9) (7), it further reaches the zygomatic bone (8) and arrives at the inner canthus, meeting the Bladder Meridian of Foot-*Taiyang* and the *Yangqiao* Meridian (9).

2) Symptoms

Drowsiness and retention of urine.

3) Acupoints to be met

The Kidney Meridian of Foot-*Shaoyin*: *Zhaohai* (KI 6) and *Jiaoxin* (KI 8); the Bladder Meridian of Foot-*Taiyang*: *Jingming* (BL 1).

Fig. 2-103 *Dai* Meridian (Belt Vessel)

6. The *Yangqiao* Meridian (*Yang* Heel Vessel)
(Fig. 2-105)
1) Traveling route

The meridian starts from the lateral side of the heel (1), passes the lateral malleolus (2) and the posterior side of the fibula, and runs along the medial side of the thigh. It then arrives at the shoulder from behind the costal region. Passing through the neck and the corner of mouth, it reaches the inner canthus to meet the *Yinqiao* Meridian. Finally it runs along the Foot-*Taiyang* Meridian to the forehead and meets the Gallbladder Meridian at *Fengchi* (GB 20) (3).

2) Symptoms

Ophthalmalgia starting from the inner canthus, and insomnia.

3) Acupoints to be met

The Bladder Meridian of Foot-*Taiyang*: *Shenmai* (BL 62), *Pucan* (BL 61) and *Fuyang* (BL 59); the Gallbladder Meridian of Foot-*Shaoyang*: *Juliao* (GB 29); the Small Intestine Meridian of Hand-*Taiyang*: *Naoshu* (SI 10); the Large Intestine Meridian of Hand-*Yangming*: *Jianyu* (LI 15) and *Jugu* (LI 16); the *Sanjiao* Meridian of Hand-*Shaoyang*: *Tianliao* (SJ 15); the Stomach Meridian of Foot-*Yangming*: *Dicang* (ST 4), *Juliao* (ST 3) and *Chengqi* (ST 1); and the Bladder Meridian of Foot-*Taiyang*: *Jingming* (BL 1).

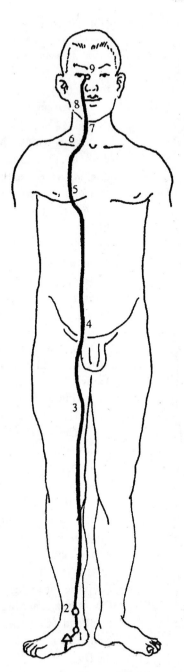

Fig. 2-104 *Yinqiao* Meridian
(*Yin* Heel Vessel)

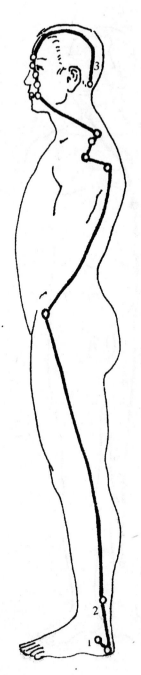

Fig. 2-105 *Yangqiao* Meridian
(*Yang* Heel Vessel)

7. The *Yinwei* Meridian (*Yin* Link Vessel)

(Fig. 2-106)

1) Traveling route

The meridian starts at the medial side of the leg (1), ascends along the medial side of the thigh (2) to the abdomen, and meets the Spleen Meridian of Foot-*Taiyin* (3). Then it passes through the chest (4) and meets the *Ren* Meridian at the neck (5).

2) Symptoms

Cardialgia and melancholy.

3) Acupoints to be met

The Kidney Meridian of Foot-*Shaoyin*: *Zhubin* (KI 9); the Spleen Meridian of Foot-*Taiyin*: *Fushe* (SP 13), *Daheng* (SP 15) and *Fuai* (SP 16); the Liver Meridian of Foot-*Jueyin*: *Qimen* (LR 14); and the *Ren* Meridian: *Tiantu* (RN 22), and *Lianquan* (RN 23).

8. The *Yangwei* Meridian (*Yang* Link Vessel)

(Fig. 2-107)

1) Traveling route

The meridian starts at the the lateral side of the heel (1), passes the lateral malleolus (2) and ascends along the Gallbladder Meridian to the hip (3). Then it runs behind the hypochondrium (4) and reaches the shoulder from the posterior axillary line (5). After reaching the forehead (6), it travels behind the nape and meets the *Du* Meridian (7).

2) Symptoms

Aversion to cold, fever, and lumbago.

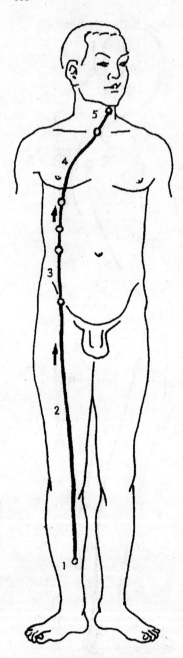

Fig. 2-106 *Yinwei* Meridian (*Yin* Link Vessel)

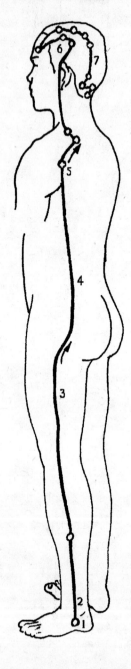

Fig. 2-107 *Yangwei* Meridian (*Yang* Link Vessel)

3) Acupoints to be met

The Bladder Meridian of Foot-*Taiyang*: *Jinmen* (BL 63); the Gallbladder Meridian of Foot-*Shaoyang*: *Benshen* (GB 13), *Yangbai* (GB 14), *Toulinqi* (GB 15), *Muchuang* (GB 16), *Zhengying* (GB 17), *Chengling* (GB 18), *Naokong* (GB 19), *Fengchi* (GB 20), *Jianjing* (GB 21) and *Yangjiao* (GB 35); the Small Intestine Meridian of Foot-*Taiyang*: *Naoshu* (SI 10); the *Sanjiao* Meridian of Hand-*Shaoyang*:

Tianliao (SJ 15); the Stomach Meridian of Foot-*Yangming*: *Touwei* (ST 8); and the *Du* Meridian: *Yamen* (DU 15) and *Fengfu* (DU 16).

Section 3
THE EXTRA ACUPOINTS

1. Acupoints of the Head and Neck (HN)

Sishencong (EX-HN 1)

Location: 1 *cun* posterior, anterior and lateral to *Baihui* (DU 20) and 4 points on the vertex of the head in all. (Fig. 2-108)

Indications: Headache, vertigo, insomnia, epilepsy, five kinds of retardation, and five kinds of flaccidity.

Method: Insert the needle horizontally, 0.5-0.8 *cun* deep.

Notes: Vasculature: The occipital arteries and veins, superficial temporal arteries and veins, and the anastomotic network formed by supraorbital arteries and veins. Innervation: The greater occipital nerve, auriculotemporal nerve and the branch of supraorbital nerve.

Yintang (EX-HN 3)

Location: At the midpoint between the eyebrows. (Fig. 2-109)

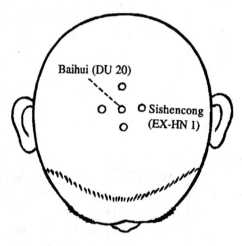

Fig. 2-108

Indications: Headache, vertigo, rhinorrhea, epistaxis, insomnia and infantile convulsion.

Method: Insert the needle horizontally downward, 0.3-0.5 *cun* deep.

Notes: Vasculature: The branches of frontal artery and vein. Innervation: The supratrochlear nerve of trigeminal nerve.

Yuyao (EX-HN 4)

Location: In the center of the eyebrow. (Fig. 2-109)

Indications: Pain in the supraorbital region, twitching eyelids, ptosis, red and swollen eyes.

Method: Insert the needle horizontally, 0.3-0.5 *cun* deep.

Notes: Vasculature: The lateral branches of frontal artery and vein. Innervation: The branches of supraorbital nerve and facial nerve.

Taiyang (EX-HN 5)

Location: 1 *cun* posterior to the midpoint between the lateral end of the eyebrow and the outer canthus. (Fig. 2-110)

Indications: Headache, red and swollen eyes, facial paralysis, toothache and trigeminal neuralgia.

Method: Insert the needle perpendicularly, 0.3-

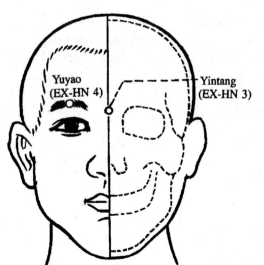

Fig. 2-109

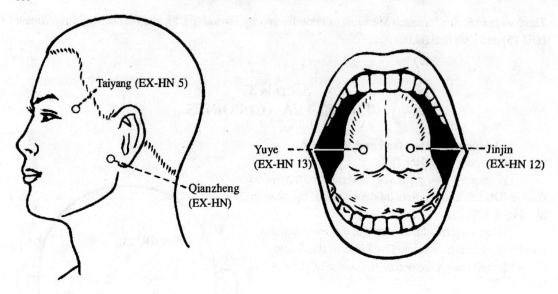

Fig. 2-110　　　　　　　　　　Fig. 2-111

0.5 *cun* deep.

Notes: Vasculature: Superficial temporal artery and vein. Innervation: The second and third branches of trigeminus, and the temporal branch of facial nerve.

Qianzheng (EX-HN)

Location: 0.5-1 *cun* anterior to the auricular lobe. (Fig. 2-110)

Indications: Facial paralysis, and toothache.

Method: Insert the needle obliquely forward, 0.5-0.8 *cun* deep.

Notes: Vasculature: The branches of masseteric artery and vein. Innervation: The branch of facial nerve.

Jinjin (EX-HN 12) and *Yuye* (EX-HN 13)

Location: On the veins on both sides of the frenulum of the tongue, with *Jinjin* on the left and *Yuye* on the right. (Fig. 2-111)

Indications: Stomatitis, swollen tongue, aphasia and diabetes.

Method: Prick the acupoint so that a little blood comes out. Moxibustion is contraindicated.

Notes: Vasculature: Hypoglossal vein. Innervation: Lingual nerve and hypoglossal nerve.

Jingbailao (EX-HN 15)

Location: 2 *cun* above and 1 *cun* lateral to *Dazhui* (DU 14). (Fig. 2-112)

Indications: Cough, hectic fever, scrofula and rigid neck.

Method: Insert the needle perpendicularly, 0.5-1 *cun* deep.

Notes: Vasculature: Occipital and vertebral arteries and veins. Innervation: The branches of greater and lesser occipital nerves.

2. Acupoints of the Back (B)

Dingchuan (EX-B 1)

Location: 0.5 *cun* lateral to *Dazhui* (DU 14). (Fig. 2-112)

Indications: Cough, asthma, and rigidity and pain in the nape and back.

Method: Insert the needle perpendicularly, 0.5-1 *cun* deep.

Notes: Vasculature: The branches of transverse cervical artery and deep cervical artery. Innervation:

The posterior branches of the seventh and eighth cervical nerves.

Jiaji (EX-B 2)

Location: 0.5 *cun* lateral to the lower border of each spinous process from the first thoracic vertebrae to the fifth lumbar vertebrae. (Fig. 2-112)

Indications: Similar to those back *shu* points. The *Jiaji* points on the upper back are indicated for disorders of the chest, heart and lung, while those on the lower back for disorders of the upper abdomen, liver, gallbladder, spleen and stomach; and those on the lumbar region are indicated for disorders of the lower abdomen, intestine, bladder and lower limbs.

Method: Insert the needle perpendicularly, 0.3-0.5 *cun* deep.

Notes: Vasculature and innervation: The posterior branches of corresponding spinal nerves and the concomitant networks of arteries and veins.

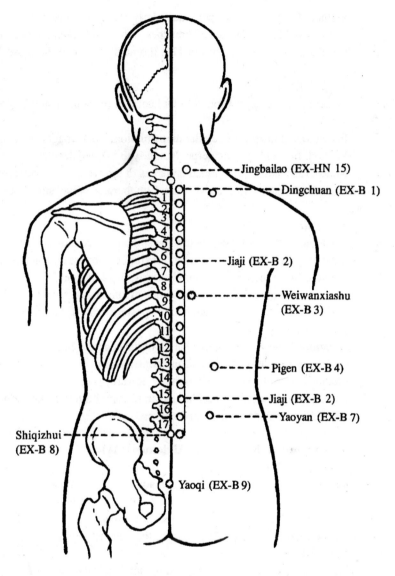

Fig. 2-112

Weiwanxiashu (EX-B 3)

Location: On the back, 1.5 *cun* lateral to the spinous process of the eighth thoracic vertebra. (Fig. 2-112)

Indications: Stomachache, abdominal pain, vomiting, and pain in the chest and hypochondriac region.

Method: Insert the needle perpendicularly, 0.5-0.8 *cun* deep.

Notes: Vasculature: The medial branches of the dorsal ramus of the eighth intercostal artery and vein. Innervation: The medial and lateral branch of the posterior ramus of the eighth thoracic nerve.

Pigen (EX-B 4)

Location: 3.5 *cun* lateral to the posterior midline and below the spinous process of the first lumbar vertebra. (Fig. 2-112)

Indications: Abdominal mass, hepatosplenomegaly and lumbago.

Method: Insert the needle perpendicularly, 0.5-1 *cun* deep.

Notes: Vasculature: The dorsal branches of the first lumbar artery and vein. Innervation: The lateral branch of the posterior ramus of the 12th thoracic nerve and the posterior ramus of the first lumbar nerve.

Yaoyan (EX-B 7)

Location: In the depression 3-4 *cun* lateral to the spinous process of the fourth lumbar vertebra. (Fig. 2-112)

Indications: Lumbago, irregular menstruation, leukorrhagia and consumptive disease.

Method: Insert the needle perpendicularly, 0.5-1 *cun* deep.

Notes: Vasculature: The dorsal branches of the second lumbar artery and vein. Innervation: The lateral branch of the posterior ramus of the 12th thoracic nerve and the lateral branch of the first lumbar nerve.

Shiqizhui (EX-B 8)

Location: In the depression below the spinous process of the fifth lumbar vertebra. (Fig. 2-112)

Indications: Pain in the lumbosacral region, numbness and pain in the lower limbs, and enuresis.

Method: Insert the needle perpendicularly, 0.5-1 *cun* deep.

Notes: Vasculature: The posterior branch of lumbar artery, and network of subcutaneous interspinal veins. Innervation: The medial branch of the posterior ramus of lumbar nerve.

Yaoqi (EX-B 9)

Location: 2 *cun* directly above the tip of the coccyx. (Fig. 2-112)

Indications: Epilepsy, headache and constipation.

Method: Insert the needle horizontally upward, 1-1.5 *cun* deep.

Notes: Vasculature: The second and third sacral arteries and veins. Innervation: The posterior branches of the second and third sacral nerves.

3. Acupoints of the Chest and Abdomen (CA)

Sanjiaojiu (EX-CA)

Location: An equilateral triangle is made on the abdomen, with each side of the triangle equals to the breadth of the patient's mouth. When the vertex angle is located in the center of the patient's umbilicus, the acupoints are where the other two angles locate. (Fig. 2-113)

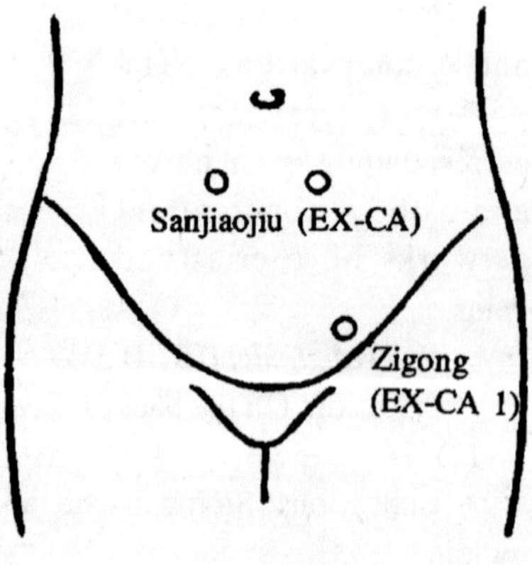

Indications: Hernia, pain around the umbilicus, and infertility.

Method: Only moxibustion is suitable for this acupoint.

Notes: Vasculature: The muscular branches of inferior epigastric artery and vein. Innervation: The tenth intercostal nerve.

Zigong (EX-CA 1)

Location: 3 *cun* lateral to *Zhongji* (RN 3). (Fig. 2-113)

Indications: Metroptosis, irregular menstruation, dysmenorrhea and hernia.

Fig. 2-113

Method: Insert the needle perpendicularly, 1-1.5 *cun* deep.

Notes: Vasculature: Superficial epigastric artery and vein. Innervation: Iliohypogastric nerve.

4. Acupoints of the Upper Extremities (UE)

Zhongkui (EX-UE 4)

Location: Clench the fist and the acupoint is at the dorsal midpoint of the proximal interphalangeal

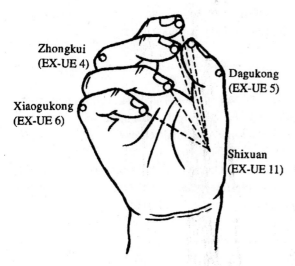

Fig. 2-114

joint of the middle finger. (Fig. 2-114)

Indications: Dysphagia, regurgitation, vomiting, hiccup and toothache.

Method: Only moxibustion is suitable for this acupoint.

Notes: Vasculature: Dorsal digital artery. Innervation: Dorsal digital nerve.

Dagukong (EX-UE 5)

Location: On the dorsal midpoint of the interphalangeal joint of the thumb. (Fig. 2-114)

Indications: Corneal nebula, ophthalmalgia and epistaxis.

Method: Only moxibustion is suitable for this acupoint.

Notes: Vasculature and innervation: The same as those of *Zhongkui* (EX-UE 4).

Xiaogukong (EX-UE 6)

Location: Clench the fist and the acupoint is at the dorsal midpoint of the proximal interphalangeal joint of the little finger. (Fig. 2-114)

Indications: Red and swollen eyes, corneal nebula, and pain in the interphalangeal joints.

Method: Only moxibustion is suitable for this acupoint.

Notes: Vasculature and innervation: The same as those of *Zhongkui* (EX-UE 4).

Shixuan (EX-UE 11)

Location: At the tips of the ten fingers and about 0.1 *cun* distal to the nails. (Fig. 2-114)

Indications: Coma, syncope, sunstroke, febrile diseases and sore throat.

Method: Prick the acupoint so that a little blood comes out.

Notes: Vasculature: The arterial and venous networks formed by proper palmar digital arteries and veins. Innervation: Proper palmar digital nerves and profuse algesireceptors.

Zhongquan (EX-UE 3)

Location: Between *Yangxi* (LI 5) and *Yangchi* (SJ 4) and in the depression on the radial side of the tendon of common extensor muscle of the fingers. (Fig. 2-115)

Indications: Distensive pain in the chest and hypochondriac region, stomachache, cough, asthma, and hematemesis.

Method: Insert the needle perpendicularly, 0.3-0.5 *cun* deep.

Notes: Vasculature: The dorsal carpal branch of radial artery, and the dorsal carpal venous network. Innervation: The superficial ramus of radial nerve.

Baxie (EX-UE 9)

Locations: Four points on the dorsum of each hand, and in the web between each finger. (Fig. 2-115)

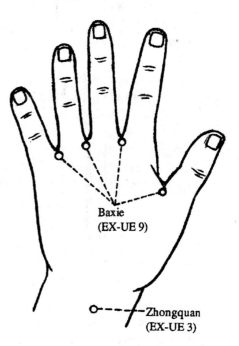

Fig. 2-115

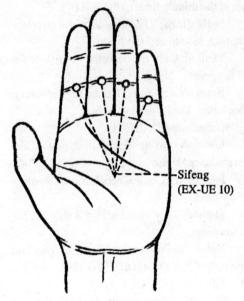

Fig. 2-116

Indications: Swelling and pain on the dorsum of the hand, numbness and spasmodic pain in the interphalangeal joints.

Method: Insert the needle obliquely upward, 0.5-0.8 *cun* deep.

Notes: Vasculature: The dorsal venous network of hand, and dorsal metacarpal artery. Innervation: The dorsal branches of ulnar and radial nerves.

Sifeng (EX-UE 10)

Location: On the palmar side of the index, middle, ring and little fingers and at the center of the proximal interphalangeal joints. (Fig. 2-116)

Indications: Infantile malnutrition and pertussis.

Method: Prick the needle, 0.1-0.2 *cun* deep until yellowish mucus comes out.

Notes: Vasculature: The branches of proper palmar digital artery and vein. Innervation: Proper palmar digital nerve.

Erbai (EX-UE 2)

Location: On the palmar side of the forearm, 4 *cun* proximal to the transverse crease of the wrist and on both sides of the tendon of the radial flexor muscle of wrist. (Fig. 2-117)

Indications: Hemorrhoids and prolapse of the rectum.

Method: Insert the needle perpendicularly, 0.5-0.8 *cun* deep.

Notes: Vasculature: Radial artery and vein, volar interosseous artery and vein. Innervation: Medial and lateral cutaneous nerves of forearm, and median nerve and radial nerve.

Jianqian (EX-UE)

Location: At the midpoint of the line connecting the end of the anterior axillary fold and *Jianyu* (LI 15). (Fig. 2-117)

Indications: Pain and motor impairment of the shoulder, motor impairment of the upper limbs.

Method: Insert the needle perpendicularly, 0.5-1 *cun* deep.

Notes: Vasculature: Thoracoacromial artery and vein, and anterior and posterior humeral circumflex arteries and veins. Innervation: The posterior branch of the supraclavicular nerve and axillary nerve.

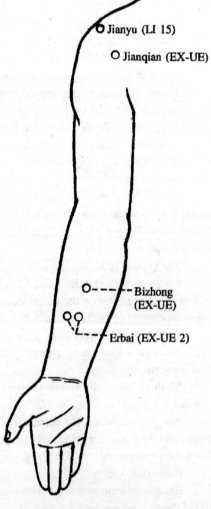

Fig. 2-117

5. Acupoints of the Lower Extremities (LE)

Baichongwo (EX-LE 3)

Location: 3 *cun* above the medial superior corner of the patella. (Fig. 2-118)

Indications: Ascariasis and cutaneous pruritus.

Method: Insert the needle perpendicularly, 0.5-1 *cun* deep.

Notes: Vasculature: Femoral artery and vein. Innervation: The anterior cutaneous branch of femoral nerve, and muscular branch of femoral nerve.

Xiyan (EX-LE 5)

Location: When the knee is flexed, the acupoint is in the two depressions on the lateral side of the patellar ligament, with four acupoints in all. (Fig. 2-118)

Indications: Disorders of the knee joint, and pain in the lower limbs.

Method: Insert the needle obliquely towards the center of the knee, 0.5-1 *cun* deep.

Notes: Vasculature: The arterial and venous network around the knee joint. Innervation: The branches of saphenous nerve and lateral cutaneous nerve of thigh, and the branch of tibiofibular nerve.

Dannang (EX-LE 6)

Location: The pressure pain point about 1 *cun* directly below *Yanglingquan* (GB 34). (Fig. 2-118)

Indications: Pain in the hypochondriac region, jaundice, pain and weakness of the lower limbs.

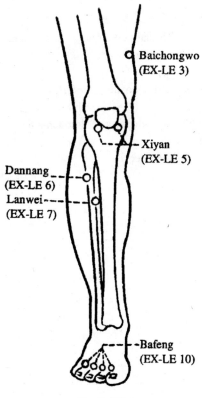

Fig. 2-118

Method: Insert the needle perpendicularly, 1-1.5 *cun* deep.

Notes: Vasculature: The branches of anterior tibial artery and vein. Innervation: Lateral cutaneous nerve of calf and superficial peroneal nerve.

Lanwei (EX-LE 7)

Location: The pressure pain point between *Zusanli* (ST 36) and *Shangjuxu* (ST 37). (Fig. 2-118)

Indications: Appendicitis, stomachache, pain and weakness in the lower limbs.

Method: Insert the needle perpendicularly, 0.5-1.2 *cun* deep.

Notes: Vasculature: Anterior tibial artery and vein. Innervation: Lateral cutaneous nerve of calf and deep peroneal nerve.

Bafeng (EX-LE 10)

Location: Eight points on the instep of both feet, and at the web ends between the five toes. (Fig. 2-118)

Indications: Swollen instep, numbness and spasmodic pain in the interphalangeal joints.

Method: Insert the needle obliquely, 0.5-0.8 *cun* deep.

Notes: Vasculature: Dorsal digital artery and vein. Innervation: Superficial and deep peroneal nerves.

Duyin (EX-LE 11)

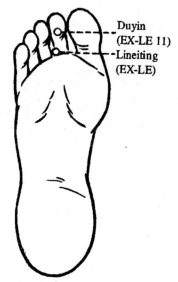

Fig. 2-119

hypochondriac region, dead fetus and retention of placenta.

Method: Insert the needle perpendicularly, 0.1-0.2 *cun* deep.

Notes: Vasculature: Medial plantar artery and vein. Innervation: Medial plantar nerve and proper plantar digital nerve.

Lineiting (EX-LE)

Location: On the plantar side, between the second and third toes and opposite to *Neiting* (ST 44). (Fig. 2-119)

Indications: Pain in the interphalangeal joints, infantile convulsion, epilepsy and stomachache.

Method: Insert the needle perpendicularly, 0.3-0.5 *cun* deep.

Notes: Vasculature: Lateral plantar artery. Innervation: Medial plantar nerve.

PART TWO
MANIPULATION OF ACUPUNCTURE AND MOXIBUSTION

Chapter One
MANIPULATION OF FILIFORM NEEDLE

Section 1
STRUCTURE, SPECIFICATIONS AND STORAGE OF FILIFORM NEEDLE

1. Structure

Filiform needle is one of the nine needles available in ancient times. First mentioned in *The Inner Canon of the Yellow Emperor*, it has since then been improved from time to time by doctors of later generations. Today, the filiform needle is still used in acupuncture practice. It is usually made of stainless steel, so it is solid, elastic, rust-proof, heat-proof and corrosion-resistant. In addition to stainless steel, gold, silver and alloy are also used to make filiform needle.

A filiform needle consists of five parts: the handle (the part wrapped with copper or aluminum wire), the tail (the round part at the end of the handle), the tip (the sharp point of the needle), the body (the part between the handle and the tip), and the stalk (the part connecting the handle and the body). (Fig. 3-1)

Fig. 3-1 The Structure of Filiform Needle

2. Specifications

The specifications of a filiform needle are usually decided according to its length and thickness. Needles 25 mm to 75 mm long with diameters from 0.32 mm to 0.38 mm are often used in clinical practice. (Table 3 and Table 4)

Table 3 Specifications of Filiform Needles in Length

Old specifications (*cun*)		0.5	1	1.5	2	2.5	3	4	5	6
New specifications										
Length of needle body (mm)		15	25	40	50	65	75	100	125	150
Length of needle handle (mm)	Long	25	35	40	40	40	40	55	55	55
	Medium		30	35	35					
	Short	20	25	25	30	30	30	40	40	40

Table 4 Specifications of Filiform Needles in Diameter

No.	26	27	28	29	30	31	32	34
Diameter (mm)	0.45	0.42	0.38	0.34	0.32	0.30	0.28	0.23

3. Storage

The needle should be kept with great care when it is not in use. It should be dried and smeared with oil or wax before being placed in a small box with layers of gauze at the bottom. It can also be kept in a tube with cotton balls at both ends. Take care not to damage the tip or press the body of the needle lest it should be deformed.

The maintenance of needles is very important and regular check up is recommended. Needles which bend slightly can be straightened up, while those greatly bent, eroded and with loose handles should be cast away. Oilstone can be used to sharpen needles with dull tips.

In order to avoid cross infection, needles must be sterilized before and after use.

Section 2
NEEDLING PRACTICE

Since the filiform needle is fine and flexible, it is necessary for beginners to practice finger force in order to insert and manipulate the needle smoothly with least pain and achieve good results.

Inserting exercise may be done on a wad of paper, a cotton ball or a cake of soap. As a beginner, you may fold some soft paper into a small wad about 8 cm^3 and 2 cm in thickness, and twine it tightly with threads. You can also make a small cotton ball, 6 cm in diameter and wrapped with a piece of gauze. At the beginning, a short needle is preferable with which you can practice such methods of manipulation as insertion, withdrawal, rotation and lifting-thrusting. When you become quite skillful, you can use a longer one. (Figs 3-2 and 3-3)

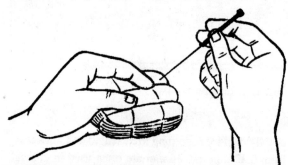

Fig. 3-2 Practising needling on a wad of paper

When you have gained some force on your fingers and become skillful with manipulation methods, you can practice needling on your own body or on other fellow students. In this way you will know the relationship between needle manipulation and sensation, and the reactions from different acupoints. It is required that the insertion causes no pain, the needle body remains straight, and there is a strong sensation upon needling radiating towards a certain direction. Only when you are familiar with different manipulation methods can you treat patients by means of acupuncture.

Section 3
PREPARATIONS FOR ACUPUNCTURE THERAPY

1. Selecting Needles

When selecting filiform needles, quality is the most important thing. The following are points for attention:

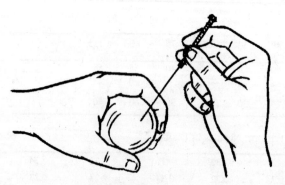

Fig. 3-3 Practising needling on a cotton ball

1) Filiform needles should be chosen according to the patient's stature, the state of illness (mild or severe, exterior or interior, deficiency type or excess type), and the locations of acupoints.

2) The needle tip must be sharp and slightly rounded but not necessarily be dull.

3) The needle must be smooth and straight, without any erosion.

4) The needle stalk must be firm, otherwise the needle is likely to break at the eroded place.

5) Moderate sized needle handle is desirable.

2. Selecting Postures

The postures of patients play an important role in locating acupoints accurately, manipulating needle smoothly, retaining the needle in an acupoint, and preventing accidents (such as faint during acupuncture, bending, sticking or breaking of needles). Generally, an ideal posture enables the doctor to locate acupoints correctly and insert the needle smoothly. Patients feel comfortable staying in the same place for a long time. The commonly used postures are as follows:

Supine position: Suitable for selecting acupoints on the head and face, chest and abdomen, and on the four limbs. (Fig. 3-4)

Fig. 3-4 Supine position

Fig. 3-5 Lying on one's side

Fig. 3-6 Prone position

Lying on one's side: Suitable for selecting acupoints on the lateral side of the body. (Fig. 3-5)

Prone position: Suitable for selecting acupoints on the head, nape, back, lumbar region, buttocks, and posterior side of the lower limbs. (Fig. 3-6)

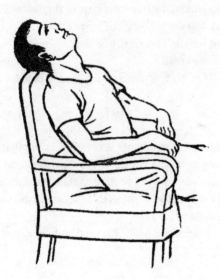 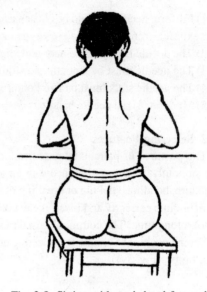

Fig. 3-7 Sitting with one's head back

Fig. 3-8 Sitting with one's head forward

Sitting with one's head back: Suitable for selecting acupoints on the head, face, neck, chest and the four limbs. (Fig. 3-7)

Sitting with one's head forward: Suitable for selecting acupoints on the head, nape and back. (Fig. 3-8)

Sitting with one's head on one's hands: Suitable for selecting acupoints on the temporal region, ear and cheek. (Fig. 3-9)

Fig. 3-9 Sitting with one's head on one's hands

3. Sterilization

Needles should be sterilized strictly in an autoclave for more than 15 minutes with an atmospheric pressure of 15 pounds, and a temperature at 120°C. The tray and forceps which may contact the needles should also be sterilized in 2% lysol solution for 30-60 minutes.

The area for insertion can be sterilized with 75% alcohol-cotton balls. If bleeding is required using a three-edged needle, the area must be sterilized first with 2% iodine solution and then an alcohol-cotton ball.

Before needling, the operator should first wash his hands with soap water, and then clean them with 75% alcohol-cotton balls.

Section 4
METHODS OF INSERTION

Generally, the needle is held by the thumb, index and middle fingers of the right hand which is known as the "inserting hand". The right hand holds and manipulates the needle. The left hand known as the "pressing hand" locates the acupoint and can reduce pain during insertion if the operator is skillful. (Fig. 3-10)

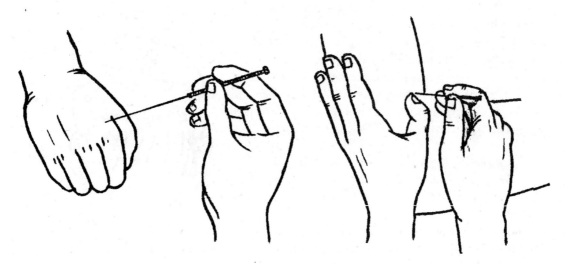

Fig. 3-10 Holding the needle   Fig. 3-11 Fingernail-pressing insertion

1. Methods of Insertion

The following are commonly used methods of insertion:

1) Fingernail-pressing insertion: Press the skin around the acupoint with the nail of the left thumb and insert the needle against the nail with the right hand. This method is suitable for short needles. (Fig. 3-11)

2) Hand-holding insertion: Hold the needle body with a cotton ball with the thumb and index fingers of the left hand, exposing the tip of the needle. Insert the needle by rotating the handle with the right hand. This method is suitable for long needles. (Fig. 3-12)

3) Stretching insertion: Stretch the skin around the acupoint with the thumb and index fingers of the left hand, and then insert the needle with the right hand. This method is often used when the skin (on the abdomen, for example) is loose or creased. (Fig. 3-13)

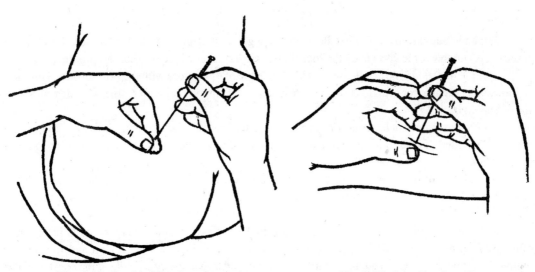

Fig. 3-12 Hand-holding insertion   Fig. 3-13 Stretching insertion

4) Pinching insertion: Pinch the skin around the acupoint with the thumb and index fingers of the left hand, and insert the needle with the right hand. This method is often used for superficial (face, for example) insertion. (Fig. 3-14)

There are other methods of insertion, but the basic ones are swift insertion and rotating insertion. All these methods help locate the acupoints precisely and reduce pain as much as possible.

2. Inserting Angle, Direction and Depth

Correct angle, direction and depth are three important factors influencing the sensation and results. They can also prevent accidents during insertion. The inserting angle, direction and depth are usually decided by the diseased area, the state of the illness, and the patient's constitutions.

1) Angle of insertion: This refers to the angle formed by the needle and the skin surface. The size of the angle is usually determined by the location of the acupoint and the purpose of treatment. Generally, there are three insertion angles: perpendicular, oblique and transverse (horizontal). (Fig. 3-15)

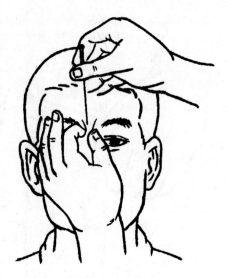

Fig. 3-14 Pinching insertion

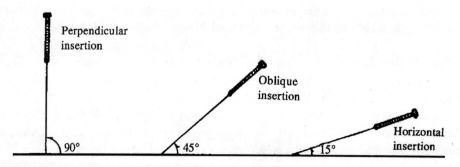

Fig. 3-15 Angle of Insertion

Perpendicular insertion: The needle forms an angle of 90 degrees with skin surface. This kind of insertion is suitable for acupoints on the four limbs and abdomen where the muscles are thick.

Oblique insertion: The needle is inserted at an angle of 45 degrees with the skin surface. This kind of insertion is suitable for acupoints close to the bones or the important internal organs, such as those on the chest and back.

Transverse or horizontal insertion: The needle is inserted at an angle of 15 degrees with the skin surface. This kind of insertion is suitable for areas with thin muscles. It is also used in point-to-point acupuncture on the head or face.

2) Direction of insertion: The direction of insertion is mainly determined by the location of the acupoints and meridians as well as the tissue to be punctured. The direction of insertion may influence the needling sensation.

The direction of insertion is closely related with the angle of insertion. Perpendicular insertion is often used for acupoints around the eyes as well as on the abdomen, lumbar region and four limbs; oblique insertion is used for acupoints on the neck, nape, and throat, the lateral side of the chest, and the back; transverse or horizontal insertion is used for acupoints on the head and face, and those on the midline of the chest.

3) Depth of insertion: This refers to how far the needle is inserted into the skin. Generally, the insertion should on the one hand cause a needling sensation, on the other not hurt the internal organs. We have talked about the depth of insertion of each individual acupoint in the first part of the book. Points for attention are as follows:

Physical constitution: Since human beings are different in constitution, the depth of insertion should differ accordingly. Shallow insertion is suitable for those of delicate constitution, while deep insertion for those of strong constitution.

Age: Because old people often suffer from deficient *qi* and blood, and infants from delicate constitution, therefore shallow insertion is recommended. But for young and middle-aged people with exuberant *qi* and blood, deep insertion is more suitable.

Location: For acupoints on the head, face, chest and back, shallow insertion is suitable; but for those on the four limbs, buttocks and abdomen, deep insertion is recommended.

Pathological condition: Generally, shallow insertion is suitable for the *yang* syndrome, external syndrome and a newly contracted disease, while deep insertion is applicable to the *yin* syndrome, internal syndrome and a lingering disease.

As for acupoints on the chest, back, nape, and those around the eyes, attention should be paid to the inserting angle, direction and depth for there are important organs here.

3. Manipulating the Needle and the Gaining of *Qi*

Manipulating the needle refers to different methods of needle operation for the purpose of arousing a needling sensation after the insertion. When the needle is inserted into an acupoint, the patient feels a stream of *qi* accompanied by sore, numb, heavy and distensive sensations around the acupoint or along the meridian, while the doctor feels a tightness under the needle tip. This kind of feeling is called the gaining of *qi*. If this stream of *qi* doesn't appear, the doctor will have an empty feeling under the needle tip, and the patient have no such needling sensation at all. *Biaoyou Verses* says: "When the patient obtains a needling sensation, he will feel heavy like a floating bait pulled down by a fish; when he has no needling sensation at all, he will feel quiet and empty like staying in a secluded place."

Studies show that whether the patient obtains a needling sensation or not, whether his sensation comes early or not and whether his sensation is strong or not greatly influence the results of treatment. Generally, a quick obtaining of *qi* and a strong feeling of being needled forecast good results, while a slow gaining of *qi* and a weak feeling of being needled indicate relatively poor results. For the latter occasion, it is very important to find out the cause. If the cause is inaccurate location of the acupoint, improper insertion angle, direction or depth, these factors should be readjusted so that a needling sensation can be obtained. If the cause is deficient *qi* due to protracted disease and weak constitution, auxiliary methods such as massaging along the meridian, scraping or flicking the needle, and moxibustion could be used to quicken the flow of *qi*. The primary and secondary methods of needle manipulation are as follows:

1) Primary methods of manipulation

a) Lifting-thrusting method: After the needle tip has reached a certain depth, thrust the needle from the superficial layer to the deep layer, then lift it from the deep layer to the superficial one. This kind of frequent lifting and thrusting method is called lifting-thrusting manipulation. Generally, a frequent, wide range of movement causes a strong stimulation, and vice versa. (Fig. 3-16)

b) Rotating method: After the needle tip has reached a certain depth, rotate the needle to the left and right repeatedly. A big angle of rotation and frequent movements will cause a strong stimulation, and vice versa. Generally the rotating angle is from 180 degrees to 360 degrees. Take care not to rotate in

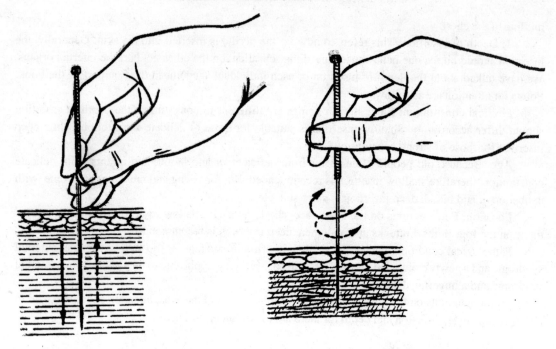

Fig. 3-16 Lifting-thrusting method   Fig. 3-17 Rotating method

one direction for that may get the fiber tissue twisted around the needle, resulting in pain and difficult needle manipulation. (Fig. 3-17)

    2) Secondary methods of manipulation

    a) Handle-scraping method: After the needle tip has reached a certain depth, press the needle tail with the thumb and scrape the handle gently with the index or middle finger nail. Or press the tail with the index and middle fingers and scrape the handle with the thumbnail. This method can strengthen the needling sensation and promote its spread. (Fig. 3-18)

    b) Massaging method: This method is used for acupoints along the meridians. Massage gently with the finger along the meridian to promote the flow of *qi* and quicken the obtaining of á needling sensation. (Fig. 3-19)

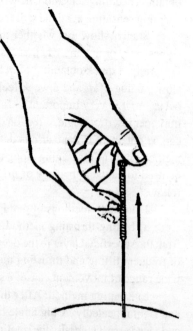

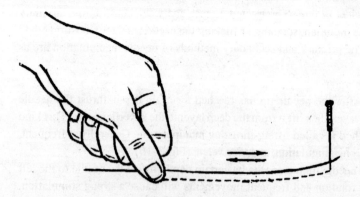

Fig. 3-19 Massaging method   Fig. 3-18 Handle-scraping method

c) Flicking method: Flick the needle tail to cause light vibrations which may strengthen the needling sensation. This method is suitable for those who need slight stimulations when the needle is retained in the skin. (Fig. 3-20)

d) Shaking method: Shake the needle body slightly to promote the flow of *qi* and help the needling sensation spread in a certain direction. (Fig. 3-21)

e) Flying method: Rotate the needle three times in a wide range, then remove the hand from the needle by opening the thumb and index finger. Repeat the above movement several times to promote the flow of *qi* and strengthen the needling sensation. (Fig. 3-22)

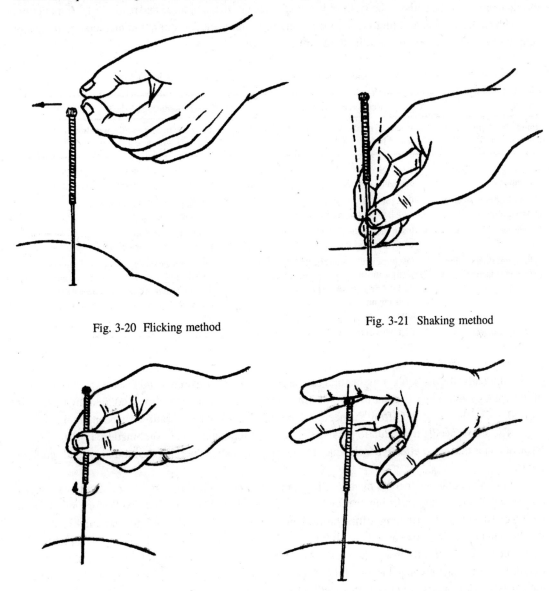

Fig. 3-20 Flicking method   Fig. 3-21 Shaking method

Fig. 3-22 Flying method

f) Trembling method: Hold the needle handle with the thumb, index and middle fingers, then lift, thrust and rotate the needle swiftly within a narrow range to cause slight vibrations. This method helps strengthen the needling sensation.

4. Reinforcement and Reduction

Methods of reinforcement and reduction are developed from the principle mentioned in the *Miraculous Pivot*. According to this book, an excess syndrome should be treated by means of purgation or reduction, while a deficiency syndrome by replenishment or reinforcement. As for heat, cold and collapse syndromes, swift needle manipulation, retaining of the needle, and moxibustion should be used respectively. The reinforcement and reduction methods use different needle manipulations to promote the changes inside the patient's body according to his constitution, condition and response to acupuncture.

Physicians in ancient times developed many reinforcement and reduction methods by means of acupuncture. The commonly used methods are as follows:

Table 5 Commonly Used Methods of Reinforcement and Reduction

Name	Reinforcing Method	Reducing Method
Rapid-slow reinforcement and reduction	Insert the needle slowly, withdraw it rapidly with a little twirling.	Insert the needle swiftly, withdraw it slowly with repeated twirling.
Breathing reinforcement and reduction	Insert the needle when the patient exhales and withdraw it when the patient inhales.	Insert the needle when the patient inhales and withdraw it when the patient exhales.
Open-close reinforcement and reduction	Press the hole immediately after withdrawing the needle.	Swing the needle to enlarge the hole when withdrawing it.
Facing-against reinforcement and reduction	Insert the needle obliquely towards where the meridian goes.	Insert the needle obliquely against the direction of a meridian.
Lifting-thrusting reinforcement and reduction	Insert the needle superficially then deeply, with the thrusting movement stronger than the lifting movement. Keep the lifting-thrusting movement within a narrow range and at a slow pace.	Insert the needle deeply then superficially, with the lifting movement stronger than the thrusting movement. Keep the lifting-movement in a wide range and at a rapid pace.
Rotating reinforcement and reduction	Gently twirl the needle counterclockwise in a small angle.	Twirl the needle clockwise in a big angle and with force.

Clinically, the *qi*-conducting method can be used to treat *qi* disorders and diseases without excess or deficiency syndromes. Similar to the uniform reinforcement-reduction, this *qi*-conducting method is carried out by thrusting and lifting the needle slowly after a needling sensation has been obtained.

The above needle manipulations can be either used separately or in combination. It is from these basic methods that many effective techniques are developed, such as "burning the mountain" and "cooling the sky."

In clinical practice, needle manipulations are different in terms of force. For patients with weak constitutions, the lifting, thrusting or rotating movements should be slow and gentle; for patients with strong constitutions, the rotating, lifting or thrusting movement should be forceful and quick. Take care that both manipulations are carried out after the needling sensation is obtained. In order to replenish the deficiency, doctors usually insert the needle first superficially then deeply, rotating it within a narrow range. The thrusting movement is forceful and quick while the lifting action is slow and gentle. To reduce the excesses, doctors usually insert the needle first deeply then superficially, rotating in a wide range. The thrusting movement is slow and gentle while the lifting action is forceful and quick. In addition, when applying the reinforcement and reduction method, doctors should also take into consideration other factors such as the traveling direction of the meridian, the direction of rotation, the respiration of the patient as well as whether the acupoint is pressed or not after the needle is withdrawn.

5. Needle Retention and Withdrawal

1) Needle retention: After insertion, keep the needle inside the acupoint for some time so as to strengthen the needling sensation and the effect. For those who has a delay in obtaining *qi*, needle retention can help promote the flow of *qi*. Usually needle retention lasts from about 10 to 20 minutes. During this period, doctors can give intermittent stimulations to the needle. For diseases like fever in children and common cold, the needle is removed as soon as a needling sensation is obtained, while for those chronic diseases with pain and spasm such as acute abdomen, the needle retention may last longer, even several hours.

2) Needle withdrawal: When the desired results have been achieved in treatment, the needle is withdrawn from the acupoint. To remove the needle, lift it to the superficial layer under the skin with right hand, wait a moment, then with left hand press the needle hole with sterilized cotton stick and pull out the needle. Press the hole immediately after removing the needle to avoid bleeding. If the reinforcement method is used, the acupoint should be pressed immediately after the needle is withdrawn; if the reduction method is used, the acupoint needs not to be pressed so that the pathogenic factors can be released.

Section 5
PRECAUTIONS AND EMERGENCY HANDLING

Generally, acupuncture is a safe way to treat diseases, but accidents may occur due to various reasons such as poor quality of needles, unskillful needle manipulations, improper postures, and nervousness of the patient.

1. Faint During Acupuncture

Manifestations: During acupuncture, the following symptoms suddenly occur such as palpitation, dizziness, nausea, cold sweat, pallor, lassitude and feeble pulse. In severe cases, patients may even manifest cold limbs, dropping of blood pressure, incontinent urine and defecation, and unconsciousness.

Causes: Mental stress, fear, weak constitution, fatigue, hunger, improper posture, incorrect manipulation.

Solutions: Stop needling immediately and withdraw all needles. Let the patient lie down on a flat pillow and keep him warm. If the case is not serious, these symptoms will disappear after a short rest and a drink of warm water or tea; if the case is severe, pinch or needle at *Shuigou* (DU 26), *Hegu* (LI 4), *Neiguan* (PC 6) and *Zusanli* (ST 36) or apply moxibustion to *Baihui* (DU 20), *Qihai* (RN 6), *Guanyuan* (RN 4) and *Yongquan* (KI 1). Other emergency measures can be adopted in combination if necessary.

Precautions: First, doctors should take into consideration the patient's constitution, facial expression, response to needling and endurance. For patients who are very nervous or who receive the acupuncture treatment for the first time, explanations are needed to relieve the anxiety. When needling, the movement should be gentle while the patient lies flat. Needle retention should be avoided or kept within a few minutes. Acupuncture treatment is not suitable for those who are hungry or tired. During the treatment, if there are signs like pale complexion, sweating and dizziness, doctors must take immediate measures.

2. Bending of Needles

Manifestations: The needle body is bent and the inserting direction is changed. There is difficulty in lifting, thrusting, rotating and withdrawing the needle, and the patient feels painful.

Causes: The patient changes his posture while the needle retains in the skin; the needle handle is pressed; the sticking of needles is not handled in time; the needle manipulation is not skillful with the needle running into the hard tissue.

Solutions: Stop lifting, thrusting and rotating immediately after the needle is bent. If it is caused by improper posture, ask the patient to resume the correct one slowly. If the needle body is slightly bent, the needle can be withdrawn bit by bit; if it is heavily bent, the doctor should first gently shake the needle body and massage the area around the acupoint to relax the muscles, then withdraw the needle in accordance with the bending direction. If the needle has more than one bend, it should be withdrawn section by section. Take care not to withdraw forcefully. Steady, accurate, gentle and slow manipulations are recommended to handle the bending of needles.

Precautions: Select a comfortable posture before acupuncture; keep the same position during the retention of needles; the needling area and the needle handle should avoid being pressed; solve the sticking of needles properly and in time; the needle manipulation should be skillful with gentle and even force.

3. Sticking of Needles

Manifestations: After insertion, it is hard to rotate, lift, thrust or withdraw the needle.

Causes: The doctor uses too much force when inserting, or uses uneven force when rotating, lifting and thrusting; the needle is rotated in one direction continuously so that the muscle fibers are twisted around the needle body; the needle is inserted into the tendons; the patient is so nervous that muscular spasm occurs; the posture is changed after insertion.

Solutions: Massage gently the muscles around the needle or keep the needle in the skin for a longer time to relax the muscles, and then withdraw the needle. Or insert another needle near the acupoint to promote blood circulation and relieve muscular spasm. If the problem is caused by the improper posture, the patient must resume the correct position slowly, then the doctor may insert the needle gently.

Precautions: Do not insert forcefully; avoid rotating the needle in one direction or insert it into the tendons; make necessary explanations to help the patient relax. Ask the patient to keep the same posture after insertion.

4. Breaking of Needles

Manifestations: The needle body is broken with some part left outside or the broken part totally under the skin.

Causes: Needles are of poor quality with the stalk or needle body eroded; the whole needle body is inserted into the skin; acute muscular spasm caused by forceful needle manipulations such as lifting, thrusting or rotating, or a sudden increase in the current intensity; the patient changes his posture; the bending or sticking of needles are not handle in time and properly; the needle handle or body is pressed or knocked.

Solutions: The patient should keep calm and in the same position if the needle breaks. This is to prevent the broken part from further entering the muscles. If part of the broken needle is left outside, pick it out with fingers or a pair of forceps; if the end of the broken part is at the same level of the skin, press the area surrounding the hole so that part of it can be seen, then pull it out with forceps; if the end of the broken part is totally inside the muscles, a surgical operation is needed.

Precautions: Examine needles carefully and get rid of those bad ones. Be sure to keep part of the needle body outside. Do avoid pulling out the needle forcefully if it is bent or stuck in the skin. The patient should not change the posture during the retention of needles, and the needle body should not be pressed or knocked.

5. Hematoma

Manifestations: After withdrawing the needle, the punctured area is purple and black due to subcutaneous bleeding, and there is swelling and pain.

Causes: Small vessels are injured during acupuncture, especially when the needle tip is bent.

Solutions: Bleeding or hematoma, if not serious, may stop or disappear spontaneously. If local swelling and pain are severe, cold compress or pressure bandage can be applied first to stop bleeding, and then hot compress can be used to relieve blood stasis.

Precautions: Examine the needle tip carefully; get familiar with the local anatomy to avoid puncturing the blood vessels.

6. After-effect

Manifestations: After withdrawing the needle, there still is a feeling of soreness, heaviness and numbness in the area around the acupoint.

Causes: The stimulation is too great; the patient is too sensitive to needling; the retention of needles is too long.

Solutions: If the condition is not serious, massage the area gently and the symptoms will disappear; if it is very serious, warm moxibustion can be applied in addition to massage treatment.

Precautions: The stimulation should be kept within limits, and the retention of needles should not last long. After withdrawing the needle, massage can be applied to prevent the above symptoms from happening.

7. Damage to Internal Organs

Manifestations: During or after acupuncture there appear different symptoms, such as chest pain, palpitation, short breath, dyspnea, abdominal pain, hematuria, sensory and motor impairment of the four limbs, paralysis, unconsciousness or shock.

Causes: The doctor is not familiar with the anatomical position of acupoints and his needle manipulation is not skillful. Therefore, when needling acupoints on the neck, nape, chest, back and upper abdomen, there are errors in the inserting angle, direction and depth, which damage the lung, resulting in pneumothorax or hemothorax; or damage the heart, liver, spleen and kidney, resulting in pain or radiating pain in the corresponding area; or damage the nerve trunk and spinal cord. Besides, if the patient suffers from hepatomegaly, splenomegaly, gastroptosis and nephroptosis, it is likely that his internal organs are easily to be damaged. Sometimes this damage to internal organs can also be caused by the changing of postures during the needle retention period, or the press or knock given to the needle body, which change its inserting angle, direction and depth.

Solutions: If the condition is not serious, let the patient lie on bed to have a rest, and the symptoms will disappear spontaneously. During this period, the patient should be kept under observation. If there are symptoms such as cough caused by the damage to the lung, an effective treatment must be carried out in time; if hemorrhage appears, the patient's blood pressure and condition must be observed carefully, hemostatic and cold compress can be applied to the patient if necessary.

If the condition is very serious, emergency measures should be taken immediately. If there is dyspneic respiration, cyanosis and shock caused by pneumothorax, thoracocentesis should be used together with oxygen administration and anti-shock therapy; if there appears shock caused by bleeding of the internal organs, or headache, nausea, vomiting and coma caused by the trauma of brain and spinal cord, relevant emergency treatment should be applied in time.

Precautions: Take care with the inserting angle, direction and depth when needling acupoints on the chest, back, nape and abdomen. The doctor should be skillful in needle manipulation and keep the lifting and thrusting movements within limits. During the needle retention period, the patient should keep the same posture so as not to press the needle body.

Section 6
POINTS FOR ATTENTION

1. Acupuncture treatment should not be carried out on patients who are extremely tired, hungry or nervous; if the patient is weak, the stimulation should be kept within control and the lying position is recommended.

2. Acupuncture is contraindicated for acupoints on the abdomen and lumbosacral region of pregnant women, and those which may cause uterus contraction, such as *Hegu* (LI 4) and *Sanyinjiao* (SP 6). During menstrual period, if it is not for the purpose of regulating menstruation, acupuncture is contraindicated.

3. Acupuncture is contraindicated for acupoints on the vertex of children whose fontanel has not yet closed. In addition, retention of needles is not suitable for children because they cannot cooperate with the doctor. Therefore, a quick needle manipulation is recommended.

4. When needling, avoid vessels so as to prevent bleeding. Acupuncture treatment is not suitable for patients with hemorrhagic diathesis.

5. Acupuncture is not applicable to areas with ulcer, scar or infections.

6. When inserting the needle if the patient feels pain, or as if hit by an electric current, or the hard tissue is injured, the doctor should stop needling and withdraw all the needles.

7. Pay attention to the inserting angle, direction and depth when needling acupoints around the eyes, on the nape, chest, back and hypochondriac region.

Chapter Two
MANIPULATIONS OF THE THREE-EDGED AND DERMAL NEEDLES

Section 1
MANIPULATION OF THE THREE-EDGED NEEDLE

The three-edged needle is a special kind of acupuncture tool with a triangular body and sharp tip. Known as "lance needle" in the ancient times, it is used to let out a little blood by prompt prick. It is also used in collateral pricking therapy.

1. Manipulation

The three-edged needle, usually made of stainless steel, is 6 cm long with a sharp triangular tip. Before use, it must be sterilized in an autoclave or soaked in 75% alcohol solution for about 30 minutes. The area around the acupoint should first be sterilized with 2% iodine solution and then with 75% alcohol solution before acupuncture. (Fig. 3-23 and Fig. 3-24)

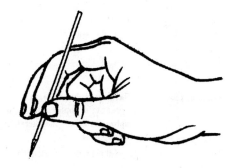

Fig. 3-23 Holding a three-edged needle

The manipulation methods are as follows:

1) Prompt prick

First massage the area around the acupoint to cause congestion. Then hold tightly the skin with the thumb, index and middle fingers of the left hand, while the thumb, index and middle fingers of the right hand hold the needle handle, exposing the needle tip 0.3-0.5 cm long. Prick the acupoint quickly and withdraw the needle at once. Squeeze the surrounding area so that a little blood comes out, then press the hole with an alcohol cotton ball. This method is often used for acupoints on fingers such as *Shixuan* (EX-UE 11) and *Shierjing* (EX-UE).

Fig. 3-24 A three-edged needle

2) Scattered needling

As known as "circling prick", this method is to prick several points around the affected area. The number of needling is determined by the size of the area. Scattered prick usually starts from the outer circle and moves gradually to the center area to relieve swelling and congestion, remove blood stasis, and clear the meridian passage. It is often used to treat local blood stasis, hematoma and protracted skin diseases.

3) Bloodletting prick

First tie the area closest to the heart with a rubber tube or a belt, and press the opposite area of the affected body part with the thumb of the left hand, while the right hand hold the needle, exposing the tip. Then insert the needle quickly into the vein under the sterilized area and withdraw the needle immediately, letting out a little blood. This method aims at dispersing toxins and removing blood stasis. It is often used for patients with strong constitution but affected by pathogenic factors or those who suffer from acute pain due to sprain and contusion.

Table 6 Acupoints for Bloodletting and Their Indications

Acupoints	Distribution of Blood Vessels	Method	Indications
Shixuan (EX-UE 11)	At the finger tips, network of the proper palmar digital arteries and veins	Prompt prick	Fever, coma, sunstroke, unconsciousness, numbness of hand and foot
Shierjing (hand)	Behind the corner of the fingernails, network of the proper palmar digital arteries and veins	Prompt prick	Fever, coma, sore throat, tonsillitis
Sifeng (EX-UE 10)	Network of the proper palmar digital arteries and veins	Squeeze out the yellowish-white liquid after prompt prick	Infantile malnutrition, dyspepsia, pertussis
Yuji (LU 10)	Reflux branch of the cephalic vein in the thumb	Prompt prick or scattered prick	Fever, sore throat, tonsillitis
Chize (LU 5)	Cephalic vein	Prompt prick	Sunstroke, acute vomiting and diarrhea
Quze (PC 3)	Cephalic vein	Prompt prick	Sunstroke, a suffocating feeling in the chest, fidgets
Weizhong (BL 40)	The great saphenous vein in the medial aspect of the popliteal fossa, the small saphenous vein in the lateral aspect of the popliteal fossa	Prompt prick	Sunstroke, acute vomiting and diarrhea, systremma
Bafeng (EX-LE 10)	Dorsal venous network of foot	Prompt prick	Swelling, pain and numbness of foot, snakebite
Baxie (EX-UE 9)	Dorsal subcutaneous venous network of hand	Prompt prick	Swelling, pain and numbness of hand, snakebite
Yintang (EX-HN 3)	Branches of the medial frontal artery and vein	Prompt prick	Headache, dizziness, red and swollen eyes, rhinitis
Taiyang (EX-HN 5)	Venous plexus inside temporal fascia	Prompt prick or scattered prick	Headache, red and swollen eyes
Baihui (DU 20)	Anastomotic network of the left and right superficial temporal artery and vein, and occipital artery and vein	Prompt prick	Headache, dizziness, coma, hypertension
Ear apex, Supratragic apex and Earback	Posterior auricular artery and vein	Prompt prick	Fever, tonsillitis, red and swollen eyes, hypertension
Jinjin (EX-HN 12) *Yuye* (EX-HN 13)	Lingual vein	Prompt prick	Apoplexy, stiff tongue and stuttering

4) Skin prick

Press the area around the acupoint with the left hand, and hold the needle with right hand. Prick the skin of the acupoint and insert the needle deep inside. Then turn the needle obliquely towards the subcutaneous tissue, and sway or twirl the needle to strengthen the stimulation. Finally, break some fiber-like substances, get the area sterilized and cover it with a piece of gauze.

2. Indications

The three-edged needle therapy can help remove obstruction in meridians and collaterals, induce resuscitation, disperse heat, and relieve swelling and pain. It is indicated for excess and heat syndromes, blood stasis and pain.

3. Points for Attention

1) The acupuncture operation should be carried out in an aseptic environment so as to prevent infection.

2) When using prompt prick or scattered prick therapy, the movement should be gentle and rapid, and the insertion superficial. Accuracy is especially important in bloodletting prick. Doctors must take care not to insert too deep, hurt arteries, or let out too much blood.

3) The three-edged needle therapy is not suitable for patients with weak constitution, or who have just given birth to children, or who are susceptible to bleeding.

SECTION 2
MANIPULATION OF THE DERMAL NEEDLE

Also known as the "plum-blossom needle" and the "seven-star needle", the dermal needle is made with a bundle of stainless steel needles (five to seven) fixed vertically at the end of a handle. Belonging to superficial acupuncture, the dermal needle therapy is developed from different needle manipulations prevailing in ancient China. It can clear the meridian passage, and regulate the flow of *qi* and blood by tapping the skin surface.

1. Manipulation

Before use, the dermal needle should be sterilized in 75% alcohol solution for 30 minutes. To start treatment, hold the handle with the right hand, with the ring and little fingers gripping the end of the handle. Meanwhile, hold the handle with the thumb and middle fingers, and fix the needle body by putting the index finger on the stalk (Fig. 3-25). Tap the acupoint with the needle, using wrist strength. Make sure that the needle is tapped perpendicularly and lifted immediately, because oblique insertion and lifting will add pain to the patient. The frequency of tapping is 70 to 90 times per minute and the distance between two taps is about 1.0 to 1.5 cm.

The tapping intensity may be classified as gentle, moderate and forceful. Gentle tap makes the skin to become red, using slight wrist strength; forceful tap causes local congestion or even slight bleeding, using full wrist strength; and moderate tap causes local congestion without bleeding.

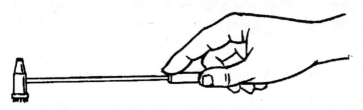

Fig. 3-25 Holding a dermal needle

There are three types of tapping: Along the meridian; on the local area or selecting relevant points; on the whole body. These methods can either be used separately or in combination. The tapping order of each part is as follows:

Head: Along the *Du* Meridian, the Bladder Meridian and the Gallbladder Meridian, from the anterior hairline to *Naohu* (DU 17), *Yuzhen* (BL 9) and *Fengchi* (GB 20) near the posterior hairline. The tapping on both sides of temples should proceed from the upper part to the lower one.

Neck: First, tap the posterior border of sternocleidomastoid muscle; second, tap downward from the anterior border of the sternocleidomastoid muscle; third, tap forward from the posterior side of the mandible angle.

Nape: Tap from *Naohu* (DU 17) to *Dazhui* (DU 14), and from *Fengchi* (GB 20) and *Tianzhu* (BL 10) to both sides of the spinous process of the sixth cervical vertebra.

Scapula: First, tap downward from the medial border of the scapula; second, tap outward from the upper border of scapular spine; third, tap outward from the lower border of scapular spine. If the arms are difficult to raise, the tapping can be centered around the shoulder joint.

Back: First, tap the first line of the Bladder Meridian on both sides of the spinal column, then tap its second line.

Sacral region: Tap outward and upward from both sides of the coccyx tip, three times on each side.

Upper limbs: Tap along the routes of the three *yin* and three *yang* meridians of hand. Circling tap can be applied to the joints.

Face: Local tap.

Around the eyes: First, tap along the eyebrow from the medial end to the outer end; second, passing the upper eyelids, tap from the inner canthus to *Tongziliao* (GB 1); third, passing the infraorbital ridge, tap from the inner canthus to *Tongziliao*.

Nose: The tapping is centered around the columella on both sides of the nose.

Ear: Tap the areas behind the lobe and in front of the ear.

2. Indications

This method is mainly used for insomnia, headache, pain in the hypochondriac region, alopecia areata, protracted skin diseases, hypertension and neurodermatitis. To treat insomnia, tap both sides of the spine, *Xinshu* (BL 15), *Feishu* (BL 13), the Heart Meridian of Hand-*Shaoyin* and the Pericardium Meridian of Hand-*Jueyin*; for dreaminess and palpitation, tap *Fengchi* (GB 20) and *Sanyinjiao* (SP 6) together with both sides of the spine, *Xinshu* (BL 15), *Feishu* (BL 13), the Heart Meridian of Hand-*Shaoyin* and the Pericardium Meridian of Hand-*Jueyin*; for headache, tap the nape, head, areas with pain, and remote sensitive region along the related meridians; for migraine, tap the nape, areas with pain, and sensitive region along the related meridians; for pain in the chest and hypochondrium, tap both sides of thoracic vertebrae on the back, especially *Geshu* (BL 17) and *Ganshu* (BL 18); for chest pain, tap the affected area and along the ribs; for hypochondriac pain, tap *Zhigou* (SJ 6) and *Taichong* (LR 3); for numbness and pain in the upper limbs, tap both sides of thoracic vertebrae, shoulder and elbow joints; for pain in the lower limbs, tap both sides of lumbar vertebrae and the affected area. For treatment of other diseases, please refer to relevant chapters in the third part of this book.

3. Points for Attention

1) Check the dermal needles regularly to make sure that all the tips are in good shape. When tapping, the needles should be kept vertically towards the skin surface so as to alleviate pain.

2) The needle and the skin should be sterilized carefully before tapping. After a forceful tapping, the skin surface should be sterilized to avoid infection.

3) Tapping is contraindicated if there is wound or ulcer on the skin.

Appendix: Manipulation of Intradermal Needle

The intradermal needle is made of stainless steel wire in shapes like a thumbtack or wheat. It is embedded subcutaneously to give out a continuous stimulus to the acupoint, and therefore is also called "needle-embedding therapy." (Fig. 3-26)

1. Manipulation

Since the needle is embedded subcutaneously for a long time, the needle and the skin should be sterilized to prevent infection.

The thumbtack-shaped needle, also known as the "pressing needle", is mainly used for the ear region. The manipulation is as follows: Hold the annular handle with forceps and insert the needle proper into the acupoint after the skin is sterilized and then fix it with a piece of adhesive plaster. Or put the annular handle of the needle on a piece of

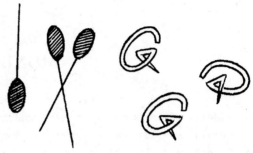

Fig. 3-26 Thumbtack-shaped and wheat-shaped intradermal needle

adhesive plaster. Or put the annular handle of the needle on a piece of adhesive plaster first, then hold the plaster with a forceps and insert the needle body into the acupoint, leaving the annular handle on the skin. Then use an adhesive plaster to fix the handle. Usually the needle is kept under skin from three to seven days, during which the needle must be pressed several times a day to add stimulus.

The wheat-shaped needle can be used for most of the acupoints. The manipulation is as follows: Hold the handle with a forceps and insert the needle into the sterilized acupoint about 0.5 to 1.0 cm deep. Take care that the inserting direction does not influence the free movement of the local area. Then fix the remaining needle body and handle on the skin with an adhesive plaster and cover it with a piece of gauze.

2. Indications

The intradermal needle treatment is suitable for chronic or painful diseases which need continuous stimulus given by needle retention, such as headache, stomachache, asthma, insomnia, enuresis, menoxenia and dysmenorrhea.

3. Points for Attention

1) The intradermal needle treatment is not suitable for body area with purulent inflammation or ulcer.

2) The area for needle embedment should be easy to fix, and causes no inconvenience to body movement. Usually, needle embedment is not applied to areas around the joints for fear of causing pain or influencing movement.

3) During the needle retention period, the area should be kept clean. In summer, the duration of needle embedment should be shorter so as to prevent infection.

CHAPTER THREE
MOXIBUSTION

Moxibustion uses moxa wool as the main material, which is made into a cone or stick. Moxa wool is burned in a specially made container placed on or above the skin surface. In this way, the meridians are warmed and dredged, the circulation of *qi* and blood promoted, the patient's resistance to diseases strengthened and the invading pathogenic factors dispelled.

Chinese mugwort plant is warm in nature and gives out aromatic odor. According to *The Dictionary of Chinese Materia Medica*, it can help regulate *qi* and blood, expel cold and dampness, warm the meridians, stop bleeding and calm the fetus. The reason why moxa wool is selected as the main material for moxibustion is that it is inflammable and the heat produced is mild but penetrating.

SECTION 1
EFFECTS OF MOXIBUSTION

1. Warm and dredge the meridians, promote the circulation of *qi* and blood, and expel cold and dampness. It can be used for arthralgia due to wind, cold and dampness; vertigo, anemia and amenorrhea due to deficiency of *qi* and blood; and deficiency of *yang*.

2. Warm the middle *jiao*, recuperate the depleted *yang* and relieve collapse. It is effective for profuse perspiration, cold limbs and faint pulse caused by the collapse of *yang-qi*; it is also effective for protracted diarrhea and dysentery, prolapse of anus, metrorrhagia, prolapse of uterus and enuresis. In addition, ginger moxibustion is effective for vomiting, diarrhea and abdominal pain of the cold-deficiency type, while aconite moxibustion helps warm the kidney and strengthen *yang* and is effective for seminal emission and impotence.

3. Remove blood stasis and dissipate masses. It is indicated for mastitis, furuncles, scrofula and cellulitis.

4. Prevent diseases and keep healthy. Burning a moxa stick on *Dazhui* (DU 14), *Guanyuan* (RN 4), *Gaohuang* (BL 43) and *Zusanli* (ST 36) regularly can enhance the patient's resistance, prevent diseases and keep healthy.

SECTION 2
CLASSIFICATION AND APPLICATION

There are various kinds of moxibustion treatment either using a moxa cone, stick, container or medicinal herbs. Yet the one which burns a moxa cone is the most popular. The following chart shows different kinds of moxibustion:

Table 7 The Classification of Moxibustion

Moxibustion method:
- Moxa cone moxibustion
  - Direct moxibustion—Purulent moxibustion, non-purulent moxibustion
  - Indirect moxibustion—Ginger moxibustion, salt moxibustion, garlic moxibustion, aconite moxibustion
- Moxa stick moxibustion—Mild moxibustion, pecking moxibustion
- Moxibustion with warming needle
- Mild moxibustion with moxa tube—Various kinds of moxa tubes
- Moxibustion with medicinal herbs—Using Herba Ranunculi Japonici, Mylabris, Semen Sinapis Albae, etc.
- Moxibustion with burning Medulla Junci
- Other moxibustions—Instrument for warming needle moxibustion, far-infrared therapeutic instrument for warm moxibustion

1. Moxibustion with Moxa Cone

Moxa cone moxibustion refers to a kind of moxibustion which burns cone-shaped moxa wool. It can be divided into two categories: direct moxibustion (with moxa wool touching the skin surface) and indirect moxibustion (with medicinal herbs placed between the moxa wool and the skin surface). The time taken for burning a moxa cone is called one *zhuang* (a unit in moxibustion), and the size of a moxa cone and the number of moxa cones are determined by the illness and the method of moxibustion. Generally, non-purulent moxibustion burns a small cone as big as a grain of wheat or a medium-sized cone as big as a soybean; while purulent moxibustion burns a big cone (1 cm in height and 0.8 cm in diameter). Usually, there are three to nine *zhuang* moxa cones been burned during one treatment. (Fig. 3-27)

Fig. 3-27 Moxa Cone

1) Direct moxibustion

A moxa cone is placed on the skin surface and burned. This method can be further classified into purulent moxibustion and non-purulent moxibustion. Since the former may leave scars on the skin, it is also called scar-producing moxibustion; while the latter which leaves no mark is called non-scarring moxibustion. (Fig. 3-28)

a) Non-purulent moxibustion: Quite popular in clinical practice, this method is suitable for various diseases in need of moxa treatment. The method of operation is: Spread medical ointment or vaseline on the skin, and then burn a moxa cone on the area. When two-thirds of the cone is burned and the

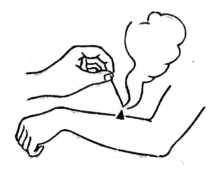

Fig. 3-28 Direct Moxibustion

patient feels a scorching pain, remove the remaining cone and place a new one to burn. The treatment ends when the skin shows congestion without blister after three to seven cones.

b) Purulent moxibustion: This method is suitable for chronic diseases such as asthma, dysplasia and stubborn pain. It can also help prevent diseases and build up the body. Before treatment, apply garlic juice or vaseline to the acupoint, and then place a moxa cone on it and get the cone burned. When the cone is burned up completely, remove it and place a new one to burn. If the patient feels a scorching pain, the doctor may tap the area around the acupoint to relieve pain. One treatment usually burns one to three cones on one or two acupoints. Purulent moxibustion is not suitable for areas near blood vessels, on the head, face and joints. Generally, better results can be achieved if there is a sore left on the skin after moxa treatment. Since it is difficult for patients with weak constitution to have their sores fully developed, the doctor may ask them to take some nutritious food or herbs which replenish *qi* and blood.

The sore should be kept clean to avoid infection. It may be covered with a piece of sterilized gauze or some ointment which must be renewed every day. After five or six weeks, the sore will heal and the scab come off, leaving a scar on the skin.

2) Indirect moxibustion

This kind of moxibustion places medicinal materials between the moxa cone and the skin surface. These materials include ginger, salt, garlic, aconite and so on. Generally, a moxa cone for indirect moxibustion is as big as a peanut.

a) Ginger moxibustion

Prepare a piece of ginger, 2-3 cm in diameter and 0.3 cm in thickness, and prick some holes on it. Place the ginger on the acupoint and burn a moxa cone on the ginger piece. When the moxa cone is burned up or the patient feels a scorching pain, renew a moxa cone to burn. The treatment ends when all the cones are used and the skin is red. This method can help warm the middle *jiao* and expel cold, and is therefore effective for abdominal pain due to cold, vomiting, diarrhea and arthralgia. (Fig. 3-29)

b) Salt moxibustion

This is often used for moxibustion on the umbilicus. Fill the naval with clean salt first and then place a moxa cone on it to burn. When the cone is burned up, renew a cone to burn. The treatment ends when all the cones are used. This method can help warm the middle *jiao* and restore *yang*. It is often used for sweating, cold limbs and hidden pulse due to acute vomiting and diarrhea, or for apoplexy and puerperal bleeding. (Fig. 3-30)

Fig. 3-29 Ginger Moxibustion

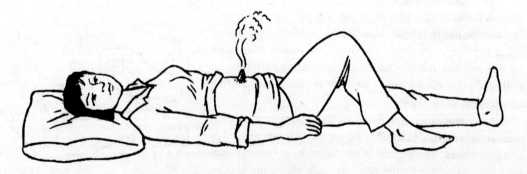

Fig. 3-30 Salt Moxibustion

c) Garlic moxibustion

Prepare a piece of garlic, 3 cm thick, and prick some holes on it. Place the garlic piece on the acupoint and burn a moxa cone on it. When the cone is burned up, renew a cone to burn. The treatment ends when all the cones are used. This method can help reduce swelling and stop pain, and is therefore effective for pyogenic infection and ulceration of skin in early stage, cellulitis and scrofula.

d) Aconite moxibustion

Grind aconite into powder, mix it with wine, and make a cake 0.3 cm thick and 3 cm in diameter. Then prick some holes on the cake and place it on the acupoint. Burn a moxa cone on the cake, and renew a cone only after it is burned completely. The treatment ends when all the cones are used. This method can help warm the kidney to invigorate *yang*, and is therefore effective for impotence, seminal emission, prospermia, sterility, cellulitis and suppurative inflammation of skin.

2. Moxibustion with Moxa Stick

Moxa stick moxibustion burns a moxa stick made from moxa wool near the acupoint so as to cause a warm sensation. It can be classified into mild moxibustion and pecking moxibustion.

1) Mild moxibustion: Burn one end of a moxa stick near the area at a distance of 1.5 to 3.0 cm to cause a warm and comfortable feeling to the patient. Usually the duration lasts 10 to 20 minutes on each acupoint with the skin turning red. This method is suitable for all diseases in need of moxa treatment. (Fig. 3-31)

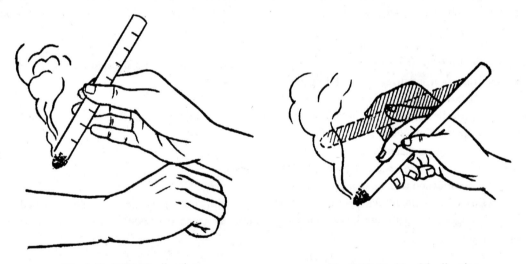

Fig. 3-31 Mild Moxibustion   Fig. 3-32 Pecking Moxibustion

2) Pecking moxibustion: Burn a moxa stick and peck it up and down or to and fro on the area. This method is suitable for numbness and pain in the limbs. (Fig. 3-32)

Besides, there is also a type of moxibustion using medicinal moxa stick such as *Taiyi* moxa-cigar and *Leihuo* (thunder-fire) needle. This kind of moxibustion is effective for numbness and pain.

3. Moxibustion with Warming Needle

Combining needling and moxibustion, this method is suitable for patients in need of needle retention and moxibustion. The operation is like this: Insert the needle into the acupoint. When a needling sensation is obtained, the filiform needle is kept at an appropriate depth. Then wrap some moxa wool or a moxa stick around the needle handle and burn it completely. (Fig. 3-33)

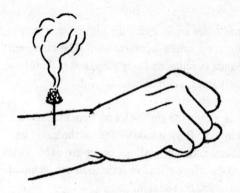

Fig. 3-33 Moxibustion with Warming Needle

4. Mild Moxibustion with Moxa Tube

Tool: A special container made of metal, consisting of two tubes with holes. The inner tube holds moxa wool while the outer one in shape of a cylinder is attached with a handle and stand. Nowadays, there are many kinds of moxa tubes in use, but the basic structure is the same.

Manipulation: Burn the moxa wool in the inner tube, and meanwhile move the container to and fro on the acupoint or area. If the container has a stand, fix it in a certain distance to the acupoint. The treatment ends when the skin is warm and congested.

This method is suitable for diseases in need of moxa treatment on a big area of skin. It is especially applicable to women, children and people afraid of moxa treatment.

5. Moxibustion with Medicinal Herbs

This therapy is to apply medicinal herbs on certain acupoints so as to cause blisters. The medicinal herbs could be used singly or in combination.

1) Moxibustion with Herba Ranunculi Japonici

Pulp Herba Ranunculi Japonici (fresh leaves) and spread it on *cunkou* (the place on the wrist over the radial artery where pulse is felt), and blisters will appear the next day. This method is effective for malaria.

2) Moxibustion with Mylabris

Soak Mylabris in vinegar or alcohol, and then apply the solution to the affected area. It is effective for tinea infection and diseases exhibiting pain.

3) Moxibustion with Herba Ecliptae

Pulp Herba Ecliptae and apply it to the acupoint to cause blisters. It is effective for malaria.

4) Moxibustion with mashed garlic

Mash garlic and apply it to *Yuji* (LU 10) to cause blisters. It is effective for sore throat. If apply mashed garlic to *Yongquan* (KI 1), it can treat hemoptysis.

5) Moxibustion with Semen Sinapis Albae

Grind Semen Sinapis Albae into powder and mix it with ginger juice. Apply it to the affected area to cause congestion and blisters. It is effective for cellulitis, subcutaneous nodule and swollen and painful knee joint.

6. Moxibustion with Burning Medulla Junci

Soak Medulla Junci in sesame oil and burn it. Apply the burning Medulla Junci directly over the skin. This method helps expel wind, promote the flow of *qi*, resolve phlegm, alleviate mental depression, induce resuscitation and stop convulsion. It is mainly used for pediatric diseases. For acute infantile convulsion with opisthotonos, apply the burning Medulla Junci to the fontanelle and glabellar; for convulsion with eyes staring upward, apply it to the area around the navel; for unconsciousness, apply it to the center of the palm and sole; for trismus, apply it to the area around the mouth and the center of the palm and sole; for mumps, apply it to *Jiaosun* (SJ 20).

Nowadays, medical apparatus have been introduced to replace moxibustion with moxa cone or stick, and they prove very effective in clinical practice.

Section 3
POINTS FOR ATTENTION

1. When carrying out moxibustion treatment, take care that no moxa wool drops on the skin or clothes.

2. Purulent moxibustion is not suitable for acupoints on the face, on the five sense organs, near bone joints or large vessels.

3. Moxibustion is not suitable for the abdominal region, lumbosacral region and some sensitive acupoints of pregnant women.

4. Moxibustion is not suitable for those who are hungry, tired, restless or who have had too much food.

5. Moxibustion treatment should be carried out according to the condition of illness (excess syndrome, heat syndrome or fever due to *yin* deficiency.

6. After moxibustion treatment, avoid wind-cold and have a rest.

Appendix: Cupping

Cupping, which is called "horn cupping" in ancient times, refers to the method of applying a vacuumized cup or jar to the affected body surface to cause warm stimulus and local congestion.

1. Types of Cups

The following are three frequently used cupping tools in clinical practice: (Fig. 3-34)

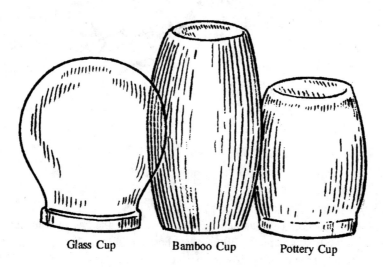

Fig. 3-34 The Types of Cups

1) Bamboo cup

Make a 3-5 cm thick bamboo into a 8-10 cm long, waist drum shaped cup with one end open and polished. Since the bamboo cup is light in weight, it can be used on areas around joints or with thin skin. The cup can also serve as a decocting pot. However, the bamboo cup is easy to crack and leak air, and it is difficult to observe the condition of skin congestion from outside.

2) Pottery cup

The pottery cup is made of potter's clay. It has smooth rim and strong suction. However, it is easy to break and difficult to suck on a small area.

3) Glass cup

The ball-shaped glass cup is made of glass, and has different sizes ranging from big, medium to small. The cup is transparent and smooth, which makes it convenient to clean and observe the condition of skin congestion. However, it is easy to break.

2. Manipulation

The commonly used cupping methods are as follows:

1) Fire-throwing method

Light a piece of paper or a cotton ball soaked with alcohol and throw it into the cup quickly. Then press the cup on the affected area. This method is suitable for side cupping.

2) Flash-fire method

Hold a burning alcohol cotton ball with forceps and circle it inside the cup. Then withdraw the burning cotton ball quickly and press the cup on the affected area. Since this method is safe and convenient, it is quite popular in clinical practice. (Fig. 3-35)

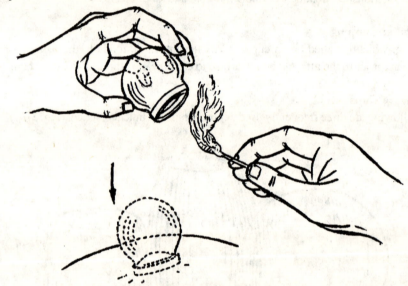

Fig. 3-35 Flash-fire Method

3) Pot-boiling method

Put prescribed herbs in a small bag and tie it up. Then boil the bag in water until the desired solution with appropriate density is ready. Boil the bamboo cup in the solution for about 15 minutes, and then take out the cup and dry it. Press the cup on the affected area while it is still hot. This method is effective for arthralgia due to wind-dampness and disorders of soft tissues. The medicinal herbs used for decoction can dispel wind and promote blood circulation.

Usually the cup is kept on the skin for 10 to 15 minutes until the skin is congested. When taking off the cup, hold the cup with the left hand and press the skin around the rim with the right hand so as to let in the air, and the cup will fall off. Do not pull or rotate the cup violently lest it should hurt the skin.

In clinical practice, there are other cupping methods according to the illness:

Cup-pushing method: Apply lubricant oil on the affected area and press the cup on it following the above procedures. Then push the cup in all directions around the area until the skin becomes hyperemic. This cupping method is suitable for a large area. (Fig. 3-36)

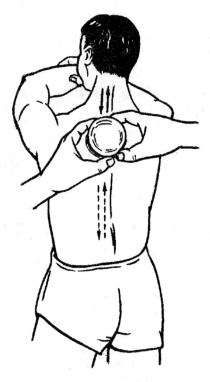

Fig. 3-36 Cup-pushing Method

Bloodletting method: Sterilize the affected area and prick it to let out a little blood using a dermal needle. Then press a cup on the area following the above procedures. This method can help promote blood circulation, remove blood stasis, remove swelling and alleviate pain.

3. Indications

The cupping therapy can help warm the meridians, promote the flow of *qi* and blood, eliminate cold and dampness, and relieve swelling and pain. It is often used for arthralgia (pain in the waist, legs, shoulder and back), gastrointestinal disorders (stomachache and abdominal pain) and lung diseases (cough and asthma).

The bloodletting method is effective for acute sprain with blood stasis, pyogenic infection and ulcers, and dermatosis such as erysipelas and neurodermatitis.

4. Points for Attention

1) Select a comfortable position. Cups with different rim sizes should be chosen according to the affected area; different types of cups should be chosen according to the condition of illness. Select areas with thick muscles and without hair and bones to carry out the cupping treatment so that the cup will not fall off. The operation should be steady, accurate and quick.

2) Cupping is contraindicated for areas with ulcers, edema, or large blood vessels; it is also contraindicated for the abdominal and sacral regions of pregnant women.

3) Cupping treatment is not suitable for patients suffering hemorrhagic diseases.

Chapter Four
ELECTROACUPUNCTURE, ACUPOINT INJECTION AND ACUPOINT MAGNETOTHERAPY

Section 1
ELECTROACUPUNCTURE

Electroacupuncture sends a weak current to the inserting needle so as to add stimulus to the acupoint and achieve certain therapeutic effects.

1. Apparatus

The electric stimulator is usually made up of transistors and produces pulse current through a transistor oscillator. Its voltage varies from 40 to 80 v and its current intensity is less than 1 milliampere.

2. Manipulation

The filiform needles for electric stimulator are either made of stainless steel or silver. Their sizes range from No. 26 to No. 28.

Before use, switch the output button to zero. Then insert needles into the acupoints. When a needling sensation is obtained, connect two output wires with two needle handles separately. Turn on the power, select the wave form and frequency, and increase the current intensity gradually until the patient gets a tolerably sore and distensive feeling in the affected area. The treatment lasts from 10 to 20 minutes each time. For symptoms exhibiting pain, the treatment may last a little longer or be given twice a day. When the treatment finishes, resume the output button to zero, turn off power, disconnect the output wires from the needles, and withdraw the needles from the skin.

3. Indications

Electroacupuncture can stimulate nerves and muscles, promote blood circulation and alleviate pain. It is not only effective for symptoms exhibiting pain, arthralgia and *wei*-syndrome but can be used for acupuncture anesthesia. Different forms of wave will bring out different therapeutic effects.

Sharp wave: It is easy to penetrate the skin and spread to tissues and organs. It can help stimulate motor nerves and muscles, improve blood circulation, nourish muscles and tissues, and enhance metabolism and nerve regeneration. It is mainly used for *wei*-syndrome in clinical practice.

Square wave: It can diminish inflammation, relieve pain, alleviate spasm, recover body functions, stop itching, bring down blood pressure, and promote tissue absorption. It is used for spasmodic diseases, pain and inflammation.

Sine wave: It can regulate the tension of nerves and muscles. It is often used for neuralgia, neuritis, myositis and myotrophy.

The common features of these waves are monotonous and periodic repetition, and therefore they are easy to be accepted by the human body. In addition, each individual wave can form a new type of wave if combined with other waves.

Waves often seen on electroacupuncture apparatus are continuous, sparse-dense, intermittent and undulatory waves.

It is believed that the dense wave has an inhibitory effect, the sparse wave can stimulate the body, and the sparse-dense wave can stop pain, promote blood circulation and increase exudate absorption. The intermittent wave, a kind of sparse wave appearing rhythmically at regular intervals, can stimulate muscular fibers. The undulatory wave is a kind of deformed intermittent wave, and its effect is mild. In clinical practice, the dense wave is used for pain and arthralgia; the sparse or intermittent wave for *wei*-syndrome; and the sparse-dense wave for inflammation.

In order to reduce the adaptability of the human body and achieve a better result, doctors can either change the frequency and form of electric waves or apply a complex wave with everchanging amplitude, width, frequency, rhythm and parameter. (Fig. 3-37)

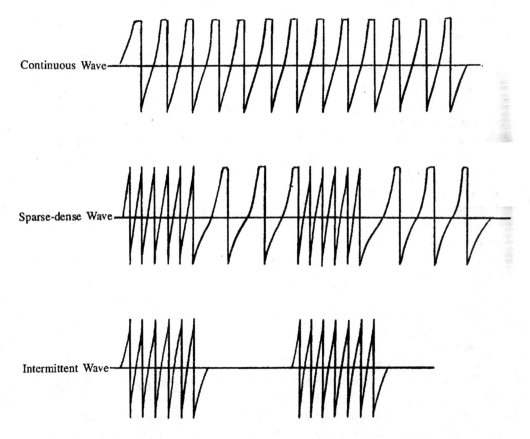

Fig. 3-37 A sketchmap of electric waves often seen on the electroacupuncture apparatus

4. Points for Attention

1) Increase the current intensity gradually lest muscles should contract violently, resulting in faint during acupuncture, bending or breaking of needles.

2) Keep the output voltage under 40 v and the current intensity within 1 milliampere lest electric shock should occur.

3) For patient with heart disease, take care that current circuit does not pass the heart. Each pair of output wires should be connected with the limbs on the same side. When applying electroacupuncture to areas near the medulla oblongata and spinal cord, the current intensity should be small lest it should

hurt the patient.

4) Regular maintenance of the electroacupuncture apparatus is recommended.

Section 2
ACUPOINT INJECTION

Acupoint injection therapy regulates the body function and treats illness by injecting medicinal solution into an acupoint.

1. Apparatus and Medicine

The selection of syringe is determined by the solution quantity. The sizes of syringe range from 1 ml, 2 ml, 5 ml, 10 ml to 20 ml, and the syringe sized 2 ml or 5 ml is often used in clinical practice. The syringe needle should be chosen according to the area and depth. The commonly used syringe needle ranges from No. 4, No. 5 to No. 6, as well as the one sized No. 5 for dentistry and the long syringe needle for blockade.

The medicinal solution for acupoint injection must be suitable for intramuscular injection. The commonly used solutions are as follows: (1) Herbal preparations such as Inj. Radix Angelicae Sinensis Co., Inj. Radix Salviae Miltiorrhizae Co., Inj. Radix Bupleuri and Inj. Caulis Erycibes. (2) Vitamin preparations such as Vitamin B_1, B_6, B_{12} and Vitamin D calcii collodiali. (3) Other preparations such as glucose, procaine hydrochloride and distilled water. (See Tables 8, 9 and 10).

2. Selection of Acupoints

1) Select acupoints according to the principle of syndrome differentiation of acupuncture and moxibustion.

2) Select tender points for injection.

3) Select reaction points by inspection and palpation, such as nodules and papules on the back *shu* points (*Feishu* [BL 13], *Xinshu* [BL 15], *Ganshu* [BL 18] and *Weishu* [BL 21]), front *mu* points on the chest and abdomen (*Zhongwan* [RN 12], *Juque* [RN 14], *Tianshu* [ST 25] and *Qimen* [LR 14]), *yuan*, *xi* and *he* points on the four limbs.

3. Manipulation

Select an appropriate syringe and needle according to the injection area and the dosage of solution. After sterilizing the skin, insert the needle into the point quickly with the required angle, direction and depth of filiform acupuncture, and lift and thrust if necessary. When the patient gets a sore and distensive feeling and there is no blood drawn out by the syringe, inject the medicinal solution into the acupoint.

The solution is usually driven in at a moderate speed. If the patient is weak due to chronic diseases, the injection speed should be slow; for patients with strong constitution and who suffer from acute diseases, the injection should be quick so as to get a strong needling sensation. The dosage of solution depends on the illness, the injection area and the nature and density of medicine. For most acupoints, 1-2 ml solution is required; acupoints on the head or areas with thin muscles only need 0.3-0.5 ml; acupoints on the limbs and lumbar region with thick muscles need a relatively large dosage, 10-20 ml of 10-20% glucose solution for example.

The acupoint injection is usually given every day or every other day, ten injections as a course of treatment. The second course of treatment may start after several days' rest.

4. Indications

Acupoint injection is effective for many diseases, such as cough, asthma, arthralgia, stomachache, pain in the lumbar region and lower limbs, trigeminal neuralgia and soft tissue injury.

5. Points for Attention

1) Manipulation should be taken out in an aseptic environment so as prevent infection.

2) Pay attention to the nature and pharmacological action of the solution, its density, dosage, incompatibility, side effect and allergic reaction. A skin test should be taken first if the medicine is likely to cause allergy, such as procaine and penicillin. Medicine with strong side effects should be used with caution. Some traditional Chinese herbs may cause certain reactions, therefore, the doctor must observe carefully for any emergency signs when giving injection.

3) Check the expiry date of solutions before use. Do not use solutions which have deteriorated.

4) Explain to the patient the reactions that may occur after injection. There will be a sore and distensive sensation in the local area; an uncomfortable feeling in the local area for 4-8 hours or more. However, the uncomfortable sensation should disappear after 24 hours. Take emergency measures if the skin becomes red, swollen and feverish due to infection.

5) Do not inject medicine into the articular cavity, spinal cord or blood vessels lest it should cause unfavorable results or accidents.

6) Keep the syringe needle away from the nerve stem when giving injection. When injecting, if the patient feels getting an electric shock, the doctor should pull out the needle a little and change its direction.

7) Do not give deep injection to acupoints on the trunk lest it should hurt the internal organs.

8) Acupoint injection is not suitable for the lower abdomen, lumbosacral region and some sensitive points like *Hegu* (LI 4) and *Sanyinjiao* (SP 6) on pregnant women. For old and weak patients, select fewer acupoints to give injection and keep the stimulus moderate lest any emergencies should occur.

Appendix: Commonly Used Drugs for Acupoint Injection

Table 8 Herbal Preparations

Name	Action	Dosage
Inj. Radix Angelicae Sinensis Co. (1 ml=0.5 g crude Radix Angelicae Sinensis, 0.5 g Safflower and 0.5 g Rhizoma *Chuanxiong*)	Invigorating blood circulation, nourishing blood and regulating menstruation	2-4 ml/dose
Inj. Radix Salviae Miltiorrhizae (1 ml=1.5 g crude drug) Inj. Radix Salviae Miltiorrhizae Co. (1 ml=1 g Radix Salviae Miltiorrhizae and 1 g Rose Wood)	Invigorating blood circulation, eliminating blood stasis, regulating menstruation, alleviating pain, nourishing the heart to calm the mind	2-4 ml/dose
Inj. Radix Bupleuri Co. (2 ml=5 g Radix Bupleuri and 0.5 g Herba Asari)	Subsiding fever and alleviating pain	1-2 ml/dose
Inj. Caulis Erycibes (1 ml=2.5 g crude drug)	Eliminating rheumatism, invigorating blood circulation and alleviating pain	2-4 ml/dose
Inj. Isatis Root (1 ml=2 g crude drug)	Eliminating heat-toxins	2-4 ml/dose
Inj. Houttuynia (1 ml=2 g crude drug)	Eliminating heat-toxins and inflammation	2-4 ml/dose
Inj. Flos Lonicerae and Radix Scutellariae (1 ml contains 25 mg extract of Flos Lonicerae and 20 mg Radix Scutellariae)	Eliminating heat-toxins and inflammation	1-2 ml/dose

Table 9 Vitamins

Name	Action	Dosage
Inj. Vitamin B$_1$ (thiamine hydrochloride) 50 mg/injection or 100 mg/injection	Maintaining normal functions of the nerves, heart and digestive system, promoting carbohydrate metabolism; effective for deficiency of vitamin B$_1$, neuritis and anorexia	50-100 mg/dose with strong sensation
Inj. Thiamine furan hydrochloride (long-acting vitamin B$_1$) 20 mg/injection	The effect is quicker and longer than vitamin B$_1$; effective for neuralgia, migraine and neuritis	20-40 mg/dose
Inj. Vitamin B$_6$ (pyridoxine hydrochloride) 25 mg/injection or 50 mg/injection	Participating in the metabolism of amino acid and axungia; effective for neuritis and vomiting of pregnancy	25-50 mg/dose, or together with Vitamin B$_1$
Inj. Vitamin D calcii collodiali (contains 500μ Vitamin D and calcii collodiali; 0.5 mg/injection (1 ml)	Promoting absorption of calcium and phosphorus in intestinal canal, keeping the balance of calcium and phosphorus in blood; effective for rachitis, osteomalacia and bronchitis	1 ml/dose
Inj. Vitamin B$_{12}$ 0.1 mg/injection (1 ml) or 0.5 mg/injection (1 ml)	Acting on the metabolism of carbohydrate, protein and axungia; effective for anemia, neuritis and malnutrition	0.1 mg/dose

Table 10 Other Commonly Used Drugs

Name	Action	Dosage
5-10% glucose 500 ml/bottle, 25% glucose 20 ml/injection	5-10% glucose is often used for replenishing moisture and heat. Acupoint injection treats diseases by adding stimulus caused by osmotic pressure of the solution to the acupoints. The higher the density, the greater the stimulation. 25% glucose can be used if necessary.	5-20 ml/dose of 5-10% glucose for deep injection or together with other drugs
Injection water (distilled water) 2 ml/injection	Giving a strong stimulus to acupoints and making the sore, distensive and painful feeling last long	0.5-1 ml/dose; since injecting distilled water may cause pain, it is seldom used except when combined with other drugs.
Procaine Hydrochloride 0.5% 20 ml/injection, 1% 20 ml/injection, 2% 2 ml/injection	Inhibiting nerve fiber conduction and dilating vessels; 0.5-1% solution for acupoint injection and 2% solution for nerve block	1-2 ml/dose; a hypersensitive test should be done before use.
Adenosine triphosphate (ATP)	As a kind of coenzyme, taking part in and supplying energy for the metabolism of axungia, protein, carbohydrate, nucleic acid and nucleotide; effective for coronary heart disease, migraine and myodystophy	10-20 mg/dose
Coenzyme A	As a kind of coenzyme produced by acetylation, influencing the metabolism of carbohydrate, axungia and protein; effective for leukopenia, purpura, hepatitis, coronary heart disease and renal-function decrease	25-50 μ/dose
Atropine Sulfate 0.5 mg/injection	Eliminating spasm of the smooth muscle, inhibiting glandular secretion, eliminating the inhibition of vagus nerve on the heart, relieving vasospasm, mydriasis and exciting the apneustic center	0.2 mg/dose
Reserpine 1 mg/injection	Exhausting noradrenalin, lowering high blood pressure slowly, mildly and permanently, calming the central nerves; effective for hypertension and maniacal psychosis	0.5 mg/dose

Section 3
ACUPOINT MAGNETOTHERAPY

Acupoint magnetotherapy, also known as "meridian magnetic field therapy" or "acupoint magnetic bead therapy", uses a magnetic field to act on the meridians and acupoints so as to cure diseases. In ancient China, magnets were used as a kind of mineral medicine to treat diseases. As the number of natural magnets is limited, artificial magnets were developed to treat diseases in the 1960s. Since the 1970s, further studies have been made on the effects of magnetic field on the human body, and as a result many electromagnetic therapeutic machines are developed.

1. Apparatus
1) Magnetic sheet/bead

It is usually made of barium-iron, strontium-iron, aluminum-nickel-cobalt, cerium-cobalt-copper, samarium-cobalt or some other permanent-magnet alloy. The magnetic field intensity varies from 300 to 3,000 gauss. Generally the strontium-iron permanent-magnet alloy is better than other magnets, because its surface magnetic field intensity reaches 1,000 gauss and its magnetism lasts long. Although the barium-iron permanent-magnet alloy is cheap, its surface magnetic field intensity is only several hundreds of gauss which is suitable for old and weak patients. Magnets with a magnetic field intensity from 500 to 2,000 gauss are often used in clinical practice.

There are three sizes of magnetic sheets: large, medium and small. The diameter of a large magnetic sheet is more than 30 mm; a medium one is between 10 mm and 30 mm; and the small one is no more than 10 mm. The shape of magnetic sheets may be round, hemispherical or rectangular, with the round ones widely used in clinical practice. The thickness of a magnetic sheet usually suits its size. In hospital, magnetic sheets 2-4 mm in thickness are often used, while those for ear acupoints is as small as a pearl, 2 mm in thickness and 3 mm in diameter.

Since the magnetic field intensity decreases after a long time use, doctors should take care to maintain its intensity. The following are points for attention: handle the magnetic sheets with care; do not force the same poles of two magnetic sheets together; do not put two magnetic sheets with different intensity together; do not sterilize the sheets with high temperature; if the intensity is decreasing, it can be remagnetized.

2) Rotary magnetotherapy device

Its structure is very simple with several rotary permanent magnets driven by a small electric motor, forming an alternating magnetic field or a pulsating magnetic field.

Samarium-cobalt alloy cylinders, with a surface intensity of 3,000-4,000 gauss, 5-10 mm in diameter and 5-7 mm in length, are usually used for rotary magnetotherapy device.

When operating the device, keep the rotary tray away from the skin, the rotating speed more than 1,500 revolutions per minute, and the time of treatment about 20 minutes.

3) Electric magnetotherapy device

Its main component is an electromagnetic coil or electromagnet which allows electric current to run through and form a constant or alternating magnetic field. The electric magnetotherapy device widely used at hospitals is the one with enamel-insulated wire around a silicon-steel sheet. After the motor is started, it can produce an alternating magnetic field. Its frequency is usually 50 revolutions per second and magnetic intensity 500 to 3,000 gauss. There are various kinds of magnetic heads, with the round one for chest, abdomen and limbs, the concave one for lumbar region, the annular one for knee joints and the bar-like one for acupoints and perineal region.

2. Manipulation

1) Magnetostatic therapy

Place one or several magnetic sheets on the acupoint so as to produce a constant magnetic field.

a) Direct contact: Place magnetic sheets directly on acupoints or pain spots. Different methods of placement can be applied according to the illness. When placing one magnetic sheet, put the sheet on the surface of an acupoint and fix it with a piece of adhesive plaster. This method is suitable for superficial disorders. When placing two sheets, you can either put them in a way that their opposite poles face each other (such as *Neiguan* (PC 6) and *Waiguan* (SJ 5), *Neixiyan* (EX-LE 4) and *Waixiyan* (EX-LE), and the internal and external sides of the auricle) or with the same pole facing each other. Depending on the theory that unlike electric charges attract each other and two like charges repel each other, this two kinds of placement drive magnetic force deep into the tissue to help cure diseases. (Fig. 3-38)

b) Indirect contact: Place a magnetic sheet in a bag, watchband or a sole so that it gets near certain parts of the body. This method is effective for diseases like neurasthenia and hypertension. It is also suitable for those who manifest allergic reactions when using direct-contact method.

c) Magneto-acupuncture: Insert an intradermal or filiform needle into an acupoint or a pain spot. Then place a magnetic sheet on the needle tail and fix it on the skin with a piece of adhesive plaster. In this way, the magnetic force runs deep into the tissues through the needle tip. It is suitable for tenosynovitis and some other diseases exhibiting swelling and pain.

2) Magnetodynamic therapy

a) Pulsating magnetotherapy: This method uses the pulsating magnetic field produced by the rotary magnetotherapy device to cure diseases. With superficially affected area, one rotary magnetotherapy device is enough; with deeply affected area, two devices can be put opposite, such as areas near joints. In this way, the magnetic force runs through the affected area and thus improves the therapeutic effects.

b) Alternating magnetotherapy: This method uses the low-frequency alternating magnetic field produced by the electric magnetotherapy device to cure diseases. When carrying out the treatment, the operator should first select a suitable magnetic head, and then place it on the affected area. Strict observation should be taken during the treatment to see if the area is overheated. If there are overheated symptoms, a piece of gauze can be applied or the magnetic head be changed to prevent scald.

3. Effects and Indications

1) Effects

a) Clearing meridian passages, promoting the circulation of *qi* and blood, relieving swelling and pain; effective for pain in the internal organs or pain caused by sprain, contusion and arthralgia.

b) Regulating the *ying* and *wei* systems and tranquilizing the mind; effective for insomnia, palpitation and amnesia due to derangement of *qi* and blood, and nasal obstruction, rhinorrhea, cough and short breath due to the hypofunction of defensive energy.

c) Nourishing kidney *yin*; effective for dizziness, tinnitus, numb hands and feet, and poor vision.

2) Indications

Internal medicine: Hypertension, coronary heart disease, bronchitis, asthma, chronic enteritis, gastritis, dysfunction of gastrointestine, neurasthenia, arthritis, headache, trigeminal neuralgia and sciatica.

Surgery: Acute or chronic sprain and contusion, scapulohumeral periomethritis, tennis elbow, traumatic arthritis, lumbar muscular strain, cervical spondylosis, nephrolithiasis, cholelithiasis, and hyperplasia of mammary glands.

Dermatology: Herpes zoster, neurodermatitis and chronic skin troubles.

Gynecology and pediatrics: Dysmenorrhea, infantile indigestion, enuresis, etc.

Five sense organs: Allergic rhinitis, pharyngitis, hordeolum and acute conjunctivitis.

MANIPULATION OF ACUPUNCTURE AND MOXIBUSTION 161

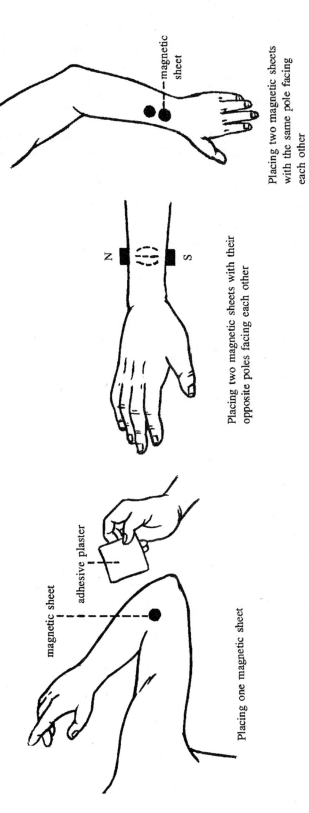

Fig. 3-38 Direct Contact

4. Points for Attention

1) Acupoint magnetotherapy selects points the same way as acupuncture. Generally, selecting local acupoints and selecting points along a meridian are used together, while the former is mainly used when there is pain caused by trauma.

2) The intensity of magnetic field can be a little greater with patients who are young and strong and who exhibit acute and painful symptoms; the intensity should be smaller with patients who are old and weak and who suffer from chronic diseases.

For each magnetic sheet, the intensity of 200-1,000 gauss is considered small, 1,000-2,000 gauss moderate, and over 2,000 large. However, as for the total intensity of all magnetic sheets, which can be accepted by a patient, less than 4,000 gauss is considered small, 4,000-6,000 gauss moderate and over 6,000 gauss large.

3) The time and courses of treatment depend on the condition of illness. If treated with magnetic sheets, the treatment will last three to seven days; if a magnetotherapy device is used, it usually lasts 20-30 minutes each time, and two to four weeks for a whole course of treatment. The patient rests for a week and then starts a new course of treatment if necessary.

4) Before or during the magnetotherapy treatment, if the white blood cell count of the patient is less than 4,000/mm^3, this kind of treatment should stop.

5) The magnetotherapy is contraindicated for patients who exhibit high fever and acute symptoms such as acute myocardial infarction, acute abdomen and hemorrhage.

6) During the treatment, if there occur serious side effects such as dizziness, palpitation, lassitude, low fever, vomiting, or even dyspnea, this kind of therapy should stop.

Chapter Five
EAR AND SCALP ACUPUNCTURE

Section 1
EAR ACUPUNCTURE

Ear acupuncture uses needle insertion or other methods to stimulate acupoints on the auricle so as to prevent and cure diseases.

The idea that the auricle is closely related with other parts of the body through meridians was mentioned in ancient Chinese medical works. Doctors of later generations have developed ear acupuncture on the basis of this idea as well as through clinical practice and researches.

1. Structure and Components of the Auricle

1) Structure of the auricle

As part of the external ear, the auricle is made up of elastic cartilage, perichondrium, ligament, degenerated muscles, hypodermis and skin. There are lots of nerves, blood vessels and lymphs under the skin of the auricle.

2) Components of the auricle (Fig. 3-39)

Helix: The prominent rim of the auricle.

Helix tubercle: A small tubercle at the posterosuperior aspect of the helix.

Helix crus: A transverse ridge of helix running backward to the ear cavity.

Helix cauda: The inferior part of the helix, at the junction of the helix and earlobe.

Antihelix: An elevated ridge with divergence opposite to the helix. It includes the trunk, superior crus and inferior crus.

Trunk of antihelix: The main vertical part of the antihelix.

Superior crus of antihelix: A superior branch of the antihelix.

Inferior crus of antihelix: An inferior branch of the antihelix.

Triangular fossa: The triangular depression between the two crura of the antihelix.

Scapha: The narrowly curved depression between the helix and the antihelix.

Tragus: A small curved flap in front of the ear cavity.

Antitragus: Above the earlobe, a small tubercle opposite to the tragus.

Supratragic notch: The depression between the helix crus and the upper border of the tragus.

Intertragic notch: The depression between the tragus and antitragus.

Helix notch: The depression between the antitragus and antihelix.

Earlobe: The lowest part of the auricle where there is no cartilage.

Concha: The depression formed by the antitragus, the trunk and inferior crus of antihelix.

Cymba concha: The concha superior to the helix crus.

Cavum concha: The concha inferior to the helix crus.

Orifice of the external auditory meatus: The opening in the cavum concha shielded by the tragus.

Superior auricular root: The area where the upper border of auricle attaches to the scalp.

Inferior auricular root: The area where the earlobe attaches to the face.

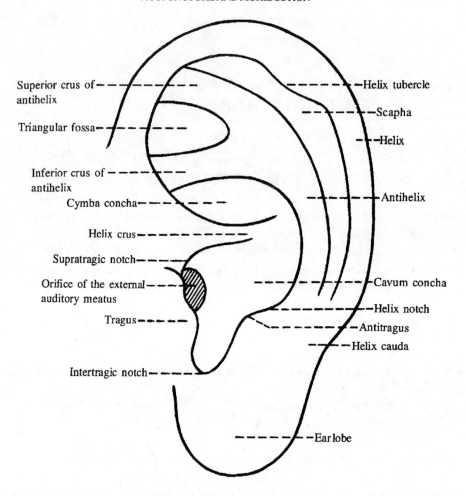

Fig. 3-39 Components of the Auricle

2. Relationship Between the Ear and *Zang-Fu* Meridians

Traditional Chinese medicine holds that the human body is an organic whole. Therefore the auricle is closely related with *zang-fu* organs and their meridians, as explained in *The Inner Canon of the Yellow Emperor* and *The Classic of Questions*. The ear is closely related with the twelve meridians, some of which enter the auricle and some spread around it. The branches of the Small Intestine Meridian of Hand-*Taiyin*, the *Sanjiao* Meridian of Hand-*Shaoyang*, the Gallbladder Meridian of Foot-*Shaoyang* and the Large Intestine Meridian of Hand-*Yangming* all enter the ear; the Stomach Meridian of Foot-*Yangming* and the Bladder Meridian of Foot-*Taiyang* run to the front of the ear and to the temple respectively. The six *yin* meridians also indirectly connect with the ear through the divergent meridians.

3. Distribution of Ear Acupoints

Ear acupoints are some specific stimulant spots on the auricle. Acupoints on the ear lobe correspond to the head and facial region; acupoints on the scapha correspond to the upper limbs; acupoints on the trunk of the antihelix correspond to the trunk of the body; acupoints on the two crura of antihelix correspond to the lower limbs; and those on the cavum concha and cymba concha correspond to the internal organs. The detailed distribution is as follows: (Fig. 3-40)

MANIPULATION OF ACUPUNCTURE AND MOXIBUSTION 165

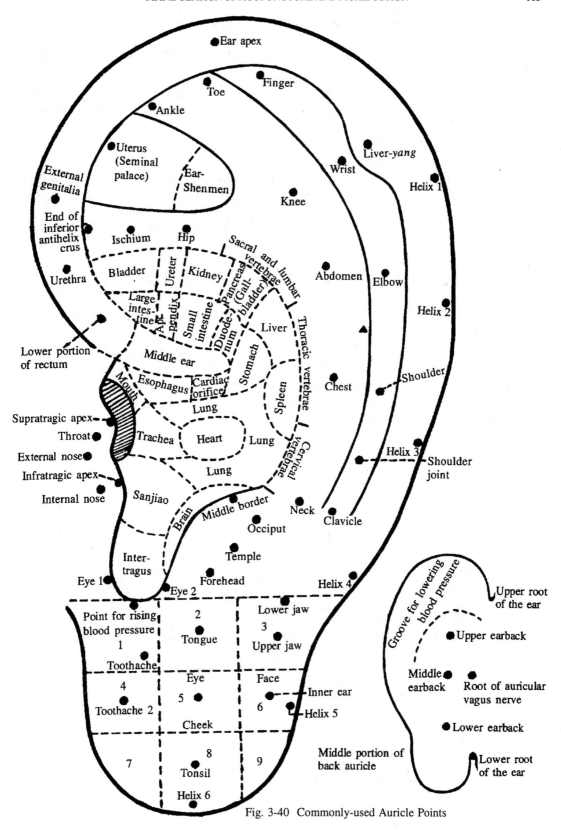

Fig. 3-40 Commonly-used Auricle Points

Helix: Lower rectum, urethra, external genitalia, ear apex, helix 1-6, and middle ear (on helix crus).

Scapha: Corresponding to the upper limbs such as finger, wrist, elbow, shoulder, shoulder joint and clavicle.

Antihelix: Corresponding to the trunk and lower limbs, such as abdomen, chest, neck and spinal column on the trunk of antihelix; toe, ankle and knee on superior crus of antihelix; and hip, ischium and end of inferior antihelix crus.

Tragus: External nose on the lateral side, supratragic apex and infratragic apex on the margin, throat and internal nose on the medial side.

Antitragus: Forehead, temple and occiput on the lateral side; point for soothing asthma at the tip of its border; brain stem at the junction of antitragus and antihelix; middle border between the brain stem and the point for soothing asthma; and brain and testis (ovary) on the medial side.

Orifice of the external auditory meatus: Intertragus near the intertragic notch; two eye acupoints at the antero-inferior and postero-inferior side of the intertragic notch.

Triangular fossa: Ear-*Shenmen* and uterus (seminal palace).

Cymba concha and cavum concha: Corresponding to the internal organs; mouth posterior to the orifice of the external auditory meatus; esophagus, cardiac orifice, stomach, duodenum, small intestine, appendix and large intestine around the helix crus; stomach acupoint at the place where helix crus terminates; liver posterior to the stomach and duodenum acupoints; kidney superior to the small intestine acupoint; bladder superior to the large intestine; pancreas and gallbladder between the liver and kidney acupoints; spleen close to the border of antihelix and inferior to the liver acupoint; heart in the center of cavum concha; lung in the U-shaped area superior, inferior and posterior to the heart acupoint; trachea between the heart and mouth acupoints; and *Sanjiao* surrounded by the orifice of the external auditory meatus, intertragus, brain and lung acupoints.

Earlobe: Eye in the center of earlobe; two points for toothache anterosuperior to the eye acupoint; upper jaw and lower jaw posterosuperior to the eye acupoint; inner ear posterior to the eye acupoint; and tonsil directly below the eye acupoint.

Earback: Groove for lowering blood pressure, upper root of the ear, lower root of the ear, root of auricular vagus nerve, upper earback, middle earback and lower earback.

Table 11 Locations and Indications of Ear Acupoints

Auricle Part	Name	Location	Indications
Helix crus	Middle ear	At the helix crus	Hiccups, dermatosis
Helix	Lower portion of rectum	At the place where helix starts and near the supratragic notch	Constipation, prolapse of rectum, tenesmus
Helix	Urethra	At the same level of the lower border of the inferior crus of antihelix	Enuresis, frequent urination, urinary retention
Helix	External genitalia	At the same level of the upper border of the inferior crus of antihelix	Testitis, vaginitis, impotence
Helix	Ear apex	At the tip of the auricle when the ear is folded towards tragus	Ophthalmia, fever, hypertension
Helix	Helix 1, 2, 3, 4, 5, 6	Evenly distributed from the lower border of auricular tubercle to the lower midpoint of the earlobe	Fever, infection of the upper respiratory tract
Scapha	Finger	Superior to the helix tubercle and inside the scapha	Pain in the corresponding area
Scapha	Wrist	At the same level of the prominence of the helix tubercle	Pain in the corresponding area

Scapha	Urticarial spot	Between the finger and wrist acupoints	Relieving itching, antianaphylaxis
Scapha	Shoulder	At the same level of supratragic notch and inside the scapha	Scapulohumeral periarthritis, stiff neck
Scapha	Elbow	Between the wrist and shoulder acupoints	Pain in the corresponding area
Scapha	Clavicle	At the same level of the incisure of helix and near the helix cauda	Pain in the corresponding area
Scapha	Shoulder joint	Between the shoulder and clavicle acupoints	Scapulohumeral periarthritis
Superior crus of antihelix	Toe	Superolateral corner of the superior crus of antihelix	Pain in the toe, paronychia
Superior crus of antihelix	Ankle	Medial and superior corner of the superior crus of antihelix	Pain in the corresponding area, sprains
Superior crus of antihelix	Knee	At the place where the superior crus of upper antihelix begins, at the same level of the border of the inferior crus of antihelix	Pain in the corresponding area, sprains
Inferior crus of antihelix	Hip	Lateral 1/2 to the upper border of the inferior crus of antihelix	Sciatica
Inferior crus of antihelix	Ischium	Medial 1/2 of the upper border of the inferior crus of antihelix	Sciatica
Inferior crus of antihelix	End of inferior antihelix crus	The juncture of the inferior crus of antihelix and the medial helix	Spasmolytic and pain-relieving effect on internal organs
Triangular fossa	Ear-*Shenmen*	In front of the point where the superior and inferior crus of antihelix cross, lateral 1/3 to the triangular fossa	Tranquilizing, calming the mind, allaying inflammation and relieving pain
Triangular fossa	Uterus (seminal palace)	In the depression close to the midpoint of helix	Gynecological diseases, impotence
Trunk of antihelix	Abdomen	At the same level of the lower border of the inferior crus of antihelix	Accessory points for diseases in the pelvic and abdominal cavities
Trunk of antihelix	Chest	At the same level of supratragic notch	Chest pain, costal pain, neurodynia, mammitis
Trunk of antihelix	Neck	On the helix notch near the lateral scapha	Stiff neck, sprains of neck
Trunk of antihelix	Vertebrae	A curved line from the level of lower portion of rectum acupoint to the level of shoulder joint acupoint, with the upper 1/3 corresponding to the sacral and lumbar vertebrae, the middle 1/3 corresponding to the thoracic vertebrae, and the lower 1/3 corresponding to the cervical vertebrae	Pain in the corresponding area
Tragus	External nose	In the center of the lateral tragus	Allergic rhinitis
Tragus	Throat	Superior 1/2 inside the tragus	Acute and chronic pharyngitis, tonsillitis
Tragus	Internal nose	Inferior 1/2 inside the tragus	Rhinitis, common cold
Tragus	Supratragic apex	At the protuberance outside the upper tragus	Toothache, strabismus
Tragus	Infratragic apex	At the lower tubercle on the border of the tragus	Raising blood pressure, antiallergy
Helix notch	Brainstem	In the center of the helix notch	Headache, dizziness
Antitragus	Point for soothing asthma	At the antitragus apex	Asthma, mumps
Antitragus	Middle border	At the midpoint of the line connecting the brainstem acupoint and point for soothing asthma	Enuresis, insomnia, metrorrhagia and metrostaxis
Antitragus	Brain	On the medial aspect of the antitragus	Tranquilizing and relieving pain
Antitragus	Testicle (Ovary)	On the anteroinferior side of the antitragus, a part of the brain acupoint	Epididymitis, menstrual disorders

Antitragus	Forehead	On the anteroinferior side of the lateral antitragus	Headache, dizziness, insomnia
Antitragus	Occiput	On the superoposterior side of the lateral antitragus	Headache, neurasthenia
Antitragus	Temple	At the midpoint of the line connecting the forehead and occiput acupoints	Headache, migraine, dizziness
Helix crus	Esophagus	At the front 2/3 of the lower border of helix crus	Dysphagia
Helix crus	Cardiac orifice	At the back 1/3 of the lower border of helix crus	Vomiting, nausea
Helix crus	Stomach	At the place where the helix crus ends	Stomachache, vomiting, dyspepsia
Helix crus	Duodenum	At the back 1/3 of the superior helix crus	Duodenal ulcer, pylorospasm
Helix crus	Small intestine	At the middle 1/3 of the superior helix crus	Palpitation, dyspepsia
Helix crus	Large intestine	At the front 1/3 of the superior helix crus	Diarrhea, constipation, dysentery
Helix crus	Appendix	Between the small intestine and large intestine	Acute simple appendicitis
Cymba concha	Bladder	On the lower border of the inferior crus of antihelix, directly above the large intestine acupoint	Enuresis, urinary retention
Cymba concha	Kidney	On the lower border of the inferior crus of antihelix, directly above the small intestine acupoint	Lumbago, tinnitus, hypoacusis, urinary, reproductive and gynecological diseases
Cymba concha	Ureter	Between the kidney and bladder acupoints	Ureteral diseases
Cymba concha	Liver	Posterior to the stomach and duodenum acupoints	Eye disorders, hypochondriac pain
Cymba concha	Spleen	Below the liver point, close to the rim of the antihelix	Abdominal distention, dyspepsia, menstrual disorders, stagnation of liver-*qi*
Cymba concha	Pancreas and gallbladder	Between the liver and kidney acupoints	Dyspepsia, biliary tract diseases, stomachache
Cavum concha	Mouth	Close to the back of the orifice of the external auditory meatus	Facial paralysis, stomatocace
Cavum concha	Heart	In the center of the cavum concha	Hysteria, palpitation
Cavum concha	Lung	Superior, inferior and back of the heart acupoint	Cough, asthma, skin diseases and common cold
Cavum concha	Trachea	Between the mouth and heart acupoints	Cough and asthma
Cavum concha	Intertragus	Inferoposterior to the orifice of the external auditory meatus, near the intertragic notch	Dysmenorrhea, menstrual disorder, disorders of reproductive system, dermatosis
Cavum concha	*Sanjiao*	Between the orifice of the external auditory meatus, intertragus, brain and lung acupoints	Constipation, edema
Earlobe	Eye 1	Inferoanterior to the intertragic notch	Glaucoma, pseudomyopia, stye
Earlobe	Eye 2	Inferoposterior to the intertragic notch	Glaucoma, pseudomyopia, stye
Earlobe	Eye	In the center of the fifth section of the earlobe	Glaucoma, pseudomyopia, stye
Earlobe	Toothache 1	At the inferoposterior corner of the first section of the earlobe	Toothache, paradentitis, tooth-extracting anesthesia
Earlobe	Toothache 2	In the center of the fourth section of the earlobe	Toothache, paradentitis, tooth-extracting anesthesia
Earlobe	Upper and lower jaw	In the center and superior to the third section of the earlobe	Toothache, arthritis of the temporo-mandibular joint
Earlobe	Inner ear	In the center of the sixth section of the earlobe	Tinnitus, hypoacusis
Earlobe	Tonsil	In the center of the eighth section of the earlobe	Tonsillitis
Earlobe	Face and cheek	Around the juncture of the fifth and sixth sections of the earlobe	Facial paralysis, trifacial neuralgia
Earback	Groove for lowering blood pressure	In the groove of the inferior crus of antihelix	Hypertension

Earback	Yangwei	Slightly above the root of auricular vagus nerve, at the junction of retroauricle and mastoid	Tinnitus, deafness
Earback	Root of auricular vagus nerve	At the junction of retroauricle and mastoid, at the same level of the helix crus	Headache, stuffy nose, biliary ascariasis
Earback	Upper earback	At the most protruding part of the cymba concha	Lumbago and pain in the back, dermatosis
Earback	Middle earback	At the midpoint of the line connecting the upper earback and lower earback acupoints	Lumbago and pain in the back, dermatosis
Earback	Lower earback	The most protruding part of cavum concha	Lumbago and pain in the back, dermatosis
Earback	Upper root of the ear	On the superior border of the auricular root	Relieving pain and treating paralysis
Earback	Lower root of the ear	On the inferior border of the auricular root	Relieving pain and treating paralysis

4. Application of Ear Acupoints

Ear acupoints correspond to the internal organs, trunk and limbs of the human body. Needling at these acupoints may help treat illness in relevant body parts. Moreover, these points can also be used to assist diagnosis and acupuncture anesthesia.

1) Diagnosis

Inspection: Abnormal reactions, such as discoloration, desquamation, papule and deformation, can be seen on the auricle when the *zang-fu* organs, trunk and four limbs are affected. These manifestations, together with other symptoms help doctors make diagnosis. If a small and round papule appears on the ear acupoint corresponding to the stomach, together with uncomfortable feelings in the upper abdomen, eructation and acid regurgitation, it's likely that the disease is gastric ulcer; if there are oblique creases on the earlobe of a patient who is over forty and often feels uncomfortable in the precordial region, the diagnosis is likely to be coronary heart disease.

Pain on pressure: In clinical practice, patients suffering from headache and dizziness usually show pain on pressure in the forehead and occiput regions. For patients suffering stomachache, the tender spot is usually at the stomach acupoint on the auricle; for patients suffering hiccup, it is likely at the middle ear; for patients suffering lumbago and pain in the legs, it is usually at the hip and ischium acupoints on the auricle. A tender spot can be found in this way: hold the probe and press it from top to bottom, outside to the center with even and light force until the most sensitive spot is found. If a tender spot is found around the lung acupoint on the auricle, the illness may be disorders of the lung and large intestine or skin diseases, and the patient's medical history must be taken into consideration before making a diagnosis.

Electric detection: Since auricular points have a low electrical resistance but high conductivity, a transistor tester can be used to detect a tender spot. When looking for a tender spot, the patient holds the electrode panel and the doctor searches the auricle with the detector. Once that the detector touches a sensitive point, the indicator light will flash. This method is simple and effective, but sometimes the indicator may flash on benign acupoints. For this reason, the doctor need to make a diagnosis according to the comprehensive clinical symptoms.

2) Application

a) Indications:

Pain: Headache, trigeminal neuralgia, intercostal neuralgia, sciatica and trauma.

Inflammation: Laryngopharyngitis, tonsillitis, enteritis, dysentery, pelvic inflammation, pulmonary infection and rheumatic arthritis.

Functional disturbances: Neurasthenia, gastrointestinal neurosis, hyperhidrosis and irregular menstruation.

Allergic diseases: Allergic dermatosis, urticaria, asthma and allergic rhinitis.

Endocrine diseases: Hyperthyroidism, simple goiter and menopausal syndrome.

Others: Hypertension, arrhythmia and indigestion.

b) Principles of acupoint selection

• Selecting acupoints according to syndrome differentiation

This method follows the theories of *zang-fu* and meridians, for example, selecting the lung acupoint on the auricle to treat dermatosis since the lung dominates the skin and hair; selecting the kidney acupoint on the auricle to treat bone diseases since kidney dominates bones.

• Selecting acupoints according to diseases

This method is based on the physiology and pathology of modern medicine, for example, selecting the intertragus acupoint to treat irregular menstruation and the brain acupoint to treat neurasthenia.

• Selecting acupoints according to the affected area

This method is based on the diagnosis of a certain disease, for example, selecting the eye acupoint on the auricle to treat eye diseases and the stomach acupoint on the auricle to treat stomachache.

• Selecting acupoints according to experiences

Doctors usually select the middle ear acupoint to treat phrenospasm, blood and skin diseases, and ear-*Shenmen* to alleviate pain and tranquilize the mind.

c) Examples of acupoint selection in ear acupuncture

Stomachache: Auricular acupoints such as stomach, end of inferior antihelix crus, ear-*Shenmen*, spleen and brain.

Diarrhea: Auricular acupoints such as large intestine, small intestine, end of inferior antihelix crus and spleen.

Constipation: Auricular acupoints such as large intestine, lower portion of rectum and the end of inferior antihelix crus.

Sprain and bruise: Acupoints around the injured area, auricular acupoints such as ear-*Shenmen* and brain.

Red and swollen eyes: Auricular acupoints such as eye, liver and ear apex.

Tympanitis: Auricular acupoints such as inner ear, intertragus, occiput and kidney.

Chronic pain in lumbar region and lower limbs: Auricular acupoints such as hip, ischium and kidney, and ear-*Shenmen*.

Pain in the shoulder and arms: Auricular acupoints such as shoulder, shoulder joint, elbow, ear-*Shenmen* and brain.

Neurasthenia: Auricular acupoints such as ear-*Shenmen*, brain and heart.

Reaction during fluid infusion: Auricular acupoints such as infratragic apex and intertragus.

d) Manipulation

• Location of acupoints: Make a prescription according to the illness. Select certain tender spots, spots with positive reaction or low electrical resistance as the stimuli for treatment.

•. Sterilization: The tools for ear acupuncture should be sterilized carefully and the auricle cleaned with 2% iodine tincture and then 75% alcohol solution. Sterilization must be strictly carried out for the auricle is liable to get infected.

• Treatment

Needling: A 0.5-*cun* long needle can be used for ear acupuncture. Fix the auricle with the left hand and insert the needle into the acupoint. Take care that the needle tip does not penetrate the auricle. Rotating or handle-scraping methods can be applied, but lifting and thrusting methods are contraindicated. After insertion, most patients get a hot and distensive feeling around the acupoint, and a few patients have a cool, numb and burning sensation along the meridian. Keep the needle under the skin for 15-30 minutes or longer when treating a chronic disease. Press the acupoint after withdrawing the needle to prevent bleeding and sterilize it with alcohol if necessary. The treatment should be carried out every day, and a whole course of treatment includes ten days. The second course of treatment may start after some rest.

Electroacupuncture: Turn on the current after inserting the needle into an acupoint so as to add stimulus to the muscles and achieve better results. This method is effective for disorders of nerve system, colic pain of viscera and asthma. It can also be used for ear acupuncture anesthesia.

Needle embedment: The method of embedding intradermal needles into auricular points is often used in ear acupuncture. It is effective for chronic, nervous and functional diseases. The method is like this: Insert the intradermal needle into a certain acupoint and then fix it with a piece of adhesive plaster. Keep the needle under the skin for three to five days during which the patient may press the needle several times a day. Pay attention to the sterilization of local area where the needle is embedded. After being wetted, the needle and adhesive plaster should be changed. If there is a distensive pain in the local area, the doctor should take immediate measures so as to avoid infection. Acupoints with the same name on both ears can be needled together or one after another. The needle embedment method is safe with little side effect. A complete course of treatment includes ten times and if necessary, the second course may start after some rest.

Seed embedment: This method embeds granular herbs or seeds on the ear acupoints so as to add stimulus and achieve therapeutic results. Since this method is safe with little side affect, it is suitable for both young and old people.

Besides, other methods like bloodletting method, mild moxibustion with moxa stick can also be applied on the ear acupoints.

e) Points for attention

• Sterilization should be strictly carried out to avoid infection. Ear acupuncture treatment is not suitable for those with auricular cold injury or inflammation. Immediate measures should be taken if the local area turns red and swollen after the treatment, such as applying 2% iodine tincture or taking antibiotics.

• Ear acupuncture treatment is not suitable for old or weak patients and pregnant women who suffer habitual abortion.

• Take care with faint during acupuncture and handle it promptly.

• Pay attention to patients who suffer insomnia caused by needle embedment or change it with seed embedment method if necessary.

Section 2
SCALP ACUPUNCTURE

Scalp acupuncture treats cerebral diseases by way of needling certain stimulation areas on the scalp.

1. Stimulation Areas and Indications

For the convenience of locating stimulation areas, doctors suppose that there are two standard lines on the scalp:

Anteroposterior midline: The line connecting the glabella and the lower border of external occipital protuberance through the vertex.

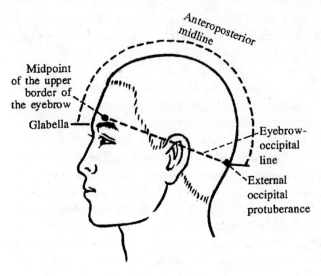

Fig. 3-41 Standard Lines

Eyebrow-occipital line: The line on the lateral head connecting the midpoint of the upper border of eyebrow and the tip of the external occipital protuberance. (Fig. 3-41)

1) Motor area

Location: The upper point is 0.5 cm posterior to the midpoint of the anteroposterior midline, and the lower point is at the crossing point of the eyebrow-occipital line and the anterior hairline on the temple, and the line connecting this two points is the motor area. The motor area is divided into five equal parts, with the upper 1/5 corresponding to the lower limb on the other side and trunk, the middle 2/5 corresponding to the upper limb on the other side, and the lower 2/5 corresponding to the face. (Fig. 3-42)

Indications: The upper 1/5 is effective for paralysis of the lower limb on the other side, the middle 2/5 for paralysis of the upper limb on the other side, and the lower 2/5 for central facial paralysis on the other side, motor aphasia, salivation and dysphonia. (The lower 2/5 of the motor area is also called Speech Area I.)

2) Sensory area

Location: It refers to the parallel 1.5 cm posterior to the motor area. The sensory area is also divided into five equal parts. The upper 1/5 corresponds to the lower limb on the other side, head and trunk, the middle 2/5 to the upper limb on the other side, and the lower 2/5 to the face. (Fig. 3-43)

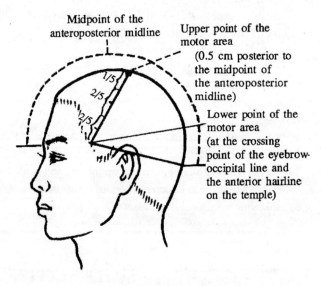

Fig. 3-42 Motor Area

Indications: The upper 1/5 is effective for pain, numbness and paresthesia of the loin and lower limb on the other side, headache, pain in neck and nape; the middle 2/5 for pain, numbness and paresthesia of the upper limb on the other side; the lower 2/5 for facial numbness, migraine, trigeminal neuralgia, toothache and temporomandibular arthritis on the other side.

3) Control area for chorea and tremor

Location: It refers to the parallel 1.5 cm anterior to the motor area. (Fig. 3-43)

Indications: Chorea, tremor and Parkinson's syndrome.

4) Vertigo and audition area

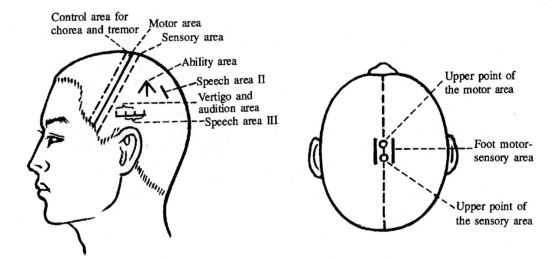

Fig. 3-43 Stimulation Area (on the side)   Fig. 3-44 Stimulation Area (on the vertex)

Location: It refers to the 4-cm-long horizontal line, with the midpoint 1.5 cm above the ear apex. (Fig. 3-43)

Indications: Vertigo, tinnitus and hypoacusis.

5) Speech area II

Location: It refers to the 3-cm-long parallel of the anteroposterior midline, with the starting point 2 cm inferoposterior to the parietal eminence. (Fig. 3-43)

Indication: Nominal aphasia.

6) Speech area III

Location: It refers to the 4-cm-long line starting from the midpoint of the vertigo and audition area. (Fig. 3-43)

Indication: Sensory aphasia.

7) Ability area

Location: Suppose a vertical line starting from the parietal eminence, and the two lines 3 cm in length and each forming a 40-degree-angle with the vertical line are where the ability area locates. (Fig. 3-43)

Indication: Apraxia.

8) Foot motor-sensory area

Location: It refers to the two 3-cm-long lines, each starting from a spot 1 cm lateral to the midpoint of the anteroposterior midline and running backward. (Fig. 3-44)

Indications: Pain, numbness and paralysis of lower limb on the other side, acute lumbar sprain, cortical polyuria, nocturia and metroptosis.

9) Visual area

Location: It refers to the two 4-cm-long parallels of the anteroposterior midline, with their lowest point at spots 1 cm lateral to the top of the external occipital protuberance. (Fig. 3-45)

Indication: Visual disturbance of cortical origin.

10) Equilibrium area

Location: It refers to the two 4-cm-long parallels of the anteroposterior midline, with their highest point at spots 3.5 cm lateral to the tip of the external occipital protuberance. (Fig. 3-45)

Indication: Disequilibrium.

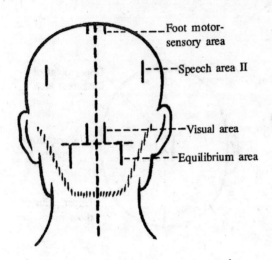

Fig. 3-45 Stimulation Area (at the back)   Fig. 3-46 Stimulation Area (in front)

11) Stomach area

Location: It refers to the two 2-cm-long parallels of the anteroposterior midline, with starting points on the anterior hairline being vertical to the pupils. (Fig. 3-46)

Indications: Acute and chronic gastritis and duodenal ulcer.

12) Thorax area

Location: It refers to the two 4-cm-long lines between the stomach area and the anteroposterior midline, parallel to the anteroposterior midline. This two lines start from the anterior hairline, 2 cm above and 2 cm below the hairline. (Fig. 3-46)

Indications: Asthma, chest pain and upset, palpitation and coronary heart disease.

13) Genital area

Location: It refers to the two 2-cm-long parallels of the anteroposterior midline, with the starting points at the frontal eminence. (Fig. 3-46)

Indications: Dysfunctional uterine bleeding, metroptosis and pelvic inflammatory disease.

2. Manipulation

Select stimulation areas and posture according to the disease. After local sterilization, insert quickly a 1.5-2 *cun* filiform needle at an angle of 30 degrees into the skin surface and push it down the galea aponeurotica. Usually the insertion depth equals the length of the area. The rotating method can be used at a frequency of 200 times per minute, which lasts 2-3 minutes. The needle should be kept under the skin for 5-10 minutes and the manipulation can be repeated twice or three times. Ask the patient or his relatives to help him move the affected limb so as to activate its functions. Withdraw the needle and press the acupoint to prevent bleeding.

An electroacupuncture device can also be used at a frequency of 200-300 per minute. The current intensity must be kept moderate. For suitable wave forms, refer to relevant chapters.

The treatment can be carried out every day or every other day, and one course includes ten times treatment. The second course of treatment may start after several days rest.

3. Indications

The head is where the six *yang* meridians meet, with the Hand-*Yangming* and Foot-*Yangming* meridians passing the forehead and face, the Hand-*Shaoyang* and Foot-*Shaoyang* meridians passing the lateral side of the head, and the Hand-*Taiyang* and Foot-*Taiyang* meridians passing the vertex and nape. As to the six *yin* meridians, Hand-*Shaoyin* and Foot-*Jueyin* all travel on the head and face, and the other four *yin* meridians also connect with the *yang* meridians and pass the head and face. Besides, the *Du* Meridian, *Yangqiao* Meridian and *Yangwei* Meridian also connect with the head. All this shows that the head has a close relationship with the meridians and acupoints, and it can be used to treat diseases on the body. Clinical practice shows that scalp acupuncture is effective for diseases of cerebral origin such as numbness, hemiparalysis and aphasia. In addition, it can also help treat vertigo, pain in the loins and lower limbs, nocturia. Scalp acupuncture anesthesia further provides surgical operations with a new method.

4. Precaution

1) Scalp acupuncture is contraindicated for patients suffering cerebral hemorrhage unless the blood pressure is lowered and the illness is kept under control.

2) Do not give scalp acupuncture treatment to patients suffering high fever or heart failure.

3) Press the acupoint with a sterilized cotton ball after withdrawing the needle to prevent infection.

4) Keep the stimulation moderate and observe the patient's reaction carefully to prevent faint.

PART THREE
THERAPEUTICS

Chapter One
INTRODUCTION

Section 1
PRINCIPLES OF SYNDROME DIFFERENTIATION

Syndrome differentiation in traditional Chinese medicine refers to an overall analysis of symptoms, including the cause, nature, and location of a disease and the physical condition of a patient. In order to make correct differentiation, doctors may use methods like inspection, auscultation and olfaction, interrogation and palpation.

Syndrome differentiation and treatment are closely related, with syndrome differentiation being the basis and the effect of treatment being a tester of the former. It is only when syndrome differentiation is correct and treatment appropriate that an ideal therapeutic effect can be achieved.

There are many methods of syndrome differentiation, and each of them has its own characteristic and emphasis. Differentiating syndromes according to the eight principles is the guiding principle of differentiation, which is widely used in clinical practice. Differentiating syndromes in accordance with the pathological changes of the *zang-fu* organs serves as the basic principle, which is further supplemented by the differentiation according to the state of *qi*, blood and body fluid. The differentiation in accordance with the state of meridians and collaterals is the basic principle for acupuncture treatment.

1. Syndrome Differentiation in Accordance with the State of the *Zang-Fu* Organs

This is a basic method of diagnosis which analyzes symptoms, physiological function and pathological changes of *zang-fu* organs. This kind of differentiation includes syndrome differentiation of *zang-fu* organs and their corresponding body surface. Since the *zang-fu* organs in the human body are closely interrelated, doctors must take the overall condition into consideration when differentiating syndromes. Pathological changes taking place in the *zang-fu* organs are complicated with various syndromes, and in this section we are going to introduce those often seen in acupuncture and moxibustion treatment.

1) Differentiation of diseases in the heart and small intestine

As the seat of mind the heart controls blood circulation, and has a specific opening in the tongue. Since the heart and small intestine are interior-exteriorly related, all disorders concerning blood vessels and mental state such as palpitation, amnesia, insomnia, coma and mania can be considered syndromes of the heart.

a) Insufficient heart-*yang*

Manifestations: Palpitation, short breath, listlessness, dyspnea, spontaneous sweating or oppression and pain of the chest, dark complexion, petechiae on the tongue, knotted and intermittent pulse.

Treatment: To benefit *qi* and invigorate *yang*, warm the meridians and restore pulse. Select the back *shu* point of the heart and those on the Heart Meridian of Hand-*Shaoyin* and *Ren* Meridian to apply acupuncture (using the reinforcing manipulation) and moxibustion.

b) Deficiency of heart-*yin*

Manifestations: Dim complexion, pale lips and tongue, palpitation, amnesia, insomnia, dream-disturbed sleep, dizziness, feverish sensation in the palms, soles and chest, and night sweat.

Treatment: To nourish blood and *yin*, and tranquilize the mind. Select the back *shu* acupoint and those on the Heart Meridian of Hand-*Shaoyin* and the Pericardium Meridian of Hand-*Jueyin* to apply acupuncture, using the reinforcing manipulation.

c) Hyperactivity of heart-fire

Manifestations: Buccal aphthae, flushed face, thirst, sore throat, bitter taste, haematemesis, epistaxis, mania, delirium, difficult and painful urination with reddish urine or hematuria.

Treatment: To disperse heat in the pericardium and purge pathogenic fire. Select acupoints on the Heart Meridian of Hand-*Shaoyin*, the Small Intestine Meridian of Hand-*Taiyang* and the Pericardium Meridian of Hand-*Jueyin* to apply acupuncture (using the reducing manipulation) or prompt prick with a three-edged needle to let out a little blood.

d) Mental disturbance due to phlegm and fire

Manifestations: Restlessness, insomnia, mania, aggressive and violent behavior, coma, delirium, mental disorder, flushed face, red tongue, constipation, and dark urine.

Treatment: To disperse heart-fire and resolve phlegm. Select acupoints on the Heart Meridian of Hand-*Shaoyin* and the Pericardium Meridian of Hand-*Jueyin* to apply acupuncture (using the reducing method) or prick the twelve *jiing* points to let out a little blood.

e) Heat in the small intestine

Manifestations: Restlessness, thirst, difficulty and pain in micturition, buccal aphthae, bitter taste, dry throat and foul breath.

Treatment: To disperse heart-fire, promote diuresis and relieve stranguria. Select acupoints on the Heart Meridian of Hand-*Shaoyin*, the Small Intestine Meridian of Hand-*Taiyang* and the Bladder Meridian of Foot-*Taiyang* to apply acupuncture, using the reducing manipulation.

2) Differentiation of diseases in the lung and large intestine

The lung is in charge of *qi* and performs the function of respiration, disseminating vital energy, cleansing the inspired air and keeping the pathway of air unobstructed and the flow of *qi* downward. Therefore, dyspnea, gasping, short breath and hemoptysis all indicate lung diseases. The function of the large intestine is to pass its content on and finally eliminate the waste. The large intestine and the lung are exterior-interiorly related, with the meridians of the former connecting with the lung. Symptoms like constipation, diarrhea, tenesmus, bloody stools, abdominal pain and prolapse of rectum all indicate diseases of the large intestine.

a) Deficiency of lung-*qi*

Manifestations: Pale complexion, lassitude, dyspnea, weak cough, spontaneous sweating, aversion to cold, low voice, and liability to catching cold.

Treatment: To invigorate lung and kidney-*qi*. Select the back *shu* point and those on the Lung Meridian of Hand-*Taiyin*, the Kidney Meridian of Foot-*Shaoyin* and the *Ren* Meridian to apply acupuncture (using the reinforcing manipulation) or apply moxibustion if necessary.

b) Deficiency of lung-*yin*

Manifestations: Emaciation, dry cough or blood-tinged sputum, dry throat, thirst, hoarse voice, afternoon fever, feverish sensation in the chest, palms and soles, malar flush, night sweat, and poor sleep.

Treatment: To nourish *yin*, moisturize the lung and suppress fire. Select the back *shu* points and those on the Lung Meridian of Hand-*Taiyin* to apply acupuncture.

c) Invasion of the lung by pathogenic cold

Manifestations: Headache, pain in the whole body, thin nasal discharge, cough with thin sputum, fever, chilliness and poor appetite.

Treatment: To ventilate the lung and disperse cold. Select acupoints on the Lung Meridian of Hand-*Taiyin*, the Large Intestine Meridian of Hand-*Yangming* and the Bladder Meridian of Foot-*Taiyang* to apply acupuncture, using superficial insertion with reducing manipulation. Uniform reinforcement and reduction can be applied to patients with weak constitution. Moxibustion can also be used if necessary.

d) Retention of pathogenic heat in the lung

Manifestations: Cough with thick and yellow sputum, noisy breathing, sore throat, thirst, chilliness, fever, pain in the chest, expectoration with foul and bloody sputum, constipation, scanty and dark urine.

Treatment: To ventilate the lung and disperse heat, and relieve cough and asthma. Select acupoints on the Lung Meridian of Hand-*Taiyin* and the Large Intestine Meridian of Hand-*Yangming* to apply acupuncture, using the reducing manipulation. Or prick with a three-edged needle to let out a little blood. Moxibustion is contraindicated.

e) Dampness-heat in the large intestine

Manifestations: Abdominal pain, tenesmus, diarrhea with bloody and mucous discharge, or chilliness and fever, dysentery with sudden onset of watery discharge, burning sensation in the anus, and oliguria.

Treatment: To disperse heat and dampness. Select the front *mu* points and lower confluent points corresponding to the large intestine, and those on the Large Intestine Meridian of Hand-*Yangming* and the Stomach Meridian of Foot-*Yangming* to apply acupuncture, using the reducing manipulation. Moxibustion is contraindicated.

3) Differentiation of diseases in the spleen and stomach

The spleen is in charge of digestion and transportation, and controls the flow of blood in the vessels. The stomach receives water and food, digests and transforms them into chyme. The spleen and stomach are interior-exteriorly related. The spleen keeps the *qi* going upward and the stomach sends it down. The spleen and stomach are in charge of the reception, digestion, transportation and transformation of food and distribution of nutrients. They are therefore considered as the source of *qi* and blood, which provide the material basis of the acquired constitution. Disorders in the spleen may lead to edema, emaciation, hemafecia or metrorrhagia, while those in the stomach result in abdominal upset, belching, acid regurgitation, hiccup or vomiting.

a) Deficiency of spleen and stomach-*qi*

Manifestations: Abdominal fullness, loss of appetite, speechlessness, lassitude, dim complexion, emaciation, pale tongue with white coating, and weak pulse.

Treatment: To reinforce *qi*, invigorate the spleen and stomach. Select the back *shu* and front *mu* points corresponding to the spleen and stomach, and those on the Spleen Meridian of Foot-*Taiyin* and the Stomach Meridian of Foot-*Yangming* to apply acupuncture, using the reinforcing manipulation. Moxibustion is used more often than acupuncture.

b) Dampness-heat in the spleen and stomach

Manifestations: Abdominal fullness and distention, lassitude, loss of appetite, nausea, vomiting, loose stools, scanty and dark urine, jaundice, skin itching, sore with yellowish exudation, eczema, intermittent fever which does not subside after sweating, yellow and sticky tongue coating, soft and rapid pulse.

Treatment: To disperse heat and eliminate dampness. Select acupoints on the Bladder Meridian of Foot-*Taiyang* and the Stomach Meridian of Foot-*Yangming* to apply acupuncture, using the reducing manipulation.

c) Cold in the stomach

Manifestations: Persistent cold and pain in the stomach which become serious when exposed to cold but relieved by warmth, thin taste without the thirsty feeling, regurgitation of clear fluid, colic, borborygmus, vomiting after eating, pale tongue with white and smooth coating, taut or slow pulse.

Treatment: To warm the stomach and spleen and disperse cold. Select the back *shu* point and those on the Stomach Meridian of Foot-*Yangming* to apply acupuncture, using the reinforcing manipulation. Moxibustion can be used at the same time.

d) Heat (fire) in the stomach

Manifestations: Stomachache, thirst with a desire for cold drinks, hyperorexia with emaciation, bitter taste, foul breath, acid regurgitation, erosion of buccal mucosa and lips, swelling and bleeding in the gums, constipation, red tongue with yellow coating, smooth and rapid pulse.

Treatment: To disperse stomach-fire. Select the front *mu* point and those on the Stomach Meridian of Foot-*Yangming* to apply acupuncture, using the reducing manipulation.

e) Spleen's failure to control blood

Manifestations: Pale or sallow complexion, poor appetite, lassitude, dizziness, short breath, hemorrhage (menorrhagia, metrorrhagia, hemafecia, hematuria and hematohidrosis), pale tongue, thready and weak pulse.

Treatment: To reinforce the spleen and keep blood flow in the vessels. Select acupoints on the Spleen Meridian of Foot-*Taiyin* and the Stomach Meridian of Foot-*Yangming*. Moxibustion is recommended.

f) Sinking of spleen-*qi*

Manifestations: Dizziness, low and timid voice, short breath, lassitude, spontaneous sweat, loss of appetite, distention after eating, abdominal pain with tenesmus, constant urgency of defecation, prolapse of rectum after prolonged diarrhea, or prolapse of uterus.

Treatment: To invigorate the spleen, benefit and elevate the *qi*. Select acupoints on the Spleen Meridian of Foot-*Taiyin*, the Stomach Meridian of Foot-*Yangming* and the *Du* Meridian to apply acupuncture, using the reinforcing manipulation. Moxibustion should be used.

4) Differentiation of diseases in the liver and gallbladder

The liver stores blood, smoothes and regulates the flow of *qi*, and controls the tendons. Since emotions greatly influence the liver, it tends to function well when one is optimistic and get impaired by depression. The liver has a specific body opening in the eyes. The gallbladder is a *fu* organ that contains bile. The liver and gallbladder are situated in the hypochondriac region, with the latter attaching to the former. They are interior-exteriorly related.

Disorders of the liver may exhibit symptoms such as dizziness, eye diseases, fullness in the chest, hypochondriac pain, hiccup, convulsion, facial paralysis and muscular twitching, while bitter taste, dry throat, deafness, hypochondriac pain, alternating episodes of chills and fever, and jaundice indicate gallbladder disorders. Furthermore, digestive abnormal functions also indicate diseases in the liver and gallbladder.

a) Stagnant liver-*qi*

Manifestations: Mental depression, irritability, depression in the chest, frequent sighing, distensive pain in the chest, hypochondria, epigastrium and breasts, dysmenorrhea, irregular menstruation, retching, acid regurgitation, sore throat, goiter on the nape and neck.

Treatment: To disperse stagnant liver-*qi* and relieve mental depression. Select acupoints on the Liver Meridian of Foot-*Jueyin*, the Gallbladder Meridian of Foot-*Shaoyang*, the Spleen Meridian of Foot-*Taiyin* and the Stomach Meridian of Foot-*Yangming* to apply acupuncture, using the uniform reinforcement and reduction manipulation.

b) Hyperactive liver-fire

Manifestations: Headache, red and swollen eyes, bitter taste, dry throat, deafness, tinnitus, burning pain in the costal and hypochondriac regions, irritability, insomnia, hematemesis, epistaxis, constipation and dark urine.

Treatment: To clear the liver and disperse the fire. Select the acupoints of Liver Meridian of Foot-*Jueyin* to apply acupuncture, using the reducing manipulation. Moxibustion cannot be used.

c) Endogenous wind stirring in the liver

Manifestations: Headache, tremor and numbness in the limbs, sudden fainting, convulsion, opisthotonos, facial paralysis, hemiplegia, dysphasia, irritability, high fever and loss of consciousness.

Treatment: To disperse heat, subdue the hyperactivity of the liver and calm endogenous wind. Select acupoints on the Liver Meridian of Foot-*Jueyin* and *Du* Meridian, and the twelve *jiing* points to apply acupuncture, using the reducing manipulation. Or prick with a three-edged needle to let out a little blood.

d) Insufficiency of liver-blood

Manifestations: Pallor, dizziness, restlessness, palpitation, dream-disturbed sleep, tinnitus, dry eyes, blurred vision, night blindness, numbness or spasm in the limbs, pallor of digits, oligomenorrhea and amenorrhea.

Treatment: To nourish liver-*yin* and liver-blood. Select acupoints on the Liver Meridian of Foot-*Jueyin* and the Kidney Meridian of Foot-*Shaoyin* to apply acupuncture, using the reinforcing manipulation.

e) Dampness-heat in the liver and gallbladder

Manifestations: Distention and fullness in the chest and hypochondria, fever, bitter taste, nausea, vomiting, irregular bowel movement, scanty and dark urine, jaundice, eczema on the scrotum, swollen testes, foul leukorrhea.

Treatment: To disperse heat, eliminate dampness, soothe the liver and activate the gallbladder. Select acupoints on the Gallbladder Meridian of Foot-*Shaoyang*, the Liver Meridian of Foot-*Jueyin* and the Spleen Meridian of Foot-*Taiyin* to apply acupuncture, using the reducing manipulation. Moxibustion is not suitable.

5) Differentiation of diseases in the kidney and bladder

The kidney regulates water metabolism, stores the essence of life, and controls the bone and the fire of the vital gate, therefore, it is known as an organ of water and the foundation of constitution. Abnormal development, reproduction and water metabolism, and disorders of the brain, marrow, bones, respiration, hearing, defecation and urination all indicate kidney diseases.

a) Deficiency of kidney-*yang*

Manifestations: Pale complexion, cold limbs, listlessness, lumbago, pain in the knees, impotence, prospermia, female sterility, oliguria, edema, poor appetite, loose stools, palpitation and short breath.

Treatment: To warm *yang*, nourish the kidney and induce diuresis. Select the back *shu* point and those on the Kidney Meridian of Foot-*Shaoyin* and *Ren* Meridian to apply acupuncture, using the reinforcing manipulation. Moxibustion can be used as the main method of treatment.

b) Deficiency of kidney-*yin*

Manifestations: Dizziness, tinnitus, deafness, lumbago, pain in the knees, blurred vision, insomnia, amnesia, dry throat and mouth, feverish sensation in the palms, soles and chest, afternoon fever, malar flush, night sweat, female sterility, amenorrhea and nocturnal emission.

Treatment: To replenish kidney-*yin*. Select the back *shu* point and those on the Kidney Meridian of Foot-*Shaoyin*, the Gallbladder Meridian of Foot-*Jueyin* and the Lung Meridian of Hand-*Taiyin* to apply acupuncture, using the reinforcing manipulation.

c) Kidney's failure to promote respiration

Manifestations: Short breath, dyspnea, prolonged expiration and difficulty in inspiration, sweating, dislike of speaking, cold limbs, dizziness, lumbago and pain in the knees.

Treatment: To warm the kidney, replenish the *qi* and conduct it to its origin. Select the back *shu* point and those on the *Ren* and *Du* meridians to apply acupuncture, using the reinforcing manipulation. Moxibustion is often used for this case.

d) Dampness-heat in the bladder

Manifestations: Dark urine, urgent and frequent urination, dysuria, hematuria and discharge of stones in the urine (accompanied by fever, chilliness and lumbago).

Treatment: To disperse heat, promote diuresis and relieve stranguria. Select the back *shu* and front *mu* points corresponding to the bladder and those on the *Ren* and three *yin* meridians of foot to apply acupuncture, using the reducing manipulation. Moxibustion is not suitable.

2. Syndrome Differentiation in Accordance with the State of *Qi*, Blood and Body Fluid

Qi, blood and body fluid, products of the *zang-fu* organs, are the material base of human activity. Therefore, they are easily influenced by any pathological changes in the *zang-fu* organs, and likewise if the *qi*, blood and body fluid are diseased, the functions of the *zang-fu* organs will be impaired. That is to say the *qi*, blood and body fluid are closely connected with the *zang-fu* organs.

1) Deficiency and sinking of *qi*

Manifestations: Dizziness, fatigue, dislike of speaking, spontaneous sweating, palpitation, dyspnea and sinking of *qi* (accompanied by prolapse of rectum or uterus).

Treatment: To benefit and elevate *qi*. Select acupoints on the *Du* and *Ren* meridians and the Stomach Meridian of Foot-*Yangming* to apply acupuncture, using the reinforcing manipulation. Moxibustion is often used for this case.

2) Stagnation of *qi*

Manifestations: Oppression, distention and pain (usually with oppression more prominent than pain).

Treatment: To promote the flow of *qi*. Select acupoints on the Liver Meridian of Foot-*Jueyin* and the Stomach Meridian of Foot-*Yangming* to apply acupuncture, using the uniform reinforcement and reduction.

3) Upward flow of unhealthy *qi*

Manifestations: Cough, dyspnea, belching, hiccup, dizziness, headache, faint and hematemesis.

Treatment: To send the unhealthy *qi* downward. Select acupoints on the Liver Meridian of Foot-*Jueyin*, the Stomach Meridian of Foot-*Yangming* or the Lung Meridian of Hand-*Taiyin* to apply acupuncture, using the reducing manipulation.

4) Deficiency of blood

Manifestations: Pale complexion and lips, whitish tongue, dizziness, blurred vision, palpitation, amnesia, troubled sleep, numb limbs, hypomenorrhea and amenorrhea.

Treatment: To replenish the blood. Select acupoints on the Stomach Meridian of Foot-*Yangming* and the Liver Meridian of Foot-*Jueyin* to apply acupuncture, using the reinforcing manipulation. Moxibustion can be used if necessary.

5) Heat in the blood

Manifestations: Restlessness, insomnia, mania, fever, thirst with no desire to drink, crimson tongue and hemorrhage.

Treatment: To disperse heat and cool blood. Select acupoints on the Pericardium Meridian of Hand-*Jueyin*, the Liver Meridian of Foot-*Jueyin* and the Bladder Meridian of Foot-*Taiyang* to apply acupuncture, using the reducing manipulation.

6) Stagnation of blood

Manifestations: Fixed pain like being punctured by a needle, which becomes severe during night, tenderness, swollen and palpable mass, dark complexion, petechiae on the tongue, and squamous and dry skin in obstinate cases.

Treatment: To promote blood circulation and eliminate blood stasis. Select acupoints on the Pericardium Meridian of Hand-*Jueyin*, the Liver Meridian of Foot-*Jueyin* and the Stomach Meridian of Foot-*Yangming*, and the local points if there is blood stasis on the skin to apply acupuncture, using the reducing manipulation. Or prick with a three-edged needle to let out a little blood.

7) Insufficiency of body fluid

Manifestations: Dry throat, tongue, lips and skin, flaccidity in the lower limbs, oliguria, constipation, vexation, thirst and red tongue.

Treatment: To replenish body fluid. Select acupoints on the Bladder Meridian of Foot-*Taiyang* and the Stomach Meridian of Foot-*Yangming* to apply acupuncture, using the uniform reinforcement and reduction.

8) Accumulation of body fluid

Manifestations: Abdominal distention, loss of appetite, lassitude, tastelessness, dysuria and loose stools caused by dampness in the spleen *yang*, cough; profuse sputum, dizziness, palpitation, short breath caused by phlegm retention; edema and abdominal distention caused by deficiency of spleen and kidney-*yang*.

Treatment: To invigorate the spleen and eliminate stasis, warm the kidney and induce diuresis, activate *yang* and resolve phlegm. Select the back *shu* point and those on the Spleen Meridian of Foot-*Taiyin*, the Kidney Meridian of Foot-*Shaoyin* and the Lung Meridian of Hand-*Taiyin* to apply acupuncture, using the reinforcing manipulation. Moxibustion is often used for this case.

3. Syndrome Differentiation in Accordance with the Doctrine of Meridians and Collaterals

The doctrine of meridians and collaterals is developed through the practice of acupuncture and moxibustion, and serves as a basic theory guiding the clinical practice. The meridians and collaterals connect with the *zang-fu* organs on the one hand and link up with the joints and limbs on the other. They help transport *qi* and blood, nourish *yin*, *yang*, tendons and bones, and soothe the joints. According to *Miraculous Pivot*, meridians and collaterals should be unimpeded for they are vital to human beings in treating diseases and regulating the balance of deficiency and excess.

The doctrine of meridians and collaterals can be used as follows:

1) Identifying the affected meridian according to the location of pathological changes

As each meridian travels in its own direction and passes certain areas, it is possible to identify which meridian is diseased by studying the location of the symptoms. For example, frontal headache indicates disorders of the *Yangming* meridian; pain on the vertex indicates disorders of the *Jueyin* meridian; migraine indicates disorders of the *Shaoyang* meridian; and pain in the occipital region and neck shows disorders of the *Taiyang* meridian.

2) Identifying the affected *zang-fu* organs according to the pathological changes of meridians and collaterals

Any disorders of the *zang-fu* organs will be reflected by the meridians and collaterals on the body surface. There will be tender spots, sensitive belt, nodule, or radiating pain along the meridian. This phenomenon helps doctors to make diagnosis.

a) Identifying the affected *zang-fu* organ according to syndromes of the meridians and collaterals

As the *zang-fu* organs are linked with the body surface through meridians and collaterals, it is possible to identify any disorders of the *zang-fu* organs by studying the pathological changes of a specific body area. For example, swollen gums indicate hyperactive stomach-fire; red and swollen eyes indicate flaring-up of liver-fire; ear pain and deafness reflect hyperactive gallbladder-fire. Ideal therapeutic effect will be achieved when the affected *zang-fu* organ is identified correctly.

b) Identifying the affected *zang-fu* organ according to the tender spots, sensitive belts, nodules and radiating pain

Usually, any disease in the *zang-fu* organ will be reflected on the meridian to which it belongs. For example, when the lung is affected, a tender spot will appear at *Zhongfu* (LU 1) on the Lung Meridian of Hand-*Taiyin*; in company with angina pectoris, there is usually radiating pain along the Heart Meridian of Hand-*Shaoyin*; and in company with biliary colic, there is usually pain spreading to *Jianjing* (GB 21) on the right side. However, there are some diseases which exhibit sensitive spots on other meridians rather than on its own meridian. For example, the tender point of acute appendicitis can be found at *Lanwei* (EX-LE 7), two *cun* below *Zusanli* (ST 36) of the Stomach Meridian of Foot-*Yangming* because the Stomach Meridian of Foot-*Yangming* and Large Intestine Meridian of Hand-*Yangming* coordinate the digestive function. The tender spots and sensitive nodules of peptic ulcer usually appear at *Pishu* (BL 20) and *Weishu* (BL 21) of the Bladder Meridian of Foot-*Taiyang*, because the back *shu* points are where the *qi* of the corresponding *zang* or *fu* organ is transmitted. As for disorders of the liver and gallbladder, sensitive belts and pain usually appear at *Qimen* (LR 14) and *Riyue* (GB 24), because this two front *mu* points are where the *qi* of the corresponding *zang* and *fu* organs meets.

c) Identifying acupoints and meridians with an electric device

Recent studies show that the electric resistance of acupoints is low, and its electric conductivity can be determined by an electric device. Analyzing the conductivity of some typical acupoints such as *yuan*, *jiing*, *xi* and back *shu* points, doctors can learn the state of *qi* and blood in the corresponding meridians. If the electric conductivity of an acupoint is 1/3 higher than the average conductivity, that meridian exhibits excess syndrome; if the electric conductivity of an acupoint is 1/3 lower than the average conductivity, the meridian exhibits deficiency syndrome; and if the electric conductivity of acupoints on both sides of the same meridian differs greatly, the meridian must be diseased. This method, together with other differentiating principles, may help doctors make correct diagnosis of a disease.

Section 2
THERAPEUTIC EFFECTS

1. Regulating *Yin* and *Yang*

According to *Miraculous Pivot*, acupuncture can be used to balance *yin* and *yang* inside the human body. Generally, *yin* and *yang* maintain an equilibrium, but this equilibrium will be upset by exogenous harmful factors and internal changes, resulting in excessive *yin* or *yang*. Therefore, apply acupuncture to certain points on the body surface will activate the flow of *qi* and blood in the meridians and collaterals, thus recovering the balance between *yin* and *yang* and curing diseases.

When carrying out acupuncture treatment, doctors must select suitable acupoints and apply appropriate manipulations, such as reinforcement and reduction. Meanwhile, doctors should also pay attention to the state of internal organs, patients' response to acupuncture so as to keep the stimulus within control.

2. Strengthening Body Resistance and Dispelling Pathogenic Factors

The development of a disease is, in a sense, a struggle between body resistance and pathogenic factors. If pathogenic factors prevail, the disease will get worse; if the body resistance is strong, the disease will be cured. Therefore, when treating diseases, the main task for doctors is to increase body resistance and dispel pathogenic factors, which is an important principle in acupuncture treatment.

The body resistance and invading pathogenic factors decide whether a disease belongs to an excess type or a deficiency one. When pathogenic factors are in abundance, the disease is of excess type; when the body resistance is severely damaged, the disease is of deficiency type. For excess syndrome, purgation and reduction methods are recommended, such as acupuncture with reducing manipulation or bloodletting with a three-edged needle; for deficiency syndrome, reinforcement and replenishing methods can be used, such as acupuncture with reinforcing manipulation or moxibustion. In addition, the special effects of some acupoints can also be used, for example, *Gaohuang* (BL 43), *Qihai* (RN 6) and *Mingmen* (DU 4) are selected to strengthen body resistance; *Shixuan* (EX-UE 11), *Zhongji* (RN 3) and *Shuigou* (DU 26) are used to dispel pathogenic factors. Reinforcing the body resistance and dispelling the pathogenic factors can be used separately or in combination. As for cases hard to differentiate, uniform reinforcement and reduction can be applied.

3. Removing Obstructions in Meridians and Collaterals

Meridians and collaterals connect the body surface with the internal organs and the upper body with the lower one, and activate the flow of *qi* and blood. This is because the twelve regular meridians and their branches crisscross in the body and the eight extra meridians link with the twelve regular meridians, the tendons and muscles, and the twelve skin areas. They turn different body parts into an integrated unity. In addition, the meridians and collaterals serve as the pathways of *qi* and blood, providing the *zang-fu* organs, tendons, bones, limbs, joints, skin and hairs of the human body with nourishment so as to maintain their normal functions.

Since the meridians and collaterals have their own traveling routes and corresponding internal organs, pathogenic factors may invade the body through these pathways. For example, when cold invades the body surface, symptoms such as chilliness, fever, headache and lumbago appear first, followed by lung disorders such as cough, dyspnea, chest pain and expectoration. Likewise, disorders of internal organs may reflect on the body surface through meridians and collaterals. For example, liver disorders usually exhibit hypochondriac and lower abdominal pain because the Liver Meridian of Foot-*Jueyin* runs through these areas.

It is based on this mutual influence of meridians and *zang-fu* organs that acupuncture and moxibustion achieve the therapeutic effect of removing obstructions in meridians and collaterals and regulating the flow of *qi* and blood.

Section 3
THE PRINCIPLES OF TREATMENT

The principles of treatment in acupuncture and moxibustion are based on the organic conception, syndrome differentiation, and the theory of meridians and collaterals. Since there are various clinical manifestations due to complicated pathogenic changes, and acute and chronic illness influenced by different climate, geographical location and individual constitution, doctors must focus on the leading cause of a disease while taking into consideration the clinical manifestations so as to give proper treatment. The following are the basic principles for acupuncture and moxibustion.

1. Reinforcing Deficiency and Reducing Excess

Reinforcing deficiency means to strengthen the body resistance. Deficiency refers to the lack of *yin*, *yang*, *qi* and blood, and its manifestations include pale complexion, lassitude, cold limbs and faint breath. Acupuncture with the reinforcing manipulation is suitable for these syndrome, while moxibustion activates the flow of *qi* for cases with *qi* and *yang* deficiency.

Reducing excess means to dispel the pathogenic factors. Excess refers to the hyperactivity of pathogenic factors. It includes *yin* and *yang* types as well as swelling and pain in some body areas. These symptoms can be treated by acupuncture with the reducing manipulation or bloodletting.

When applying the principle of reinforcing deficiency and reducing excess, the selection of acupoints is also very important. Doctors can make use of the five *shu* acupoints, back *shu*, front *mu*, *yuan*, *luo*, eight influential points and *xi* points to bring out a better therapeutic result.

2. Dispersing Heat and Cold

The principle of dispersing heat and cold is also mentioned in *The Inner Canon of the Yellow Emperor*. For invasion of the body surface by pathogenic heat or loss of consciousness due to the blockage of the upper orifices, acupuncture with superficial insertion or prompt prick to let out a little blood with a three-edged needle can be applied to disperse heat. But when pathogenic cold invade or appear inside the body, the doctor had better insert the needle quite deep into an acupoint and keep the needle in the acupoint for a longer time, or in cooperation with moxibustion. Besides, the doctor can also use other methods such as cooling the sky for heat syndrome and burning the mountain for cold syndrome.

3. Treating the Incidental and Fundamental

Treating the incidental and fundamental is a basic principle in syndrome differentiation. The fundamental and incidental have various meanings—they can be body resistance and pathogenic factors, the cause of a disease and its manifestations, the primary onset of a disease and its complications.

Generally speaking, the fundamental is treated first because manifestations are usually complicated, and only when the cause of a disease is found can the doctor select suitable treatment and achieve good result. Take headache for example, there are many factors which may cause headache, such as exogenous pathogenic factors, blood deficiency, phlegm-dampness, blood stasis and hyperactive liver-*yang*. Doctors must conduct an overall analysis so as to find the root cause and take effective measures, including dispelling pathogenic factors from the body surface, nourishing blood, eliminating dampness and resolving phlegm, promoting blood circulation to remove blood stasis, and calming the liver to check exuberant *yang*.

However, there are times when symptoms are so acute that the patient will be in great danger if the doctor does not take any emergency measures. In emergency cases, the doctor should treat the acute symptoms first, and when these symptoms are relieved, he should treat the root cause. For example, when treating gastric disease together with hematemesis, to check bleeding is the first step. Some patients with chronic diseases contract common cold, therefore the cold should be treated first and then the chronic disease.

If both the fundamental and incidental are serious, they should be treated at the same time. Take febrile diseases caused by exogenous pathogenic factors for example, heat of excess type greatly influences the *yin* fluid, resulting in fever, restlessness, abdominal pain, constipation, thirst and dry mouth. The treatment should nourish the *yin* fluid while dispersing heat. If the exogenous pathogenic factors are further complicated by internal syndrome, and they all exhibit acute symptoms, the treatment should focus on both at the same time.

4. Treating the Same Disease with Different Methods and Different Diseases with the Same Method

This principle is based on the similarities and differences of pathogenesis. For example, for headache caused by hyperactive liver-*yang*, select acupoints on the Gallbladder Meridian of Foot-*Shaoyang* and the Liver Meridian of Foot-*Jueyin* to apply acupuncture with the reducing manipulation or prompt prick with a three-edged needle to let out a little blood. Therefore, the liver will be soothed and the function of the gallbladder be promoted. If the headache is caused by blood deficiency, select acupoints on the *Du* Meridian, the Stomach Meridian of Foot-*Yangming* and the Bladder Meridian of Foot-*Taiyang* to apply acupuncture with the reinforcing manipulation. Moxibustion can also be used to strengthen *qi* and nourish blood, regulate collaterals and relieve pain. This two different treatment shows the principle of treating the same disease with different methods. While the same treatment can be applied to different diseases if their pathogenesis is the same. For example, headache and vertigo are two different diseases, but if they are both caused by hyperactive liver-*yang*, doctors can apply the same treatment, that is to needle at the acupoints on the Liver Meridian of Foot-*Jueyin* and the Gallbladder Meridian of Foot-*Shaoyang*. Proctoptosis, hysteroptosis and gastroptosis are all caused by the sinking of the spleen-*qi*, acupuncture can be applied to acupoints like *Baihui* (DU 20), *Zhongwan* (RN 12), *Zusanli* (ST 36) and *Qihai* (RN 6) with the reinforcing manipulation to elevate the spleen-*qi*. Moxibustion should be used.

SECTION 4
ACUPOINT SELECTION IN ACUPUNCTURE AND MOXIBUSTION

1. Principles of Acupoint Selection

Based on syndrome differentiation, these principles guide doctors to select appropriate acupoints, insertion methods and moxibustion so as to achieve desired results. The commonly used principles are as follows:

1) Selecting faraway acupoints

It refers to selecting acupoints which are far from the diseased area. According to *The Inner Canon of the Yellow Emperor*, in order to treat diseases on the upper part of the body, select acupoints on the lower body and vice versa; for diseases on the head, select acupoints on the foot; and for diseases in the lumbar region, select acupoints on the back of the knee. In clinical practice, this principle is applied in two ways:

a) Selecting acupoints on the diseased meridian

For example, *Zusanli* (ST 36) of the Stomach Meridian of Foot-*Yangming* is used for gastric diseases and *Neiting* (ST 44) for toothache.

b) Selecting acupoints on other meridians

It refers to selecting acupoints on meridians relevant to the diseased meridians or *zang-fu* organs. For example, for vomiting caused by the unhealthy stomach and liver-*qi*, *Taichong* (LR 3) can be punctured together with acupoints on the Stomach Meridian of Foot-*Yangming* to soothe the liver and check the unhealthy *qi*; for tinnitus and deafness caused by the flaring-up of gallbladder-fire, *Zhongzhu* (SJ 3) on the *Sanjiao* Meridian of Hand-*Shaoyang* can be punctured; for cough caused by the invasion of the lung by exogenous pathogenic factors, *Hegu* (LI 4) on the Large Intestine Meridian of Hand-*Yangming* can be punctured.

2) Selecting nearby acupoints

Select acupoints around the diseased *zang-fu* organs, five sense organs or limbs to apply acupuncture. Tender spots can also serve as acupoints. For example, *Yintang* (EX-HN 3) is for frontal headache; *Jingming* (BL 1) for eye disorders; *Yingxiang* (LI 20) for nasal disorders; *Shenshu* (BL 23) for lumbago; *Jianyu* (LI 15) and *Tianzong* (SI 11) for shoulder pain; *Xiyan* (EX-LE 5), *Zusanli* (ST 36) and *Xuehai* (SP 10) for pain in the knee joint; *Zhongwan* (RN 12), *Weishu* (BL 21) and *Pishu* (BL 20) for stomachache; and *Danzhong* (RN 17) and *Feishu* (BL 13) for cough and asthma. Aiming at regulating the flow of *yin*, *yang*, *qi* and blood of the diseased *zang-fu* organ, this method is widely used in clinical practice.

3) Selecting acupoints according to the syndrome

This method is used to relieve certain syndrome. For instance, applying moxibustion to *Zhiyin* (BL 67) can treat abnormal fetal position; applying acupuncture at *Sifeng* (EX-UE 10) for infantile malnutrition; *Dazhui* (DU 14) for high fever; and *Shuigou* (DU 26) for coma. In addition, the eight influential points also have some special therapeutic effects.

Table 12 Acupoints for Common Symptoms

Symptoms	Acupoints
Fever	*Dazhui* (DU 14), *Quchi* (LI 11), *Hegu* (LI 4)
Coma	*Renzhong* (DU 26), *Shixuan* (EX-UE 11), *Yongquan* (KI 1)
Collapse	Applying moxibustion to *Baihui* (DU 20), *Shenque* (RN 8) and *Guanyuan* (RN 4); needling at *Zusanli* (ST 36)
Profuse sweating	*Hegu* (LI 4), *Fuliu* (KI 7)
Night sweat	*Houxi* (SI 3), *Yinxi* (HT 6)
Insomnia	*Shenmen* (HT 7), *Sanyinjiao* (SP 6), *Taixi* (KI 3)
Dream-disturbed sleep	*Xinshu* (BL 15), *Shenmen* (HT 7), *Taichong* (LR 3)
Aphonia	*Futu* (LI 18), *Hegu* (LI 4), *Jianshi* (PC 5)
Lockjaw	*Xiaguan* (ST 7), *Jiache* (ST 6), *Hegu* (LI 4)
Stiff tongue	*Yamen* (DU 15), *Lianquan* (RN 23), *Hegu* (LI 4)
Inflammation of the throat	*Shaoshang* (LU 11), *Hegu* (LI 4)
Salivation	*Renzhong* (DU 26), *Jiache* (ST 6), *Hegu* (LI 4)
Palpitation	*Neiguan* (PC 6), *Ximen* (PC 4)
Chest pain	*Danzhong* (RN 17), *Neiguan* (PC 6)
Cough	*Tiantu* (RN 22), *Lieque* (LU 7)
Dysphagia	*Tiantu* (RN 22), *Neiguan* (PC 6)
Suffocating feeling in the chest	*Zhongwan* (RN 12), *Neiguan* (PC 6)
Nausea and vomiting	*Neiguan* (PC 6), *Zusanli* (ST 36)
Vomiting	*Geshu* (BL 17), *Neiguan* (PC 6), *Laogong* (PC 8)
Abdominal distention	*Tianshu* (ST 25), *Qihai* (RN 6), *Neiguan* (PC 6), *Zusanli* (ST 36)
Hypochondriac pain	*Zhigou* (SJ 6), *Yanglingquan* (GB 34)
Dyspepsia	*Zusanli* (ST 36), *Gongsun* (SP 4)
Anuresis	*Sanyinjiao* (SP 6), *Yinlingquan* (SP 9)
Emission and impotence	*Sanyinjiao* (SP 6), *Guanyuan* (RN 4)
Prospermia	*Sanyinjiao* (SP 6), *Guanyuan* (RN 4)
Incontinence of urine	*Qugu* (RN 2), *Sanyinjiao* (SP 6)
Constipation	*Tianshu* (ST 25), *Zhigou* (SJ 6)
Prolapse of the rectum	*Changqiang* (DU 1), *Chengshan* (BL 57)
Spasm	*Chengshan* (BL 57), *Yanglingquan* (GB 34)
Skin pruritus	*Quchi* (LI 11), *Xuehai* (SP 10), *Sanyinjiao* (SP 6)
Asthenia	*Guanyuan* (RN 4), *Zusanli* (ST 36)

2. The Combination of Acupoints

This is in fact the prescription for acupuncture. According to the principle of acupoint selection and the state of illness, doctors choose more than two points to apply acupuncture. The following are some commonly used acupoint combination:

1) Combination of back *shu* and front *mu* points

Each *zang* or *fu* organ has its own back *shu* and front *mu* points. Located on the back, back *shu* points are where the *qi* of the internal organs flows to. The front *mu* points are situated on the chest and abdomen where the *qi* of the corresponding organs concentrates. Since the back *shu* points are of *yang* nature and the front *mu* points of *yin* nature, the combination of this two improves the balance between *yin* and *yang*, and helps cure diseases of the *zang-fu* organs. For example, *Qimen* (LR 14) and *Ganshu* (BL 18) are used together for liver diseases; *Zhongwan* (RN 12) and *Weishu* (BL 21) for gastric disorders. This kind of acupoint combination can be further extended to acupoints on the front and back, such as *Tiantu* (RN 22) and *Danzhong* (RN 17) on the chest with *Ganshu* (BL 18) and *Danshu* (BL 19) on the back to treat asthma.

2) Combination of acupoints on the left and right sides

The distribution of meridians is symmetrical, therefore the same acupoints on both sides are used to treat disorders of the internal organs and regulate the *qi* inside meridians. For instance, *Zusanli* (ST 36) on both sides can be used to treat gastric diseases. In addition, since each meridian intersects with itself, doctors can puncture the acupoints on the right side for diseases on the left, and vice versa. For instance, *Hegu* (LI 4) on the right side can be needled to treat facial paralysis on the left side, and vice versa.

3) Combination of acupoints on the upper and lower body parts

The upper refers to the upper limbs and the part above the lumbus, while the lower refers to the lower limbs and the part below the lumbus. This kind of acupoint combination is widely used in clinical practice. For instance, *Shenmen* (HT 7) on the upper limbs is used together with *Sanyinjiao* (SP 6) on the lower limbs for palpitation and insomnia; *Hegu* (LI 4) on the upper limbs together with *Neiting* (ST 44) on the lower limbs for toothache and sore throat. Besides, the eight confluent points can also be used together, such as *Neiguan* (PC 6) on the upper limbs can be used together with *Gongsun* (SP 4) on the lower limbs for disorders of the stomach, heart and chest.

4) Combination of acupoints near or away from the affected area

This combination may be more effective for certain diseases. For example, *Zhongwan* (RN 12) and *Weishu* (BL 21) near the affected part are used together with *Neiguan* (PC 6), *Zusanli* (ST 36) and *Gongsun* (SP 4) far away from it to cure gastric diseases.

3. Specific Points and Their Application

1) The five *shu* points

On the twelve regular meridians below the elbow and knee, the five *shu* points include *jiing*, *ying*, *shu*, *jing* and *he* points. Since they are where the *qi* and blood of the meridians enter and exit, they can help treat disorders of the *zang-fu* organs and meridians.

According to *The Inner Canon of the Yellow Emperor*, *jiing* points are selected for disorders of the five *zang* organs; *ying* points for unhealthy complexion; *shu* points for intermittent diseases; *jing* points for disorders of the voice; and *he* points for disorders of the stomach caused by improper diet. *The Classic of Questions* mentioned that *jiing* points are indicated for fullness in the chest; *ying* points for febrile diseases; *shu* points for lassitude and painful joints; *jing* points for dyspneic cough, fever and chills; and *he* points for unhealthy *qi*. In addition, the five *shu* points can also be used in the light of the five *zang* organs and the Five Elements. For example, *Xingjian* (LR 2), a *ying* (fire) point, can be punctured with the reducing manipulation to treat excess syndrome of the liver; *Ququan* (LR 8), a *he* (water) point, can be punctured with the reinforcing manipulation to treat deficiency syndrome of the liver. The above syndrome can also be relieved by other means: *Shaofu* (HT 8), a *ying* point of the Heart Meridian of Hand-*Shaoyin*, can be punctured with the reducing manipulation to treat excess syndrome of the liver; *Yingu* (KI 10), a *he* point of the Kidney Meridian of Foot-*Shaoyin*, can be punctured with the reinforcing manipulation to treat deficiency syndrome of the liver.

Table 13 The Five Shu Points of the *Yin* Meridians

Yin Meridians	Five *Shu* Points				
	Jiing (wood)	*Ying* (fire)	*Shu* (earth)	*Jing* (metal)	*He* (water)
Lung Meridian of Hand-*Taiyin*	*Shaoshang* (LU 11)	*Yuji* (LU 10)	*Taiyuan* (LU 9)	*Jingqu* (LU 8)	*Chize* (LU 5)
Pericardium Meridian of Hand-*Jueyin*	*Zhongchong* (PC 9)	*Laogong* (PC 8)	*Daling* (PC 7)	*Jianshi* (PC 5)	*Quze* (PC 3)
Heart Meridian of Hand-*Shaoyin*	*Shaochong* (HT 9)	*Shaofu* (HT 8)	*Shenmen* (HT 7)	*Lingdao* (HT 4)	*Shaohai* (HT 3)
Spleen Meridian of Foot-*Taiyin*	*Yinbai* (SP 1)	*Dadu* (SP 2)	*Taibai* (SP 3)	*Shangqiu* (SP 5)	*Yinlingquan* (SP 9)
Liver Meridian of Foot-*Jueyin*	*Dadun* (LR 1)	*Xingjian* (LR 2)	*Taichong* (LR 3)	*Zhongfeng* (LR 4)	*Ququan* (LR 8)
Kidney Meridian of Foot-*Shaoyin*	*Yongquan* (KI 1)	*Rangu* (KI 2)	*Taixi* (KI 3)	*Fuliu* (KI 7)	*Yingu* (KI 10)

Table 14 The Five *Shu* Points of the *Yang* Meridians

Yang Meridians	Five *Shu* Points				
	Jiing (metal)	*Ying* (water)	*Shu* (wood)	*Jing* (fire)	*He* (earth)
Large Intestine Meridian of Hand-*Yangming*	*Shangyang* (LI 1)	*Erjian* (LI 2)	*Sanjian* (LI 3)	*Yangxi* (LI 5)	*Quchi* (LI 11)
Sanjiao Meridian of Hand-*Shaoyang*	*Guanchong* (SJ 1)	*Yemen* (SJ 2)	*Zhongzhu* (SJ 3)	*Zhigou* (SJ 6)	*Tianjing* (SJ 10)
Small Intestine Meridian of Hand-*Taiyang*	*Shaoze* (SI 1)	*Qiangu* (SI 2)	*Houxi* (SI 3)	*Yanggu* (SI 5)	*Xiaohai* (SI 8)
Stomach Meridian of Foot-*Yangming*	*Lidui* (ST 45)	*Neiting* (ST 44)	*Xiangu* (ST 43)	*Jiexi* (ST 41)	*Zusanli* (ST 36)
Gallbladder Meridian of Foot-*Shaoyang*	*Qiaoyin* (GB 44)	*Xiaxi* (GB 43)	*Zulinqi* (GB 41)	*Yangfu* (GB 38)	*Yanglingquan* (GB 34)
Bladder Meridian of Foot-*Taiyang*	*Zhiyin* (BL 67)	*Tonggu* (BL 66)	*Shugu* (BL 65)	*Kunlun* (BL 60)	*Weizhong* (BL 40)

2) The back *shu* and front *mu* points

The back *shu* points are where the *qi* of the internal organs flows to. They spread on both sides of the spinal column at the back, and most of them are located near the corresponding *zang* or *fu* organs. If an internal organ is diseased, its corresponding back *shu* point will show abnormal reactions such as pain on pressure. It is for this reason that the back *shu* points are used to treat disorders of the internal organs.

The front *mu* points are located on the chest and abdomen, where the *qi* of the respective internal organs is concentrated. If an internal organ is diseased, pathological reactions such as pain on pressure will be observed at the corresponding point. Therefore, they can be used to regulate the function of *zang-fu* organs.

Table 15 Back *Shu* and Front *Mu* Points

Zang and *Fu* Organs	Back *Shu* Points		Front *Mu* Points	
	Name	Meridian	Name	Meridian
Lung	*Feishu* (BL 13)	Bladder Meridian of Foot-*Taiyang*	*Zhongfu* (LU 1)	Lung Meridian of Hand-*Taiyin*
Pericardium	*Jueyinshu* (BL 14)	Bladder Meridian of Foot-*Taiyang*	*Danzhong* (RN 17)	*Ren* Meridian
Heart	*Xinshu* (BL 15)	Bladder Meridian of Foot-*Taiyang*	*Juque* (RN 14)	*Ren* Meridian
Liver	*Ganshu* (BL 18)	Bladder Meridian of Foot-*Taiyang*	*Qimen* (LR 14)	Liver Meridian of Foot-*Jueyin*
Spleen	*Pishu* (BL 20)	Bladder Meridian of Foot-*Taiyang*	*Zhangmen* (LR 13)	Liver Meridian of Foot-*Jueyin*
Kidney	*Shenshu* (BL 23)	Bladder Meridian of Foot-*Taiyang*	*Jingmen* (GB 25)	Gallbladder Meridian of Foot-*Shaoyang*
Gallbladder	*Danshu* (BL 19)	Bladder Meridian of Foot-*Taiyang*	*Riyue* (GB 24)	Gallbladder Meridian of Foot-*Shaoyang*
Stomach	*Weishu* (BL 21)	Bladder Meridian of Foot-*Taiyang*	*Zhongwan* (RN 12)	*Ren* Meridian
Sanjiao	*Sanjiaoshu* (BL 22)	Bladder Meridian of Foot-*Taiyang*	*Shimen* (RN 5)	*Ren* Meridian
Large intestine	*Dachangshu* (BL 25)	Bladder Meridian of Foot-*Taiyang*	*Tianshu* (ST 25)	Stomach Meridian of Foot-*Yangming*
Small intestine	*Xiaochangshu* (BL 27)	Bladder Meridian of Foot-*Taiyang*	*Guanyuan* (RN 4)	*Ren* Meridian
Bladder	*Pangguangshu* (BL 28)	Bladder Meridian of Foot-*Taiyang*	*Zhongji* (RN 3)	*Ren* Meridian

The back *shu* points are often used to treat disorders of the five *zang* organs, while the front *mu* points are chosen to treat diseases in the six *fu* organs. For instance, *Feishu* (BL 13) on the back is effective for disorders of the Lung Meridian of Hand-*Taiyin* such as cough, chest pain, dyspnea and expectoration. *Zhongwan* (RN 12), a front *mu* point on the abdomen, is used to treat disorders of the Stomach Meridian of Foot-*Yangming* such as stomachache, vomiting and belching. The back *shu* and front *mu* points can be used separately or in combination. Moreover, the back *shu* points corresponding to the five *zang* organs can also help treat diseases in the limbs and five sense organs. Since the liver controls the tendons and has its specific body opening in the eyes, *Ganshu* (BL 18) is effective for disorders of the eyes, tendons and vessels. Likewise, since the kidney is in charge of the bone and has a specific body opening in the ear, *Shenshu* (BL 23) can be used to treat disorders of the ear and bone.

3) The *yuan* points

The *yuan* points, closely related with *sanjiao* (triple energizer), are where the condition of the *qi* is reflected. Needling at *yuan* points can help promote the flow of *qi* in *sanjiao* and regulate the function of the internal organs. Among the six *yang* meridians, the *yuan* points are located behind the *shu* points;

while among the six yin meridians, the *shu* points serve as the *yuan* points.

Table 16 Twelve *Yuan* Points

Meridians	*Yuan* points	Meridians	*Yuan* points
Lung Meridian	*Taiyuan* (LU 9)	Pericardium Meridian	*Daling* (PC 7)
Heart Meridian	*Shenmen* (HT 7)	Liver Meridian	*Taichong* (LR 3)
Spleen Meridian	*Taibai* (SP 3)	Kidney Meridian	*Taixi* (KI 3)
Bladder Meridian	*Shugu* (BL 65)	Stomach Meridian	*Chongyang* (ST 42)
Gallbladder Meridian	*Qiuxu* (GB 40)	Small Intestine Meridian	*Wangu* (SI 4)
Sanjiao Meridian	*Yangchi* (SJ 4)	Large Intestine Meridian	*Hegu* (LI 4)

4) The *luo* points

Twelve regular meridians as well as the *Ren* and *Du* meridians each has a *luo* point, and the Spleen Meridian has two *luo* points, hence fifteen in all. They connect the respective yin and yang meridians interior-exteriorly and are therefore used to treat diseases of corresponding internal organs. For instance, *Gongsun* (SP 4), a *luo* point of the Spleen Meridian of Foot-*Taiyin*, is effective for disorders along the Spleen Meridian and the Stomach Meridian of Foot-*Yangming*. And *Changqiang* (DU 1), *Jiuwei* (RN 15) and *Dabao* (SP 21) are used to treat disorders in certain areas or the *zang-fu* organs.

Table 17 Distribution and Indications of the Fifteen *Luo* Points

Meridians	*Luo* Points	Location	Neighbouring Meridians	Indications - Excess Syndrome	Indications - Deficiency Syndrome
Branch of Hand-*Taiyin*	*Lieque* (LU 7)	1.5 *cun* above the crease of the wrist	Connecting with the *Yangming* Meridian	Feverish sensation in the hand	Dribbling urination
Branch of Hand-*Shaoyin*	*Tongli* (HT 5)	1 *cun* proximal to the crease of the wrist	Connecting with the *Taiyang* Meridian	Epigastric flatulence	Aphasia
Branch of Hand-*Jueyin*	*Neiguan* (PC 6)	2 *cun* above the crease of the wrist	Connecting with the *Shaoyang* Meridian	Cardiac pain	Rigidity of the head (fidgets)
Branch of Hand-*Taiyang*	*Zhizheng* (SI 7)	5 *cun* proximal to the dorsal crease of the wrist	Entering the *Shaoyin* Meridian	Motor impairment of the joints and limbs	Scabies
Branch of Hand-*Yangming*	*Pianli* (LI 6)	3 *cun* above the crease of the wrist	Connecting with the *Taiyin* Meridian	Dental caries, deafness	Cold feeling in the teeth
Branch of Hand-*Shaoyang*	*Waiguan* (SJ 5)	2 *cun* proximal to the dorsal crease of the wrist	Connecting with the *Jueyin* Meridian	Elbow problems	Motor impairment of the arms and limbs
Branch of Foot-*Taiyang*	*Feiyang* (BL 58)	7 *cun* proximal to the malleolus	Connecting with the *Shaoyin* Meridian	Stuffy nose, pain in the back of the head	Epistaxis
Branch of Foot-*Shaoyang*	*Guangming* (GB 37)	5 *cun* above the tip of the external malleolus	Connecting with the *Jueyin* Meridian	Syncope	Flaccidity, motor impairment of the legs
Branch of Foot-*Yangming*	*Fenglong* (ST 40)	8 *cun* above the tip of the external malleolus	Entering the *Taiyin* Meridian	Inflammation of the throat and aphonia due to the reversed flow of *qi*; Manic-depressive psychosis	Motor impairment of the legs
Branch of Foot-*Taiyin*	*Gongsun* (SP 4)	1 *cun* posterior to the metatarsophalangeal joint	Connecting with the *Yangming* Meridian	Cholera due to the attack by pathogenic factors; Acute intestinal pain	Tympany

Branch of Foot-Shaoyin	Dazhong (KI 4)	Posterior and inferior to the medial malleolus, in the depression medial to the attachment of the Achilles tendon	Connecting with the Taiyang Meridian	Irritability due to the reversed flow of qi Retention of urine	Lumbago
Branch of Foot-Jueyin	Ligou (LR 5)	5 cun above the tip of the medial malleolus	Connecting with the Shaoyang Meridian	Swollen testis and hernia due to the reversed flow of qi Prolapse of uterus	Severe itching
Branch of the Ren Meridian	Jiuwei (RN 15)	Below the xiphosternal synchondrosis	Spreading over the abdomen	Pain in the skin of the abdomen	Severe itching
Branch of the Du Meridian	Changqiang (DU 1)	Below the tip of the coccyx, at the midpoint of the line connecting the tip of the coccyx and anus	Spreading over the head	Rigidity of the spinal column	Heavy sensation of the head
The main luo point of the spleen	Dabao (SP 21)	3 cun below the axilla	Spreading over the chest and hypochondrium	Overall pain	Flaccidity of all joints

5) The xi points

Xi points are where the qi of the meridian accumulates deep. Each of the twelve regular meridians, together with the Yinwei, Yangwei, Yinqiao and Yangqiao, has a xi point, hence sixteen in all. Xi points are effective for critical and stubborn diseases in the relevant zang or fu organs. For example, Kongzui (LU 6) is effective for hemoptysis caused by lung diseases; Ximen (PC 4) can treat chest pain. In addition, xi points are often used together with the eight influential points, for instance, Kongzui, a xi point on the Lung Meridian of Hand-Taiyin, is used together with Danzhong (RN 17) for dyspnea; and Liangqiu (ST 34), a xi point on the Stomach Meridian of Foot-Yangming, is used together with Zhongwan (RN 12) for acute stomachache.

Table 18   The Sixteen Xi (Cleft) Points

Meridians of Hand	Lung Meridian of Hand-Taiyin—Kongzui (LU 6)
	Heart Meridian of Hand-Shaoyin—Yinxi (HT 6)
	Pericardium Meridian of Hand-Jueyin—Ximen (PC 4)
	Large Intestine Meridian of Hand-Yangming—Wenliu (LI 7)
	Small Intestine Meridian of Hand-Taiyang—Yanglao (SI 6)
	Sanjiao Meridian of Hand-Shaoyang—Huizong (SJ 7)
Meridians of Foot	Spleen Meridian of Foot-Taiyin—Diji (SP 8)
	Kidney Meridian of Foot-Shaoyin—Shuiquan (KI 5)
	Liver Meridian of Foot-Jueyin—Zhongdu (LR 6)
	Stomach Meridian of Foot-Yangming—Liangqiu (ST 34)
	Bladder Meridian of Foot-Taiyang—Jinmen (BL 63)
	Gallbladder Meridian of Foot-Shaoyang—Waiqiu (GB 36)
Eight Extra Meridians	Yangwei Meridian—Yangjiao (GB 35)
	Yinwei Meridian—Zhubin (KI 9)
	Yangqiao Meridian—Fuyang (BL 59)
	Yinqiao Meridian—Jiaoxin (KI 8)

6) The eight influential points

This eight important points are closely related with the *zang*, *fu*, *qi*, blood, tendons, vessels, bones and marrows respectively. They are used to treat disorders in the corresponding area, such as *Zhongwan* (RN 12) for disorders of *fu* organs, and *Danzhong* (RN 17) for *qi* disorders.

Table 19 The Eight Influential Points

Eight Influential Points	
	Fu organs—*Zhongwan* (RN 12)
	Zang organs—*Zhangmen* (LR 13)
	Qi—*Danzhong* (RN 17)
	Blood—*Geshu* (BL 17)
	Tendon—*Yanglingquan* (GB 34)
	Pulse and vessels—*Taiyuan* (LU 9)
	Bone—*Dazhu* (BL 11)
	Marrow—*Xuanzhong* (GB 39)

7) The eight confluent points

Located in the wrist and ankle regions, these points are where the twelve regular meridians intersect with the eight extra meridians. They can be used in pairs to treat disorders of the relevant meridians and extra meridians. For example, *Neiguan* (PC 6) links with the *Yinwei* Meridian, and *Gongsun* (SP 4) with the *Chong* Meridian, and the *Yinwei* and *Chong* meridians cross each other in the chest, heart and stomach. Therefore, *Neiguan* and *Gongsun* are used in combination to treat disorders of the heart, chest and stomach, such as distention in the chest and abdomen, epigastric pain and poor appetite. *Lieque* (LU 7) links with the *Ren* Meridian, and *Zhaohai* (KI 6) with the *Yinqiao* Meridian, and the *Ren* and *Yinqiao* meridians cross each other in the respiratory system, throat and diaphragm. Therefore, *Lieque* and *Zhaohai* are used together to treat sore throat, chest pain and cough.

Table 20 The Eight Confluent Points and Their Indications

Eight Extra Meridians	Intersected Meridians	Name	Indications
Chong Meridian	Spleen Meridian of Foot-*Taiyin*	*Gongsun* (SP 4)	Disorders in the chest, heart and stomach
Yinwei Meridian	Pericardium Meridian of Hand-*Jueyin*	*Neiguan* (PC 6)	
Ren Meridian	Lung Meridian of Hand-*Taiyin*	*Lieque* (LU 7)	Disorders in the respiratory system and throat
Yinqiao Meridian	Kidney Meridian of Foot-*Shaoyin*	*Zhaohai* (KI 6)	Disorders in the chest and diaphragm
Du Meridian	Small Intestine Meridian of Hand-*Taiyang*	*Houxi* (SI 3)	Disorders in the inner canthus of the eyes and the neck
Yangqiao Meridian	Bladder Meridian of Foot-*Taiyang*	*Shenmai* (BL 62)	Disorders in the nape, ear and shoulder
Dai Meridian	Gallbladder Meridian of Foot-*Shaoyang*	*Zulinqi* (GB 41)	Disorders in the outer canthus of the eyes and the earback
Yangwei Meridian	*Sanjiao* Meridian of Hand-*Shaoyang*	*Waiguan* (SJ 5)	Disorders in the shoulder, neck and cheek

8) The lower confluent points

Located on the three *yang* meridians of the foot, these six points correspond to the six *fu* organs and are therefore used to treat disorders of the *fu* organs. For instance, *Shangjuxu* (ST 37), the lower confluent point of the large intestine, is effective for diseases in the large intestine; and *Zusanli* (ST 36), the lower confluent point of the stomach, can be used to treat diseases of the stomach.

Table 21 The Lower Confluent Points

Six *Fu* Organs	Lower Confluent Points
Large Intestine	*Shangjuxu* (ST 37)
Small Intestine	*Xiajuxu* (ST 39)
Sanjiao	*Weiyang* (BL 39)
Stomach	*Zusanli* (ST 36)
Gallbladder	*Yanglingquan* (GB 34)
Bladder	*Weizhong* (BL 40)

Chapter Two
TREATMENT OF VARIOUS KINDS OF DISEASES

Section 1
INTERNAL DISEASES

1. The common cold

The common cold is usually caused by exogenous pathogenic factors. It may occur in four seasons, especially in spring and winter when the weather changes suddenly.

1) Etiology and pathogenesis

The common cold is usually caused by weak constitution, fatigue, protracted illness, and the attack of pathogenic factors due to weather changes.

2) Syndrome differentiation

a) Wind-cold syndrome: Chilliness, fever, headache, pain in the limbs, nasal stuffiness, running nose, anhidrosis, thin and white tongue coating, superficial and tense pulse.

b) Wind-heat syndrome: Fever, chilliness, cough with profuse expectoration, sore throat, thirst, sweating, dry nose, thin and yellowish tongue coating, superficial and rapid pulse.

3) Treatment

a) Wind-cold syndrome

Principles: To dispel wind and cold and ventilate the lung.

Methods: Select acupoints on the Lung Meridian of Hand-*Taiyin*, the Large Intestine of Hand-*Yangming* and the Bladder Meridian of Foot-*Taiyang* to apply acupuncture, using the reducing manipulation. Uniform reduction and reinforcement can be applied to patients with weak constitution; moxibustion can also be used if necessary.

Notes: Apply shallow insertion at acupoint *Lieque* (LU 7), the *luo* point of the Lung Meridian of Hand-*Taiyin*, so as to ventilate the lung, relieve cough and alleviate headache and neck pain. Needling at *Fengmen* (BL 12) can help regulate the flow of *qi* in *Taiyang* meridians. *Fengmen* and *Fengchi* (GB 20) together can dispel wind and cold. *Hegu* (LI 4), the *yuan* point of the Large Intestine Meridian of Hand-*Yangming*, can help promote the flow of *qi* and ventilate the lung since the *Yangming* and *Taiyin* meridians are interrelated.

b) Wind-heat syndrome

Principles: To dispel wind and heat, and send the unhealthy *qi* downward.

Methods: Select acupoints on the Lung Meridian of Hand-*Taiyin*, the Large Intestine Meridian of Hand-*Yangming* and the *Sanjiao* Meridian of Hand-*Shaoyang* to apply acupuncture, using shallow insertion and the reducing manipulation.

Acupoints: *Dazhui* (DU 14), *Quchi* (LI 11), *Hegu* (LI 4), *Yuji* (LU 10) and *Waiguan* (SJ 5).

Notes: *Dazhui* helps eliminate *yang* pathogenic factors and disperse heat; *Yuji*, the *ying* point of the Lung Meridian of Hand-*Taiyin*, disperses the lung fire and relieves sore throat; *Waiguan* dispels superficial pathogenic factors and heat; *Hegu* and *Quchi*, the *yuan* and *he* points of the Large Intestine Meridian of Hand-*Yangming* disperse heat and ventilate the lung.

Modified combination: For the common cold caused by wind-cold or wind-heat, *Taiyang* (EX-HN 5) and *Yintang* (EX-HN 3) can be used to treat headache; *Yingxiang* (LI 20) can be used to treat nasal stuffiness; *Tiantu* (RN 22) and *Taiyuan* (LU 9) for cough; *Tianzhu* (BL 10) and *Shaoshang* (LU 11) for sore throat; *Fenglong* (ST 40) and *Zusanli* (ST 36) for abundant expectoration; *Yinlingquan* (SP 9) and *Zusanli* (ST 36) for dampness.

4) Reference materials

a) Applying acupuncture to 373 patients who suffer from the common cold (See the *Journal of Acupuncture*, No.1 issue of 1965)

Acupoints: *Dazhui* (DU 14), *Hegu* (LI 4) and *Zusanli* (ST 36).

Methods: After a needling sensation was gained, the acupoints were punctured with strong stimulation. It was not necessary to retain the needle in the acupoints for a long time.

Effects: Fever subsided within 24 hours in 198 cases, 53.08% of the total; fever subsided within 48 hours in 124 cases, 33.24% of the total; 51 patients felt the fever had subsided within 24 hours of treatment and resumed their daily work, 13.67% of the total.

b) Applying acupuncture to 818 people to prevent influenza (See the *Shaanxi Medical Journal*, No.4 issue of 1959)

People receiving the acupuncture treatment all lived in an epidemic area of influenza and were in good health. The treatment was carried out like this: punctured *Zusanli* (ST 36) on one side, using the reinforcing manipulation, and withdrew the needle when a needling sensation was felt on the instep. After the treatment, they all remained in good health. This proves that acupuncture can help prevent influenza.

2. Cough

Cough is one of the main syndrome of lung diseases. There are two causes leading to cough — exogenous pathogenic factors and dysfunction of internal organs. Cough due to exogenous pathogenic factors may turn into a chronic disease if the treatment is not appropriate. Chronic cough will be further complicated with dyspnea if it lasts long or there is a deficiency of the *zang-qi* with old and weak patients.

1) Etiology and pathogenesis

a) Cough due to exogenous pathogenic factors: This disease usually occurs when the weather changes suddenly and the body resistance is weak. As a result, pathogenic wind-cold and wind-heat enter the body through the mouth, nose and skin and cause the stagnation of lung *qi*.

b) Cough due to dysfunction of internal organs: This disease often occurs when the *qi* and *yin* of the lung are deficient, and the lung fails to control *qi* and cleanse the inspired air. It can also be caused by disorders of other *zang-fu* organs. For example, spleen deficiency produces dampness which accumulates into phlegm, thus blocking the lung; the liver fails to regulate the flow of *qi* due to depressed emotions and this stagnation of liver *qi* damages the lung, resulting in cough.

2) Syndrome differentiation

a) Cough due to exogenous pathogenic factors

Wind-cold syndrome: Cough with thin and white expectoration, sore throat accompanied by chilliness, fever, headache, general aching, anhidrosis, nasal stuffiness and with clear discharge, white tongue coating, superficial and tense pulse.

Wind-heat syndrome: Severe cough with difficulty in expectoration, thick and yellow sputum accompanied by sore throat and dry mouth, fever, aversion to wind, sweating, thirst, thin and yellow tongue coating, superficial and rapid pulse.

b) Cough due to dysfunction of internal organs

Phlegm-dampness syndrome: Cough which is more severe in the morning, thick expectoration, chest upset, poor appetite, lassitude, white and sticky tongue coating, soft or smooth pulse.

Liver-fire syndrome: Cough with scanty but thick expectoration, chest pain, short breath, bitter taste, dry throat, flushed face, irritability, insomnia, red rim of the tongue, thin and yellow tongue coating, taut and rapid pulse.

3) Treatment

a) Wind-cold syndrome

Principles: To dispel wind and cold, ventilate the lung and relieve cough.

Methods: Select acupoints on the Lung Meridian of Hand-*Taiyin* and the Large Intestine Meridian of Hand-*Yangming* to apply acupuncture, using the reducing manipulation. Moxibustion can also be used if necessary.

Acupoints: *Lieque* (LU 7), *Feishu* (BL 13), *Hegu* (LI 4) and *Fengmen* (BL 12).

Notes: *Lieque*, the *luo* point of the Lung Meridian of Hand-*Taiyin*, together with *Feishu* help ventilate the lung; *Hegu*, the *yuan* point of the Large Intestine Meridian of Hand-*Yangming* which is closely related with the Lung Meridian of Hand-*Taiyin*, dispels wind and cold; *Hegu* and *Fengmen*, an acupoint on the Bladder Meridian of Foot-*Taiyang*, regulate the flow of *qi* of the *Taiyang* Meridian and dispel the exogenous pathogenic factors.

b) Wind-heat syndrome

Principles: To dispel wind and the lung heat, and resolve phlegm.

Methods: Select acupoints on the Lung Meridian of Hand-*Taiyin*, the Large Intestine Meridian of Hand-*Yangming* and the *Du* Meridian to apply acupuncture, using the reducing manipulation.

Acupoints: *Chize* (LU 5), *Feishu* (BL 13), *Quchi* (LI 11) and *Dazhui* (DU 14).

Notes: *Feishu* and *Chize*, the *he* point of the Lung Meridian of Hand-*Taiyin*, clear the lung and resolve phlegm; *Quchi* dispels wind and heat; *Quchi* and *Dazhui* regulate the flow of *yang-qi* and disperse the heat from the exterior.

c) Phlegm-dampness syndrome

Principles: To invigorate the spleen, resolve dampness, eliminate phlegm and relieve cough.

Methods: Select acupoints on the Lung Meridian of Hand-*Taiyin*, the Spleen Meridian of Foot-*Taiyin* and the Stomach Meridian of Foot-*Yangming* to apply acupuncture, using the reinforcing manipulation. Moxibustion can also be used.

Acupoints: *Feishu* (BL 13), *Pishu* (BL 20), *Taibai* (SP 3), *Fenglong* (ST 40) and *Zhangmen* (LR 13).

Notes: *Pishu* and *Zhangmen* invigorate the spleen; *Pishu* and *Taibai* resolve dampness and phlegm; *Fenglong* resolves phlegm; *Feishu* eliminates phlegm and relieves cough. If these acupoints are used together, they help invigorate the spleen, resolve dampness, eliminate phlegm and stop cough.

d) Liver-fire syndrome

Principles: To calm the liver, suppress fire, clear the lung and resolve phlegm.

Methods: Select acupoints on the Lung Meridian of Hand-*Taiyin* and the Liver Meridian of Foot-*Jueyin* to apply acupuncture, using the reducing manipulation.

Acupoints: *Feishu* (BL 13), *Ganshu* (BL 18), *Taichong* (LR 3) and *Chize* (LU 5).

Notes: *Feishu* regulates lung *qi*; *Feishu* and *Chize*, the *he* point of the Lung Meridian of Hand-*Taiyin*, clear the lung and resolve phlegm; *Ganshu* calms the liver; *Ganshu* and *Taichong* calm the liver and suppress fire. If these four acupoints are used together, they can help disperse heat, resolve phlegm and relieve cough.

4) Other remedies

Ear acupuncture

Acupoints: Auricular points for the lung, trachea, liver, and the ear-*Shenmen* point.

Methods: Puncture at both ears with moderate stimulation and keep the needle in the points for 10-20 minutes. The treatment should be carried out once a day, and a whole course includes ten treatment. Needle embedment method can be applied to patients suffer from chronic cough.

5) Reference materials

a) Applying acupoint injection to 228 patients with chronic bronchitis

According to *A Selection of Clinical Experiences in Acupuncture and Moxibustion*, the treatment was carried out like this: inject 100 mg vitamin B_1 solution into *Feishu* (BL 13), *Zhongfu* (LU 1) and two spots showing positive reactions once a day. One course included five treatment. This treatment proved effective in 94.7% cases, with 80 patients recovering from the disease, another 80 feeling much better, 56 improving a little bit, and 12 ineffective.

b) Applying herbal medicine to acupoints to treat 380 cases with chronic bronchitis

According to *A Selection of Clinical Experiences in Acupuncture and Moxibustion*, patients were divided into two groups, with one group (160 patients) receiving point application treatment in July and August for one to three years, and another group (220 patients) receiving point application together with cupping treatment in months except July and August. Acupoints for Group A are *Feishu* (BL 13), *Xinshu* (BL 15) and *Geshu* (BL 17); and *Dazhui* (DU 14), *Gaohuang* (BL 43), *Danzhong* (RN 17), *Mingmen* (DU 4) and *Lingtai* (DU 10) for Group B. The herbal medicines were applied once every five days, and a whole course included three treatment. Acupoints for Group A were punctured during the first and third treatment, and those for Group B were punctured during the second. The medicines were removed 24 or 48 hours later. Cold, raw and pungent food and cold bath were contraindicated during the treatment.

The herbal medicines for acupoint application were Semen Sinapis Albae, Radix Kansui, Rhizoma Corydalis, Herba Asari, Lignum Aquilariae Resinatum, Rhizoma Zingiberis, Flos Daturae, Phenergan and camphora.

The point application treatment proved very effective in 25 cases, 10% of the total; the condition of illness improved in 97 cases, 66.2% of the total; ineffective in 38 cases, 23.7% of the total. The point application together with cupping treatment proved very effective in 56 cases, 25.4% of the total; the condition of illness improved in 135 cases, 61.4% of the total; and ineffective in 29 cases, 13.2% of the total.

3. Asthma

Asthma is a recurrent illness characterized by paroxysmal dyspnea and wheezing.

1) Etiology and pathogenesis

a) Weak spleen and stomach coupled with improper diet (overeating greasy and sweet food or sea food) lead to the dysfunction of the spleen and stomach, thus producing phlegm. The phlegm moves upward, blocking the airway and causes asthma.

b) Exposure to seasonal pathogenic factors, pollen, smoke and dust may impair the lung's function, resulting in the accumulation of phlegm which blocks the air passage and leads to asthma.

c) Phlegm caused by the deficiency of the spleen and kidney, fatigue and emotional upset can also cause asthma.

2) Syndrome differentiation

a) Excess syndrome: Chilliness, headache, anhidrosis, thirstlessness, cough with thin or white and thick sputum, fullness in the chest, thin and white tongue coating, superficial and tense pulse in wind-cold cases; short breath, choking cough, thick and yellow sputum, restlessness, fever, thirst, sweating, constipation, red tongue with yellow and sticky coating, smooth and rapid pulse in phlegm-heat syndrome.

b) Deficiency syndrome: Prolonged illness leads the deficiency of lung *qi*. If induced by weather changes, asthma is likely to occur. The manifestations are nasal clear discharge, chilliness, spontaneous perspiration, short breath, feeble voice, pale tongue, superficial and feeble pulse; asthma due to spleen deficiency shows the following syndrome, poor appetite, gastric fullness, lassitude, profuse sputum and loose stool; asthma due to kidney deficiency shows the following syndrome, lumbago, weak lower limbs, dizziness, blurred vision, tinnitus, dyspnea, sweat, cold limbs, deep and thready pulse.

3) Treatment

a) Excess syndrome

Principles: To ventilate the lung and resolve phlegm, relieve cough and asthma.

Methods: Select acupoints on the Lung Meridian of Hand-*Taiyin*, the Large Intestine Meridian of Hand-*Yangming* and the Bladder Meridian of Foot-*Taiyang* to apply acupuncture, using the reducing manipulation. If necessary, moxibustion and cupping therapy can be applied to acupoints on the back.

Acupoints: *Feishu* (BL 13), *Chize* (LU 5) and *Dingchuan* (EX B 1). *Fengmen* (BL 12) can be used in combination for wind-cold syndrome; *Fenglong* (ST 40) and *Hegu* (LI 4) for phlegm-dampness; *Tiantu* (RN 22) and *Neiguan* (PC 6) for asthma accompanied by dyspnea.

Notes: *Feishu* ventilates the lung and resolves phlegm; *Chize*, the *he* point of the Lung Meridian of Hand-*Taiyin*, ventilates the lung; *Dingchuan* relieves asthma. If used together, the above three points can help ventilate the lung, send the unhealthy *qi* downward, and relieve cough and asthma. *Fengmen* dispels pathogenic factors from the exterior; *Fenglong*, the *luo* point of the stomach, resolves phlegm and eliminates turbidity; *Hegu* disperses the lung heat; *Tiantu* relieves dyspnea and sends the unhealthy *qi* downward. If *Tiantu* and *Neiguan* are used together, they can help relieve asthma and cough, regulate the flow of *qi* and soothe the chest.

b) Deficiency syndrome

Principles: To warm the lung, invigorate the spleen, nourish the kidney, resolve phlegm and relieve asthma.

Methods: Select acupoints on the Lung Meridian of Hand-*Taiyin* and back *shu* points, using the reinforcing manipulation or the reinforcing and reducing method. Moxibustion therapy can also be used if necessary.

Acupoints: *Feishu* (BL 13), *Gaohuang* (BL 43), *Pishu* (BL 20), *Zusanli* (ST 36), *Qihai* (RN 6) and *Shenshu* (BL 23).

Notes: Applying moxibustion therapy to *Feishu* and *Gaohuang* can replenish the lung *qi* and relieve asthma; *Pishu* and *Zusanli* invigorate the spleen and stomach, and nourish the acquired energy; *Qihai* and *Shenshu* nourish the kidney *qi*. If used together, the above acupoints can help strengthen the spleen and stomach, nourish the lung and kidney, thus preventing the recurrence of asthma.

4) Other remedies

a) Ear acupuncture

Acupoints: Auricular points for asthma, infratragic apex, lung, brain, intertragic apex and the ear-*Shenmen* point.

Methods: Select two or three points each time to apply acupuncture with strong stimulation. Electroacupuncture device can also be adopted, using the dense or sparse-dense wave and keeping the needle in the acupoints for 10-20 minutes. The ear acupuncture treatment can be carried out once a day, and a complete course includes ten treatment. Needle embedment can also be used in the following way: select two to three points each time and carry out the treatment every three to five days. Both ears should be punctured in turn until the illness is relieved.

b) Skin acupuncture

Location: On the thenar, the forearm where the Lung Meridian of Hand-*Taiyin* travels, and sternocleidomastoid muscles.

Methods: Use a dermal needle to tap the area where the Lung Meridian of Hand-*Taiyin* runs and then tap the sternocleidomastoid muscles until the skin becomes red. Tap each area for about 15 minutes.

5) Notes

a) Medicinal treatment can be used in combination with acupuncture for severe and prolonged asthma. Dispel exogenous pathogenic factors if there are evident syndrome.

b) Since asthma is very likely to recur, patients should pay attention to the weather changes and take care not to contact anything allergic.

c) Scar-producing moxibustion: Select two or three points from among *Dazhui* (DU 14), *Fengmen* (BL 12), *Feishu* (BL 13), *Danzhong* (RN 17), *Gaohuang* (BL 43) and *Tiantu* (RN 22) and burn three to five moxa cones at each point. This treatment should be given every 10 days, and a whole course includes three treatment. asthma will improve in several months and even be brought under control if this treatment is carried out in July and August every year.

d) Applying moxibustion to 157 patients with bronchial asthma (See *Shanghai Journal of Traditional Chinese Medicine*, No.11 issue of 1963)

Acupoints: *Dazhui* (DU 14), *Feishu* (BL 13), *Tiantu* (RN 22), and *Lingtai* (DU 10).

Notes: *Lingtai* can be used for young patients; *Zhongwan* (RN 12) for patients with cold in the stomach; *Danzhong* (RN 17) and *Qihai* (RN 6) for patients with *qi* deficiency. Moxibustion treatment was given once a day, four or five points each time. A whole course of treatment included four or five days, which was usually carried out during July and August every year. This treatment proved effective in 125, 79.6% of the total patients; 48 patients recovered from the disease completely, 30.6% of the total.

e) Applying purulent moxibustion to 985 cases with bronchial asthma (See *Chinese Acupuncture and Moxibustion*, No.1 issue of 1981)

Acupoints: *Tiantu* (RN 22), *Lingtai* (DU 10) and *Feishu* (BL 13) were used for the first time; *Fengmen* (BL 12) and *Dazhui* (DU 14) for the second time; and *Dazhu* (BL 11) and *Danzhong* (RN 17) for the third time.

Notes: Moxibustion treatment was given to the patients once a year or three times every two years. 505 patients recovered from the disease completely and the condition of illness improved in 425 cases. The treatment proved effective in 94.4% cases. The therapeutic effect depended largely on whether or not the moxibustion treatment made the acupoints purulent. Local anesthesia brought no bad influence on the therapeutic effect.

4. Epigastric pain

Epigastric pain often occurs together with acute and chronic gastritis, peptic ulcer and gastric neurosis.

1) Etiology and pathogenesis

a) Attack of the stomach by liver *qi*: The stagnation of liver *qi* caused by anxiety attacks the stomach, thus leading to the obstruction of stomach *qi* and stomachache. In addition, prolonged stagnation of *qi* may also produce blood stasis and damage the blood vessels, resulting in hematemesis and hemafecia.

b) Deficiency-cold of the spleen and stomach: Weak constitution, prolonged illness, deficiency of *yang-qi* and improper diet can all damage the spleen and stomach; exogenous pathogenic factors such as cold attacks the body and accumulates in the middle *jiao*, resulting in the dysfunction of digestion and absorption. The cold-dampness thus produced blocks the flow of *qi* and causes stomachache.

2) Syndrome differentiation

a) Attack of the stomach by liver *qi*: Gastric pain and distention spreading to the hypochondria, belching, acid regurgitation, white tongue coating and taut pulse. The symptoms become more serious with anxiety and fatigue, and alleviate when the patient takes a good rest.

b) Deficiency-cold of the spleen and stomach: Recurring dull pain in the epigastrium after improper diet, regurgitation of thin fluid, lassitude, pale tongue with white coating, taut pulse, preference for warmth and press.

3) Treatment

a) Attack of the stomach by liver *qi*:

Principles: To release stagnant liver *qi*, regulate the stomach and send the unhealthy *qi* downward.

Methods: Select acupoints on the Liver Meridian of Foot-*Jueyin* and the Stomach Meridian of Foot-*Yangming* to apply acupuncture, using the reducing manipulation.

Acupoints: *Zhongwan* (RN 12), *Zusanli* (ST 36), *Neiguan* (PC 6), *Qimen* (LR 14) and *Taichong* (LR 3).

Notes: *Zhongwan* (the front *mu* point of the stomach) and *Zusanli* (the lower confluent point of the stomach) disperse the stagnant stomach *qi* and turbidity when used together. *Neiguan* which is on the branch of the Pericardium Meridian of Hand-*Jueyin* and connects with *Shaoyang* meridians, soothes the chest and relieves the stagnation; *Neiguan* and *Zusanli* can regulate the middle *jiao* and check the unhealthy stomach *qi*; *Qimen* (the front *mu* point of the liver) and *Taichong* (the *yuan* point of the Liver Meridian) regulate the flow of liver *qi*.

b) Deficiency-cold of the spleen and stomach:

Principles: To warm and invigorate the spleen and stomach.

Methods: Select acupoints on the *Yangming* meridians and the back *shu* and front *mu* points of the spleen and stomach to apply acupuncture, using the reinforcing manipulation. Moxibustion can also be used.

Acupoints: *Pishu* (BL 20), *Weishu* (BL 21), *Zhongwan* (RN 12) and *Zusanli* (ST 36).

Notes: *Zhongwan* and *Weishu* are the front *mu* and back *shu* points of the stomach respectively; *Pishu*, the back *shu* point of the spleen, regulates the spleen; *Zusanli* is the lower confluent point of the stomach. Moxibustion is often used at these four points to warmly invigorate the spleen and stomach.

4) Other remedies

a) Cupping

Apply the cupping treatment to the upper abdomen and the back after acupuncture. It promotes the flow of *qi* and blood, warms the meridians and relieves pain.

b) Point injection

Inject 2-5 ml of 20% glucose or 0.5 ml atropine added with 2 ml distilled water into the above back *shu* points or *Zusanli* (ST 36) once a day or every other day. This treatment can relieve pain.

5) Notes

a) Since acute stomachache sometimes exhibits the same symptoms as liver and gallbladder disorders and angina pectoris, syndrome differentiation should be conducted with great care so as to apply correct treatment.

b) Patients should pay attention to diet after the treatment and avoid pungent food. Emergency measures such as surgical operation should be taken for cases complicated by bleeding and perforation.

6) Reference materials

Applying point injection to 186 patients with peptic ulcer (see *Journal of Acupuncture*, No.1 issue of 1965)

Of the 186 cases of peptic ulcer, 165 patients had taken barium meal X-ray examination, and 153 patients, 92.7% of the total, had a positive focus in addition to the common symptoms.

Acupoints: *Pishu* (BL 20) and *Weishu* (BL 21).

Methods: 5 ml of 0.25-1% Novocain solution was injected into each point once a day. A whole course of treatment included ten days. Usually, the disease was cured after two or three courses.

Effects: Of the 186 patients, 87 patients, 52.2% of the total, recovered from the disease after one to four courses of treatment; the illness greatly improved in 78 cases, 41.9% of the total; the illness improved a little in 11 cases, 5.9% of the total. An X-ray examination showed that niche had disappeared in 90.9% cases. During the first course, 122 patients, 65.6% of the total, felt the pain relieved, and 65 patients, 34.9% of the total, felt the pain disappeared. During the second course, 24 patients, 12.9% of the total felt the pain relieved, and 77 patients, 41.4% of the total felt the pain disappeared. Of all the 186 cases, 162 patients, 80% of the total, felt the pain disappeared.

5. Vomiting

Vomiting is an accompanied symptom of various diseases. It is usually caused by the failure of stomach in sending down preliminarily digested food. The causes are the attack of exogenous pathogens such as wind, cold, summer-heat and dampness, improper diet or emotional upset. Vomiting can also be caused by the accumulation of cold-dampness in the middle *jiao* and retention of phlegm and fluid due to the deficiency of the spleen and stomach.

This part will mainly deal with vomiting due to acute and chronic gastritis, pyloric obstruction and gastric neurosis. For vomiting caused by other diseases, please refer to the relevant chapters.

1) Etiology and pathogenesis

a) Attack of the stomach by exogenous pathogenic factors: The stomach receives water and food, digests and transforms food into chyme, and sends the chyme down. Therefore, if attacked by exogenous pathogenic factors, the stomach can hardly send food downward, thus leading to vomiting.

b) Impairment of the stomach by improper diet: Improper diet and eating unclean, raw, cold, sweet or greasy food may damage the stomach and prevent stomach *qi* from descending, thus causing vomiting.

c) Attack of the stomach by liver *qi*: Hyperactive liver-*qi* due to emotional upset attacks the stomach; anxiety impairs the spleen, resulting in the dysfunction of the spleen in transport and retention of food. They can all cause vomiting.

d) Retention of phlegm and fluid: Hypofunction of the spleen and stomach leads to the accumulation of cold-dampness in the middle *jiao* and retention of phlegm and fluid. The phlegm and fluid thus produced go upward and cause vomiting.

2) Syndrome differentiation

a) Excess syndrome: When the stomach is attacked by exogenous pathogenic factors, vomiting is often accompanied by fever, chilliness, headache, general aching, distention and oppression in the chest and abdomen, and superficial pulse. If vomiting is caused by improper diet, vomitus is usually foul and undigested food accompanied by distention and oppression in the epigastrium and abdomen, belching, acid regurgitation, comfortable feeling after vomiting and possibly diarrhea. If vomiting is caused by cold-dampness or retention of phlegm and fluid, it is usually accompanied by salivation, chest upset, dizziness, palpitation, white and greasy tongue coating, and taut and smooth pulse. When the stomach is attacked by liver *qi*, vomiting is often accompanied by distention and oppression in the chest and hypochondria, belching, acid regurgitation, insomnia, red outer edges of the tongue and taut pulse.

b) Deficiency syndrome: Patients with spleen and stomach deficiency often exhibit the following symptoms, pale complexion, lassitude, preference for warmth and pressure, dizziness, loose stools, poor appetite, abdominal distention, pale tongue coating, and weak pulse. When the stomach *yin* is deficient, vomiting is often accompanied by dry mouth and throat, hunger but without appetite, retching, aphthae, flushed face, thready and rapid pulse.

3) Treatment

a) Excess syndrome

Principles: To dispel superficial pathogenic factors, eliminate dampness, relieve stagnation, soothe the liver, regulate the stomach and send the unhealthy *qi* downward.

Methods: Select acupoints on the Stomach Meridian of Foot-*Yangming* and the front *mu* point of the stomach to apply acupuncture, using the reducing manipulation.

Acupoints: *Zhongwan* (RN 12), *Neiguan* (PC 6), *Zusanli* (ST 36) and *Gongsun* (SP 4). For retention of undigested food, these four points can be used together with *Xiawan* (RN 10); for retention of phlegm and fluid, they can be used together with *Fenglong* (ST 40); for the attack of the stomach by liver *qi*, they can be used together with *Yanglingquan* (GB 34) and *Taichong* (LR 3); for affection of exogenous pathogenic factors, they can be used together with *Hegu* (LI 4).

Notes: *Zhongwan* is the front *mu* point of the stomach. *Neiguan*, the *luo* point of the Pericardium Meridian of Hand-*Jueyin*, connects with *sanjiao* through the diaphragm. The *Yinwei* Meridian controls the internal organs and therefore can promote the flow of *qi* in the upper and middle *jiao*. If *Neiguan* and *Zhongwan* are used together, they help send the stomach *qi* downward. *Zusanli* (the *he* point of the Stomach Meridian of Foot-*Yangming*) and *Gongsun* (the *luo* point of the Spleen Meridian of Foot-*Taiyin*) regulate the stomach and invigorate the spleen. *Xiawan* helps promote the flow of *qi* and resolve food retention; *Yanglingquan* calms the liver and regulates the stomach; *Taichong* regulates the stagnant liver *qi*; and *Hegu* disperses the exogenous pathogenic factors.

b) Deficiency syndrome

Principles: To warm the middle *jiao* and strengthen the spleen, regulate the stomach and send the unhealthy *qi* downward.

Methods: Select acupoints on the Spleen Meridian of Foot-*Taiyin* and the Stomach Meridian of Foot-*Yangming* and the back *shu* and front *mu* points to apply acupuncture, using the reinforcing manipulation or uniform reinforcement and reduction. Moxibustion can also be used.

Acupoints: *Pishu* (BL 20), *Yinbai* (SP 1), *Zhongwan* (RN 12) and *Zhaohai* (KI 6).

Notes: *Pishu* (the back *shu* point of the Spleen Meridian of Foot-*Taiyin*) and *Yinbai* (the *jiing* point of the Spleen Meridian of Foot-*Taiyin*) help invigorate the spleen when used together. Applying moxibustion treatment to *Zhongwan*, the front *mu* point of the stomach, can warm the middle *jiao* and regulate the stomach. *Zhaohai*, the *jing* point of the Kidney Meridian of Foot-*Shaoyin*, nourishes the kidney *yin* and arrests vomiting caused by *yin* deficiency.

4) Other remedies

a) Ear acupuncture

Acupoints: Auricular points for the stomach, liver, brain and end of inferior antihelix crus, and ear-*Shenmen*.

Methods: Select two or three points to apply acupuncture with strong stimulation and keep the needle in the acupoints for 20-30 minutes. The treatment can be carried out once a day or every other day.

b) Acupoint injection

Acupoints: *Zhiyang* (DU 9), *Zusanli* (ST 36) and *Lingtai* (DU 10).

Methods: Select two points each time to inject 2 ml of normal saline. The treatment should be carried out once a day.

5) Reference materials

According to *A Concise Book of Acupuncture and Moxibustion*, a 26-year-old woman named Zhou complained that she had stomachache and vomiting of undigested food for six months. Yet the X-ray examination showed no pathological change in the stomach. The disease was finally diagnosed as neurogenic vomiting. Since many therapeutic methods were in vain, she sought help from acupuncture treatment. Points selected were *Neiguan* (PC 6), *Zhongwan* (RN 12), *Zusanli* (ST 36) and *Weishu* (BL 21). While puncturing these acupoints, the doctor used the cooling-the-sky manipulation. Needles were kept in the acupoints except *Weishu* (BL 21) for 15 minutes after a needling sensation was obtained. Vomiting alleviated after three times treatment. It stopped after six times treatment, and the patient recovered completely after receiving the acupuncture treatment for eight times.

6. Abdominal pain

Abdominal pain is a common symptom of disorders in the *zang-fu* organs.

This part will deal with abdominal pain caused by acute and chronic enteritis, enterospasm and intestinal neurosis. For abdominal pain due to other reasons, please refer to the relevant chapters.

1) Etiology and pathogenesis

a) Accumulation of cold: Overeating raw and cold food impairs the spleen and stomach and causes stagnation of cold and *qi*, resulting in abdominal pain; exposure to the exogenous cold leads to intestinal spasm and *qi* stagnation which results in abdominal pain.

b) Retention of food: Improper diet leads to stagnation of food which produces heat in the intestine and blocks the flow of *qi* in the *fu* organs, resulting in abdominal pain.

c) Stagnation of liver *qi*: Emotional upset causes stagnation of liver *qi*, resulting in abdominal pain.

d) Deficiency of *yang* in the *zang-fu* organs: Deficiency of *yang* in the spleen and stomach impairs the digestive function and leads to the lack of nutrients in the regenerative process; deficiency of *yang* in the kidney fails to provide the *zang-fu* organs with warmth and the meridians with nutrient, resulting in abdominal pain of the deficiency type.

2) Syndrome differentiation

a) Accumulation of cold: Acute abdominal pain, preference for warmth and aversion to cold, cold limbs, loose stools, pale tongue with white coating, deep and taut pulse.

b) Retention of food: Abdominal distention, pain and tenderness, anorexia, belching, acid regurgitation, vomiting and diarrhea which relieve the pain, greasy tongue coating, and smooth pulse.

c) Stagnation of liver *qi*: Abdominal pain spreading to the hypochondriac region, abdominal distention, belching, loss of appetite, bitter taste, red outer edges of the tongue and white coating, and taut pulse.

d) Deficiency of *yang* in the *zang-fu* organs: Intermittent and dull abdominal pain, preference for warmth and pressure, pale complexion, lassitude, cold limbs, loose stools, lumbago and pain in the knees, pale and swollen tongue with tooth marks on the edge, deep and slow pulse.

3) Treatment

a) Accumulation of cold

Principles: To warm meridians, expel cold, and relieve pain.

Methods: Select acupoints on the Large Intestine of Hand-*Yangming*, the Stomach Meridian of Foot-*Yangming* and the Spleen of Foot-*Taiyin* to apply acupuncture and moxibustion.

Acupoints: *Zhongwan* (RN 12), *Zusanli* (ST 36), *Gongsun* (SP 4) and *Shenque* (RN 8).

Notes: *Zhongwan* and *Zusanli* help warm the middle *jiao* and disperse cold. *Gongsun*, the *luo* point of the Spleen Meridian of Foot-*Taiyin*, connects with the Stomach Meridian of Foot-*Yangming* and therefore can invigorate the spleen and stomach. Applying moxibustion to *Shenque* can warm the middle *jiao* and stop diarrhea.

b) Retention of food

Principles: To resolve the stagnation, promote the flow of *qi* and alleviate the pain.

Methods: Select acupoints on the Large Intestine Meridian of Hand-*Yangming* and the Stomach Meridian of Foot-*Yangming* and the front *mu* points to apply acupuncture, using the reducing manipulation.

Acupoints: *Tianshu* (ST 25), *Zhongwan* (RN 12), *Zusanli* (ST 36) and *Neiting* (ST 44).

Notes: *Zhongwan* and *Tianshu* are the front *mu* points of the stomach and large intestine respectively. If they are used together, they can help regulate the flow of *qi* in the stomach and intestines. *Zusanli* invigorates the stomach and resolves stagnation. *Neiting* disperses stagnation and relieves pain.

c) Stagnation of liver *qi*

Principles: To regulate the liver and the circulation of *qi*.

Methods: Select acupoints on the Pericardium Meridian of Hand-*Jueyin*, the Liver Meridian of Foot-*Jueyin* and the *Ren* Meridian to apply acupuncture, using the uniform reinforcement and reduction.

Acupoints: *Danzhong* (RN 17), *Taichong* (LR 3), *Neiguan* (PC 6) and *Yanglingquan* (GB 34).

Notes: *Danzhong* (an influential point of *qi*) and *Taichong* (the *yuan* point of the Liver Meridian of Foot-*Jueyin*) can help disperse stagnant liver *qi*; *Neiguan* regulates the stomach, resolves stagnation and sends the unhealthy *qi* downward; *Yanglingquan* resolves stagnation and relieves vexation.

d) Deficiency of *yang* in the *zang-fu* organs

Principles: To warm and replenish the spleen and kidney.

Methods: Select back *shu* and front *mu* points and those on the *Ren* Meridian to apply moxibustion treatment.

Acupoints: *Pishu* (BL 20), *Zhangmen* (LR 13), *Shenshu* (BL 23) and *Guanyuan* (RN 4).

Notes: *Pishu* (a back *shu* point) and *Zhangmen* (a front *mu* point) help invigorate the spleen and replenish the spleen *qi*; *Shenshu* warms the kidney and *Guanyuan* invigorates the *yang*. When the spleen and stomach functions normally, there will be sufficient nutrients in the regenerative process and the kidney *yang* is warm. This leads to the free flow of *qi* and blood in the *zang-fu* organs and meridians, and the abdominal pain will be relieved.

4) Other remedies

Acupoint injection

Methods: Inject 10 ml of 20% glucose solution into *Zusanli* (ST 36) on both sides. The treatment can be carried out once a day or every other day.

5) Reference materials

Applying acupuncture to 77 patients suffering abdominal pain caused by intestinal adhesion after operation (see *Fujian Journal of Traditional Chinese Medicine*, No.2 issue of 1965)

Acupoints: *Ashi* points, *Tianshu* (ST 25), *Dachangshu* (BL 25) and *Zusanli* (ST 36).

Methods: The acupoints were punctured with uniform reinforcement and reduction manipulation. The needles were kept in the acupoints for 20-30 minutes after a needling sensation was felt around the acupoint or along the meridian. The treatment was given every other day and a complete course included 10 times treatment.

Effects: 57 patients recovered from the disease; the illness improved a little bit in 13 cases; the treatment proved in vain in seven cases. Point injection therapy was effective in 90.9% cases.

7. Diarrhea

Diarrhea refers to abnormal frequency and liquidity of fecal discharge as often seen in acute and chronic enteritis, and allergic colitis. Diarrhea with discharge of blood and mucus does not belong to this category. The organs involved are chiefly the spleen, stomach, large and small intestines.

1) Etiology and pathogenesis

a) Acute diarrhea: It is often caused by eating and drinking something cold, raw and contaminated and the attack of exogenous pathogenic dampness and the summer-heat. As a result, there appears the disorder of *qi* and dysfunction of the stomach and intestines. The waste of digested food fails to be sent down and the essence cannot be transported upward, thus occurs diarrhea.

b) Chronic diarrhea: It is often caused by the dysfunction of the middle *jiao* due to weak spleen and stomach, deficient *qi* due to prolonged illness, hypoactive kidney *yang* or dysfunction of digestion.

2) Syndrome differentiation

a) Acute diarrhea: Frequent bowel movements and feces in large quantity. Acute diarrhea of the dampness-heat type is often accompanied by urgency or difficulty in defecation, abdominal pain, yellow and fetid stools, burning sensation in the anus, fever, thirst, oliguria with reddish urine, reddened tongue with yellow and greasy coating, soft and rapid or smooth and rapid pulse. Acute diarrhea of the cold-dampness type is often accompanied by watery diarrhea, abdominal pain, borborygmus, gastric upset, poor appetite, white, thin or greasy tongue coating, soft and retarded pulse.

b) Chronic diarrhea: Diarrhea lasting for a long time. Chronic diarrhea due to weak spleen is often accompanied by loose stools, frequent bowel movements when the patient eats more, sometimes even discharge of undigested food, abdominal distention, sallow complexion, lassitude, pale tongue with white coating, thready and weak pulse. Chronic diarrhea due to deficient kidney *yang* is often accompanied by morning diarrhea with abdominal pain and borborygmus, aversion to cold, cold limbs, lumbago, soreness in the knee joints, pale tongue with white coating, deep and thready pulse.

3) Treatment

a) Acute diarrhea

Principles: To disperse heat and remove dampness in cases of the dampness-heat type; to warm the middle *jiao* and expel cold and dampness in cases of the cold-dampness type.

Methods: Select acupoints on the Stomach Meridian of Foot-*Yangming* and the front *mu* points of the stomach and intestines to apply acupuncture, using the reducing manipulation.

Acupoints: *Zhongwan* (RN 12), *Tianshu* (ST 25), *Shangjuxu* (ST 37) and *Xiajuxu* (ST 39).

Notes: *Zhongwan* and *Tianshu* are the front *mu* points of the stomach and large intestine respectively. Since the front *mu* points are where the *qi* of the *zang-fu* organs converges, puncturing at this two acupoints can regulate the function of gastrointestines. *Shangjuxu* and *Xiajuxu* are the lower confluent points of the large and small intestines respectively. Since the lower confluent points can treat diseases in the *fu* organs, puncturing at this two points can help check diarrhea.

b) Chronic diarrhea

Principles: To invigorate the spleen and activate the stomach, warm and invigorate kidney *yang*.

Methods: Select acupoints on the Spleen Meridian of Foot-*Taiyin* and *Ren* Meridians, using the reinforcing manipulation. Moxibustion treatment can also be used.

Acupoints: *Pishu* (BL 20), *Zhangmen* (LR 13), *Zusanli* (ST 36), *Zhongwan* (RN 12), *Tianshu* (ST 25), *Mingmen* (DU 4) and *Guanyuan* (RN 4).

Notes: Since *Pishu* and *Zhangmen* are the back *shu* and front *mu* points of the Spleen Meridian of Foot-*Taiyin*, they can invigorate the spleen and replenish *qi*. Applying acupuncture and moxibustion to *Zusanli* (the lower confluent point of the stomach), *Zhongwan* (the front *mu* point of the stomach) and *Tianshu* (the front *mu* point of the large intestine) can help restore the function of spleen *yang* and promote digestion and absorption. Moxibustion treatment at *Mingmen* and *Guanyuan* can invigorate the kidney *yang*. To warm and invigorate the spleen and kidney is the guiding principle in treating diarrhea.

4) Other remedies

a) Scraping (*guasha*)

This is a popular treatment for diarrhea due to summer-heat. The method is as the following: select a suitable tool such as a smooth spoon or comb. Dip it in cooking oil or water and then scrape the skin along the spinal column, neck, intercostal spaces, shoulder, arms, armpits and popliteal fossae until the skin shows deep red.

b) Ear acupuncture

Acupoints: Auricular points for the stomach, spleen, small and large intestines, end of inferior antihelix crus, and ear-*Shenmen*.

Method: Select two or three points to apply needle embedment. The treatment can be given every three to five days, and a complete course includes ten treatment. This method proves effective for chronic diarrhea.

5) Notes

Patients suffering acute diarrhea should keep a restricted diet. Fluid infusion can be applied if the bowel movements are frequent and the patient gets dehydrated.

6) Reference materials

Applying acupuncture to 55 patients suffering diarrhea (see *Shanghai Journal of Traditional Chinese Medicine*, No.10 issue of 1965)

Of these 55 patients, 47 were two months to one year old; five were one year to five years old; and three were over 20 years old. There were 37 patients suffering from diarrhea for one to five days; 14 patients for five days to one month; three patients for one to two months for three; and one patient for six months. Among the 55 cases, 45 were caused by indigestion or cold; seven by weak spleen and stomach; and three by deficiency of kidney *yang*.

Acupoints: *Fuxie* (0.5 *cun* below *Shenque* [RN 8] and 1 *cun* above *Qihai* [RN 6]) as the main point and *Zusanli* (ST 36), *Tianshu* (ST 25) and *Zhongwan* (RN 12) as the accessory points.

Method: *Fuxie* was punctured 0.3-0.8 *cun* deep with the reinforcing manipulation. Needle retention is not necessary. The accessory points were used when the main point could not relieve diarrhea.

Effects: There were 47 patients who completely recovered after the first treatment. After the second treatment, diarrhea stopped in the other eight cases.

8. Dysentery

Dysentery is an intestinal infectious disease that often occurs in summer and autumn. Traditional Chinese medicine holds that eating contaminated food or the accumulation of dampness and turbidity in the spleen and stomach may cause dysentery. Its main symptoms are abdominal pain, tenesmus and stools containing blood and mucus.

The principles here mentioned can be used to treat acute and chronic bacillary dysentery as well as amebic dysentery in Western medicine.

1) Etiology and pathogenesis

Dysentery is often caused by the attack of exogenous dampness-heat, pestilent agent and the damage of spleen and stomach by raw and cold food. The accumulation of exogenous pathogenic factors and undigested food impairs the normal function of intestines, while the combined action of dampness-heat and the stagnation of *qi* and blood hurt the vessels of *zang-fu* organs, resulting in discharge of blood and mucus. People with exuberant *yang* are susceptible to pathogenic dampness-heat and if they contract dampness-heat, it is very likely to turn into pathogenic heat; while people with deficient *yang* are susceptible to pathogenic cold-dampness and if they contract cold-dampness, it is very likely to turn into pathogenic cold. Excessive heat damages the vessels so that more blood than mucus is discharged; while excessive dampness impairs *qi* so that more mucus than blood is discharged. The blockage of *qi* leads to abdominal pain and tenesmus.

2) Syndrome differentiation

a) Dampness-heat dysentery: abdominal pain, discharge of blood and mucus, tenesmus, a burning sensation in the anus, oliguria with reddish urine, aversion to cold, fever, vexation and thirst, reddened tongue with yellow and greasy coating, smooth and rapid pulse.

b) Cold-dampness dysentery: Discharge of sticky mucus, preference for warmth and aversion to cold, fullness in the chest and epigastrium, distention and dull pain in the abdomen, tastelessness, thirstlessness, pale tongue with white and greasy coating, soft, retarded or slow pulse.

3) Treatment

a) Dampness-heat dysentery

Principles: To disperse heat, expel toxins, resolve dampness, promote the circulation of *qi* and blood and relieve food retention.

Methods: Select acupoints on the Large Intestine Meridian of Hand-*Yangming* and the Stomach Meridian of Foot-*Yangming* to apply acupuncture, using the reducing manipulation.

Acupoints: *Hegu* (LI 4), *Quchi* (LI 11), *Tianshu* (ST 25), *Shangjuxu* (ST 37) and *Neiting* (ST 44).

Notes: *Hegu* (the *yuan* point of the Large Intestine of Hand-*Yangming*) and *Quchi* (the *he* point of the same meridian) can help disperse the dampness-heat in the intestine and stomach. *Tianshu* and *Shangjuxu*, the front *mu* point and lower confluent point of the large intestine, can help activate the flow of *qi* in the large intestine, eliminate dampness and relieve food retention. *Neiting*, a *ying* point of the Stomach Meridian of Foot-*Yangming*, can alleviate pain.

b) Cold-dampness dysentery

Principles: To warm and eliminate cold and dampness, and activate the circulation of *qi*.

Methods: Select acupoints on the Stomach Meridian of Foot-*Yangming* and *Ren* Meridian and the back *shu* points to apply acupuncture, using the reinforcing manipulation. Moxibustion treatment can also be used.

Acupoints: *Tianshu* (ST 25), *Zusanli* (ST 36), *Zhongwan* (RN 12), *Qihai* (RN 6) and *Pishu* (BL 20).

Notes: *Zusanli*, the *he* point of the Stomach Meridian of Foot-*Yangming*, can regulate the function of the stomach and intestine when used together with *Tianshu*. Applying moxibustion treatment to *Pishu*, the back *shu* point of the Spleen Meridian of Foot-*Taiyin*, can help strengthen the spleen, warm the middle *jiao* and expel cold. *Zhongwan* can regulate stomach *qi* and eliminate dampness. Applying moxibustion treatment to *Qihai* can regulate *qi* to remove stagnation and warm *yang*.

4) Other remedies

Acupoint injection

Inject 2-5 ml of 20% glucose solution or 100 mg of vitamin B_1 added with 500 microgram of vitamin B_{12} into *Tianshu* (ST 25) and *Zusanli* (ST 36) on both sides alternately and the treatment is carried out once a day.

5) Notes

a) Recurrent dysentery is caused by deficiency of *qi* of the middle *jiao*, cold or improper diet. Treatment should be given according to syndrome differentiation. Acupoints for strengthening the body resistance can be punctured. For cases with cold-dampness, *Guanyuan* (RN 4), *Shenshu* (BL 23) and *Weishu* (BL 21) can be punctured to invigorate the kidney *qi*.

b) Dysentery due to the invasion of exogenous pestilent agent is usually acute and often occurs in children, with symptoms like high fever, restlessness, thirst, abdominal pain, convulsion, coma, discharge of bright or purplish blood and mucus. In addition to the treatment for dampness-heat dysentery mentioned above, *Shixuan* (EX-UE 11), *Weizhong* (BL 40) and *Taichong* (LR 3) can be punctured to disperse heat and relieve convulsion; *Shuigou* (DU 26) and *Yongquan* (KI 1) can be punctured to bring back consciousness to patients. Chinese and Western medicine should be used in combination for acute cases.

6) Reference materials

Applying acupuncture to more than 1,000 patients with acute bacillary dysentery (see *New Developments in Acupuncture and Moxibustion Research*)

Acupuncture treatment was applied to 645 patients whose bacteria culture of stools showed positive. Compared with 281 patients who orally took furazolidone, symptoms like tenesmus, abdominal pain and diarrhea disappeared earlier in the acupuncture group. Patients whose bacteria culture turned negative in seven days were more than those taking Western medicine. The acupoints were almost the same as the above, and the reducing manipulation was applied. A study on the indices of immunity activity was carried out, including serum protein electrophoresis, serum total complement content, serum lysozyme content, phagocytosis of reticuloendothelial system of liver, etc. The study showed that the immunity activity of the patients steadily increased during the course of acupuncture treatment, especially the humoral immunity. An experiment on animals with bacillary dysentery was also carried out, and the number of bacteria was found reduced after acupuncture treatment. This further proved that acupuncture can help improve the protective mechanism of the human body.

9. Constipation

Constipation is a disorder of the large intestine due to various reasons and its manifestations are abnormal (over two days) or difficult evacuation of feces.

1) Etiology and pathogenesis

a) Excess type: Exuberant *yang* inside the human body, overdrinking and eating too much pungent and greasy food lead to the accumulation of heat in the intestine and stomach. It may also caused by the consumption of body fluid due to febrile diseases. Anxiety and stagnation of *qi* lead to the abnormal distribution of body fluid and dysfunction of the intestine and stomach, and constipation thus occurs.

b) Deficiency type: This is usually caused by the stagnation of *qi* in the intestinal tract due to internal damage, deficiency of blood and *qi* after illness, childbirth, old-age or weakness, or deficient *yang-qi* in the lower *jiao* and accumulation of cold.

2) Syndrome differentiation

a) Excess type: Bowel movement every three to five days or more, discharge of dry stools, difficulty in defecation, internal hemorrhoid or anal fissure with bleeding. Constipation due to heat accumulation exhibits the following symptoms such as fever, irritability, thirst, foul breath, reddened tongue with yellow and dry coating, taut and rapid pulse. Constipation due to *qi* stagnation often exhibits symptoms such as distensive pain in the abdomen and hypochondria, belching, poor appetite, reddened edges of the tongue with thin and greasy coating, and taut pulse.

b) Deficiency type: Patients with deficient *qi* exhibit the following symptoms, pale complexion, lassitude, disability to defecate, pale tongue with white coating and feeble pulse; those with blood deficiency often exhibit lusterless complexion, dizziness, palpitation, dry stools, pale lips and tongue, thready and weak pulse; those with exuberant cold due to *yang* deficiency exhibit cold pain in the abdomen, soreness and coldness in the back, cold limbs, frequent urination with clear urine, difficulty in defecation, pale tongue with white and thick or greasy coating, deep and slow pulse.

3) Treatment

a) Excess type

Principles: To disperse heat, remove stagnant *qi* and promote defecation.

Methods: Select acupoints on the Large Intestine Meridian of Hand-*Yangming* and the back *shu* and front *mu* points of the large intestine to apply acupuncture, using the reducing manipulation.

Acupoints: *Dachangshu* (BL 25), *Tianshu* (ST 25) and *Zhigou* (SJ 6) are used together with *Hegu* (LI 4) and *Shangjuxu* (ST 37) for heat accumulation; *Dachangshu*, *Tianshu* and *Zhigou* are used together with *Taichong* (LR 3) and *Zhongwan* (RN 12) for cases with *qi* stagnation.

Notes: *Tianshu* and *Dachangshu*, the front *mu* and back *shu* points of the Large Intestine Meridian of Hand-*Yangming*, can be used together to activate the flow of *qi* in the large intestine. *Zhigou*, a point on the *Sanjiao* Meridian of Hand-*Shaoyang*, can promote the flow of *qi* in *sanjiao* and further the flow of *qi* in the large intestine, thus relieving constipation. *Hegu* (the *yuan* point of the Large Intestine Meridian of Hand-*Yangming*) and *Shangjuxu* (the lower confluent point of the large intestine) may promote the function of the large intestine. *Taichong*, a *shu* point of the Liver Meridian of Foot-*Jueyin*, helps soothe the liver *qi*. When used together with *Zhongwan*, the influential point of the *fu* organs, it help regulate the flow of *qi* in the *fu* organs and relieve constipation.

b) Deficiency type

Principles: To replenish *qi* and nourish blood, warm *yang* and relieve constipation.

Methods: Select acupoints on the Stomach Meridian of Foot-*Yangming*, the Spleen Meridian of Foot-*Taiyin* and the Kidney Meridian of Foot-*Shaoyin* to apply acupuncture, using the reinforcing manipulation. Moxibustion treatment can also be used.

Acupoints: *Pishu* (BL 20), *Weishu* (BL 21), *Dachangshu* (BL 25), *Tianshu* (ST 25) and *Zhaohai* (KI 6). For patients with deficient *yang* moxibustion can be applied to *Weishu* (BL 21), *Shenque* (RN 8) and *Qihai* (RN 6).

Notes: A basic treatment for constipation of deficiency type is to puncture at *Pishu* and *Weishu* to invigorate the spleen and stomach and further the production of *qi* and blood. *Zhaohai*, an acupoint on the Kidney Meridian of Foot-*Shaoyin*, helps activate the production of fluid and moisturize the intestines. If *Zhaohai*, *Dachangshu* and *Tianshu* are used together, they can help activate the *qi* in the *fu* organs and relax the bowels. Applying moxibustion treatment to *Shenque* and *Qihai* can regulate the flow of *qi* in *sanjiao* and eliminate *yin* cold. *Shenque*, *Qihai*, and *Shenshu* can be used together to warm the *yang* and relax the bowels.

4) Other remedies

Ear acupuncture

Acupoints: Auricular points for lower portion of rectum, large intestine, end of inferior antihelix crus and brain.

Methods: Insert the needle intermittently, giving moderate or strong stimulation to the acupoints. Keep the needles in the skin for 10-20 minutes.

5) Notes

a) Patients with constipation should form a good living habit, which means to eat more fibrous food such as vegetables, fruits and oats and have bowel movements regularly.

b) Patients with constipation should take up physical training and do labor work so as to promote intestinal preistalsis. Patients can also do self-massage in the following way: press the abdomen around the umbilicus clockwise with the left palm several times a day and 15 minutes each time.

6) Reference materials

Applying acupuncture to 40 patients suffering habitual constipation (see *A Selection of Clinical Experiences in Acupuncture and Moxibustion*)

Of the 40 patients, 16 were males and 24 females, and most of them were 20-40 years old.

Acupoints: *Zusanli* (ST 36) and *Zhigou* (SJ 6) for the first time; *Dachangshu* (BL 25) for the second time; *Tianshu* (ST 25) and *Fenglong* (ST 40) for the third time. Points on both limbs were punctured.

Method: Mild stimulation was adopted to promote intestinal peristalsis while strong stimulation was used to treat constipation due to intestinal spasm. After a needling sensation was obtained, the needle was lifted and thrust repeatedly for three to five minutes and then withdrawn. For some cases, the needle was left in the skin for 15 minutes. Moxibustion treatment could be given to *Dachangshu* on both sides for five to ten minutes, three times a week. Moxibustion treatment should not be given to *Tianshu* lest it should lead to dry stools. Cathartics were contraindicated during acupuncture treatment.

Therapeutic effects: Effects came slow in patients with long history of constipation, but were apparent in acute cases. The treatment was believed effective if the interval of bowel movement shortened and the patients relaxed the bowels one or two days after the treatment. The treatment proved effective in 36 cases and invalid in four cases. The frequency of treatment varied from four sessions to twenty.

10. Prolapse of rectum

Prolapse of rectum refers to the protrusion of the rectal mucous membrane through the anus in varying degrees, which often occurs in children, old men or multiparous women.

1) Etiology and pathogenesis

The illness is usually caused by deficiency of *qi* and blood, and collapse of spleen *qi*, which leads to the weak contraction of the rectum. Deficiency of *qi* and blood in the old people, prolonged diarrhea, weak constitution after childbirth, or giving birth to several children can all cause the lack of primordial *qi* and result in prolapse of rectum.

2) Syndrome differentiation

This disease may be mild or serious with slow development. In mild cases, patients feel something swollen falling out of the anus when having bowel movement, and the feeling disappears after bowel movement. In serious cases, the protrusion of the rectal mucous membrane can hardly go back even with the help of a hand. Protracted prolapse of rectum is likely to recur if induced by fatigue. The accompanied symptoms are lassitude, weak limbs, sallow complexion, dizziness, palpitation, pale tongue with white coating, soft, superficial and thready pulse.

3) Treatment

Principles: To replenish *qi* and elevate spleen *yang* to cure collapse.

Methods: Select acupoints on the *Du* Meridian and the back *shu* points to apply acupuncture, using the reinforcing manipulation. Moxibustion treatment is strongly recommended.

Acupoints: *Baihui* (DU 20), *Changqiang* (DU 1) and *Dachangshu* (BL 25).

Notes: *Baihui* is a crossing point of the *Du* Meridian and three *yang* meridians. Applying moxibustion treatment to *Baihui* can help replenish *qi* and elevate spleen *yang*. Located near the anus, *Changqiang* is the *luo* point of the *Du* Meridian, which can be used to treat local diseases. *Dachangshu*, the back *shu* point of the Large Intestine Meridian, can help replenish *qi* in the large intestine. The above three points can be used together to elevate spleen *yang* to cure collapse.

4) Other remedies

Prompt prick

Select positive points on the longitudinal line 1.0-1.5 *cun* lateral to the posterior midline between the third lumbar vertebra and the second sacral vertebra and prick them with needles.

5) Notes

a) If the prolapse of rectum is caused by chronic dysentery or enteritis, the treatment should seek to cure the primary disease.

b) Since the illness is often caused by weak constitution, moxibustion treatment is applied to *Zusanli* (ST 36) and *Qihai* (RN 6) to reinforce the constitution; tonics can also be taken to achieve a better result.

6) Reference materials

Applying acupuncture to 35 cases of prolapse of rectum (see *A Selection of Clinical Experiences in Acupuncture and Moxibustion*)

These 35 patients were all males suffering from prolapse of rectum for a long time, and what had gone out of the rectum, 3-4 cm long, failed to resume the normal position.

Acupoints: Three groups of acupoints were selected. The first group included *Baihui* (DU 20), *Zusanli* (ST 36), *Changqiang* (DU 1) and *Chengshan* (BL 57); the second included *Changqiang* (DU 1), *Chengshan* (BL 57) and *Huanmen* (on both sides of the anus between the white and red skin); the third included *Changqiang* (DU 1), *Huanmen*, *Chengshan* (BL 57) and *Baihui* (DU 20).

Methods: With the patient taking the prone position, inserted the needle 1.5 *cun* deep into the acupoints, using the reinforcing manipulation. The needle were kept in the skin for three to five minutes. The treatment was carried out every other day.

Therapeutic effects: Of the 10 cases receiving acupuncture on the first group of acupoints, four cases completely recovered and six improved. After adding *Huanmen* point, four cases of the former six recovered. Of the 16 cases receiving acupuncture on the second group of acupoints, 14 cases recovered, one case improved, and one case proved ineffective. Of the nine cases receiving acupuncture on the third group of acupoints, six cases recovered and three cases improved. The total effectiveness is 97.1%. The follow-up visits to 22 patients 1-12 months later showed no relapse of the illness.

11. Hypochondriac pain

Hypochondriac pain is a common syndrome occurring in one or both sides of the chest. Chronic cases may be accompanied by a dull pain while acute cases manifest a sharp pain.

The illness is often accompanied with acute and chronic diseases of the liver, gallbladder and pleura as well as intercostal neuralgia.

1) Etiology and pathogenesis

a) Stagnation of liver *qi*: Emotional upset disturbs the liver *qi* and causes stagnation.

b) Accumulation of dampness-heat in the liver and gallbladder: Exogenous pathogenic factors accumulate in the Gallbladder Meridian of Foot-*Shaoyang*, which in turn causes stagnation of *qi*. Improper diet leads to the accumulation of dampness-heat in the liver and gallbladder, which in turn disturbs the liver *qi*.

c) Stagnation of *qi* and blood: Prolonged stagnation of *qi* and blood results in the accumulation of blood stasis. Overburden damages the vessels in the hypochondriac region, and contusion gives rise to blood stasis which blocks the *qi*.

d) Insufficiency of liver *yin*: Prolonged illness leaves the blood and collaterals in lack of nourishment; stagnant *qi* turns into fire and impairs the *yin*; the retention of dampness heat impairs the *yin* and leaves the meridians in lack of nourishment.

2) Syndrome differentiation

a) Stagnation of liver *qi*: Distensive and moving pain which is closely related with emotional changes and spreads in the hypochondriac region, irritability, bitter taste, dry throat, insomnia, chest upset, belching, acid regurgitation, thin tongue coating and taut pulse.

b) Accumulation of dampness-heat in the liver and gallbladder: Hypochondriac pain accompanied by bitter taste, chest upset, poor appetite, fever, chilliness, nausea, vomiting, conjunctival congestion, jaundice, dark urine, yellow and greasy tongue coating, taut and rapid pulse.

c) Stagnation of *qi* and blood: Fixed stabbing pain in the hypochondriac region for a long time, tenderness over the hypochondriac region with a history of trauma, lumps, dark purplish tongue, deep and taut pulse.

d) Insufficiency of liver *yin*: Dull pain over the hypochondriac region, vexation, restlessness, dry throat, dizziness, blurred vision, reddened tongue with little coating, taut, thready and rapid pulse.

3) Treatment

a) Stagnation of liver *qi*

Principles: To disperse liver *qi*.

Methods: Select acupoints on the Liver Meridian of Foot-*Jueyin* and the Gallbladder Meridian of Foot-*Shaoyang* to apply acupuncture, using the reducing manipulation.

Acupoints: *Ganshu* (BL 18), *Qimen* (LR 14), *Xiaxi* (GB 43) and *Neiguan* (PC 6).

Notes: *Qimen* (the front *mu* point of the liver) and *Ganshu* (the back *shu* point of the liver) can regulate the liver *qi*. *Xiaxi*, the *ying* point of the gallbladder, can eliminate liver-fire. *Neiguan*, the *luo* point of the Heart Meridian of Hand-*Shaoyin*, can regulate the *qi* and soothe the chest.

b) Accumulation of dampness-heat in the liver and gallbladder

Principles: To disperse heat, eliminate dampness, soothe the liver and gallbladder.

Methods: Select acupoints on the Liver Meridian of Foot-*Jueyin*, the *Sanjiao* Meridian of Hand-*Shaoyang*, and the Gallbladder Meridian of Foot-*Shaoyang* to apply acupuncture, using the reducing manipulation.

Acupoints: *Qimen* (LR 14), *Zhigou* (SJ 6), *Yanglingquan* (GB 34), *Zusanli* (ST 36), *Taichong* (LR 3) and *Riyue* (GB 24).

Notes: *Qimen* and *Taichong* of the Liver Meridian of Foot-*Jueyin* together with *Riyue*, *Zhigou* and *Yanglingquan* of the Gallbladder Meridian of Foot-*Shaoyang* can disperse stagnant *qi* in the liver and gallbladder meridians. *Qimen* and *Riyue* are the front *mu* points of the liver and gallbladder meridians respectively. *Zhigou* and *Yanglingquan* can relieve hypochondriac pain, while *Zusanli* helps strengthen the spleen and disperse dampness-heat.

c) Stagnation of *qi* and blood

Principles: To promote blood circulation, remove obstruction in the collaterals, activate the flow of *qi* and alleviate pain.

Methods: Select acupoints on the Liver Meridian of Foot-*Jueyin* and the Gallbladder Meridian of Foot-*Shaoyang* as main points and those on the Small Intestine Meridian of Foot-*Taiyang* and the back *shu* points as accessory points to apply acupuncture, using the reducing manipulation.

Acupoints: *Xingjian* (LR 2), *Geshu* (BL 17), *Sanyinjiao* (SP 6), *Yanglingquan* (GB 34) and *Riyue* (GB 24).

Notes: *Geshu*, the influential point related to blood, helps promote blood circulation when used together with *Sanyinjiao*; *Xingjian* soothes the liver and *Riyue* promotes the function of gallbladder; *Yanglingquan* promotes the flow of *qi* and further the circulation of blood. As a result, smooth collateral passages relieve the hypochondriac pain.

d) Insufficiency of liver *yin*

Principles: To invigorate the liver, nourish blood and smooth the collateral passages.

Methods: Select acupoints on the Liver Meridian of Foot-*Jueyin* and the back *shu* points to apply acupuncture, using the reinforcing manipulation.

Acupoints: *Qimen* (LR 14), *Ganshu* (BL 18), *Xuehai* (SP 10), *Shenshu* (BL 23) and *Sanyinjiao* (SP 6).

Notes: *Qimen* and *Ganshu*, the front *mu* and back *shu* points of the Liver Meridian of Foot-*Jueyin* respectively, regulate the liver *qi*, nourish and soften the liver; *Xuehai* and *Sanyinjiao* are used together to invigorate *yin* and nourish blood which provides nutrients for the meridians. *Shenshu* invigorates the kidney and nourishes the *yin*. As a result, the liver receives adequate nutrients and the hypochondriac pain is relieved.

4) Other remedies

a) Ear acupuncture

Acupoints: Auricular points for the liver, gallbladder, ear-*Shenmen* and chest.

Methods: Puncture the ear on the affected side, giving strong stimulation if the case is of excess type and mild stimulation if the case is of deficiency type. Keep the needle in the skin for 30 minutes or use the needle embedment method.

b) Plum-blossom needle acupuncture

Tap the sore point in the hypochondrium while simultaneously stimulating the back *shu* point located at the same level with the sore area. Meanwhile, tap the two other back *shu* points situated equidistantly above and below the initial back *shu* point. Cupping therapy can also be applied.

5) Reference materials

a) Applying ear acupuncture treatment to 26 patients suffering posthepatitic syndrome (see *Journal of Acupuncture and Moxibustion*, No.1 issue of 1965)

Although the liver and spleen functioned well and their sizes were normal, there appeared symptoms like distensive pain in the hypochondriac region, lassitude and poor appetite.

Methods: The positive points on the ear were punctured every day or every other day, 1-3 points each time. Needle embedment therapy was used every 2-3 days. One course of treatment included 10 days and 1-3 courses were carried out.

Therapeutic effects: 15 patients recovered from the illness; the treatment were effective in six cases; and the conditions of two patients improved.

b) Applying acupuncture to a male patient named Yang of 33 (a case at Hospital of Traditional Chinese Medicine in Jiangsu Province)

After a mitral commissurotomy, the patient suffered a persistent intercostal neuralgia to which analgesics proved ineffective. Then he received acupuncture treatment 14 days after the operation. Acupoints such as *Xinshu* (BL 15), *Zhigou* (SJ 6) and *Shenmen* (HT 7) were punctured every day. The pain was greatly relieved one day after the acupuncture treatment and the patient completely recovered after the eighth treatment.

12. Palpitation

Palpitation manifests symptoms such as rapid heartbeat, chest upset and susceptibility to fright. Palpitation caused by neurosis and cardiac diseases can be treated according to the following descriptions.

1) Etiology and pathogenesis

a) If induced by sudden fear and fright, timidity due to heart deficiency or insufficiency of blood in the heart due to protracted illness can all lead to uncontrollable palpitation.

b) Accumulation of dampness due to the impairment of the spleen and stomach by improper diet turns into phlegm and further fire. Anxiety causes the stagnation of *qi* which disturbs the phlegm and results in palpitation.

c) Protracted illness leads to the obstruction of meridians by pathogenic factors which attack the heart, leaving the heart vessels blocked. The stagnation of *qi* and blood causes severe palpitation or even the deficiency of heart *yang*.

2) Syndrome differentiation

a) Palpitation due to the deficiency of *qi*: A void in the heart, rapid heartbeat, short breath and lassitude, susceptibility to fright, thin and white tongue coating, thready and rapid pulse.

b) Palpitation due to the deficiency of blood: Lusterless complexion, dizziness, uncontrollable palpitation due to anxiety, slightly red tongue, thready and weak pulse. Cases with hyperactive fire due to *yin* deficiency often exhibit vexation, insomnia, dreaminess, thirst, tinnitus, flushed face, red tip of the tongue, thready and rapid pulse.

c) Palpitation due to phlegm-fire: Chest upset, dizziness, restlessness, intermittent palpitation which even reaches the chest and the area round the umbilicus, insomnia, bitter taste, cough with thick sputum, yellow urine, constipation, yellow and greasy tongue coating, smooth and rapid pulse.

d) Palpitation due to blood stasis: Continuous palpitation which gets worse as time goes on, short breath upon exertion, paroxysmal chest pain, sallow complexion, cyanotic lips and tongue, thready, knotted and intermittent pulse. Deficiency of heart *yang* often exhibits palpitation, aversion to cold, cold limbs, cough with dyspnea, orthopnea, cold sweat, edema and weak pulse.

3) Treatment

a) Palpitation due to the deficiency of *qi*

Principles: To invigorate *qi* and calm the mind.

Methods: Select acupoints on the Heart Meridian of Hand-*Shaoyin* and the Pericardium Meridian of Hand-*Jueyin* and the back *shu* and front *mu* points to apply acupuncture, using the reinforcing manipulation.

Acupoints: *Xinshu* (BL 15), *Juque* (RN 14), *Jianshi* (PC 5), *Shenmen* (HT 7) and *Daling* (PC 7).

Notes: *Xinshu* and *Juque*, the back *shu* and front *mu* points respectively, regulate and reinforce the heart *qi*. *Jianshi* and *Shenmen* help calm the mind and relieve pain in the chest. *Daling*, the *luo* point of the Pericardium Meridian of Hand-*Jueyin*, helps regulate *qi*, calm the mind and relieve convulsion.

b) Palpitation due to the deficiency of blood

Principles: To nourish blood and calm the mind.

Methods: Select acupoints on the Stomach Meridian of Foot-*Yangming* and the Heart Meridian of Hand-*Shaoyin* and the back *shu* points to apply acupuncture, using the reinforcing manipulation. Moxibustion treatment can also be used.

Acupoints: *Geshu* (BL 17), *Pishu* (BL 20), *Zusanli* (ST 36), *Tongli* (HT 5) and *Taixi* (KI 3).

Notes: *Pishu* and *Zusanli* help invigorate the spleen and stomach, enriching the source of metabolism. *Geshu*, the influential point related to blood, helps nourish the blood and calm the mind. *Tongli* helps calm the mind and relieve palpitation. For cases with *yin* deficiency, *Taixi* is added to strengthen the kidney *yin* and suppress heart-fire.

c) Palpitation due to phlegm-fire

Principles: To disperse fire and eliminate phlegm.

Methods: Select acupoints on the Lung Meridian of Hand-*Taiyin*, the Heart Meridian of Hand-*Shaoyin*, the Pericardium Meridian of Hand-*Jueyin*, and the Stomach Meridian of Foot-*Yangming* to apply acupuncture, using the reducing manipulation.

Acupoints: *Ximen* (PC 4), *Chize* (LU 5), *Feishu* (BL 13) and *Fenglong* (ST 40).

Notes: *Chize*, the *he* point of the Lung Meridian of Hand-*Taiyin*, is used together with *Feishu* to disperse fire. *Ximen*, the *xi* point of the Pericardium Meridian of Hand-*Jueyin*, helps regulate the mental activities, calm the mind and relieve palpitation. *Fenglong* helps resolve phlegm.

d) Palpitation due to blood stasis

Principles: To promote the flow of blood, remove blood stasis and strengthen the heart.

Methods: Select acupoints on the Heart Meridian of Hand-*Shaoyin*, the Pericardium Meridian of Hand-*Jueyin*, the Spleen Meridian of Foot-*Taiyin* and the Stomach Meridian of Foot-*Yangming* to apply acupuncture, using the reducing manipulation. Moxibustion treatment can also be used if necessary.

Acupoints: *Neiguan* (PC 6), *Shaohai* (HT 3), *Sanyinjiao* (SP 6), *Danzhong* (RN 17) and *Zusanli* (ST 36).

Notes: *Neiguan* promotes the flow of *qi* and soothes the chest; *Shaohai* relieves palpitation and alleviates pain. *Danzhong*, the influential point related to *qi*, helps replenish *qi* and strengthen the heart. *Sanyinjiao* promotes the flow of blood and removes blood stasis; and *Zusanli* strengthens the spleen and relieves edema.

4) Other remedies

Ear acupuncture

Acupoints: Auricular points for the heart, ear-*Shenmen*, brain and end of inferior antihelix crus.

Methods: Give a moderate stimulation to the acupoints and keep the needles in the skin for 15-30 minutes. The treatment should be given once a day, and a complete course of treatment includes 10 sessions.

5) Notes

Applying acupuncture to treat palpitation can not only relieve all symptoms but also cure the causes. As for palpitation due to organic heart diseases, a combination of different therapy can be used to achieve a better result.

6) Reference materials

Applying acupuncture to a 43-year-old female patient who suffered palpitation after uterine curettage (see *A Concise Book of Acupuncture and Moxibustion*)

After receiving the operation, the patient felt dizzy and a pain in the precordial region accompanied by palpitation. A test taken at that time showed that her heartbeat was 184 beats per minute without any pulse deficit, enlargement of the heart or rales. Her blood pressure was 98/70mm Hg. The diagnosis was paroxysmal tachycardia with no response to pressure on the carotid sinus and eyeballs. Acupuncture treatment was applied to *Shenmen* (HT 7), *Danzhong* (RN 17), *Daling* (PC 7) and *Juque* (RN 14). The needles were removed from the skin right after the treatment. The symptoms disappeared three minutes after the acupuncture and the heartbeat resumed normal rate (84/min.). The follow-up visits four months later showed no recurrence.

13. Insomnia

Insomnia refers to the inability to have a normal sleep. Mild insomnia includes the difficulty in falling asleep or shallow sleep, while severe insomnia refers to the inability to fall asleep for the whole night.

Insomnia due to neurasthenia or anemia can be treated according to the prescription in this part.

1) Etiology and pathogenesis

a) Stagnation of liver *qi* due to emotional upset turns into fire which disturbs the mind.

b) The damage of the spleen and stomach by improper diet leads to retention of food and further the adverse flow of *qi* which disturbs a sound sleep.

c) General debility or protracted illness leads to the deficiency of *yin* and hyperactivity of fire. As a result, the kidney fails to control heart-fire. Emotional upset destroys the balance between kidney and heart, resulting in a disturbed mind.

d) Failure of blood to nourish the heart due to the deficiency of the heart and spleen leads to a wandering mind; deficiency of heart *qi* and timidity also lead to insomnia.

2) Syndrome differentiation

a) Excess syndrome: Usually, the causes are stagnant liver *qi* turning into fire, turbid phlegm due to the retention of food, and indigestion. The symptoms are irritability, poor appetite, bitter taste, vexation or heaviness in the head, abundant expectoration, chest upset, belching, acid regurgitation, red tongue with yellow and greasy coating, taut and rapid pulse.

b) Deficiency syndrome: The causes are insufficiency of *yin* blood, such as hypofunction of the heart and spleen, and deficiency of liver *yin* and kidney *yin*, which leads to hyperactive fire and disturbs the mind. The symptoms are palpitation, amnesia, lassitude, pale complexion, dizziness, tinnitus, sore and weak loins and knees, feverish sensation in the palms, soles and the chest, dreaminess; pale tongue with thin coating, thready and rapid pulse are often found in cases of deficient heart and spleen.

3) Treatment

Principles: To calm the mind is the main principle. To promote digestion, regulate the stomach and disperse phlegm-fire in cases of excess syndrome; to replenish *qi*, nourish the blood, and invigorate the liver and kidney in cases of deficiency syndrome.

Methods: Select the *yuan* points of the corresponding meridians and the back *shu* points to apply acupuncture, using the reducing or reinforcing manipulation. Moxibustion can be used together if necessary.

Acupoints: *Shenmen* (HT 7) and *Sanyinjiao* (SP 6). For cases with deficiency of the heart and spleen, *Xinshu* (BL 15) and *Pishu* (BL 20) can be used together with *Shenmen* and *Sanyinjiao*; *Xinshu* (BL 15), *Shenshu* (BL 23), *Taixi* (KI 3) and *Neiguan* (PC 6) for the imbalance between the heart and kidney; *Ganshu* (BL 18) and *Taichong* (LR 3) for hyperactivity of liver-fire; and *Weishu* (BL 21) and *Zusanli* (ST 36) for disorder of the spleen and stomach.

Notes: *Shenmen*, the *yuan* point of the Heart Meridian of Hand-*Shaoyin*, calms the mind; *Sanyinjiao* promotes the balance between *yin* and *yang* of the three *yin* meridians of foot. Applying acupuncture or moxibustion treatment to *Xinshu* and *Pishu* can invigorate the heart and kidney; *Shenshu* and *Xinshu* are used to invigorate the kidney and calm the mind so as to achieve the balance between *yin* and *yang*. *Taixi* helps invigorate the kidney, thus controlling hyperactive liver-fire; *Neiguan* calms the heart and mind; *Ganshu* and *Taichong* relieve the stagnation of *qi* and check the liver-fire; *Weishu* and *Zusanli* promote the function of stomach.

4) Other remedies

a) Ear acupuncture

Acupoints: Auricular points for heart, ear-*Shenmen*, brain and end of inferior antihelix crus.

Methods: Select two or three points to apply needle embedment every 2-3 days. Treatment should be given to both sides alternately, and one course includes ten times treatment.

b) Plum-blossom needle therapy

Gently tap the neck, eyes, temples, and the back along both sides of the spine once a day, and one course includes ten times treatment.

5) Notes

Acupuncture, ear acupuncture and plum-blossom needle therapy can all treat insomnia, and a better effect can be achieved if these three are used in combination.

6) Reference materials

Applying ear acupuncture to 73 patients suffering insomnia due to various reasons (see *Jiangsu Journal of Traditional Chinese Medicine*, No.5 issue of 1962)

Since hypnotics was in vain, these patients received ear acupuncture treatment.

Methods: Acupuncture treatment was applied to the tender points in the subcortex. The needles were inserted perpendicularly with rotation until the patient felt pain in the region and the needles did not penetrate the ear. The treatment was given at bedtime once a day and the needles were kept in the skin for 20-30 minutes each time.

Effects: The treatment was effective in 90% cases. The frequency of treatment varied from one session to eleven sessions, with an average of three to eight times.

14. Epilepsy

Epilepsy is a kind of paroxymal mental disorder.

1) Etiology and pathogenesis

Fright and anger lead to the stagnation of *qi* in the heart and liver. The fire produced by stagnant *qi* and the phlegm due to the deficiency in the spleen attack the meridians and block the upper orifices, resulting in the disorder of the *yin* and *yang* and epilepsy.

2) Syndrome differentiation

Before the disease attacks, the patient feels dizzy, tired and oppressed in the chest. When it occurs, the patient manifests the following symptoms, such as faint on a sudden, unconsciousness, lockjaw, pale complexion, eyes staring up, tetany, sialorrhea, crying and screaming, incontinence of urine and feces in severe cases. When the attack is over, the patient feels tired and aching all over. The patient looks healthy again after a rest.

Recurring epilepsy may cause deficiency of healthy *qi*. Although the illness frequently occurs, muscular spasm alleviates. There is difficulty in breathing accompanied by snoring, cold sweat and incontinence of urine. After the attack, symptoms like fatigue, dizziness, palpitation, poor appetite and dementia, thready and weak pulse will appear.

3) Treatment

Principles: To calm the liver and suppress the endogenous wind, invigorate the spleen and resolve phlegm, induce resuscitation and relieve mental stress.

Methods: Select acupoints on the Liver Meridian of Foot-*Jueyin*, the Stomach Meridian of Foot-*Yangming* as well as the *Ren* and *Du* meridians, using the reducing manipulation.

Acupoints: *Dazhui* (DU 14), *Jiuwei* (RN 15), *Yaoqi* (EX-B 9), *Taichong* (LR 3), *Jianshi* (PC 5), *Fenglong* (ST 40) and *Sanyinjiao* (SP 6).

Notes: *Dazhui* (the crossing point of six *yang* meridians) and *Jiuwei* (the *luo* point of the *Ren* Meridian) can be used together to coordinate *yin* and *yang*. *Yaoqi*, a time-tested point for epilepsy, helps achieve a better result when used together with *Jiuwei*. *Taichong* helps calm the liver to suppress the endogenous wind, induce resuscitation and relieve mental stress when used with *Jianshi*. *Fenglong* and *Sanyinjiao* help invigorate the spleen and resolve phlegm.

4) Other remedies

Ear acupuncture

Acupoints: Auricular points for the stomach, brain, middle-border, ear-*Shenmen*, heart and occiput.

Methods: Every time select two or three points to give strong stimulation, keep the needles in the skin for 30 minutes and rotate it from time to time. The treatment is given once every other day, and a complete course includes ten times treatment. Needle embedment can also be used every three to five days, and a complete course includes ten times treatment.

5) Reference materials

Applying acupoint injection therapy to 110 patients suffering epilepsy (see *Journal of Shandong's Medicine*)

Methods: The acupoints were divided into two groups. Among the first group of acupoints, *Jianshi* (PC 5) and *Waiguan* (SJ 5) were the main points, *Jiuwei* (RN 15) and *Baihui* (DU 20) the accessory points, and *Zhangmen* (LR 13), *Benshen* (GB 13) and *Daling* (PC 7) the optional points. Of the second group, *Shenmen* (HT 7) and *Houxi* (SI 3) were the main points, *Yuji* (LU 10) and *Yangxi* (LI 5) the accessory points, *Zusanli* (ST 36) and *Fenglong* (ST 40) the optional points. The main points and accessory points were used every time and the optional points were used according to the condition of illness.

Solution: 0.5% novocain in normal saline.

Methods: The above two groups of acupoints were used alternately with one group a day. Each point required 5 ml solution except *Zusanli* and *Jianshi* which required 10 ml solution. A complete course included ten times treatment and the second course could only start after five days rest. Usually the condition of illness improved after two or three courses of treatment. When the illness had been under control for one to three months, another course of treatment was carried out to stabilize the effect.

Effects: Of the 110 patients, 89 recovered, 80.9% of the total patients; the illness was almost kept under control in 12 cases, 10.9% of the total; the condition of illness improved in five cases, 4.5% of the total; and therapy was in vain for four cases, 3.03% of the total.

15. Retention of urine

In Chinese, retention of urine is known as *long-bi*. *Long* refers to mild dysuria when the patient only passes small amounts of urine and experiences dripping urination, while *bi* is more acute, when urine is completely retained. Since it is hard to tell one from the other, they are usually taken as one disease. Clinically, this illness includes dysuria and retention of urine caused by the organic diseases or functional disorders of the urinary bladder, urethra, prostate and kidney.

1) Etiology and pathogenesis

Although the urinary bladder is primarily responsible for retained urine, the disease is closely related to the kidney, lung and spleen. Since the lung is the upper source of body fluid, too much heat accumulates in the lung may block the water passage and prevent body fluid from entering the urinary bladder. When the spleen functions abnormally, dampness-heat will gather in the middle *jiao* and further attack the urinary bladder, causing obstruction of *qi* in the bladder. If the kidney *qi* is deficient, body essence and blood will also become deficient. The decline of fire from the vital gate leads to the hypofunction of urinary bladder. In addition, the disease may also be caused by trauma or surgical operation.

2) Syndrome differentiation

a) Accumulation of lung-heat: Fever, chilliness, cough, short breath, thirst with a desire to drink, difficult urination or retention of urine, reddened tongue and lips, thin and yellow tongue coating, superficial and rapid pulse.

b) Attack of dampness-heat: Chest upset, abdominal distention, loose stools or constipation, oliguria with reddish urine, dysuria with a burning sensation, or even retention of urine, thirst, reddened tongue with yellow coating, soft, superficial and rapid pulse.

c) Insufficiency of kidney *qi*: Pale complexion, cold limbs, lassitude, soreness and weakness in the loin and knees, dizziness, tinnitus, dripping of urine, pale tongue coating, deep and thready pulse, and weak pulse at the cubit.

d) Trauma: Patients with a history of trauma or surgical operation often exhibit distention and fullness in the lower abdomen, difficult urination or hematuria.

3) Treatment

a) Accumulation of lung-heat

Principles: To disperse lung-heat and smooth water passage.

Methods: Select acupoints on the Lung Meridian of Hand-*Taiyin* and the Large Intestine Meridian of Hand-*Yangming* to apply acupuncture, using the reducing manipulation.

Acupoints: *Chize* (LU 5), *Hegu* (LI 4) and *Zhongji* (RN 3).

Notes: *Chize*, the *he* point of Hand-*Taiyin* Meridian, is used to smooth the flow of lung *qi*. Since the lung and the large intestine are interior-exteriorly related, *Hegu*, the *yuan* point of the Large Intestine Meridian, is used to regulate the *qi* in the meridian, disperse pathogenic heat and restore the function of lung so that the body fluid goes downward. *Zhongji*, the front *mu* point of the bladder, helps promote the circulation of *qi* and smooth urination.

b) Attack of dampness-heat

Principles: To disperse heat and dampness, and promote diuresis.

Methods: Select acupoints on the Spleen Meridian of Foot-*Taiyin* and the Stomach Meridian of Foot-*Yangming* to apply acupuncture, using the reducing manipulation.

Acupoints: *Sanyinjiao* (SP 6), *Zusanli* (ST 36), *Pangguangshu* (BL 28) and *Zhongji* (RN 3).

Notes: *Sanyinjiao* of the Spleen Meridian and *Zusanli* (the lower confluent point of the Stomach

Meridian) are used to invigorate the spleen and stomach and disperse dampness-heat. *Zhongji* (a front *mu* point) and *Pangguangshu* (a back *shu* point) are used to regulate the flow of *qi* in the urinary bladder and disperse dampness-heat.

c) Insufficiency of kidney *qi*

Principles: To warm *yang*, benefit *qi*, replenish the kidney and promote diuresis.

Methods: Select the back *shu* points of the *Ren* Meridian to apply acupuncture, using the reinforcing manipulation. Moxibustion may also be used if necessary.

Acupoints: *Shenshu* (BL 23), *Guanyuan* (RN 4), *Qihai* (RN 6) and *Sanjiaoshu* (BL 22).

Notes: *Shenshu* is used to invigorate kidney *qi*; *Sanjiaoshu* regulates the flow of *qi* in *sanjiao*; *Guanyuan* and *Qihai* of the *Ren* Meridian warm and invigorate *yang-qi* in the lower *jiao*. Applying moxibustion to *Guanyuan* and *Qihai* can achieve a even better result. When kidney *qi* is restored and the flow of *qi* becomes smooth, urine will be discharged normally.

d) Trauma

Principles: To promote the flow of *qi*, remove blood-stasis and relieve stranguria.

Methods: Select acupoints on the *Ren* Meridian and the Spleen Meridian of Foot-*Taiyin* to apply acupuncture, using the reducing manipulation.

Acupoints: *Qugu* (RN 2), *Zhongji* (RN 3) and *Sanyinjiao* (SP 6).

Notes: *Zhongji*, the front *mu* point of urinary bladder, is used together with *Sanyinjiao* (the crossing point of the Liver Meridian of Foot-*Jueyin*, the Kidney Meridian of Foot-*Shaoyin* and the Spleen Meridian of Foot-*Taiyin*) to regulate the flow of *qi* in the lower *jiao*. *Qugu*, located near the pubic symphysis, may help relieve stranguria.

4) Other remedies

a) Moxibustion together with massage

After applying moxa stick moxibustion to *Guanyuan* (RN 4) and *Qihai* (RN 6) for 20 minutes to promote the circulation of *qi*, rub the acupoints with the thumb to invigorate the flow of *qi* in the meridians so as to relieve stranguria.

b) Acupoint injection

Inject 10-20 ml of 10% glucose solution into *Zusanli* (ST 36) on both sides. This method has proved effective for acute and functional retention of urine.

5) Notes

a) Acupuncture is more effective in treating functional retention of urine, especially in children, than those caused by organic diseases such as prostatic hypertrophy, urolithiasis and tumor.

b) According to syndrome differentiation, acupoints running through the Lung, Spleen, Kidney and *Sanjiao* Meridians are selected to treat the disease. They are the crossing point *Sanyinjiao* (SP 6), front *mu* points *Zhongji* (RN 3) and *Guanyuan* (RN 4), back *shu* points *Shenshu* (BL 23), *Pangguangshu* (BL 28) and *Sanjiaoshu* (BL 22), and *he* points *Yinlingquan* (SP 9) and *Zusanli* (ST 36).

6) Reference materials

Applying acupuncture treatment to 86 patients suffering postoperative retention of urine (see *A Selection of Clinical Experiences in Acupuncture and Moxibustion*)

Before receiving the treatment, all the patients had applied a hot compress to their lower abdomen or changed the body posture when urinating, but these methods were in vain.

Acupoints: *Guanyuan* (RN 4), *Qugu* (RN 2), *Zusanli* (ST 36), *Sanyinjiao* (SP 6) and *Yinlingquan* (SP 9). One or two points were used each time. *Zusanli* on both sides and *Guanyuan* proved more effective than other points.

Effects: Of the 86 patients, 59 passed urine within 30 minutes after acupuncture, 68.6% of the total; the acupuncture therapy proved in vain in 27 cases, 31.4% of the total.

16. Spermatorrhea

Spermatorrhea is usually classified as nocturnal emission and spontaneous emission. It is quite normal for a single man or a married man who does not live together with his wife has seminal emission once or twice every month. Seminal emission caused by neurasthenia or orchitis can be treated according to the prescriptions in this part.

1) Etiology and pathogenesis

a) Deficiency of *yin* and hyperactivity of fire due to mental stress.

b) Deficiency of the kidney and the loss of essence due to indulgence in sexual activity.

c) The downward flow of dampness-heat and the loss of essence due to indulgence in alcohol and greasy food.

2) Syndrome differentiation

a) Deficiency of *yin* and hyperactivity of fire: Vexation, insomnia, aphthae, nocturnal emission, oliguria, reddened tongue, thready and rapid pulse.

b) Deficiency of the kidney and the loss of essence: Frequent emission or even spermatorrhea, dizziness, blurred vision, tinnitus, soreness and weakness in the loin and knees, pale tongue, thready and weak pulse.

c) The downward flow of dampness-heat: Nocturnal emission accompanied by chest upset and abdominal fullness, insomnia, bitter taste or thirst, poor appetite, painful and hot discharge of urine, yellow and greasy tongue coating, soft, superficial and rapid pulse.

3) Treatment

Principles: To purge fire to nourish *yin* and invigorate the kidney to keep essence. To disperse heat and resolve dampness if there is fever of the deficiency type.

Methods: Select acupoints on the Kidney Meridian of Foot-*Shaoyin*, the Spleen Meridian of Foot-*Taiyin* and the *Ren* Meridian to apply acupuncture, using the reducing or mild reinforcement and reduction manipulation.

Acupoints: *Guanyuan* (RN 4), *Dahe* (KI 12), *Zhishi* (BL 52), *Taichong* (LR 3), *Neiguan* (PC 6), *Shenshu* (BL 23), *Taixi* (KI 3) and *Shenmen* (HT 7). *Yinlingquan* (SP 9) and *Sanyinjiao* (SP 6) for cases with dampness-heat.

Notes: *Neiguan* and *Taichong* are used to disperse heart-fire and liver-fire. *Guanyuan*, the crossing point of three *yin* meridians of foot and the *Ren* Meridian, is the source of primordial *qi* and therefore is used to invigorate kidney *qi*. *Taixi*, the *shu* point of the Kidney Meridian of Foot-*Shaoyin*, is used together with *Shenshu* to nourish *yin* and invigorate the kidney. *Shenmen*, the *shu* point of the Heart Meridian of Foot-*Shaoyin*, helps calm the mind. *Dahe*, the crossing point of the Kidney Meridian of Foot-*Shaoyin* and the *Chong* Meridian, helps strengthen the kidney and check seminal emission. *Yinlingquan*, the *he* point of the Spleen Meridian, is used together with *Sanyinjiao* to disperse dampness-heat.

4) Other remedies

a) Ear acupuncture

Points: Auricular points for uterus (seminal vesicle), tragic apex, ear-*Shenmen*, heart, and kidney.

Methods: Select two or three points to give mild stimulation and keep the needles in the skin for 30-50 minutes. Rotate the needles every 10-15 minutes.

b) Point injection

Inject certain amount of medicinal solution into *Guanyuan* (RN 4) and *Zhongji* (RN 3). When injecting Radix Angelicae Sinensis or normal saline, special attention should be taken to turn the needle towards external genitalia and then push in the solution. The treatment is given once a day, and a complete course includes ten times treatment.

5) Notes

Spermatorrhea for the most part is due to functional disorder, so it is necessary to dispel the patient's anxiety and worries. If spermatorrhea is caused by an organic disease, the treatment should seek to cure the cause as well as the symptoms.

6) Reference materials

Applying acupuncture treatment to 42 patients suffering nocturnal emission or spermatorrhea (see *Journal of Acupuncture and Moxibustion*, No.1 issue of 1965)

The age of these patients ranged from 20 to 35. There were four patients who had suffered the disease for one year and 38 patients for one to three years. Of the 42 cases, two were diagnosed as nocturnal emission and 40 spermatorrea.

Points: Four pairs of points — *Shangliao* (BL 31), *Zhongliao* (BL 33), *Ciliao* (BL 32) and *Xialiao* (BL 34) on both sides of the body.

Methods: The above acupoints were punctured with the reducing manipulation. The needles were lifted swiftly and thrust slowly for about 30 seconds before being inserted deep into the skin. A number of accessory points were used, such as *Guanyuan* (RN 4), *Zhongji* (RN 3), *Mingmen* (DU 4) and *Shenshu* (BL 23) for deficiency of the kidney with symptoms of nocturnal emission, lumbago, dizziness, tinnitus, cold limbs, lassitude, thready and weak pulse. These points were punctured alternately, using the reinforcing manipulation. *Qimen* (LR 14) and *Sanyinjiao* (SP 6) were punctured to treat stagnation of liver *qi* and deficiency of kidney with symptoms of dreaminess, insomnia, dizziness, bitter taste, listlessness, taut pulse in the *guan* position and weak pulse in the *chi* position. *Zusanli* (ST 36), *Zhongwan* (RN 12) and *Sanyinjiao* (SP 6) were punctured with the reducing manipulation for deficiency of the spleen and stomach with symptoms of sallow complexion, listlessness, poor appetite, abdominal distention, loose stools, thick and greasy tongue coating, and feeble pulse. *Shenmen* (HT 7) and *Neiguan* (PC 6) were used to treat disorder of the heart and kidney with symptoms of nocturnal emission, lumbago, palpitation, amnesia, vexation, insomnia, reddened tongue, deep and weak pulse.

Effects: Of the 42 patients, 36 recovered completely; the condition of illness improved in five cases; and the treatment was regarded as ineffective for one patient who had stopped receiving the treatment.

17. Impotence

Impotence refers to the inability to have an erection or maintain an erection until ejaculation, which is often seen in sexual neurastenia and some chronic diseases.

1) Etiology and pathogenesis

Impotence is usually caused by the decline of fire from the gate of life and exhaustion of essence and blood as a result of early marriage, indulgence in sexual activity or frequent masturbation, damage to the kidney by fright, damage to the heart and spleen and further the Stomach Meridian of Foot-*Yangming* and *Chong* Meridian by worries. There are also some cases caused by the downward flow of dampness-heat.

2) Syndrome differentiation

Failure to have an erection or inability to maintain a satisfactory erection, premature ejaculation. The accompanying symptoms are dizziness, blurred vision, tinnitus, insomnia, pale complexion, lassitude, soreness and weakness in the loin and knees, thready and weak pulse.

3) Treatment

Principles: To invigorate kidney *qi* and benefit the heart and spleen.

Methods: Select acupoints on the Kidney Meridian of Foot-*Shaoyin* and the Stomach Meridian of Foot-*Yangming* and a back *shu* point to apply acupuncture treatment, using the reinforcing manipulation.

Moxibustion can also be used if necessary.

Acupoints: *Shenshu* (BL 23), *Zusanli* (ST 36) and *Neiguan* (PC 6).

Notes: Since the disease is chiefly due to the deficiency of kidney *qi*, *Shenshu* is used to invigorate kidney *qi* and improve the function of the Kidney Meridian. *Zusanli*, the *he* point of the Stomach Meridian of Foot-*Yangming*, helps relieve stagnation, calm the mind and invigorate the heart and spleen when used together with *Neiguan*.

4) Other remedies

a) Pricking therapy

Acupoints: *Shenshu* (BL 23), *Mingmen* (DU 4), *Shangliao* (BL 31), *Ciliao* (BL 32), *Zhongliao* (BL 33), *Xialiao* (BL 34), *Sanjiaoshu* (BL 22), *Guanyuanshu* (BL 26), *Baihui* (DU 20), *Dazhui* (DU 14), *Dazhu* (BL 11) and *Changqiang* (DU 1).

Methods: Select one to two points each time. Prompt prick and sway the needle for 5-10 minutes. Use a fine needle to prick the tendons if the patient is of weak constitution, and moxibustion treatment can be used at the same time. The treatment is given every two days, and a complete course includes five times treatment.

b) Electric acupuncture

Apply an electroacupuncture device to *Qugu* (RN 2), *Rangu* (KI 2), and four pairs of points — *Shangliao* (BL 31), *Zhongliao* (BL 33), *Ciliao* (BL 32) and *Xialiao* (BL 34) on both sides of the body, using low-frequency pulse circuit. The treatment lasts three to five minutes each time. When puncturing at *Qugu*, it's better to conduct the needling sensation towards the external genitalia.

c) Ear acupuncture

Points: Auricular points for uterus (seminal vesicle), external genitalia, testis (ovary) and internal tragic apex.

Methods: Select two to four points each time, and keep the needle in the skin for 10-20 minutes. If needle embedment therapy is used, it should last three to five days.

5) Notes

Tonics which benefit *qi* and strengthen the kidney *yang* can be taken during the acupuncture treatment to achieve a better result.

6) Reference materials (see *Needle-Pricking Therapy*)

A 27-year-old patient named Liang came to see the doctor for the first time in April 1974, complaining that he had no baby ever since he got married three years ago. He told the doctor that he had a habit of masturbation before marriage, and indulged in sexual activity after marriage. It was for these reasons that he was in trouble of impotence and sterility. The accompanying symptoms were dizziness, tinnitus, sallow complexion and listlessness. Semen examination showed that the spermatic count was 28,400,000/cm^3 and 50% sperms were inactive. He had tried many medicine including oral Chinese and western medicine, but all in vain. His wife also took a medical check and nothing abnormal was found.

Pricking therapy was applied first to *Dazhu* (BL 11) on both sides and *Guanyuan* (RN 4), and the patient felt an erection the next morning. The treatment was applied to *Shenshu* (BL 23) and *Fengfu* (DU 16) for the second time, and the patient became vigorous; *Guanyuanshu* (BL 26) on both sides and *Dazhui* (DU 14) were punctured for the third time. Sexual activity became normal in one week, and semen check after one month showed that the spermatic count was 90,750,000/cm^3 and 80% sperms were active. The couple had a boy in one year.

18. Hernia

Hernia refers to the swelling and pain in the testis, scrotum and lower abdomen. The diseased area is often along the *Ren* Meridian and the Liver Meridian of Foot-*Jueyin*. Testitis, epididymitis, spermatitis and inguinal hernia can all be treated according to the prescriptions in this part.

1) Etiology and pathogenesis

Hernia of the cold type is usually caused by exposure to cold and dampness such as cold water, rain and cold wind. The cold makes the *qi* and blood in the *Ren* Meridian and the Liver Meridian of Foot-*Jueyin* stagnant; hernia of the dampness-heat type is caused by the downward flow of dampness-heat from the liver and spleen; overburden or stress may lead to deficiency and collapse of *qi*, resulting in inguinal hernia.

2) Syndrome differentiation

a) Cold hernia: Coldness and pain in external genitalia, contracture of testis spreading to the lower abdomen or even the chest and hypochondria, cold limbs, pale complexion, thin and white tongue coating, deep and thready pulse.

b) Dampness-heat hernia: Distensive pain in the testis, reddened, swelling and hot pain in external genitalia, chilliness, fever, yellow urine, constipation, yellow and greasy tongue coating, taut and rapid pulse.

c) Inguinal hernia: Continuous distensive pain in the scrotum when standing and in the lower abdomen when lying down.

3) Treatment

a) Cold hernia

Principles: To warmly eliminate cold-dampness and smooth the meridians.

Methods: Select acupoints on the Liver Meridian of Foot-*Jueyin* and the *Ren* Meridian to apply acupuncture, using the reducing manipulation. Moxibustion may also be used if necessary.

Acupoints: *Guanyuan* (RN 4), *Sanyinjiao* (SP 6) and *Dadun* (LR 1).

Notes: Hernia is a disorder of the *Ren* Meridian. The Liver Meridian of Foot-*Jueyin* travels around the external genitalia and the three *yin* meridians of foot connect with the *Ren* Meridian. Therefore, *Guanyuan* of the *Ren* Meridian, *Dadun* of the Liver Meridian of Foot-*Jueyin* and *Sanyinjiao*, the crossing point of three *yin* meridians of foot, are used to smooth the meridians. If moxibustion is used together with acupuncture, it can warm the meridians, smooth the collaterals, dispel cold-dampness and alleviate pain.

b) Dampness-heat hernia

Principles: To disperse heat and dampness, relieve swelling and stagnation.

Methods: Select acupoints on the three *yin* meridians of foot to apply acupuncture, using the reducing manipulation.

Acupoints: *Guanyuan* (RN 4), *Taichong* (LR 3) and *Yinlingquan* (SP 9).

Notes: *Guanyuan* and *Taichong* can disperse heat in the Liver Meridian of Foot-*Jueyin* and the *Ren* Meridian; *Yinlingquan* helps disperse dampness-heat. When dampness-heat is eliminated, swelling and stagnation will disappear.

c) Inguinal hernia

Principles: To invigorate and elevate *qi*, promote the flow of *qi* and alleviate pain.

Methods: Select acupoints on the *Ren* Meridian and the Stomach Meridian of Foot-*Yangming* to apply acupuncture, using the reinforcing manipulation. Moxibustion may also be used if necessary.

Acupoints: *Guilai* (ST 29), *Guanyuan* (RN 4) and *Sanjiaojiu* (EX-CA)

Notes: The Stomach Meridian of Foot-*Yangming* is rich in *qi* and blood which nourish the external genitalia. Therefore, *Guilai* on this meridian is used together with *Guanyuan* to invigorate and elevate *qi*. Applying moxibustion treatment regularly at *Sanjiaojiu* is effective for hernia, for it can elevate *qi* and induce astringency.

4) Notes

Although acupuncture treatment can alleviate enterocele, surgical operation is recommended if the disease attacks frequently and the protruded intestines are difficult to resume the normal position.

5) Reference materials

Applying acupuncture treatment to 22 patients suffering acute epididymitis (see *Chinese Journal of Surgery*, No.2 issue of 1962)

Points: *Sanyinjiao* (SP 6), *Guanyuan* (RN 4), *Xingjian* (LR 2), *Zusanli* (ST 36), *Yanglingquan* (GB 34) and *Qugu* (RN 2).

Methods: Three to four points were punctured each time. Moderate or strong stimulation was given to the points, and the needles were kept in the skin for 30-60 minutes. The treatment was usually given once or twice a day in combination with a hot compress. During the treatment, no patients administered antibiotics except for four who received procaine block therapy.

Effects: There were 14 patients recovered from the disease; seven almost recovered; and one found the treatment ineffective.

19. Headache

Headache is a common symptom of various acute and chronic diseases. This part of the book deals with headache often seen in chronic diseases rather than headache caused by acute febrile diseases. Headache caused by neurasthenia, migraine, hypertension or brain trauma can be treated according to the descriptions of this part.

1) Etiology and pathogenesis

a) Headache due to wind-cold: Affection of wind-cold blocks the collaterals and leads to the disharmony between nutrient and defensive systems, which attacks the head and results in headache.

b) Headache due to wind-heat: Wind-heat, a pathogenic factor of the *yang* type, is liable to attack the upper part of the body and block the collaterals.

c) Headache due to wind-dampness: The stagnation of wind-dampness in the meridians on the head blocks the circulation of *qi* and blood circulation, resulting in headache.

d) Headache due to hyperactivity of liver *yang*: Anger leads to the stagnation of *qi* which turns into fire and attacks the head. The deficiency of kidney *yin* prevents the liver from being nourished, therefore hyperactive liver *yang* attacks the upper part of the body.

e) Headache due to phlegm-dampness: Dampness accumulates in people who are fat and fond of sweet and greasy food. Phlegm produced by this dampness blocks the meridians and the lucid *yang-qi*, and headache thus occurs.

f) Headache due to blood stasis: Trauma damages the collaterals and produces blood stasis; protracted illness enters the collaterals and blocks the circulation of *qi* and blood, headache thus occurs.

g) Headache due to deficiency of blood: Weak constitution, body deficiency due to protracted illness, blood deficiency due to blood loss all result in the failure of blood in nourishing the brain, and headache thus occurs.

2) Syndrome differentiation

a) Headache due to wind-cold: Headache spreading to the neck and back, pain in the joints of the limbs, aversion to wind and cold, preference to cover the head with a scarf, thin and white tongue coating, and superficial pulse.

b) Headache due to wind-heat: Headache with a distensive and bursting feeling, flushed face, reddened eyes, blue veins standing out on the temples, vexation, thirst, fever, chilliness, constipation, oliguria, reddened tongue with yellow coating, superficial and rapid pulse.

c) Headache due to wind-dampness: Headache with a feeling of being wrapped tightly by a strap, chest upset, lassitude, sleepiness, loose stools, white and greasy tongue coating, soft and superficial pulse.

d) Headache due to hyperactivity of liver *yang*: Headache on one side, dizziness, irritability, flushed face, conjunctival congestion, bitter taste, insomnia, reddened tongue with yellow coating, and taut pulse.

e) Headache due to phlegm-dampness: Headache, blurred vision, fullness in the chest and abdomen, nausea, vomiting, white and greasy tongue coating, taut and smooth pulse.

f) Headache due to blood-stasis: Lingering headache with a fixed position and needling pain and blurred vision. If the patient has a history of brain trauma, the symptoms are dark purplish tongue, and thready and knotted pulse.

g) Headache due to deficiency of blood: Headache, dizziness, pallor, blurred vision, hypoacusis, palpitation, insomnia, lassitude aggravating on strain, pale tongue with thin and white coating, thready and weak pulse.

3) Treatment

a) Headache due to wind-cold

Principles: To dispel wind and cold.

Methods: Select acupoints on the Bladder Meridian of Foot-*Taiyang* and the Large Intestine Meridian of Hand-*Yangming* to apply acupuncture, using the reducing manipulation. Moxibustion can also be used if necessary.

Acupoints: *Dazhu* (BL 11), *Fengmen* (BL 12), *Hegu* (LI 4) and *Taiyang* (EX-HN 5).

Notes: *Dazhu* helps to alleviate headache and pain in neck and back. If *Dazhu* and *Fengmen* are used together, they can dispel wind, relieve external syndrome and alleviate pain. *Hegu* dispels wind and relieves external syndrome. If *Hegu* and *Taiyang* are used together, they can smooth the meridians and relieve headache.

b) Headache due to wind-heat

Principles: To dispel wind and heat.

Methods: Select acupoints on the Large Intestine Meridian of Hand-*Yangming* and the Gallbladder Meridian of Foot-*Shaoyang* to apply acupuncture, using the reducing manipulation.

Acupoints: *Hegu* (LI 4), *Fengchi* (GB 20), *Quchi* (LI 11) and *Yangbai* (GB 14).

Notes: *Hegu* and *Quchi* help dispel wind and heat; *Fengchi* and *Yangbai* regulate the *qi* in the meridians and alleviate pain.

c) Headache due to wind-dampness

Principles: To eliminate wind, resolve dampness and smooth the meridians.

Methods: Select acupoints on the Large Intestine Meridian of Hand-*Yangming*, the *Sanjiao* Meridian of Hand-*Shaoyang*, the Stomach Meridian of Foot-*Yangming* and the Gallbladder Meridian of Foot-*Shaoyang* to apply acupuncture, using the reducing manipulation. Moxibustion can also be used if necessary.

Acupoints: *Lieque* (LU 7), *Tianzhu* (BL 10), *Shuaigu* (GB 8), *Sanyangluo* (SJ 8) and *Touwei* (ST 8).

Notes: *Sanyangluo* and *Shuaigu* are used to relieve hemicrania; *Touwei* eliminates wind and dampness and relieves frontal headache; *Lieque* relieves headache and rigid nape; *Tianzhu* relieves occipital headache. The combination of these acupoints serves to regulate *yang-qi*, warm the meridians, smooth the collaterals, and eliminate wind and dampness.

d) Headache due to hyperactivity of liver *yang*

Principles: To relieve stagnant liver-*qi*, suppress wind and *yang*.

Methods: Select acupoints on the Gallbladder Meridian of Foot-*Shaoyang*, the Liver Meridian of Foot-*Jueyin* and the Kidney Meridian of Foot-*Shaoyin* to apply acupuncture, using the reducing manipulation.

Acupoints: *Xuanlu* (GB 5), *Hanyan* (GB 4), *Taichong* (LR 3) and *Taixi* (KI 3).

Notes: Since the hyperactivity of liver *yang* is usually accompanied by the attack of the upper part of the body by wind-heat along the Gallbladder Meridian of Foot-*Shaoyang*, symptoms like pain in the temporal region appear. *Xuanlu* and *Hanyan* are used to disperse *qi* in the Foot-*Shaoyang* Meridian. *Taichong* helps purge fire and *Taixi* nourishes the kidney-*yin* to benefit the liver and suppress the hyperactive *yang*.

e) Headache due to phlegm-dampness

Principles: To resolve phlegm, disperse the turbidity, smooth the collaterals and alleviate pain.

Methods: Select acupoints on the *Ren* and *Du* meridians as well as the Stomach Meridian of Foot-*Yangming* to apply acupuncture, using the reducing manipulation. Moxibustion can also be used if necessary.

Acupoints: *Dazhui* (DU 14), *Yintang* (EX-HN 3), *Fenglong* (ST 40) and *Zhongwan* (RN 12).

Notes: *Dazhui*, the crossing point of *yang* meridians, is used to warm *yang-qi* and eliminate cold-phlegm. *Yintang* helps to activate lucid *yang*. *Fenglong* and *Zhongwan* are used to strengthen the spleen and stomach, eliminate dampness and turbidity. Moxibustion can be used to warm and disperse phlegm-dampness, smooth the collaterals and alleviate pain.

f) Headache due to blood-stasis

Principles: To promote blood circulation, remove blood stasis, activate the flow of *qi* and alleviate pain.

Methods: Select acupoints on the Large Intestine Meridian of Hand-*Yangming*, the Spleen Meridian of Foot-*Taiyin* and the Liver Meridian of Foot-*Jueyin* to apply acupuncture, using the reducing manipulation.

Acupoints: *Hegu* (LI 4), *Taichong* (LR 3), *Xuehai* (SP 10) and *Ashi* point.

Notes: *Hegu*, the *yuan* point of the Large Intestine Meridian of Hand-*Yangming*, activates the flow of *qi* and blood; *Taichong*, the *yuan* point of the Liver Meridian of Foot-*Jueyin*, removes blood stasis and alleviates pain. *Taichong* and *Xuehai* serve to promote the flow of blood; *Ashi* point helps to smooth the meridians and alleviate pain.

g) Headache due to deficiency of blood

Principles: To invigorate the spleen, replenish blood, promote the flow of *qi*, regulate collaterals and alleviate pain.

Methods: Select acupoints on the Stomach Meridian of Foot-*Yangming* and the Bladder Meridian of Foot-*Taiyang* and the back *shu* points to apply acupuncture, using the reinforcing manipulation. Moxibustion can also be used if necessary.

Acupoints: *Ganshu* (BL 18), *Geshu* (BL 17), *Sanyinjiao* (SP 6), *Zusanli* (ST 36), *Pishu* (BL 20) and *Dazhui* (DU 14).

Notes: *Zusanli* and *Pishu* strengthen the spleen and stomach and further the production of *qi* and blood. *Geshu*, an influential point related to blood, is used together with *Ganshu* to nourish the liver and replenish blood. *Sanyinjiao* and *Dazhui* help promote the circulation of *qi* and blood, and the smooth flow of *qi* and blood will relieve headache.

4) Other remedies

Plum-blossom needle therapy

Tap the head, neck, temporal region and both sides of the spine with a plum-blossom needle. Give hard knocks at the above areas in cases with acute pain of the excess type. The treatment is given once a day, and a complete course includes ten times treatment.

5) Notes

Acupuncture and moxibustion treatment are effective for chronic and recurrent headache, especially insomnia and headache caused by neurasthenia.

6) Reference materials

Applying acupuncture treatment to 73 patients suffering nervous headache (see *A Selection of Clinical Experiences in Acupuncture and Moxibustion*)

The local and remote acupoints were used in acupuncture. There were 18 patients who completely recovered and received treatment by an average of 9.3 sessions; the treatment proved effective on 28 patients who received treatment by an average of 8.4 sessions; the condition of illness improved in 23 patients who received treatment by an average of 7.6 sessions; the treatment was ineffective on two patients who received treatment by an average of 7.5 sessions; two cases didn't meet the statistical requirements. The total rate of effectiveness was 97.48%.

20. Dizziness

Dizziness refers to a feeling of something spinning within the head. In mild cases, dizziness disappears when one closes his eyes; in severe cases, there is a whirling sensation, inability to stand up, nausea, vomiting, sweating, or even fainting. Dizziness is often seen in hypertension, arteriosclerosis, anemia, neurosis and Meniere's diseases.

1) Etiology and pathogenesis

a) Hyperactivity of liver *yang*: Exuberant *yang* in one's body leads to hyperactivity of liver *yang*; fire produced by anger or depression consumes liver *yin* and liver *yang* becomes active which attacks the head; deficient kidney *yin* fails to nourish the liver and liver *yang* becomes active.

b) Deficiency of *qi* and blood: Protracted illness, blood loss and deficiency of the spleen and stomach all lead to the deficiency of *qi* and blood. Deficiency of *qi* results in the disorder of lucid *yang*, and insufficient blood fails to nourish the brain.

c) Insufficiency of kidney-essence: Congenital defect, senile debility and indulgence in sexual activity can all lead to the loss of kidney-essence. Since the brain is the sea of marrow, deficiency of marrow and the loss of kidney-essence will lead to dizziness.

d) Stagnation of phlegm-dampness: Improper diet harms the spleen and stomach and further the digestion. Food retention produces dampness and phlegm which block the middle *jiao*. As a result, lucid *yang* cannot ascend and turbid *yin* lingers, thus dizziness occurs.

2) Syndrome differentiation

a) Hyperactivity of liver *yang*: Dizziness, tinnitus, flushed face, irritability, headache with a distensive feeling which aggravates upon anger, insomnia, dreaminess, bitter taste, reddened tongue with yellow coating, and taut pulse.

b) Deficiency of *qi* and blood: Pale complexion, palpitation, insomnia, lassitude, poor appetite, dizziness which aggravates upon exertion, pale tongue, and weak pulse.

c) Insufficiency of kidney essence: Lumbago, weak knees, dizziness, tinnitus, lassitude, amnesia, insomnia, nocturnal emission. In cases of *yin* deficiency, there are symptoms of a feverish sensation in the palms, soles and chest, reddened tongue and rapid pulse; in cases of *yang* deficiency, there are symptoms such as cold limbs, pale tongue, deep and weak pulse.

d) Stagnation of phlegm-dampness: Heaviness in the head, chest upset, nausea, poor appetite, somnolence, pale and greasy tongue coating, soft and smooth pulse.

3) Treatment

a) Hyperactivity of liver-*yang*

Principles: To calm the liver and suppress *yang*.

Methods: Select acpoints on the Liver and Gallbladder Meridians to apply acupuncture, using the reducing manipulation.

Acupoints: *Ganshu* (BL 18), *Taichong* (LR 3), *Fengchi* (GB 20), *Xiaxi* (GB 43), *Taixi* (KI 3) and *Shenshu* (BL 23).

Notes: *Ganshu* (the back *shu* point of the Liver Meridian and where the *qi* of the *zang* organ is distributed) and *Taichong* (the *yuan* point of the Liver Meridian) purge liver-fire. *Xiaxi* (the *ying* point of the Gallbladder Meridian) is used together with *Fengchi* to purge the gallbladder-fire and wind-heat. *Taixi* and *Shenshu* invigorate the kidney and nourish *yin* and further suppress liver-fire.

b) Deficiency of *qi* and blood

Principles: To nourish *qi* and blood, and invigorate the spleen and stomach.

Methods: Select the back *shu* points and acupoints on *Du* and Foot-*Yangming* Meridians to apply acupuncture, using the reinforcing manipulation. Moxibustion can also be applied.

Acupoints: *Pishu* (BL 20), *Zusanli* (ST 36), *Baihui* (DU 20), *Qihai* (RN 6) and *Ganshu* (BL 18).

Notes: *Pishu* and *Zusanli* invigorate the spleen and stomach. Therefore, the production of *qi* and blood is promoted. *Baihui* and *Qihai* invigorate the *qi* and elevate *yang*. *Ganshu* nourishes the liver, blood and brain, and dizziness thus stops.

c) Insufficiency of kidney-essence

Principles: To invigorate the kidney, benefit essence, support the primordial *qi* and strengthen body resistance.

Methods: Select the back *shu* points and acupoints on the Kidney Meridian of Foot-*Shaoyin* to apply acupuncture. Moxibustion treatment can be used in cases with *yang* deficiency. The reinforcing manipulation is adopted when applying acupuncture treatment to cases with *yin* deficiency.

Acupoints: *Baihui* (DU 20), *Pishu* (BL 20), *Zusanli* (ST 36), *Guanyuan* (RN 4), *Sanyinjiao* (SP 6), *Ganshu* (BL 18) and *Shenshu* (BL 23).

Applying moxibustion treatment to *Baihui* can help elevate the lucid *yang*; *Pishu* and *Zusanli* can invigorate the spleen and stomach; *Shenshu* and *Ganshu* replenish the essence and blood. Applying moxibustion treatment to *Guanyuan* can warm and strengthen the primordial *qi*. Applying moxibustion treatment to *Sanyinjiao* and *Guanyuan* can replenish *yin* in cases of *yin* deficiency.

d) Stagnation of phlegm-dampness

Principles: To regulate the middle *jiao* and eliminate dampness.

Methods: Select acupoints on the Stomach Meridian of Foot-*Yangming* and the Spleen Meridian of Foot-*Taiyin* and the back *shu* points, using the reducing manipulation.

Acupoints: *Touwei* (ST 8), *Fenglong* (ST 40), *Zhongwan* (RN 12), *Pishu* (BL 20), *Zusanli* (ST 36) and *Neiguan* (PC 6).

Notes: *Touwei*, the crossing point of the Stomach Meridian of Foot-*Yangming* and Gallbladder Meridian of Foot-*Shaoyang*, helps to dispel wind, alleviate pain and relieve dizziness. *Fenglong* (the *luo* point of the Stomach Meridian of Foot-*Yangming*) and *Zhongwan* (the front *mu* point of the stomach) help eliminate phlegm. *Pishu* and *Zusanli* warm and resolve phlegm-dampness. *Neiguan*, which is the *luo* point of the Pericardium Meridian of Hand-*Jueyin* and links with the *Sanjiao* Meridian of Hand-*Shaoyang*, is used to disperse heart-fire, soothe the chest and relieve vomiting.

4) Other remedies

a) Head acupuncture

Area: Vertigo and audition area.

Method: After sterilization, insert the needle into the points on this area, 2 cm deep. While keeping the needle in the skin, rotate it quickly twice or three times. The treatment is given once a day and a complete course includes ten sessions. Another course will begin after an interval of three days.

b) Ear acupuncture

Points: Ear-*Shenmen*, brain, end of inferior antihelix crus, and inner ear.

Method: Two or three points are used each time. The needles are embedded for three to five days. While applying acupuncture treatment, give a moderate stimulation. The treatment is given once a day and a complete course includes ten times treatment.

5) Notes

Since there are many causes of dizziness, the doctor must first make a correct diagnosis and then select an appropriate treatment. Moxibustion with warming needle is often used to treat Meniere's disease and the effective points are *Baihui* (DU 20), *Fengchi* (GB 20), *Neiguan* (PC 6) and *Zusanli* (ST 36).

6) Reference materials

Applying ear acupuncture treatment to 550 patients suffering dizziness due to streptomycin poisoning (see *Research on Ear Acupuncture*)

After the treatment, 282 patients totally recovered from the illness; the symptoms almost disappeared in 237 patients. The effectiveness rate was 94%. There were 94 patients whose vestibular function resumed the normal state and the condition of 124 patients improved. The effectiveness rate was 85%.

Appendix: Essential hypertension

1) Etiology and pathogenesis

Imbalance between *yin* and *yang*, *qi* and blood due to anxiety, mental stress, overeating greasy food, smoking and drinking is the basic cause of hypertension.

2) Syndrome differentiation

In the initial stage of hypertension, blood pressure is not stable, and the cause is usually mental stress or fatigue. Symptoms of this period are restlessness, irritability, flushed face, headache and dizziness. In the middle stage, blood pressure keeps going up due to the deficiency of *yin* and hyperactivity of *yang*. The symptoms of this period are numbness in the limbs, dizziness, tinnitus, vexation and insomnia. In the tertiary stage due to the deficiency of *yin* and *yang*, symptoms such as a feverish sensation in the palms, soles and chest, palpitation, insomnia, dizziness, lassitude, lumbago and weakness in the knee joints appear.

3) Treatment

Principles: To calm the liver and suppress wind, nourish *yin* and invigorate the kidney, and regulate *yin* and *yang*.

Methods: Select acupoints on the Kidney Meridian of Foot-*Shaoyin*, the Liver Meridian of Foot-*Jueyin* and the Stomach Meridian of Foot-*Yangming* to apply acupuncture, using the reducing manipulation in the initial stage, the mild reinforcement and reduction in the middle stage and tertiary stages. Moxibustion can also be used.

Acupoints: *Taichong* (LR 3), *Zusanli* (ST 36) and *Yongquan* (KI 1). *Fengchi* (GB 20) is used together with the above points in treating dizziness; *Neiguan* (PC 6) is added to treat insomnia and vexation.

Notes: *Taichong*, the *yuan* point of the Liver Meridian, helps calm the liver and suppress wind. *Zusanli*, an acupoint on the Stomach Meridian, serves to regulate *qi* and blood. *Yongquan*, the *jiing* point of the Kidney Meridian, helps nourish *yin* and invigorate the kidney. Giving moxibustion treatment to *Yongquan* can send fire back to its origin (kidney). *Fengchi*, the crossing point of the *Yangwei* Meridian and the Gallbladder Meridian, can disperse fire and relieve headache. *Neiguan* disperses heart-fire and calms the mind.

4) Other remedies

Ear acupuncture

Area: The ear groove for lowering blood pressure

Methods: Puncture at the upper and lower ends of the groove and direct the needle toward the center while rotating it. Keep the needles in the skin for 15-30 minutes. The auricular points for heart and brain, and ear-*Shenmen* can also be used. This treatment is given once a day, and a complete course includes ten sessions. Besides, needle embedment therapy can also be used, with 3-5 days duration and one or two points each time. Both ears can be punctured alternately.

21. Apoplexy

Apoplexy is a disorder which causes the patient to fall to the ground all of a sudden and lose consciousness. The accompanied symptoms are contortion of the facial muscles, dysphasia and hemiplegia. It is characterized by an abrupt onset with pathological changes taking place over a very short period of time, like the time it takes for the nature of the wind to change. It is for this reason that its Chinese name is "windstroke".

It is similar to the cerebral hemorrhage and thrombosis, subarachnoid hemorrhage, cerebrovascular spasm viral encephalitis and central facial paralysis in modern medicine.

1) Etiology and pathogenesis

a) Insufficiency of healthy *qi*: When the body resistance is weak and the meridians are empty, pathogenic wind can invade them, disturbing turbid phlegm which enters the meridians.

b) Imbalance between *yin* and *yang*: Strain, weakness of the body after illness, debility due to old age can all lead to deficiency of *yin* in the lower body and hyperactivity of asthenic *yang*. The unhealthy *qi* and blood cause apoplexy.

c) Disharmony of the liver and spleen: Improper diet, strain, dysfunction of the spleen can all lead to the accumulation of dampness which turns into phlegm. Dysfunction of the liver causes the stagnation of *qi* and further fire. The phlegm and dampness attack the meridians and block the clear cavity, thus apoplexy occurs.

d) Emotional upsets: Hyperactivity of heart-fire and liver *yang* produces wind and fire which work together with *qi* and blood as they move upward.

In a word, apoplexy is closely related to deficiency (deficiency of *yin* and *qi*), fire (liver-fire or heart-fire), wind (liver-wind or exogenous wind), phlegm (wind-phlegm or dampness-phlegm), *qi* (the unhealthy *qi*) and blood (blood stasis). Its basic cause is *yin* deficiency of the liver and kidney.

2) Syndrome differentiation

The *zang-fu* organs are likely to be attacked if apoplexy is serious, and if the disease is superficial, the meridians are attacked.

a) Attack on the *zang-fu* organs

Loss of consciousness and facial hemiplegia, which usually occur after premonitory symptoms and leave sequelae. Clinically, the disease is divided into two types: one with excess syndrome and the other with prostration syndrome.

Apoplexy with excess syndrome: Fall in a fit, loss of consciousness, lockjaw, clenched fists, red face and ears, open eyes, gasp, rale, retention of urine, constipation, taut and smooth pulse.

Apoplexy with prostration syndrome: Fall in a fit, loss of consciousness, unclenched hands, open mouth, closed eyes, pale complexion, profuse perspiration, feeble breathing, incontinence of urine and feces, cold limbs, thready and weak pulse.

THERAPEUTICS

Table 22 Apoplexy with Excess Syndrome and Prostration Syndrome

	Excess syndrome	Prostration syndrome
Major symptoms	1) open eyes	1) closed eyes
	2) lockjaw	2) open mouth
	3) clenched fists	3) loose hands
	4) absence of sweat, wheezing, gasp	4) profuse perspiration
	5) constipation and ischuria	5) incontinence of stools and urine
Pulse	taut, rapid and forceful pulse	feeble pulse

b) Attack on the meridians

It refers to the mild condition of apoplexy without losing consciousness. After the attack on the *zang-fu* organs, this often occurs as its sequelae. Besides, there are cases which only involve the meridians from the very beginning, with symptoms of dyskinesia of limbs, facial paralysis, dysphasia, hemiplegia, reddened tongue with yellow coating, taut, thready and rapid pulse.

Hemiplegia: Flaccid or numb limbs, sallow complexion and petechiae over the tongue in cases of *qi* deficiency, blood stasis and obstruction of meridians; headache, dizziness, flushed face, tinnitus, rigid limbs, reddened tongue with yellow coating, taut and rapid pulse in cases of hyperactivity of liver *yang*.

Dysphasia: Stiff tongue and numb limbs in cases of the obstruction of collaterals by wind-phlegm; palpitation, short breath, lumbago and weak knee joints in cases of deficiency of the kidney essence.

Distortion of the face: Wry eyes and mouth in cases of obstruction of collaterals by wind-phlegm.

3) Treatment

a) Attack on the *zang-fu* organs

Apoplexy with excess syndrome

Principles: To restore consciousness, calm the liver, suppress wind, disperse fire and eliminate phlegm.

Methods: Select acupoints on the *Du* Meridian and the *jiing* points to apply acupuncture, using the reducing manipulation.

Acupoints: *Shuigou* (DU 26), the twelve *jiing* points, *Taichong* (LR 3), *Fenglong* (ST 40) and *Laogong* (PC 8).

Notes: *Shuigou* helps regulate the *qi* of the *Du* Meridian and restore consciousness. Prompt pricking the twelve *jing* points to let out a little blood can purge heat and suppress endogenous wind. *Taichong* sends down the unhealthy *qi* in the Liver Meridian and calms liver *yang*; *Fenglong* eliminates phlegm and dampness; *Laogong*, the *ying* point of the Pericardium Meridian, disperses heart-fire and heat.

Apoplexy with prostration syndrome

Principles: To recuperate depleted *yang* and rescue the patient from collapse.

Methods: Select certain points on the *Ren* Meridian to apply moxibustion treatment so as to strengthen the *yang-qi* in the body.

Acupoints: *Guanyuan* (RN 4), *Shenque* (RN 8), *Qihai* (RN 6) and *Baihui* (DU 20).

Notes: *Guanyuan*, *Shenque* and *Qihai* all help to restore the healthy *qi* and relieve collapse. Applying salt moxibustion to these points can recuperate depleted *yang* and rescue the patient from collapse. *Baihui* regulates the *qi* in the *Du* Meridian and restore consciousness.

b) Attack on the meridians

Hemiplegia

Principles: To promote the circulation of *qi* and blood and regulate the function of meridians.

Methods: Select acupoints on the *yang* meridians on the diseased side of the body, using the mild reinforcement and reduction manipulation.

Acupoints: *Baihui* (DU 20), *Fengchi* (GB 20) and *Dazhui* (DU 14). *Jianyu* (LI 15), *Quchi* (LI 11), *Waiguan* (SJ 5) and *Hegu* (LI 4) are used for paralysis of the upper limbs; *Huantiao* (GB 30), *Yanglingquan* (GB 34), *Zusanli* (ST 36), *Jiexi* (ST 41) and *Shenshu* (BL 23) are used for paralysis of the lower limbs.

Notes: Pathogenic wind is of the *yang* type and usually attacks the upper part of the body and the body surface, therefore *Baihui*, *Fengchi* and *Dazhui* are used to expel wind from the upper body. Since the *yang* meridians control the body surface, points along these meridians are used to promote the circulation of *qi* and blood and smooth the meridians. *Sanyinjiao* and *Xuehai* are used to invigorate *qi*, promote the circulation of blood, relieve blood stasis. *Taiyang* (EX-HN 5), *Taichong* and *Taixi* (KI 3) are used in combination to nourish *yin*, suppress *yang*, arrest wind and disperse heat in cases of *yin* deficiency of the liver and kidney and hyperactivity of liver *yang*.

Distortion of the face

Principles: To smooth meridians and regulate *qi* and blood.

Methods: Select acupoints on the Large Intestine Meridian of Hand-*Yangming*, Stomach Meridian of Foot-*Yangming*, and the Bladder Meridian of Foot-*Taiyang* to apply acupuncture, using the mild reinforcement and reduction manipulation.

Acupoints: Refer to the chapter of facial paralysis.

Dysphasia

Principles: To regulate the balance between *yin* and *yang*, *qi* and blood.

Methods: Select acupoints on the *Ren* and *Du* meridians to apply acupuncture, using the mild reinforcement and reduction manipulation or prompt prick to let out a little blood.

Acupoints: *Lianquan* (RN 23), *Yamen* (DU 15), *Jinjin* (EX-HN 12), *Yuye* (EX-HN 13) and *Guanchong* (SJ 1).

Notes: *Lianquan* and *Yamen*, acupoints on the *Ren* and *Du* meridians, are used to regulate the balance between *yin* and *yang* and smooth meridians. *Jinjin*, *Yuye* and *Guanchong* are effective for stiff tongue.

4) Other remedies

a) Head acupuncture

The treatment should be carried out when the condition of illness becomes stable and a diagnosis has been made, for the shorter the duration of illness, the better the therapeutic effect and vice versa. In addition, the treatment is more effective against the thrombosis of the branches of middle and anterior cerebral arteries than against that of deep branches and arterial stem.

Area: The motor area, sensory area, and foot motor-sensory area on the other side.

Methods: First, select an area and sterilize the skin. Then insert a filiform needle (1 *cun* to 1.5 *cun* long) into the skin, 3-5 cm deep, and twist it 220 times/min. for two to three minutes. Meanwhile, ask the patient to move his paralyzed limb so as to achieve a better result. Keep the needle in the skin for a little while and then repeat the above manipulation once or twice. One session of treatment lasts 10-20 minutes. Then withdraw the needle while pressing the hole so as to avoid bleeding. A complete course includes ten sessions of treatment, with each treatment being carried out once a day or every other day. The second session of treatment can only start after an interval of three to five days. This method is effective for hemiplegia as a sequela of apoplexy. As for cases with dysphasia, the speech areas can be used in combination.

b) Ear acupuncture

Points: Infratragic apex, ear-*Shenmen*, the auricular points for heart, kidney, liver and spleen, middle border, end of inferior antihelix crus, ear apex, the corresponding area of the paralyzed region, and the groove for lowering blood pressure.

Methods: Each time select two to three points on both ears to apply acupuncture, giving moderate stimulation. Prompt prick the ear apex to let out a little blood for cases with excess syndrome; use the needle embedment therapy for cases likely to leave sequelae. One course includes ten sessions of treatment which is carried out once a day or every other day. The second course can only start after an interval of three to five days. Skin sterilization should be carried out strictly and the acupoints punctured alternately. While puncturing, take care not to hurt the auricle.

5) Notes

a) Elderly people or people suffering *qi* deficiency, dizziness and numb fingers should pay attention to daily life and diet. Moxibustion treatment can be given to *Zusanli* (ST 36) and *Xuanzhong* (GB 39) to prevent apoplexy.

b) Acupuncture and moxibustion treatment are effective for the sequelae of apoplexy if carried out promptly. An ideal therapeutic effect can be achieved in three months of the illness. The treatment proves weak in cases lasting over one year.

c) If it is difficult to distinguish between excess syndrome and prostration syndrome, the bloodletting therapy at the twelve *jiing* points should not be used. *Shuigou* (DU 26) can be punctured to restore consciousness and *Zusanli* (ST 36) to regulate *qi* and blood.

d) For treatment of the sequelae of apoplexy, please refer to the therapeutic methods for attack on the meridians, the *wei*-syndrome and *bi*-syndrome. For protracted apoplexy with poor therapeutic effect, puncture with the reinforcing manipulation on the healthy side and with the reducing manipulation on the diseased side. For example, when treating facial paralysis on the left side, *Dicang* (ST 4), *Jiache* (ST 6), *Taiyang* (EX-HN 5) and *Yifeng* (SJ 17) on the left side are punctured with reducing manipulation; *Hegu* (LI 4) and *Quchi* (LI 11) on the right side are punctured with reinforcing manipulation.

e) According to *Epitome of Acupuncture and Moxibustion*, acupuncture treatment is given to *Shaoshang* (LU 11), *Shangyang* (LI 1), *Zhongchong* (PC 9), *Guanchong* (SJ 1), *Shaochong* (HT 9) and *Shaoze* (SI 1) when the following symptoms appear, such as fall in a fit, loss of consciousness, retention of phlegm and lockjaw. For cases with muscular contracture, pain in the medial side of the ankle and inability to walk, burn 40 moxa cones on the medial malleolus; and 30 moxa cones on the lateral malleolus for muscular contracture and pain in the lateral side of the ankle; moxibustion treatment is given to *Kunlun* (BL 60) if the patient feels no pain while walking.

6) Reference materials

Applying acupuncture treatment to a 50-year-old woman patient suffering paralysis on the right limbs for 40 days (see *Head Acupuncture*)

The patient was from Jishan County of Shanxi Province and named Yin. She told the doctor that the disease was so happened that she could hardly hold anything with her right hand or stand and walk with the right leg after getting up on the morning of November 30, 1970. Since taking Chinese and Western drugs proves ineffective, she went to the hospital for treatment on January 12, 1971. A physical exam showed the following symptoms: a clear mind, normal speech ability, difficulty in moving the right limbs, hyperactivity of deep reflex, negative pathological signs and systolic murmur coming from the tricuspid region.

Diagnosis: Cerebral thrombosis.

Area: The upper and middle 3/5 of the motor area on the left side.

Effects: After twisting the needle after insertion, the patient felt a hot stream flowing through the right arm and leg to the right hand and toes. This hot stream strengthened after rotating the needle for three minutes and the patient felt comfortable in the diseased limbs. After withdrawing the needle, her right limbs could move and she could walk by herself in a normal way.

22. Spasmodic pain over the face

This refers to a painful tic on the face. Trigeminal neuralgia can be treated according to the descriptions in this part.

1) Etiology and pathogenesis

a) The invasion on meridians by wind, cold and dampness causes the obstruction of meridians and the stagnation of *qi* and blood.

b) The invasion on facial meridians by wind-heat disturbs the circulation of *qi* and blood.

2) Syndrome differentiation

Sudden pain on one side of the cheek, in particular the maxillary and mandibular areas. The pain feels as if the cheek has been burnt by lightning or cut by a knife, and lasts only a few seconds or several minutes before it relieves spontaneously. The accompanied symptoms are facial spasm, lacrimation, running nose and salivation. The pain may occur several times a day and last for several days. It is usually caused by washing the face, brushing teeth, eating or speaking.

Patients suffering the invasion of wind, cold and dampness find the pain becomes acute on exposure to cold and alleviates on warmth, with white tongue coating and superficial pulse. In cases induced by wind-heat, patients find a burning pain, reddened eyes, lacrimation, yellow and greasy tongue coating and rapid pulse.

3) Treatment

Principles: To smooth the *Yangming*, *Taiyang* and *Shaoyang* meridians.

Methods: Select acupoints near or far from the affected area to apply acupuncture treatment, using the reducing manipulation.

Acupoints: *Cuanzhu* (BL 2), *Yangbai* (GB 14), *Touwei* (ST 8), *Shuaigu* (GB 8) and *Houxi* (SI 3) for pain around the frontal area; *Sibai* (ST 2), *Quanliao* (SI 18), *Taiyang* (EX-HN 5) and *Hegu* (LI 4) for pain around the maxillary area; and *Xiaguan* (ST 7), *Jiache* (ST 6) and *Neiting* (ST 44) for pain around the mandibular area.

Notes: Acupoints near the affected area are used as the main points for acupuncture. These points help smooth the facial meridians, dispel cold and heat, regulate the *qi* and blood and thus relieve pain. In addition, a local tender point can also be punctured so as to promote the circulation of *qi* in meridians.

4) Other remedies

Acupoint injection: Inject 0.5 ml of Vitamin B_1, B_{12} or 1% procaine into the tender points or the above acupoints. One or two points are used each time.

23. Facial paralysis

Facial paralysis or "wry mouth and eyes" is usually of the peripheral type. The disease may occur in people of all ages, especially adults. Its main symptom is flaccid muscle on one side of the face. Peripheral facial paralysis, neuritis and wry mouth and eyes as the sequelae of apoplexy can be treated according to the descriptions in this part.

1) Etiology and pathogenesis

It is usually caused by the invasion of *Yangming* and *Shaoyang* meridians by wind-cold or wind-heat which block the *qi* in the meridians and prevent them from being nourished, resulting in the flaccidity of facial muscles.

2) Syndrome differentiation

The disease occurs suddenly with one side of the face numb and stiff. The accompanied symptoms are the inability to knit the brows, expose the teeth or puff out the cheeks, wry mouth twisted to the healthy side, eyes open all the time, lacrimation, wrinkles smoothing on the forehead, shallow or obliterated nasolabial groove on the diseased side. In some cases there are pain behind and below the ear or in the face; in serious cases, taste functions may be affected on part of the tongue and hyperacusia may also occur.

3) Treatment

Principles: To eliminate wind and smooth the meridians.

Methods: Select acupoints along the Large Intestine Meridian as main points and those along the *Sanjiao*, Small Intestine, Gallbladder and Bladder meridians as accessory points. Usually two acupoints are punctured at the same time. The reducing manipulation is used for the early stage of illness, while the reinforcing manipulation and moxibustion treatment for the later stage.

Acupoints: *Dicang* (ST 4), *Jiache* (ST 6), *Yangbai* (GB 14), *Yingxiang* (LI 20), *Hegu* (LI 4) and *Yifeng* (SJ 17).

Notes: Most acupoints are chosen from the diseased area. *Dicang*, *Jiache*, *Yangbai*, *Sibai* (ST 2) and *Yingxiang* are used to promote the flow of *qi* along the meridians; *Yifeng* expels wind and alleviates pain (pain behind the ear in particular). *Hegu*, the *yuan* point of the Large Intestine Meridian, helps to regulate the flow of *qi*. Since the Large Intestine Meridian of Hand-*Yangming* is rich in *qi* and blood and circles the face before meeting the Stomach Meridian, *Hegu* along this meridian is effective against facial paralysis.

4) Other remedies

a) Plum-blossom needling therapy

Prick the above points with a plum-blossom needle, stimulating strongly in the early stage and mildly in the later stage. Points are usually pricked once every day, or every other day, each time for 10-15 minutes. Ten application would be sufficient for a course of treatment.

b) Point injection: One or two points are used each time, and 0.5-1.0 ml of Vitamin B_1 or Vitamin B_{12} is injected into each point every day, or every other day.

5) Notes

According to *Jade Dragon Verses*, a folk song in the traditional Chinese medical circles, inserting the needle into *Dicang* (ST 4) and *Jiache* (ST 6) at the same time is very effective against wry mouth with distorted eyes. Another folk song popular among Chinese doctors called *Verses for Hundred Symptoms* says: inserting the needle into *Taichong* (LR 3) with the reducing manipulation is effective against twisted lips.

6) Reference materials

Applying point-to-point acupuncture treatment to 52 patients suffering facial paralysis (see *New Journal of Medicine*, No.3 issue of 1985)

Acupoints: *Taiyang* (EX-HN 5) to *Dicang* (ST 4), *Sibai* (ST 2) to *Dicang*, the lateral end of the upper eyebrow to the medial end, the outer canthus to the inner canthus.

Method: After insertion, the needle was twisted slightly and kept in the skin for 15-20 minutes. The above treatment was given once every day or every other day. Seven to ten days later, an electrotherapeutic apparatus was used to send a small quantity of pulse current to the patient.

Effect: After treatment, 40 of the 52 cases recovered, 11 patients felt much better and only one patient found it ineffective.

24. *Bi* syndrome

Bi literally means obstruction, so *bi* syndrome refers to the obstruction of the flow of *qi* and blood caused by the invasion on the meridians by exogenous pathogenic factors. *Bi* symptoms are soreness, numbness, swelling, pain and dyskinesia on the limbs and joints. *Bi* syndrome can be seen in patients with rheumatic arthritis, rheumatoid arthritis, myofibrositis or neuralgia.

1) Etiology and pathogenesis

a) The invasion on tendons and joints by wind, cold and dampness, at a time when the body resistance is weakened.

b) The affect of wind, cold, and dampness after a prolonged stay in a wet environment or during abnormal weather.

c) The change from exogenous cold to heat affects the joints and meridians in cases with a predominance of *yin-qi* and dampness-heat, or a deficiency of *yin* and hyperactivity of *yang*.

2) Syndrome differentiation

a) *Bi* syndrome due to wind, cold and dampness: Swelling and pain on joints, or soreness, heaviness, numbness and muscle spasm. Because of the difference of body constitution and the predominance of either wind or cold or dampness, various clinical types may occur. *Bi* syndrome due to wind, cold and dampness can be divided into the following types:

Bi syndrome with migratory pain: This category is marked by predominance of wind and presents as arthralgia with migratory pain, chilliness, fever, yellow and greasy tongue coating and superficial pulse.

Bi syndrome with severe pain: This type of *bi* syndrome is marked by predominance of cold, presenting as arthralgia with severe pain all over the body. This condition is alleviated by warmth, but aggravated by cold, white tongue coating, and a taut and tense pulse.

Bi syndrome with fixed pain and heaviness: A type marked by predominance of dampness presenting as swelling, pain and numbness occurring when the patient is exposed to dampness, white and greasy tongue coating, soft, superficial, and retarded pulse.

b) *Bi* syndrome due to heat: Reddened, swelling, hotness and pain of joints with limited movement, fever, thirst, a red tongue with yellow and dry coating, a smooth and rapid pulse.

3) Treatment

Principles: To eliminate wind, cold, and dampness, dredge and activate the meridians in the case of *bi* syndrome due to wind, cold and dampness. Disperse heat, eliminate dampness and dredge the meridians in the case of *bi* syndrome due to heat.

Methods: Insert the needle into acupoints near and far from the affected part, using the reducing manipulation for *bi* syndrome with migratory pain and pain due to heat. Use moxibustion treatment for *bi* syndrome with severe pain. Acupuncture and moxibustion can be applied to treat *bi* syndrome with fixed pain and heaviness.

Acupoints: *Jianjing* (GB 21), *Jianyu* (LI 15), *Jianwaishu* (SI 14) and *Tianzong* (SI 11) in combination with the *Ashi* point for pain in the shoulders and arms. *Jianyu* (LI 15), *Quchi* (LI 11) and *Waiguan* (SJ 5) for pain in the upper limbs; *Huantiao* (GB 30), *Yanglingquan* (GB 34), *Zusanli* (ST 36), *Xuanzhong* (GB 39) for pain in the lower limbs. *Dazhu* (BL 11), *Yanglingquan* (GB 34) and *Xuanzhong* (GB 39), the influential points of bones, tendons and marrow respectively, help strengthen the tendons and bones. *Dazhui* (DU 14), *Waiguan* (SJ 5) and *Quchi* (LI 11) help eliminate wind and cold and disperse heat; *Yanglingquan* (GB 34) and *Sanyinjiao* (SP 6) are used to strengthen the spleen and expel dampness.

4) Other remedies

a) Acupoint injection: Drugs such as Radix Salviae Miltiorrhizae Co., Caulis Erycibes or Radix Angelicae Sinensis Co. can be injected into two or four points, 1 ml at each point. This should be done once every day, or every other day. Ten times would suffice the treatment. Sterilize the injector and take care not to inject the above drugs into the articular cavity.

b) Plum-blossom needle therapy: Prick the painful area around the affected joints or along the spinal column. Cupping therapy can be used. The painful area is tapped hard to enable a small amount of blood to be taken out. This procedure will help dredge the meridians and alleviate pain.

5) Notes

In general, acupuncture treatment is effective against *bi* syndrome. Treatment must be given for a long time when *bi* syndrome occurs with rheumatoid arthritis.

6) Reference materials

Applying acupuncture and moxibustion treatment to a 39-year-old male patient named Yao who suffered *bi* syndrome (see *A Concise Compilation of Acupuncture and Moxibustion*)

Yao suffered arthralgia in the knee joints and had not been able to move his limbs freely for more than one month because he felt pain on the wrist and lumbar section of the spine. The disease was diagnosed as *bi* syndrome with severe pain. The doctor inserted the needle into *Liangqiu* (ST 34), *Xiyan* (EX-LE 5), *Yanglingquan* (GB 34), *Zusanli* (ST 36), *Yangchi* (SJ 4), *Hegu* (LI 4), *Shenshu* (BL 23) and *Qihai* (RN 6) for the purpose of mild reinforcement and reduction before giving the patient moxibustion treatment. Swelling became less serious after the first round of treatment, and pain also reduced. After the second and third rounds of treatment, Yao could move his limbs quite freely. All the symptoms were gone after over 20 rounds of treatment.

Appendix 1 Sciatica

Sciatica refers to pain which can be felt along the passage and distributive area of the sciatic nerves. There are several reasons for this disease.

1) Etiology and pathogenesis

The pathogenesis of sciatica is the impairment of meridians and stagnation of *qi* and blood, which may be caused by wind, cold, dampness and heat, or trauma. If this condition is untreated for a long time, tendons and muscles will become undernourished, resulting in muscular atrophy, numbness and pain.

2) Syndrome differentiation

Burning or stabbing pain occurs paroxysmally or continuously in the buttock, posterior aspect of thigh, and the posterolateral aspect of leg and foot. Walking aggravates the condition and tenderness occurs along the passage of the Bladder and Gallbladder meridians. The leg can not be raised freely.

Patients with wind-heat syndrome experience a burning pain in the affected side, which aggravates upon exposure to warmth; patients with wind-cold syndrome feel a cold pain in the affected limb, which relieves upon exposure to warmth; patients with dampness-syndrome feel heaviness and pain in the affected limb, which aggravates on rainy days.

3) Treatment

Use acupoints along the Bladder and Gallbladder meridians as main points and together with those along the Stomach and Spleen meridians for cases with muscular atrophy. The principle is to dredge and activate meridians, to promote the flow of *qi*, and to alleviate pain. Generally, acupuncture is used for the purpose of reduction, and moxibustion or cupping may be used in combination. Electroacupuncture treatment can also be used to give the patient strong stimulation, with dense waves followed by sparse-dense waves. The commonly-used acupoints are *Shenshu* (BL 23), *Dachangshu* (BL 25), *Zhibian* (BL 54), *Huantiao* (GB 30), *Yinmen* (BL 37), *Weizhong* (BL 40), *Yanglingquan* (GB 34), *Xuanzhong* (GB 39), *Zusanli* (ST 36), *Sanyinjiao* (SP 6) and *Ashi* points.

Appendix 2 Periarthritis of shoulder

Periarthritis of shoulder, also known as frozen shoulder, refers to pain and limited movement on one side of the shoulder joint.

1) Etiology and pathogenesis

The disease is caused by deficiency of *qi* and blood, damage to the tendons and bones and local affection of wind-cold or strain and contusion, which gives rise to the stagnation of the *qi* and blood.

2) Syndrome differentiation

Such movements as raising upward and stretching backward on the part of the affected shoulder joint are limited. Pain, or to be precise, resting pain, is the main symptom in the early stage of the disease, which becomes serious at night during winter and is alleviated in the daytime after the joint has been moved. Muscular atrophy, limited movement or even "frozen" joint may occur if the disease is prolonged.

3) Treatment

Principles: To eliminate wind-cold, resolve dampness, dredge meridians, activate *qi* and alleviate pain.

Methods: Use acupoints along the *Sanjiao*, Small Intestine and Large Intestine meridians and those around the shoulder joint. Both acupuncture and moxibustion are employed. Electroacupuncture with sparse-dense waves can help diminish inflammation and relieve pain. Ginger moxibustion is more effective against shoulder pain caused by wind-cold.

Acupoints: *Jianyu* (LI 15), *Jianzhen* (SI 9), *Binao* (LI 14), *Tianzong* (SI 11), *Quchi* (LI 11), *Waiguan* (SJ 5) and *Ashi* points.

25. Wei syndrome

Wei syndrome refers to a disorder of weak muscles, flabby limbs and even limited movement and muscular atrophy, which usually occurs in the lower limbs as a result of multiple neuritis, sequelae of poliomyelitis, acute myelitis, myasthenia gravis, hysterical paralysis or periodic paralysis.

1) Etiology and pathogenesis

a) Consumption of body fluid by lung-heat: After the lung is attacked by heat and the body fluid is consumed, the tendons and muscles are deprived of fluid lubrication so that the limbs become flaccid.

b) Attack by dampness-heat: The retention of dampness after exposure to rain or damage to the spleen and stomach due to improper diet leads to the production of heat, which in turn attacks the muscles and tendons, interferes with the flow of *qi* and blood and deprives the muscles and tendons of nutrients.

c) Weak spleen and stomach: The spleen and stomach are the postnatal basis and at the same time the source of the body fluid—*qi* and blood. Weak spleen and stomach fail to provide the body with enough fluid, thus leaving the muscles and tendons undernourished.

d) Deficiency of liver and kidney: Protracted illness and indulgence in sexual activity weaken the liver and kidney, resulting in malnutrition of the tendons, bones and meridians.

2) Syndrome differentiation

a) Consumption of body fluid by lung-heat: Fever at the beginning of the illness, weakness in the limbs after the fever, irritability, thirst, cough, dry throat, scanty and yellow urine, constipation, reddened tongue with yellow coating, weak and rapid pulse.

b) Attack by dampness-heat: Lassitude, a heavy sensation in the limbs, flaccidity, slightly swollen and numb lower limbs, fever, chest upset, pain and difficulty in urination, reddened urine, yellow and sticky tongue coating, thready and rapid pulse.

c) Weak spleen and stomach: Lassitude, weakness in the limbs, poor appetite, emaciation with sallow complexion, loose stool, pale tongue with white coating, and thready pulse.

d) Deficiency of liver and kidney: Flaccidity in the lower limbs, lumbago, sore and weak knees, dizziness, tinnitus, or irregular menstruation, reddened and uncoated tongue, thready and rapid pulse.

3) Treatment

Principles: To invigorate the spleen and stomach, and nourish the tendons and muscles.

Methods: Use acupoints along the Large Intestine and Stomach meridians as main points. For patients suffering lung-heat and dampness-heat, insert a filiform needle into the acupoints for the purpose of reduction, or prick the acupoints with a plum-blossom needle in combination. For instances of deficiency of liver and kidney *yin*, apply acupuncture treatment to the acupoints. For cases due to deficiency-cold of spleen and stomach, give moxibustion treatment to the acupoints.

Acupoints: *Jianyu* (LI 15), *Quchi* (LI 11), *Hegu* (LI 4), *Yangxi* (LI 5), *Biguan* (ST 31), *Liangqiu* (ST 34), *Zusanli* (ST 36) and *Jiexi* (ST 41). *Chize* (LU 5) and *Feishu* (BL 13) are used together with the above acupoints for cases with lung-heat; *Yinlingquan* (SP 9) and *Pishu* (BL 20) for dampness-heat; *Ganshu* (BL 18), *Shenshu* (BL 23), *Xuanzhong* (GB 39) and *Yanglingquan* (GB 34) for deficiency of liver and kidney *yin*; and *Zhongwan* (RN 12) and *Sanyinjiao* (SP 6) for deficiency-cold of spleen and stomach.

Notes: The principles of selecting acupoints are based on the premise that only points along the *Yangming* meridians are used to treat *wei* syndrome (the premise is described in *The Inner Canon of the Yellow Emperor*), since those meridians are rich in *qi* and blood. *Feishu* and *Chize* are used to promote the production of body fluid and disperse lung-heat, and *Pishu* and *Yinlingquan* to strengthen the spleen and stomach, and to eliminate dampness-heat. *Xuanzhong* and *Yanglingquan* are the influential points of marrow and tendon respectively and *Ganshu* and *Shenshu* help invigorate the liver and kidney. The above four points can strengthen the tendons and bones if they are used together. As for *Zhongwan* and *Sanyinjiao*, they play a big role in strengthening and warming the spleen and stomach.

4) Other remedies

a) Plum-blossom needle therapy: Tap the spinal column with a plum-blossom needle from top to bottom, first along the first line and then the second line of the Bladder Meridian on both sides and the *Du* Meridian. The treatment is given once a day, and ten times is a typical course of treatment. A second course of treatment may be given to the patient after three days rest.

b) Acupoint injection: Vitamin B_1 and B_{12} and galanthamine are injected into the above points, two or three points each time. The treatment is given once every other day, and ten times will make up a whole course of treatment. A second course of treatment can be given to the patient after several days rest.

5) Notes

a) The principles of treating *wei* syndrome as described in *The Inner Cannon of The Yellow Emperor* are reasonable, because the *Yangming* meridians dominate the tendons and muscles responsible for the movement of joints on the one hand and connect with the spleen and stomach serving as the postnatal basis and the source of generation from which the lung-fluid, liver-blood and kidney-essence come. Therefore when the spleen and stomach produce enough *qi* and blood, the tendons and muscles will be well nourished and *wei* syndrome will be cured.

b) Use the points on the proximal region of limbs as main points and those on the distal region as accessory ones. The above method is quite effective against *wei* syndrome in the early and immediate stages.

c) Use acupoints along the meridian according to syndrome differentiation in the later stage. Take the eversion of foot for instance. This condition should be treated by inserting the needle into acupoints along the Gallbladder Meridian because there is deficiency of *qi* on the lateral side of the meridian. If there is a foot drop, that means there is deficiency of *qi* on the part of the Stomach Meridian, and the needle should be inserted into acupoints along the meridian for the purpose of reinforcement.

26. Lumbago

Lumbago is one of the common symptoms that often break out with lumbar muscle strain, rheumatism or spinal disease. This part will discuss lumbago caused by cold-dampness, muscle strain and kidney-deficiency. As for lumbago caused by other factors, please refer to other relevant parts.

1) Etiology and pathogenesis

a) Lumbago due to cold-dampness: Prolonged exposure to dampness, rain, draughts and wind after sweating may give rise to the retention of cold-dampness in the meridians and the stagnation of *qi* and blood.

b) Lumbago due to muscle strain: Inappropriate movement, prolonged fatigue, sprain or contusion may damage the tendons and bones and cause the stagnation of *qi* and blood.

c) Lumbago due to kidney-deficiency: Kidney-deficiency because of old-age, prolonged illness or too much sexual activity may give rise to insufficiency of essence and blood and malnutrition of the tendons and bones and then to pain.

2) Syndrome differentiation

a) Lumbago due to cold-dampness: The limited movement of the spine, heaviness and soreness at the lumbosacral region (which intensifies on cold and rainy days), heaviness and edema at the lower limbs, pale tongue with white and smooth coating, and taut and slow pulse.

b) Lumbago due to muscle strain: Lumbar pain (which becomes intense on exertion), the limited movement and definite tender spot in the lumbar region, white tongue coating, taut pulse, and the recurrence of an old injury or disease.

c) Lumbago due to kidney-deficiency: Dull aching at the lumbar region, and weak loins and knees. The condition is accompanied by dizziness, blurred vision, tinnitus, lassitude, cold limbs, pale tongue, or taut and thready pulse in cases of deficiency of kidney *yang*; and by vexation, insomnia, oliguria, reddened and uncoated tongue, thready and rapid pulse in cases of deficiency of kidney *yin*.

3) Treatment

Principles: To eliminate cold-dampness, invigorate the kidney, relax the tendons and activate the meridians.

Methods: Insert acupoints along the Bladder, Kidney and *Du* meridians for the purpose of reinforcement or for a mild reinforcement and reduction. Moxibustion can be used at the same time.

Acupoints: *Shenshu* (BL 23), *Weizhong* (BL 40), *Ashi*, *Yaoyangguan* (DU 3), *Yanglingquan* (GB 34), *Mingmen* (DU 4), *Ciliao* (BL 32) and *Taixi* (KI 3).

Notes: Inserting a needle into *Shenshu* can help invigorate the kidney *qi*. Moxibustion application may expel cold and dampness. *Weizhong* dredges and regulates the *qi* of the Bladder Meridian and relieves lumbago. Acupoints or *Ashi* points near the affected part dredge and regulate the *qi* in the meridian; *Yaoyangguan*, a point along the *Du* Meridian, activates *yang-qi* and enhances the effect of *Shenshu*; *Yanglingquan* relaxes muscles and tendons and activates meridians; *Ciliao* enhances the effect of *Weizhong*; *Mingmen* invigorates the kidney and strengthens the lumbar muscles; *Taixi*, the *yuan* point of the Kidney Meridian, invigorates the kidney and nourishes *yin*.

4) Other remedies

a) Plum-blossom needle and cupping therapies: Use a plum-blossom needle to tap both sides of the spine, especially the area around *Shenshu* (BL 23). Cupping therapy can be used with plum-blossom needling or separately.

b) Acupoint injection: 10 ml of 10% glucose or 2-4 ml of Vitamin B_1, or injection of Radix Angelicae Sinensis Co. are injected into two or three acupoints mentioned above. The treatment is given once every other day, and a complete course of treatment includes ten applications.

5) Notes

In general, acupuncture is highly effective against lumbago, but if there are local organic diseases, an exact diagnosis should be made and symptomatic treatment be given. For cases with tuberculosis of spine, local acupuncture is inadvisable.

6) Reference materials

a) Moxibustion treatment should be given to *Yaoshu* (DU 2) for lumbago due to cold-dampness; acupuncture treatment should be applied to *Qihai* (RN 6) for lumbago due to lumbar sprain and *qi* deficiency. (see *Selected Records of Acupuncture and Moxibustion Literature*)

b) Applying cupping and acupuncture treatment to a 45-year-old male patient named Wang who suffering lumbago and pain in the leg (see *A Concise Compilation of Acupuncture and Moxibustion*)

Due to overwork, the patient felt a pain on the right side of the lower back and leg for two years when he came to see the doctor. He said the pain became serious in winter and on rainy days, when he would be unable to bend forward by more than 70 degrees. For this reason, cupping therapy was given to *Shenshu* (BL 23), and acupuncture treatment to *Yanglingquan* (GB 34), *Kunlun* (BL 60) and *Weizhong* (BL 40) on the right side. Moxibustion treatment was given to *Huantiao* (GB 30) on the right side and sometimes *Ashi* points at the lower back after acupuncture. After receiving treatment for half a month, the patient could move his lower back and limb once again.

SECTION 2
GYNIATRICS AND PEDIATRICS

1. Irregular menstruation

Irregular menstruation indicates a problem with the menstrual cycle, and the quality and quantity of menses.

1) Etiology and pathogenesis

a) Advanced menstrual period: First, eating too much hot and pungent food or emotional depression due to exuberance of *yang* is likely to give rise to the accumulation of heat in the uterus and blood. Second, prolonged illness consumes too much *yin-qi* which in turn leads to deficiency of *yin* and internal heat, and weakens the *Chong* and *Ren* meridians.

b) Delayed menstrual period: First, deficiency of *yang* and preponderance of *yin* or the fact that the body is affected by pathogenic cold when a patient remains cold and wet for a long time during menstrual period may give rise to the accumulation of cold in the blood. Second, emotional depression, *qi* stagnation and blood stasis may affect the flow of blood in the uterus. Third, prolonged illness, multiparity or the impairment of the spleen and stomach caused by eating too much may give rise to deficiency of blood in the *Chong* and *Ren* meridians.

c) Irregular menstrual period: First, emotional depression or anger, which affects the ability of the liver to smooth and regulate the flow of *qi*, results in the dysfunction of *Chong* and *Ren* meridians. Second, sexual indulgence or multiparity causes deficiency of kidney *qi* and leads to the dysfunction of *Chong* and *Ren* meridians.

2) Syndrome differentiation

a) Advanced menstrual period: The main symptom is an irregular cycle with the menstrual period taking place one week earlier than normal, or even twice a month. In cases of excess-heat syndrome, there appear symptoms like dark or purplish red and sticky menses, vexation, chest upset, thirst, flushed face, yellow urine, constipation, reddened tongue with yellow coating, and smooth and rapid pulse. In cases of heat-stagnation syndrome, distention of the chest, hypochondria and breast, irritability, and taut and rapid pulse will appear. In cases of deficiency-heat syndrome, oligomenorrhea, thick red menses, hectic fever, feverish sensation of palms and soles, lumbago, soreness and weakness of knees, red tongue with scanty coating, and thready and rapid pulse will appear.

b) Delayed menstrual period: The main symptom is an irregular cycle with the menstrual period occurring seven or more days later than normal or even once every 40-50 days. Other symptoms are oligomenorrhea with dark red menses, cold pain in the lower abdomen (which is relieved when the patient feels warm). Cases with cold-excess syndrome exhibit symptoms such as chilliness, cold limbs, pallor, thin and white tongue coating, or deep and tense pulse. Cases with cold-deficiency syndrome exhibit symptoms such as oligomenorrhea with thin and light red menses, dull pain in the lower abdomen (which relieves when the patient feels warm or pressure on the abdomen), polyuria with clear urine, loose stools, pale tongue with thin and white coating, deep, slow and forceless pulse. Cases with blood-deficiency syndrome exhibit oligomenorrhea with thin and light red menses, dizziness, palpitation, pale or sallow complexion, pale tongue with scanty coating, thready and weak pulse.

c) Irregular menstrual period: The main symptom is that menstruation occurs at an indefinite period of time. Cases with stagnant liver-*qi* syndrome exhibit symptoms such as hypermenorrhea or oligomenorrhea, distensive pain in the chest, hypochondria and breast, belching, frequent sighing, thin and white tongue coating and taut pulse. Cases with kidney-deficiency syndrome exhibit symptoms such as oligomenorrhea with light red menses, dizziness, tinnitus, lumbago, soreness of knee joints, nocturia, pale tongue with white coating, deep and weak pulse.

3) Treatment

Principles: To regulate the flow of *qi* and blood and modulate the *Chong* and *Ren* meridians. In addition, efforts should be done to disperse heat and regulate menstruation in cases of excess-heat syndrome, nourish *yin* and disperse heat in cases of deficiency-heat syndrome, disperse heat and eliminate pathogenic factors in cases of heat-stagnancy syndrome, warm the meridians and expel cold in cases of excess-cold syndrome, warm the kidney and invigorate *yang* in cases of deficiency-cold syndrome, release *qi* of the liver in cases of stagnant liver-*qi* syndrome, and invigorate the kidney in cases of kidney-deficiency syndrome.

Methods: Select acupoints on the Spleen and *Ren* meridians to apply acupuncture, using the reducing manipulation for excess syndrome and reinforcing manipulation for deficiency syndrome. Moxibustion treatment can be used with acupuncture in cases of cold and deficiency syndromes but not in cases of excess syndrome.

Acupoints: *Qihai* (RN 6) and *Sanyinjiao* (SP 6). In cases of advanced menstrual period, *Taichong* (LR 3) and *Xuehai* (SP 10) can be used with the above acupoints for excess-heat syndrome; *Rangu* (KI 2) can be used together with the above acupoints for deficiency-heat syndrome; *Xingjian* (LR 2) for heat-stagnancy syndrome. In cases of delayed menstrual period, *Guilai* (ST 29) is indicated for excess-cold syndrome; *Mingmen* (DU 4) for deficiency-cold syndrome. In cases of irregular menstrual period, *Taichong* (LR 3) is indicated for stagnant liver-*qi* syndrome; *Shenshu* (BL 23) and *Taixi* (KI 3) for kidney-deficiency syndrome.

Notes: *Qihai*, an acupoint of the *Ren* Meridian, regulates the flow of *qi* throughout the body, *Sanyinjiao* of the Spleen Meridian, regulates the flow of *qi* and blood as well as menstruation. The above acupoints, if used together, can regulate the flow of *qi* and blood and modulate the *Chong* and *Ren* meridians. With the help of *Taichong* and *Xuehai*, they can disperse excess-heat in the *xue* system, and with the help of *Rangu*, the *ying* point of the Kidney Meridian and belonging to fire in the Five Elements, they can invigorate *yin* and disperse heat. Moreover, needling at *Xingjian* with the reducing manipulation can disperse stagnant heat in the liver and gallbladder. Giving moxibustion treatment to *Guilai* can warm the meridians and expel cold, to *Mingmen* can strengthen the kidney-*yang* to expel cold. Puncturing at *Shenshu* with the reinforcing manipulation may benefit the kidney.

4) Other remedies

Ear acupuncture

Points: The auricular points for uterus, tragic apex, liver, kidney and ovary.

Method: Each time select two or three points to apply acupuncture, giving a moderate stimulation. Keep the needles in the skin for 15-20 minutes. Needle embedment can also be used.

5) Reference materials

According to *Progress on Research in Acupuncture and Moxibustion*, the plum-blossom needle therapy is quite effective against irregular menstruation.

Tap the areas along the *Ren*, *Du*, Liver, Spleen, Kidney and *Dai* meridians at the ventral aspect below the umbilicus and the dorsal aspect below the second lumbar vertebra.

2. Dysmenorrhea

Dysmenorrhea refers to pain experienced in the underbelly and lower back before or during menstruation. It is often caused by maldevelopment of uterus, anteversion and retroversion of uterus, stenosis of cervix uteri, prolapse of endometrium, endometriosis or pelvic inflammation.

1) Etiology and pathogenesis

a) Emotional depression causes the stagnation of liver *qi* which in turn affects the flow of blood in the *Chong* and *Ren* meridians.

b) Being affected by cold or sitting on a wet ground for a long time during menstrual period gives rise to the retention of cold-dampness in uterus which in turn blocks the flow of blood.

c) Deficiency of *qi* and blood due to weak physique or prolonged illness leads to blood deficiency, resulting in the malnutrition of the uterus.

d) Weak physique, sexual indulgence or multiparity impairs the liver and kidney and further the body essence and blood which in turn causes the malnutrition of the uterus.

2) Syndrome differentiation

According to causes, time of occurrence and the nature of pain, dysmenorrhea is divided into two types: excess syndrome and deficiency syndrome.

a) Excess syndrome: Pain in the lower abdomen is severe and bleeding is not smooth before, after or during menstrual period. If dysmenorrhea is caused by blood-stasis, the pain is more severe than distention and the patient feels uncomfortable when pressing the abdomen, the blood is dark purple and clotted, and the pulse is deep and rough. Cases due to stagnant *qi* often exhibit a small amount of bleeding, a feeling of distention more prominent than pain and which spreads to the chest, hypochondria and breast, nausea, and taut pulse. Cases due to cold-dampness exhibit the following symptoms such as pale and scanty menstruation, dark and clotted menses, pain spreading to the back and spine, chilliness, loose stools, white and greasy tongue coating, deep and tense pulse.

b) Deficiency syndrome: Pain in the lower abdomen is felt during or after menstruation. The pain is not acute and relieves upon pressure. Cases with insufficient *qi* and blood exhibit pink and thin menses, pallor, lassitude, dizziness, palpitation, pale tongue with thin coating, feeble and weak pulse. Cases due to weak liver and kidney often exhibit scanty and pink menses, lumbago, weak knee joints, dizziness, tinnitus, pale tongue with white coating, deep and thready pulse.

3) Treatment

a) Excess syndrome

Principles: To soothe the liver, promote the flow of blood, activate menstruation and relieve pain if there is *qi* and blood stagnation; to expel cold from meridians, eliminate dampness, regulate menstruation and relieve pain if there is cold-dampness.

Methods: Select acupoints on the Spleen, Liver and *Ren* meridians to apply acupuncture, using the reducing manipulation. Moxibustion can be used for cases with cold-dampness.

Acupoints: *Zhongji* (RN 3), *Diji* (SP 8) and *Guilai* (ST 29). To treat cases with stagnant liver *qi*,

Taichong (LR 3) can be added.

Notes: *Zhongji* along the *Ren* Meridian helps modulate the *Chong* and *Ren* meridians. Applying moxibustion treatment at *Zhongji* can help warm and dredge the meridians. *Diji*, the *xi* point of the Spleen Meridian, regulates menstruation, relieves pain, invigorates the spleen and eliminates dampness. *Guilai* regulates the meridians and relieves pain. *Taichong* soothes the liver, promotes the flow of *qi* and relieves pain.

b) Deficiency syndrome

Principles: To invigorate *qi* and blood if there is insufficiency of *qi* and blood, and replenish the liver and kidney if there is weak liver and kidney.

Methods: Select acupoints on the Kidney, Stomach and *Ren* Meridian to apply acupuncture, using the reinforcing manipulation. Moxibustion is recommended.

Acupoints: *Guanyuan* (RN 4), *Zusanli* (ST 36), *Pishu* (BL 20), *Shenshu* (BL 23) and *Taixi* (KI 3).

Notes: *Guanyuan* warms and invigorates primordial *qi* and nourishes the *Chong* and *Ren* meridians. *Shenshu* and *Taixi* invigorate the liver and kidney. *Zusanli* and *Pishu* strengthen the spleen and stomach to benefit *qi* and blood.

4) Other remedies

Ear acupuncture

Points: The auricular points for uterus, tragic apex, kidney and brain, and ear-*Shenmen*.

Method: Give a strong stimulation and keep the needles in the skin for 15-20 minutes. Needle embedment can also be used.

5) Notes

Dysmenorrhea is classified into primary pain and secondary pain. According *Progress on Research in Acupuncture and Moxibustion*, acupuncture and moxibustion are more effective against primary dysmenorrhea than secondary dysmenorrhea.

6) Reference materials

Applying acupuncture treatment to a 37-year-old married woman named Liu who suffering dysmenorrhea (see *A Concise Compilation of Acupuncture and Moxibustion*)

The patient said she felt a severe paroxysmal pain in the lower abdomen two days before or during menstrual period. The other symptoms were lassitude, headache, dizziness and pain in the legs. But they vanished as soon as menstruation ended. She added that she had suffered from the disease for eight years, and she found it more severe a year previously. A physical exam showed no other abnormality. When her disease was diagnosed as dysmenorrhea, the analgesics she was told to take proved ineffective. She decided to ask acupuncturists for help. *Guanyuan* (RN 4), *Hegu* (LI 4) and *Sanyinjiao* (SP 6) were punctured. Her pain was relieved soon after and she received the acupuncture treatment two more times. The follow-up visits within one year found no recurrence of the disease.

3. Amenorrhea

Amenorrhea refers to the failure of menstruation to start when a woman reaches adulthood or the abnormal cessation of the periods for more than three months in a row once they have started.

1) Etiology and pathogenesis

a) Excess syndrome: First, emotional depression makes liver *qi* stagnant and blocks the flow of *qi* and blood. Second, the dysfunction of the spleen leads to the accumulation of dampness and production of phlegm. Dampness and phlegm check the *Chong* and *Ren* meridians and the vessels of uterine. Third, cold invades and blocks the vessels of uterine.

b) Deficiency syndrome: First, congenital insufficiency of kidney *qi*, sexual indulgence or multiparity impairs the liver and kidney and consumes essence and blood, thus leaving the *Chong* and

Ren meridians in malnutrition. Second, prolonged illness, blood loss or impairment of the spleen and stomach causes the insufficiency of *qi* and blood, thus leaving the *Chong* and *Ren* meridians in malnutrition.

2) Syndrome differentiation

a) Amenorrhea due to blood stagnation: Cases with stagnation of *qi* and blood exhibit the following symptoms such as ceasing of menstruation, distensive pain in the lower abdomen, mental depression, irritability, fullness in the chest and hypochondriac region, dark purple tongue, deep and taut pulse. Cases with stagnation of cold and blood exhibit the ceasing of menstruation, cold limbs and pain in the lower abdomen (which alleviates on exposure to warmth), pale tongue with white coating, deep and taut pulse. Cases with accumulation of phlegm-dampness exhibit the ceasing of menstruation, obesity, fullness in the chest and hypochondriac region, nausea, abundant expectoration, lassitude, profuse leukorrhea, greasy tongue coating and smooth pulse.

b) Amenorrhea due to blood depletion: Cases with insufficient *qi* and blood exhibit the following symptoms such as scanty menses in the later menstrual period or even ceasing of menstruation, pale or sallow complexion, dizziness, palpitation, short breath, lassitude, poor appetite, loose stools, pale lips and tongue, thready and weak pulse. Cases with weak liver and kidney often exhibit delayed menophania, scanty menses in light color, dizziness, tinnitus, lumbago, sore and weak knees, hectic fever, feverish sensation over the palms, soles and chest, reddened tongue with scanty coating, taut and thready pulse.

3) Treatment

a) Amenorrhea due to blood stagnation

Principles: To regulate *qi*, remove stagnation, strengthen the spleen, eliminate phlegm, warm the meridians and expel cold.

Methods: Select acupoints along the *Ren* and Spleen meridians to apply acupuncture, using the reducing manipulation. Moxibustion can be used to treat cases with cold-syndrome.

Acupoints: *Zhongji* (RN 3), *Zusanli* (ST 36), *Sanyinjiao* (SP 6), *Taichong* (LR 3), *Fenglong* (ST 40), *Diji* (SP 8) and *Hegu* (LI 4).

Notes: *Zhongji* regulates the *Chong* and *Ren* meridians; *Zusanli*, *Sanyinjiao*, *Diji* and *Fenglong* invigorate the spleen, activate diuresis, eliminate phlegm and promote menstruation; *Sanyinjiao* and *Hegu* activate the flow of *qi* and promote menstruation; and *Taichong* soothes the liver if punctured with the reducing manipulation.

b) Amenorrhea due to blood depletion

Principles: To invigorate *qi* and blood and nourish liver and kidney.

Methods: Select acupoints on the *Ren* Meridian and the back *shu* points to apply acupuncture, using the reinforcing manipulation. Moxibustion may also be applied.

Acupoints: *Shenshu* (BL 23), *Pishu* (BL 20), *Guanyuan* (RN 4), *Zusanli* (ST 36) and *Sanyinjiao* (SP 6).

Notes: *Pishu*, *Zusanli* and *Sanyinjiao* help invigorate the spleen and stomach and promote the generation of *qi* and blood. A sufficient body blood source will lead to normal menstruation. Giving acupuncture treatment to *Shenshu* and *Guanyuan* with the reinforcing manipulation can help invigorate the kidney and keep the essence and blood sufficient.

4) Other remedies

a) Ear acupuncture: Select auricular points for uterus, tragic apex, liver, kidney and brain to apply acupuncture, giving moderate stimulation. Three to four points are punctured each time and the needles are kept in the skin for 15-20 minutes. Needle embedment is also used.

b) Plum-blossom needle therapy: Tap both sides along the spinal column, lumbosacral region and lower abdomen with moderate stimulation, once every other day.

5) Notes

Be sure to distinguish amenorrhea from early pregnancy before giving acupuncture treatment to the acupoints. In addition, try to find the real cause of amenorrhea before applying remedies.

6) Reference materials

Applying acupuncture and moxibustion treatment to a 24-year-old married woman named Zhang who suffering amenorrhea for about eight months when she came to see the doctor (see *Clinical Experience in Acupuncture and Moxibustion*)

She said that she came down with the disorder after catching a cold during menstruation. Other symptoms included lumbago, listlessness, poor appetite, thin and white tongue coating, deep and thready pulse. The disease was diagnosed as secondary amenorrhea. Then acupuncture treatment was given three days before expected menstrual period to *Tianshu* (ST 25), *Qihai* (RN 6), *Zhongwan* (RN 12), *Zusanli* (ST 36) and *Sanyinjiao* (SP 6), and ginger moxibustion was applied to *Qihai*. The treatment continued till two days after menstruation, each treatment lasting 30 minutes. The same treatment was given to the above acupoints four days before expected menstruation. Following this treatment, the menses was small in quantity and dark in color. Everything returned to normal by the third month, after which she soon became pregnant and had a child ten months later.

4. Metrorrhagia

Metrorrhagia refers to bleeding or continuous bleeding from the uterus occurring between menstrual periods. It can be seen in dysfunctional bleeding from the uterine or inflammation and tumor in the female genital organ.

1) Etiology and pathogenesis

a) Exuberance of *yang*, invasion of heat, eating too much pungent food, or emotional depression leads to the stagnation of liver *qi* and the production of fire. The heat thus produced impairs the *Chong* and *Ren* meridians and forces the blood to go into the surrounding body tissues.

b) The deficiency of spleen or the impairment of spleen and stomach by improper diet leads to the deficiency and collapse of *qi* in the spleen and stomach and weakens the *Chong* and *Ren* meridians.

c) Sexual indulgence or multiparity impairs *qi* in the kidney and the function of essence-storing, thus leaving the *Chong* and *Ren* meridians weakened.

2) Syndrome differentiation

Excess syndrome

a) Blood-heat: Bleeding from the uterus with dark red and thick discharge, flushed face, vexation, thirst with a desire to drink, reddened tongue with yellow coating, smooth and rapid pulse. Fullness in the chest and hypochondriac region, irritability, taut and rapid pulse are the symptoms of heat stagnation.

b) Blood-stasis: Bleeding from the uterus with blood clots, pain and tenderness in the lower abdomen (which is relieved after the discharge of blood clots), dark reddened tongue or petechiae on its tip, deep and rough pulse.

Deficiency syndrome

a) Deficiency of *qi*: Bleeding from the uterus with light-colored discharge, pallor, lassitude, palpitation, short breath, loss of appetite, loose stools, pale tongue with white coating, thready and weak pulse.

b) Deficiency of kidney: If there is deficiency of *yang*, symptoms such as bleeding from the uterus with light-colored discharge, chilliness, cold limbs, cold pain in the lower abdomen, polyuria, loose stools, pale tongue with white coating, deep and thready pulse appear; if there is deficiency of *yin*, symptoms such as bleeding from the uterus with red discharge, dizziness, tinnitus, hectic fever, night sweat, vexation, insomnia, lumbago, sore and weak knees, reddened tongue with scanty coating, thready and rapid pulse appear.

3) Treatment

a) Excess syndrome

Principles: To disperse heat, cool blood and stop bleeding if there is blood-heat; to relieve stagnant liver-*qi*, disperse heat and cool blood if there is heat stagnancy; and to promote blood circulation and remove blood-stasis if there is blood-stasis.

Methods: Select acupoints along the *Ren* and Spleen meridians to apply acupuncture, using the reducing manipulation.

Acupoints: *Guanyuan* (RN 4), *Sanyinjiao* (SP 6) and *Yinbai* (SP 1). They can be used with *Xuehai* (SP 10) and *Shuiquan* (KI 5) to disperse blood heat; with *Taichong* (LR 3) to eliminate heat stagnation; and with *Qichong* (ST 30) and *Chongmen* (SP 12) to eliminate blood-stasis.

Notes: *Guanyuan*, the crossing point of the three *yin* meridians of foot and the *Chong* and *Ren* meridians, helps to regulate the *Chong* and *Ren* meridians, promote blood flow and remove blood-stasis. *Sanyinjiao* and *Yinbai* serve to regulate blood in the spleen in order to prevent blood from going out of the vessels and further into the surrounding body tissues. *Xuehai* and *Shuiquan* dispel heat in the blood; *Taichong* relieves stagnant liver-*qi*; *Chongmen* and *Qichong* regulate menstruation and remove blood-stasis.

b) Deficiency syndrome

Principles: To invigorate the spleen, supplement *qi* and stop bleeding if there is deficiency of *qi*; to warm the kidney, invigorate *yang* and stop bleeding if there is deficiency of *yang*; to nourish *yin*, strengthen the kidney and stop bleeding if there is deficiency of *yin*.

Methods: Select acupoints on the *Ren*, Spleen and Kidney meridians to apply acupuncture, using the reinforcing manipulation. Moxibustion can be applied to patients with *yang* and *qi* deficiency.

Acupoints: *Guanyuan* (RN 4), *Sanyinjiao* (SP 6) and *Zusanli* (ST 36). They can be used together with *Pishu* (BL 20) and *Baihui* (DU 20) for deficiency of *qi*, *Qihai* (RN 6) for deficiency of *yang*, *Rangu* (KI 2) and *Taixi* (KI 3) for deficiency of *yin*.

Notes: *Guanyuan* along the *Ren* Meridian serves to regulate and invigorate the *Chong* and *Ren* meridians, supplement *qi* and keep blood in the vessels. *Sanyinjiao* and *Zusanli* invigorate the spleen and stomach and enhance the effects of benefiting *qi* and keeping blood inside the vessels. Giving mild moxibustion treatment to *Qihai* can support primordial *qi* and check bleeding. *Rangu* and *Taixi*, the *ying* and *yuan* points of the Kidney Meridian, help to nourish *yin* and disperse heat.

4) Other remedies

Ear acupuncture: Select the auricular points for uterus, ovary, tragic apex and ear-*Shenmen* to give acupuncture with a moderate stimulation. Puncture three to four points each time and keep the needles in the skin for 30-60 minutes. The treatment should be given once every day or every other day. Needle embedment can also be used.

5) Notes

A thorough examination should be given to ensure there are no tumor if blood flows out of the uterus repeatedly during menopause.

6) Reference materials

Applying acupuncture treatment to a 29-year-old woman named Li who suffered dysfunctional uterine bleeding (see *A Concise Compilation of Acupuncture and Moxibustion*)

The patient suffered intermittent vaginal bleeding for four months before visiting a doctor. She said that the amount of bleeding was almost 80-100 ml, six or seven times per day. She also felt tired and dizzy and complained of abdominal pain. The physical examination showed that the patient was undernourished and the liver was palpable. There was blood stain on the vulva and blood clots in the vagina. The cervix was hypertrophied and congested and had only room for a fingertip. When placed in a horizontal position, the body of the uterus seemed quite soft and without any tenderness, and the left side of appendages appeared thicker. Hemostatic, endocrine preparations, herbal medicines, blood transfusion and uterine curettage had been used, but all in vain. Then acupuncture treatment was applied to *Xuehai* on both sides of the body, and moxibustion to *Sanyinjiao* (SP 6). After five sessions of treatment, bleeding ceased and other symptoms became much relieved.

5. Leukorrhagia

Leukorrhagia refers to the abnormal flow of blood-free discharge from the reproductive tract of the female. It may be seen in vaginitis, pelvic inflammation or cervicitis.

1) Etiology and pathogenesis

a) Improper diet impairs the function of spleen and stomach, and as a result, dampness descends and retains in the body; protracted dampness turns into heat which descends and leads to leukorrhagia.

b) Sexual indulgence and multiparity damage the kidney *qi*, and lead to the dysfunction of the *Dai* Meridian.

c) The attack of dampness and toxins during menstrual period and puerperium damages the *Ren* and *Dai* meridians.

2) Syndrome differentiation

a) Deficiency of spleen: Persistent discharge of white or yellowish viscid and odorless leukorrhea, pale or sallow complexion, lassitude, poor appetite, loose stools, pale tongue with white and greasy coating, retarded and weak pulse.

b) Deficiency of kidney: Persistent and profuse discharge of thin and white leukorrhea, lumbago, cold feeling in the lower abdomen, polyuria, nocturia, loose stools, pale tongue with thin white coating, deep and retarded pulse.

c) The attack of dampness and toxins: Profuse discharge of ricelike, green-yellowish or bloody and foul leukorrhea, pruritus, bitter taste, abdominal pain, oliguria, reddened tongue with yellow coating, smooth and rapid pulse.

3) Treatment

a) Deficiency of spleen

Principles: To strengthen the spleen, supplement *qi*, eliminate dampness and relieve leukorrhagia.

Methods: Select acupoints on the *Ren*, *Dai* and Spleen meridians to apply acupuncture, using the reinforcing manipulation. Moxibustion can also be used in treatment.

Acupoints: *Sanyinjiao* (SP 6), *Zusanli* (ST 36), *Daimai* (GB 26), *Baihuanshu* (BL 30) and *Qihai* (RN 6).

Notes: *Daimai* invigorates *qi* in the *Dai* Meridian. *Qihai* supplements *qi* and regulates the *Ren* and *Dai* meridians. *Baihuanshu* helps the urinary bladder to eliminate dampness. *Sanyinjiao* and *Zusanli* strengthen the spleen, benefit *qi* and resolve dampness.

b) Deficiency of kidney

Principles: To invigorate the kidney, strengthen *yang*, stop vaginal discharge and relieve leukorrhagia.

Methods: Select acupoints on the *Ren* and *Dai* meridians to apply acupuncture, using the reinforcing manipulation. Moxibustion can also be used.

Acupoints: *Guanyuan* (RN 4), *Daimai* (GB 26), *Shenshu* (BL 23) and *Zusanli* (ST 36).

Notes: Warmly supplementing *Guanyuan* and *Daimai* can strengthen the kidney and regulate the *Ren* and *Dai* meridians. Reinforcing *Zusanli* can strengthen the spleen and eliminate dampness. Warmly supplementing *Shenshu* can invigorate kidney *yang*, stop vaginal discharge and relieve leukorrhagia.

c) The attack of dampness and toxins

Principles: To disperse heat, remove toxins, eliminate dampness and relieve leukorrhagia.

Methods: Select acupoints on the *Ren*, *Dai* and Spleen meridians to apply acupuncture, using the reducing manipulation.

Acupoints: *Daimai* (GB 26), *Zhongji* (RN 3), *Zusanli* (ST 36), *Yinlingquan* (SP 9) and *Xingjian* (LR 2).

Notes: *Daimai* and *Zhongji* eliminate dampness-heat in the lower *jiao* and regulate the *Ren* and *Dai* meridians. *Zusanli* and *Yinlingquan* strengthen the spleen and eliminate dampness to relieve leukorrhagia. *Xingjian* disperses stagnant heat in the Liver Meridian.

4) Other remedies

Ear acupuncture: Select the auricular points for uterus, tragic apex, ovary, urinary bladder and kidney to apply acupuncture, giving a moderate stimulation and three to four points each time. Keep the needle in the skin for 15-20 minutes.

5) Notes

a) Try to find out the cause of leukorrhagia before adopting acupuncture treatment. Do not dismiss the possibility of cancer if the patient is over 40 years old and the leukorrhea is profuse in quantity, yellow-reddish in color and foul in odor.

b) According to *Progress on Research in Acupuncture and Moxibustion*, acupoint injection has been used to treat leukorrhagia in recent years. The method is to inject 0.5 ml of placental tissue fluid or 3-5 ml of novocain into each of acupoints such as *Zhongji* (RN 3), *Guilai* (ST 29), *Guanyuan* (RN 4) and *Shenshu* (BL 23). Many symptoms of the disease will subside after five to ten treatments.

6. Malposition of fetus

Malposition of fetus refers to abnormal positions of the fetus in the uterus.

1) Treatment

Acupoints: *Zhiyin* (BL 67).

Methods: Let the patient lie on her back or sit in an armchair and give moxibustion treatment to *Zhiyin* on both little toes for 15-20 minutes once or twice every day.

2) Notes

a) Give the patient a careful examination so as to find the root cause of fetal malposition. Take additional measures to moxibustion if the pelvis is contracted or the uterus is deformed.

b) According to *Progress on Research in Acupuncture and Moxibustion*, there are many records referring to the correction of fetal malposition by way of moxibustion. Other methods have also been developed to treat malposition in recent years, including acupuncture and electroacupuncture. In comparison with other methods, moxibustion is safer and easier to use with no bad side effects on the pregnant woman or fetus.

7. Prolonged labor

Prolonged labor refers to a labor lasting over 24 hours caused by the abnormal contraction of the uterus.

1) Etiology and pathogenesis

a) Uterine atony due to weak parturient with deficiency of *qi* and blood, or premature amniorrhea.

b) Mental stress due to primiparity or stagnation of *qi* and blood due to the exogenous cold.

2) Syndrome differentiation

a) Deficiency of *qi* and blood: Mild delivery pains, uterine contractions with short duration and long intermittence, discharge of profuse pale blood, pallor, lassitude, palpitation, short breath, pale tongue with thin coating, large and feeble, or deep, thready and weak pulse.

b) Stagnation of *qi* and blood: Severe labor pains, strong uterine contraction with irregular intervals, scanty discharge of dark red blood, mental stress, fullness in the chest and abdomen, nausea, dark red tongue, deep and forceful pulse with irregular intervals.

3) Treatment

Principles: To invigorate *qi* and blood to promote delivery in cases of deficiency of *qi* and blood; to activate the circulation of *qi* and blood to promote delivery in cases of stagnation of *qi* and blood.

Methods: Select acupoints on the Large Intestine and Spleen meridians to apply acupuncture treatment, using the reinforcing manipulation for the deficiency syndrome, and reducing manipulation for the excess syndrome.

Acupoints: *Sanyinjiao* (SP 6), *Hegu* (LI 4), *Zhiyin* (BL 67) and *Duyin* (EX-LE 11). *Zusanli* (ST 36) can be used together with the above points for deficiency of *qi* and blood and *Taichong* (LR 3) for stagnation of *qi* and blood.

Notes: Puncturing at *Hegu* with the reinforcing manipulation and at *Sanyinjiao* with the reducing manipulation can regulate *qi* and activate the flow of blood to promote delivery. *Duyin* and *Zhiyin* serve as oxytocic. *Zusanli* invigorates the spleen and stomach, and supplements *qi* and blood. *Taichong* promotes the flow of *qi* and blood.

4) Notes

Acupuncture and moxibustion are indicated for prolonged labor due to uterine inertia but not for that caused by uterine deformity and contracted pelvis.

5) Reference materials

Applying acupuncture treatment to 110 patients suffering prolonged labor for several days because of uterine inertia (see *A Selection of Clinical Experiences in Acupuncture and Moxibustion*)

Four groups of acupoints were used, with the first group consisting of *Hegu* (LI 4), *Sanyinjiao* (SP 6) and *Zhibian* (BL 54), the second of *Hegu* and *Sanyinjiao*, the third being *Zhibian*, and the four being *Xuanzhong* (GB 39) or the tender points on the medial side of the thigh.

As a result, 48 of them felt much better because of an increase in the frequency of uterine contractions and the completion of the birth process within eight hours for mothers giving birth for the first time, and within four hours if they had given birth before. Forty-three of them felt a little better, and the rest found no improvement. The best results were achieved in the first group due to the use of acupoints near and far from the affected part. The results in the fourth group were unsatisfactory.

8. Hypogalactia

Hypogalactia is a condition in which a mother can secrete little or no milk after giving birth to a child.

1) Etiology and pathogenesis

a) The exhaustion of *qi* and blood caused by weak constitution and blood loss during delivery.

b) The impediment in the functional activities of *qi* and obstruction of meridians caused by emotional depression.

2) Syndrome differentiation

In addition to the absence of milk, patients with deficiency of *qi* and blood exhibit symptoms such as pallor, lassitude, short breath, poor appetite, loose stools, pale tongue, thready and weak pulse; patients with stagnant *qi* exhibit symptoms such as distention in the chest and hypochondriac region, poor appetite, thin tongue coating and taut pulse.

3) Treatment

Principles: To invigorate *qi* and blood to promote the secretion of milk if there is deficiency of *qi* and blood; to disperse stagnant liver *qi* and promote the secretion of milk if there is stagnation of *qi*.

Methods: Select acupoints along the Pericardium, Large Intestine, Liver and Stomach meridians to apply acupuncture, using the reinforcing manipulation for cases with deficiency syndrome. Moxibustion can also be adopted. For cases with excess syndrome, acupuncture with the reducing manipulation is recommended.

Acupoints: *Shaoze* (SI 1), *Rugen* (ST 18) and *Danzhong* (RN 17). *Zusanli* (ST 36) and *Pishu* (BL 20) can be used together with the above points if there is deficiency of *qi* and blood; *Taichong* (LR 3) and *Neiguan* (PC 6) for cases with stagnant *qi*.

Notes: *Danzhong*, one of the influential points closely related to *qi*, helps regulate the flow of *qi* and promote milk secretion. *Rugen* helps dredge the flow of *qi* in the Large Intestine and Stomach meridians and promote milk secretion. *Shaoze* is a common point for stimulating milk secretion. Puncturing at *Zusanli* and *Pishu* with the reinforcing manipulation can help invigorate the spleen and stomach, promote the production of *qi*, blood and milk. Puncturing at *Taichong* with the reducing manipulation can disperse stagnant liver *qi*. *Neiguan* helps ease the chest and relieve stagnation.

4) Notes

In addition to acupuncture treatment, foods such as pig trotters and crucian carp soup can also be used to stimulate milk secretion.

5) Reference materials

Applying acupuncture and moxibustion treatment to a 31-year-old primipara named Lu who suffered agalactosis for more than one month (see *A Concise Compilation of Acupuncture and Moxibustion*)

Points: Acupuncture at *Zusanli* (ST 36) and *Hegu* (LI 4); acupuncture and moxibustion at *Danzhong* (RN 17); acupuncture or moxibustion at *Rugen* (ST 18); moxibustion at *Shaoze* (SI 1) after letting out a little blood with prompt prick. The secretion of milk increased after five courses of treatment, and a follow-up visit after one month found her lactation had become normal.

9. Prolapse of uterus

Prolapse of uterus refers to the displacement of the uterus so that the cervix is within or outside the vaginal orifice.

1) Etiology and pathogenesis

a) Exerting too much strength during delivery or taking physical exercises too early after delivery impairs *qi* of the spleen and stomach so that *qi* becomes insubstantial and descends, and the uterus is displaced.

b) Multiparity or sexual indulgence consumes kidney *qi* and impairs the *Dai*, *Chong* and *Ren* meridians so that the uterus is displaced.

2) Syndrome differentiation

The main symptoms are the displacement of the uterus, and the dropping and distending sensations in the lower abdomen which become more pronounced on exertion. Cases with weak spleen exhibit symptoms such as lassitude, short breath, pallor, poor appetite, leukorrhagia, pale tongue with thin coating, feeble and weak pulse; cases with weak kidney exhibit symptoms such as lumbago, sore and weak knees, dizziness, tinnitus, polyuria, pale tongue, deep and weak pulse.

3) Treatment

Principles: To replenish and elevate *qi*, and strengthen the spleen if there is deficiency of spleen; to invigorate the kidney if there is deficiency of kidney.

Methods: Select acupoints on the *Du* and *Ren* meridians to apply acupuncture, using the reinforcing manipulation. Moxibustion is also used.

Acupoints: *Baihui* (DU 20), *Qihai* (RN 6), *Weidao* (GB 28), *Zusanli* (ST 36) and *Sanyinjiao* (SP

6). *Zhaohai* (KI 6) is added for cases with deficiency of kidney.

Notes: *Baihui*, an acupoint along the *Du* Meridian at the vertex, elevates *yang-qi*. This acupoint is adopted based on the principle requiring the use of acupoints on the upper part of the body to treat disorders in the lower part, and elevating *qi* to treat disorders due to collapse. *Qihai* reinforces the primordial *qi* and regulates the *Chong* and *Ren* meridians; *Weidao* restores the prolapsed uterus back in place; *Sanyinjiao* and *Zusanli* invigorate the spleen and stomach and benefit *qi* in the middle *jiao*; *Zhaohai* invigorates the liver and kidney.

4) Other remedies

Electric acupuncture: Puncture at *Zusanli* (ST 36) with the reinforcing manipulation. Use a two-*cun*-long filiform needle to puncture at *Zigong* (EX-CA 1) obliquely towards the uterus. Then turn on the electric current for 15-20 minutes when the patient gets a pronounced sensation of being needling at the uterus.

5) Notes

a) The patient must not carry heavy loads on the back. During treatment she must stretch the levator ani muscle.

b) Acupuncture treatment has proved quite effective against mild hysteroptosis. *Baihui* (DU 20), *Qichong* (ST 30), *Weidao* (GB 28) and *Sanyinjiao* (SP 6) are the effective acupoints.

6) Reference materials

Applying acupuncture treatment to a 37-year-old patient named Wang who suffered from prolapse of uterus (see *A Concise Compilation of Acupuncture and Moxibustion*)

The condition occurred five months after she had had her sixth child, as a result of her carrying heavy loads with her hands. The condition worsened, and as a result symptoms such as abnormal menstruation, backache, pain in the lower abdomen with tenesmus appeared. The woman took both Chinese and Western medicines to no effect. An examination revealed that her cervix was four centimeters outside the vaginal orifice, and that the cervix could return to a normal position periodically. There was no any inflammation or ulceration on the surface of the cervix. During treatment, *Zhongji* (RN 3) and *Zusanli* (ST 36) on both sides were punctured and the uterus did not prolapse the next day. Following this result, *Zhongji* and *Guanyuan* (RN 4) on one side and *Zusanli* and *Sanyinjiao* (SP 6) on both sides were punctured. No recurrence was found ten days later, and the patient felt that her condition had returned to normal.

10. Acute infantile convulsion

Acute infantile convulsion refers to a disease with symptoms such as stupor, convulsion, lockjaw and opisthotonos. It often occurs with high fever, meningitis, encephalitis, atelencephalia, hypocalcemia or epilepsy, with the patients' ages ranging from one to five.

1) Etiology and pathogenesis

a) Exogenous pathogenic factors: The attack by exogenous pathogenic factors goes from the exterior to the interior, which turns stagnation into heat, and heat into wind, before stupor and convulsion occur.

b) The accumulation of phlegm-heat: Eating too much food impairs the spleen and stomach, which gives rise to internal stagnation of phlegm and produces heat and wind before stupor and convulsion occur.

c) Sudden shock: Getting frightened or falling down on hearing strange sounds can disturb the mind as a prelude stupor and convulsion occur.

2) Syndrome differentiation

At the onset of acute infantile convulsion, there is high fever, flushed face, irritability, involuntary head shaking with protruding tongue and excessive movement of limbs, and coma, eye staring, lockjaw, convulsion and opisthotonos. Symptoms are accompanied by cough, thin and yellow tongues coating, and superficial and rapid pulse when the body is affected by exogenous pathogenic factors. Symptoms of distensive pain at the epigastrium and abdomen, vomiting, wheezing sound in the throat, yellow and greasy tongue coating, and rapid pulse when phlegm-heat is accumulated. Low fever, cold limbs, unquiet or lethargic sleep, changing complexion, thin tongue coating, deep pulse, and blue purple superficial venule of the index finger when the patient gets a fright.

3) Treatment

Principles: To calm the wind and relieve convulsion, and disperse heat and eliminate pathogenous factors if the body is affected by exogenous pathogenic factors; to disperse heat and eliminate phlegm if phlegm-heat is accumulated inside the body.

Methods: Select acupoints on the *Du* Meridian, and *Shixuan* (EX-UE 11) to apply acupuncture, using the reducing manipulation or prompt prick.

Acupoints: *Shuigou* (DU 26), *Shixuan* (EX-UE 11), *Hegu* (LI 4) and *Taichong* (LR 3). *Dazhui* (DU 14) and *Quchi* (LI 11) are used together with the above points for the affection of exogenous pathogenic factors; *Zhongwan* (RN 12) and *Fenglong* (ST 40) for the accumulation of phlegm-heat; *Yintang* (EX-HN 3) and *Shenmen* (HT 7) relieve convulsion.

Notes: *Shuigou*, a point on the *Du* Meridian, induces resuscitation and relieves convulsion. *Shixuan* disperses heat and induces resuscitation. *Hegu* and *Taichong* arrest convulsion. *Dazhui* and *Quchi* disperse heat. *Zhongwan* and *Fenglong* strengthen the spleen and stomach, eliminate phlegm and promote digestion. *Shenmen* and *Yintang* tranquilize the mind.

4) Notes

Acupuncture has proved effective against convulsion, but does not cure the cause of the condition.

5) Reference materials

Applying acupuncture to a one-and-half-year-old boy named Sun who suffered acute infantile convulsion (see *Experience on Acupuncture and Moxibustion Treatment*)

The patient had a high fever and cough after catching a cold. Other symptoms were convulsion, lockjaw and opisthotonos. A physical examination showed a body temperature of 39.8°C, respiratory rate of 38/min and heart rate of 108/min. In addition, respiration was harsh, liver and spleen impalpable, throat swollen and congested, superficial venule of the finger blue and purple and convulsion paroxysmal. Though the patient's development was normal, the disease was diagnosed as hyperpyretic convulsion, also called acute infantile convulsion.

Acupuncture treatment was given to the boy, and point *Shuigou*, *Hegu* and *Dazhui* were punctured with strong stimulation. Bloodletting therapy with prompt prick was applied at *Shixuan*. The needles were kept in the skin for 20-60 minutes and twisted every ten minutes during the treatment. The convulsion stopped after acupuncture treatment. No recurrence was found within the two hours that followed. To ensure effective therapy, *Baolong* Bolus of Succinum was prescribed and taken three times a day with half a bolus each time. Fever had subsided by the third day and the condition was cured.

11. Bed-wetting

Bed-wetting is a condition in which a child who is three years old or more cannot help discharging urine while at sleep.

1) Etiology and pathogenesis

a) The physique is weak and the kidney *qi* unstable, which makes the bladder dysfunctional and unable to control urination.

b) Lung *qi* is deficient, which makes the bladder dysfunctional, or spleen *qi* is deficient, which causes the accumulation of water and dampness. These factors make it impossible to keep urination under control.

2) Syndrome differentiation

Involuntary urination which takes place once over several nights or several times every night. It is accompanied by pallor, mental retardation, polyuria, cold limbs, chilliness, pale tongue and deep and retarded pulse if there is deficiency of kidney; by pallor, lassitude, weak limbs, loss of appetite, loose stools, oliguria, pale tongue, retarded or deep and thready pulse if there is deficiency of spleen *qi* and lung *qi*.

3) Treatment

Principles: To warm and invigorate kidney *yang* if there is deficiency of kidney but to invigorate the spleen and lung if there is deficiency of spleen and lung.

Methods: Select acupoints on the *Ren* Meridian and the back *shu* points to apply acupuncture, using the reinforcing manipulation. Moxibustion can also be used in treatment.

Acupoints: *Guanyuan* (RN 4), *Zhongji* (RN 3), *Pangguangshu* (BL 28) and *Sanyinjiao* (SP 6). *Shenshu* (BL 23) can be added to the above points to treat patients with deficiency of kidney; *Zusanli* (ST 36) and *Taiyuan* (LU 9) can be added to the above points to treat patients with deficiency of spleen and lung.

Notes: *Guanyuan*, a point along the *Ren* Meridian, serves as a tonic and helps to reinforce kidney *qi* and make it stable. *Zhongji* and *Pangguangshu*, the front *mu* and back *shu* points of the bladder respectively, help to promote the functional activities of the bladder. *Sanyinjiao* serves to regulate and invigorate the spleen and kidney. *Shenshu* supplements the kidney, thus ensuring the normal function of the bladder. Puncturing at *Zusanli* with the reinforcing manipulation may invigorate the spleen and stomach. *Taiyuan*, the *yuan* point along the Lung Meridian of Hand-*Taiyin*, can be used to benefit lung *qi*.

4) Other remedies

Ear acupuncture

Points: The auricular points for kidney, gallbladder, brain and middle border.

Method: Select two to three points each time to give a moderate stimulation. Keep the needle in the skin for 15-20 minutes and the treatment is given once a day. Needle embedment can also be used.

5) Reference materials

Applying acupuncture to 42 children including 15 boys who suffered bed-wetting (see *A Selection of Clinical Experiences in Acupuncture and Moxibustion*)

There were 25 patients aging from three to five, 13 patients from six to eight, and four patients from nine to 12. Points *Sanyinjiao* (SP 6) and *Zhongji* (RN 3) were used as main points and *Shenshu* (BL 23) and *Zusanli* (ST 36) as accessory ones. *Sanyinjiao* was punctured by way of mild reinforcement and reduction so that a needling sensation can reach the medial side of the thigh. The needle was withdrawn one or two minutes after being twisted slightly. Then heat-producing needling was applied to *Zhongji*, and the needle was twirled for three minutes so that a needling sensation was felt at the genitalia. After that, *Shenshu* and *Zusanli* were punctured with the reinforcing manipulation. The above treatment was given once every day. As a result, 34 of the patients recovered, and eight reported improvements in their condition. Follow-up visits within the six months that followed showed that 30 of the children had no relapse.

12. Infantile paralysis

Infantile paralysis refers to a disease caused by such exogenous pathogenic factors as wind, dampness and heat. Categorized as seasonal febrile disease in traditional Chinese medicine, infantile paralysis has similar symptoms to fever, headache, sore throat, nausea, vomiting and melalgia in the early stages, with numbness and paralysis in the limbs later. In this part of the book infantile paralysis at the later stage is dealt with in detail.

1) Etiology and pathogenesis

The consumption of fluid in the lung, stomach, liver and kidney, and the deficiency of essence and blood makes the meridians empty and tendons and muscles undernourished, which give rise to muscular flaccidity and paralysis.

2) Syndrome differentiation

As the disease passes into the later stage, the limbs become paralyzed. It is not until one or two weeks later that paralysis is gradually relieved. The muscles will not be atrophied and deformed if the paralysis can be relieved in one and a half years.

3) Treatment

Principles: To invigorate the liver and kidney, benefit essence and blood, relax the tendons and muscles and activate meridians.

Methods: Select acupoints along the Large Intestine and Stomach meridians to apply acupuncture, using the reinforcing and reducing manipulation according to the nature of the disease.

Acupoints: *Shenshu* (BL 23), *Jiaji* (EX-B 2), *Huantiao* (GB 30), *Futu* (ST 32), *Zusanli* (ST 36) and *Yanglingquan* (GB 34) for paralysis of lower limbs. *Jianyu* (LI 15), *Quchi* (LI 11), *Hegu* (LI 4) and *Waiguan* (SJ 5) for paralysis of upper limbs.

Notes: Rich in *qi* and blood, the Large Intestine and Stomach meridians keep the tendons under control. Therefore acpoints such as *Jianyu*, *Quchi*, *Hegu*, *Futu* and *Zusanli* along this two meridians are chosen to treat paralysis, which is in conformity with the principle of selecting points along the Large Intestine and Stomach meridians for flaccidity syndrome. *Yanglingquan*, one of the eight influential point related to tendons, is used with *Huantiao* of the Gallbladder Meridian to relax the tendons and soothe the joints. *Shenshu* and *Jiaji* help invigorate the kidney and benefit essence.

4) Other remedies

Acupoint injection: The acupoints for injection are the same as those for acupuncture. The drugs that are often used in treatment are injections of 10% glucose, Vitamin B_1, furathiamine hydrochloride, Radix Angelicae Sinensis Co. and galanthamine. The 10% glucose should be injected into acupoints near thick muscles such as *Futu* (ST 32), *Zusanli* (ST 36), *Biguan* (ST 31), with 10 ml for each acupoint. As for other drugs, the amount to be injected varies from 0.5 to 1.0 ml, with two to four points each time. The treatment is given once a day or every other day, and a complete course of treatment includes 10-20 sessions.

5) Reference materials

Applying acupuncture treatment to 108 children suffering infantile paralysis (see *A Selection of Clinical Experiences in Acupuncture and Moxibustion*)

A common sequela of the disease was noted, that is the inability of the upper arms to adduct when the disease involved the upper limbs, or the liability of the feet to abduct when the disease involved the lower limbs. In the past, when treating this disease, acupoints along the *Yangming* and *Shaoyang* meridians (Large Intestine, Stomach, Sanjiao and Bladder meridians) were often used instead of those along the three *yin* meridians (Heart, Pericardium, Lung, Kidney, Spleen and Liver meridians). In this study, new methods were introduced. First, acupoints along the *yin* and *yang* meridians were used together, with *Jianyu* (LI 15), *Quchi* (LI 11), *Hegu* (LI 4), *Chize* (LU 5), *Quze* (PC 3), *Shaohai* (HT 3), *Shenmen* (HT 7) and *Daling* (PC 7) for paralysis of the upper limbs, while *Huantiao* (GB 30), *Yanglingquan* (GB 34) and *Zusanli* (ST 36), *Yinbao* (LR 9), *Xuehai* (SP 10), *Yingu* (KI 10), *Zhubin* (KI 9), *Sanyinjiao* (SP 6), *Zhongfeng* (LR 4), *Shangqiu* (SP 5) and *Taixi* (KI 3) for paralysis of the lower limbs. Second, acupoints along the *yin* and *yang* meridians were used alternately. For example, acupoints along the *yang* meridians were used in the first course of treatment while those along the *yin* meridians in the second course. Moreover, in accordance with the principle of using *shu* points to treat chronic diseases, such acupoints as *Feishu* (BL 13), *Weishu* (BL 21), *Pishu* (BL 20), *Shenshu* (BL 23), *Dachangshu* (BL 25) and *Xiaochangshu* (BL 27) were used alternately. When treating the inability of the upper limbs to adduct, acupoints along the *yin* meridians were used more often than those along the *yang* meridians, and the same method was used when treating the liability of lower limbs to abduct. After treatment, 74 of the 108 patients found the motor function of their limbs had returned to normal, 25 of them found their motor function had recovered but their feet were liable to abduct as before, and five of them still felt that their upper limbs were unable to abduct, the rest of the children found the new methods ineffective.

Section 3
SURGICAL DISEASES

1. Acute mastitis
Acute mastitis is an acute suppurative disease of the breast.

1) Etiology and pathogenesis

The attack on the breast by exogenous heat and fire, stagnation of liver *qi* after emotional depression, and the accumulation of heat in the Large Intestine and Stomach meridians as induced by overeating can all lead to the accumulation of pathogenic heat and obstruction of meridians.

2) Syndrome differentiation

The main symptoms of the disease are redness, swelling and pain at the breast. In the early stage of the disease there appears a painful lump in the breast which makes it difficult to secrete milk. It is then accompanied by chilliness, fever, and thirst. If the lump enlarges, with local redness and more pronounced pain, the disease has reached the stage of suppuration; if something soft is felt around the lump, an abscess has been formed; and if liver *qi* is stagnant, symptoms appear, such as irritability, distention in the chest and hypochondriac region, poor appetite, thin tongue coating and a taut pulse.

3) Treatment

Principles: To disperse heat, eliminate stagnation, eliminate the lump and relieve swelling.

Methods: Select acupoints on the Large Intestine, Stomach, Pericardium and Liver meridians to apply acupuncture, using the reducing manipulation.

Acupoints: *Zusanli* (ST 36), *Hegu* (LI 4), *Quchi* (LI 11), *Neiguan* (PC 6), *Jianjing* (GB 21) and *Shaoze* (SI 1). *Neiting* (ST 44) is added to treat the stagnation of heat in the Large Intestine and Stomach meridians; *Taichong* (LR 3) and *Qimen* (LR 14) are added if there is stagnation of liver *qi*.

Notes: Since the Large Intestine and Stomach meridians travel around the breast, therefore acupoints along this two meridians such as *Zusanli*, *Quchi*, *Hegu* and *Neiting* are selected to disperse heat and eliminate lumps; *Neiguan*, *Qimen* and *Taichong* promote the circulation of liver *qi* and relieve the stagnation in the chest; *Jianjing*, which relieves lumps, is an effective point for acute mastitis; *Shaoze* disperses heat and promotes secretion of milk.

4) Other remedies

When the disease is at the early stage, cover the affected area with onion or garlic mash and burn a moxa stick for 10-20 minutes every day.

5) Notes

Acupuncture can be used to treat acute mastitis with no abscess around the breast and surgical operation should be applied when an abscess is found around the breast.

6) Reference materials

Applying acupuncture treatment to a female patient named Xu suffering acute mastitis (see *A Concise Compilation of Acupuncture and Moxibustion*)

The patient felt uncomfortable and her appetite worsened gradually after she had her third child. She also felt a pain in the left breast and could not sleep. A physical examination showed that her left breast was red and swollen and that the patient felt a severe pain when the affected part was pressed. The examination also showed a high temperature 39.5°C. The disease was diagnosed acute mastitis. *Quchi* (LI 11) on both sides and *Danzhong* (RN 17) on left side were punctured and the needles were kept in the skin for 40 minutes before moxibustion treatment was given to *Danzhong* for 30 minutes. The temperature dropped and the symptoms were relieved. The next day the same treatment was applied. The left breast became less red and swollen, while the right one became red, swollen and severely painful. The patient's temperature rose to 40.2°C on the third day. Then *Danzhong* on one side and *Rugen* (ST 18) on right side were punctured and the needles were retained in the skin for 60 minutes before moxibustion treatment was given to *Danzhong* for 30 minutes. On the fourth day, *Quchi* on both sides and *Danzhong* on one side were punctured and the symptoms were again relieved.

2. Nodules of the breast

Nodules can be found at the breast when a woman suffers from lobular or chronic cystic hyperplasia.

1) Etiology and pathogenesis

The dysfunction of the liver due to emotional depression or the disharmony of the *Dai* and *Ren* meridians due to too much anxiety is liable to cause the derangement of *qi* and blood and the accumulation of phlegm-dampness blocking the milk meridian.

2) Syndrome differentiation

The main symptoms of the disease are that one or several nodules appear on one or two sides of the breast. The nodule is painless and movable, and feels quite smooth. It is usually accompanied by distensive pain in the breast, chest upset and belching. The above symptoms become more pronounced before menstruation, with relief afterwards. Symptoms can also change with emotion.

3) Treatment

Principles: To soothe the liver and regulate the flow of *qi*, relieve depression and resolve lumps.

Methods: Select acupoints along the Stomach and Liver meridians to apply acupuncture, using the mild reinforcement and reduction manipulation.

Acupoints: *Neiguan* (PC 6), *Danzhong* (RN 17), *Fenglong* (ST 40), *Zusanli* (ST 36) and *Jianjing* (GB 21).

Notes: *Neiguan*, one of the eight confluent points, helps soothe chest, resolve lumps and relieve swelling. *Danzhong*, one of the eight influential point related to *qi*, serves to promote the flow of *qi* and dredge the meridians. *Zusanli* and *Fenglong* strengthen the spleen and stomach and eliminate phlegm-dampness so as to resolve the lumps. *Jianjing* helps to remove stagnation and swelling.

4) Reference materials

According to *A Selection of Clinical Experiences in Acupuncture and Moxibustion*, acupuncture can reduce or resolve nodules in the breast, probably because it helps to eliminate old and proliferated cells, and prevents cells in the breast from growing. An experiment has shown that acupuncture can stimulate macrophages so that their phagocytic index can be enhanced.

3. Acute appendicitis

Acute appendicitis refers to a condition whose main symptom is pain felt in the right lower region of the abdomen.

1) Etiology and pathogenesis

a) Eating too much greasy food is liable to cause the functional disorders of the stomach and intestines, accumulation of dampness-heat and stagnation of *qi* and blood in the intestines.

b) Taking a fast walk after a meal is liable to cause the functional disorders of the intestines and stagnation of *qi* and blood in the intestines.

2) Syndrome differentiation

At the onset of the condition, pain is felt first in the epigastrium or around the umbilicus and then in the right lower region of the abdomen, which gives rise to local tenderness, muscular spasm and cutaneous hyperesthesia. These symptoms are usually accompanied by fever, chilliness, nausea, vomiting, dark yellow urine, constipation, reddened tongue with yellow and greasy coating and rapid and forceful pulse. Pain and tenderness may become more pronounced and the mass near the affected part may become palpable.

3) Treatment

Principles: To clear the intestines of heat, promote the flow of *qi*, remove blood-stasis and relieve pain.

Methods: Select acupoints on the Large Intestine and Stomach meridians to apply acupuncture, using the reducing manipulation.

Acupoints: *Shangjuxu* (ST 37), *Lanwei* (EX-LE 7), *Quchi* (LI 11) and *Tianshu* (ST 25). *Qihai* (RN 6) is added to treat abdominal distention, and *Neiguan* (PC 6) for vomiting.

Notes: *Shangjuxu*, the lower confluent point of the large intestine, can treat disorders of the six *fu* organs; *Tianshu*, the front *mu* point of the large intestine, can help promote the flow of *qi* in the large intestine and disperse heat in the *fu* organs. *Quchi* disperses heat and eliminates toxins. *Lanwei*, an effective point for appendicitis, helps to promote the flow of *qi* and eliminate distention with *Qihai* and soothe the chest and stop vomiting with *Neiguan*.

4) Other remedies

a) Acupoint injection

Inject 2-5 ml of 10% glucose into *Lanwei* (EX-LE 7) and the tender spot, 0.5 to 0.8 *cun* deep and once a day.

b) Ear acupuncture

Puncture with strong stimulation at the auricular points for appendix, inferior anthihelix crus and ear-*Shenmen*. Keep the needle in the skin for 30 minutes once a day.

5) Notes

Acupuncture treatment is suitable for simple appendicitis or mild suppurative appendicitis. If there is abscess, other methods including surgical operation should be used.

6) Reference materials

According to *Progress on Research in Acupuncture and Moxibustion*, research has shown that acupuncture can help regulate the state of the body, bring the various functions of vegetative nervous system back into balance, improve the circulation of blood in the appendix, eliminate harmful substance within the body, reduce local exudation and swelling, and promote the peristalsis and the circulation of blood in the appendix, thus accelerating the excretion from the appendiceal cavity and the absorption of inflammation. In addition, acupuncture can also improve the organic immunologic function, speed up the absorption of body fluid in the abdominal cavity and enhance the function of adrenal gland. In so doing, the metabolism within the body will be promoted and resistance increased.

4. Hemorrhoids

Hemorrhoids refers to a medical condition in which the varicose veins inside or outside the anus become dilated, swollen and painful and sometimes bleed.

1) Etiology and pathogenesis

Eating too much acrid and pungent food gives rise to the accumulation of dampness and heat in the intestines and stomach, or standing, sitting or walking for a long time, chronic dysentery, or constipation causes stagnation of *qi* and blood in the rectum.

2) Syndrome differentiation

There are two types of hemorrhoids.

One is internal hemorrhoid in which the pile is small and soft at the onset, with bright or dark red blood flowing out during defecation. As the pile becomes bigger, the patient will find difficulty in defecating or urinating. If this condition occurs repeatedly, resulting in the outflow of too much blood, then such symptoms as sallow complexion, short breath, loss of appetite, pale tongues and weak pulse will appear, due to a deficiency of *qi* and blood. If the pile becomes prolapsed and cannot go back into the anus, the pile may become swollen, eroded or even necrotic because of incarceration and infection.

The other type is the external hemorrhoid. The patient may or may not have a sensation of pain with this foreign growth at the anus. Bleeding is not as great as with an internal hemorrhoid when this kind of hemorrhoid occurs.

3) Treatment

Principles: To disperse heat, promote digestion, cool the blood and stop bleeding.

Methods: Select acupoints along the Bladder and *Du* meridians, using the reducing manipulation.

Acupoints: *Changqiang* (DU 1), *Dachangshu* (BL 25), *Chengshan* (BL 57) and *Erbai* (EX-UE 2). *Baihui* (DU 20) can be added to treat deficiency of *qi* and blood.

Notes: Since a branch of the Bladder Meridian passes the anus, *Chengshan* and *Dachangshu* along the meridian are used to promote the flow of *qi* and blood in the meridian, disperse heat and stagnation; *Changqiang* promotes the flow of local *qi* and blood; *Erbai* is an effective point for treating hemorrhoid; and *Baihui* helps promote the flow of *yang-qi*.

4) Other remedies

Prompt prick

Points: Sensitive points in the lumbosacral region and *Dachangshu* (BL 25).

Method: Prompt prick the subcutaneous tissue with a thick needle, one or two points each time. The treatment is carried out once every week.

5) Notes

Patients should be advised to eat less acrid or pungent food, and keep smooth bowel movements.

6) Reference materials

Applying electroacupuncture treatment to 28 patients suffering hemorrhoidal bleeding (see *A Selection of Clinical Experiences in Acupuncture and Moxibustion*)

Points: *Zhishu* (one *cun* lateral to *Mingmen*, DU 4), *Huiyang* (BL 35), *Changqiang* (DU 1) and *Chengshan* (BL 57). *Erbai* (EX-UE 2) can be added for hematochezia; *Qihai* (RN 6) and *Shenshu* (BL 23) for prolapse of rectum.

Methods: Two or three points were punctured each time, with relatively strong stimulation for most cases and moderate stimulation for cases with bleeding. After a needling sensation was obtained, an electric wave was sent to the patient. Electroacupuncture treatment lasted five minutes, twice or three times per week. Some patients administered Chinese drugs if the treatment resulted in too great a flow of blood.

Effects: Twenty-five of the 28 patients, suffering from either internal, external or mixed hemorrhoid found no blood flowing after one or two treatment. Twelve patients returned to the doctor shortly after they received treatment. In terms of pile reduction, acupuncture proved most effective against internal hemorrhoid. Four of the five patients who suffered from internal hemorrhoid recovered from their condition and one felt much better than before.

5. Sprain

Sprain refers to an injury which causes damage to the soft tissues or ligaments of the trunk and limbs. Symptoms of sprain include swelling and pain at the affected part and dyskinesia of joints.

1) Etiology and pathogenesis

The flow of *qi* and blood is stagnant, and tendons, vessels and joints are injured as caused by sudden, strenuous or other inappropriate movements of the body.

2) Syndrome differentiation

Mild cases often exhibit swelling, pain, bruise or tenderness at the affected part; severe cases exhibit redness and swelling, dyskinesia of joints and intolerable pain. The neck, shoulder, elbow, wrist, lumbus, hip, knee and ankle are liable to be affected by sprain.

3) Treatment

Principles: To promote the flow of *qi*, dredge the meridians, reduce swelling and alleviate pain.

Methods: Select acupoints near the affected area to apply acupuncture, using the reducing manipulation. Moxibustion can be used with acupuncture to treat old strain.

Acupoints: *Jianyu* (LI 15), *Jianliao* (SJ 14), *Jianzhen* (SI 9) and *Shousanli* (LI 10) are used for the shoulder sprain; *Quchi* (LI 11), *Shousanli* (LI 10), *Shaohai* (HT 3) and *Tianjing* (SJ 10) for the elbow sprain; *Yangchi* (SJ 4), *Yangxi* (LI 5) and *Yanggu* (SI 5) for the wrist sprain; *Shenshu* (BL 23), *Weizhong* (BL 40) and tender spots for the lumbus sprain; *Huantiao* (GB 30), *Chengfu* (BL 36) and *Juliao* (GB 29) for the hip sprain; *Xiyan* (EX-LE 5), *Weizhong* (BL 40), *Yanglingquan* (GB 34) and *Xiyangguan* (GB 33) for the knee sprain; *Jiexi* (ST 41), *Kunlun* (BL 60), *Qiuxu* (GB 40) and *Xuanzhong* (GB 39) for the ankle sprain.

Notes: Points near the affected part are used to promote the flow of *qi* and blood in the meridians and relieve pain.

4) Other remedies

Cupping with bloodletting. Cupping therapy is applied to the affected part after tapping with a plum-blossom needle to let out a little blood.

5) Notes

During acupuncture treatment, ask the patient to move the affected limb to achieve best results.

6) Reference materials

Applying acupuncture treatment to 300 patients suffering sprain (see *A Selection of Clinical Experiences in Acupuncture and Moxibustion*)

The affected parts included the neck, shoulder, elbow, lumbus, knee and ankle, and 33.7% of the patients suffered ankle sprain, a higher percentage than that of the patients who suffered the injury in other parts of the body. The duration of injury lasted from one day to one year, and 38.7% of them came for treatment five days after being sprained.

Points: *Fengchi* (GB 20), *Jianjing* (GB 21), *Dazhui* (DU 14), and *Jianzhongshu* (SI 15) together with *Baihui* (DU 20), *Tianzhu* (BL 10), *Shenzhu* (DU 12) and *Hegu* (LI 4) for neck sprain; *Shenshu* (BL 23), *Shangliao* (BL 31), *Dachangshu* (BL 25) and *Zhishi* (BL 52) together with *Weizhong* (BL 40) and *Mingmen* (DU 4) for lumbar sprain.

Methods: The needles were inserted into the points with twirling manipulation and kept in the skin for 20-30 minutes. During this needle retention period, the needles were twisted every ten minutes in order to maintain a persistent sensation of distending soreness.

Therapeutic effects: There were 243 patients, 81% of the total, recovered from sprain; 40 patients,

13.3% of the total, felt much better; 17 patients, 5.7% of the total, found the treatment ineffective. Of the 243 patients who recovered from their sprain, 224 (92.2%) patients received one to five sessions of acupuncture treatment.

Appendix: Torticollis

Torticollis is a muscular disorder in which the neck is twisted and the head pulled to one side. It is usually caused by a poor posture in sleep, improper turning of the neck or the obstruction of *qi* and blood circulation in the meridians due to the effect on the neck by pathogenic wind-cold.

Its symptoms include pain on one side of the neck and limited movement. The patient often feels a pain in the neck as if it were pulled by something else. When moving the neck, the pain becomes more intense, sometimes producing tenderness. In addition, the pain may spread down to the upper limb of the affected side.

Principles of treatment are to promote the flow of *qi* and blood, dredge the meridians and alleviate pain.

The method is to select acupoints along the Small Intestine and Gallbladder meridians to apply acupuncture, using the reducing manipulation.

Points: *Houxi* (SI 3), *Tianzhu* (BL 10), *Fengchi* (GB 20) and *Jianjing* (GB 21). As the Small Intestine Meridian runs along the neck, nape and shoulder, *Houxi* along this meridian can be used to promote the flow of *qi* to relieve pain. *Tianzhu*, *Fengchi* and *Jianjing*, which are situated near the affected part, can help promote the flow of *qi* around the region. Cupping treatment can be used in combination.

6. Elbow strain

Elbow strain, which falls into the category of injury of tendons in traditional Chinese medicine, refers to non-traumatic pain in the elbow regions. It is usually seen in external humeral epicondylitis.

1) Etiology and pathogenesis

The attack on the elbow joint by wind-cold gives rise to the stagnation of *qi* and blood, and to the dysfunctioning of tendons and muscles in the elbow.

2) Syndrome differentiation

The pain gradually starts to occur in the elbow joint in patients who may never have had a history of trauma. It becomes intense when the patient rotates the forearm forcefully or clenches a fist. Pain may even spread to the arm and shoulder. Swelling may not be obvious, but tenderness is quite evident on the external epicondyle of the humerus.

3) Treatment

Principles: To dredge the meridians, relax tendons and muscles and alleviate pain.

Methods: Select acupoints along the Large Intestine Meridian and areas near the affected side to apply acupuncture, using the reducing manipulation. Moxibustion can be used in combination.

Acupoints: *Ashi* points, *Quchi* (LI 11), *Shousanli* (LI 10) and *Hegu* (LI 4).

Notes: Puncturing at the above points helps promote the flow of *qi* in the affected area and the Large Intestine Meridian. Moxibustion treatment helps warm and dredge the meridians.

4) Other remedies

Acupoint injection: In the early stage of the disease, 0.5 ml of acetate hydrocortisone can be injected into the tender spot. Injections can be administered weekly, with procaine added to the dose when necessary.

5) Notes

Try to keep the patient from doing too much elbow exercise during treatment.

7. Thecal cyst

Thecal cyst usually occurs near the joint or tendon sheath at the wrist or the dorsum of foot. It is possibly caused by trauma, mechanical stimulation or chronic strain.

The progress of the disease is quite slow and results in a cyst developing into a round lump. The lump feels soft with a smooth surface and clear margins, becoming hard and tender when the cyst is full of liquid. The patient may feel tired with local pain upon slight movement or exertion.

Treatment

a) Local needling: Try to keep the cyst sterilized and fixed before inserting a three-edged needle deeply into it to break the cyst wall. Squeeze liquid from the broken cyst and bandage tightly for three to five days. Repeat the treatment if the cyst reappears within a week.

b) Surrounding needling: Insert five needles into the cyst, four from its sides and one from its top. Then apply electroacupuncture or moxibustion with warming needle treatment to the affected part. The treatment can be carried out once a day.

8. Urticaria

It is also known as *yinzhen* and *fengzhenkuai* in traditional Chinese medicine.

1) Etiology and pathogenesis

a) The attack on the skin and muscles by wind-cold or wind-heat.

b) The accumulation of heat in the intestines and stomach due to improper diet, or the stagnation of heat in the skin and muscles due to the accumulation of dampness.

c) Deficiency of *qi* and blood or the production of pathogenic wind due to deficiency of blood caused by prolonged illness.

2) Syndrome differentiation

Main symptoms are itching wheals. The wheals appear and disappear quickly at different times, leaving no trace. Cases due to the affection of wind are usually accompanied by fever, thirst, cough, thin tongue coating and superficial and rapid pulse. Cases due to stagnation of heat in the stomach and intestines are accompanied by a distensive pain in the abdomen, poor appetite, constipation, loose stools, yellow and greasy tongue coating, or smooth and rapid pulse. Cases with deficiency of blood exhibit wheals occurring intermittently, pallor, lassitude, dizziness, pale tongue and thready pulse.

3) Treatment

Principles: To disperse wind and heat and relieve itching, and purge the intestine and remove stagnation if there is the accumulation of heat in the intestines and stomach, and to invigorate *qi* and blood if there is deficiency of blood.

Methods: Select acupoints along the Large Intestine and Kidney meridians to apply acupuncture, using the reducing manipulation. Reinforcing manipulation can be used when treating cases with deficiency of blood.

Acupoints: *Quchi* (LI 11), *Hegu* (LI 4), *Xuehai* (SP 10), *Geshu* (BL 17) and *Dazhui* (DU 14). *Zusanli* (ST 36) is used together with the above points for the accumulation of heat in the stomach and intestines; *Zusanli* and *Pishu* (BL 20) for deficiency of blood.

Notes: Since urticaria is a disorder caused by the attack of exogenous wind or stagnation of heat in the Large Intestine Meridian in the skin, *Quchi* and *Hegu* along this meridian are selected to disperse wind and heat and relieve itching. *Xuehai* along the Spleen Meridian regulates blood and expels heat; *Geshu*, an influential point, helps regulate blood and is indicated for diseases caused by stagnation of heat in the *xue* system; *Dazhui* disperses wind and stagnant heat in the Large Intestine Meridian. Puncturing at *Zusanli* with the reducing manipulation can disperse heat; at *Zusanli* and *Pishu* with the reinforcing manipulation helps nourish the spleen and stomach and benefit *qi* and blood.

4) Other remedies

Ear acupuncture

Points: The auricular points for lung, tragic apex, occiput and ear-*Shenmen*.

Methods: Select two to three points each time to apply acupuncture, giving a moderate stimulation. Keep the needles in the skin for 20-30 minutes. Needle embedment can also be used.

5) Reference materials

Applying acupuncture treatment to 82 patients (36 females) suffering urticaria (see *A Selection of Clinical Experiences in Acupuncture and Moxibustion*)

Acupoints such as *Fengshi* (GB 31), *Quchi* (LI 11), *Zusanli* (ST 36), *Fengchi* (GB 20), *Yanglingquan* (GB 34) and *Hegu* (LI 4) were used. *Fengchi*, *Quchi* and *Hegu* were used for wheals on the head and trunk; *Fengshi* and *Zusanli* for those on the lower limbs; *Fengshi*, *Quchi* and *Zusanli* for those all over the body. Generally the treatment was given by way of mild reduction or reinforcement unless the the patient suffered severe itching, under which circumstance acupuncture was used by way of reduction. The needle was kept in the skin for 20 minutes. After treatment, 40 of them found they had recovered from the disease, 15 felt much better, and eight felt a little bit better. This result accounted for 76.8% of the total patients. No other method was allowed to be used during acupuncture treatment.

9. Herpes zoster

Herpes zoster is a disease which causes painful red sores to appear on the back, chest and face.

1) Etiology and pathogenesis

Emotional upset with the hyperactivity of fire in the liver and gallbladder, or prolonged stagnation of dampness in the spleen with the accumulation of dampness and heat, or the stagnation of muscles, skin, and the *ying* and *wei* systems due to the attack of exogenous dampness and toxins.

2) Syndrome differentiation

At the onset of the disease, the patient has a slight fever and feels tired. Just before and after rashes appear, he may feel sore as if something is burning around the affected part of the body. As soon as they appear, the rashes (about the size of mung bean or soy bean) turn into vesicles, scattered in the form of belts on one side of the lumbus, hypochondrium and chest. The color of the skin unaffected by vesicles remains normal. Petechiae or bloody vesicles can be seen when the disease progresses. At later stages of the disease, vesicles appear on the face. If fire is hyperactive in the liver and gallbladder, there will be symptoms such as sharp pain, flushed face, bitter taste, dizziness, headache, irritability, yellow and greasy tongue coating, taut and rapid pulse; if dampness-heat is accumulated in the spleen and stomach, symptoms such as blisters with profuse exudation, loss of appetite, epigastric distention, yellow and greasy tongue coating, soft, superficial and rapid pulse.

3) Treatment

Principles: To clear the liver and gallbladder of dampness-heat or eliminate dampness-heat, reduce swelling and alleviate pain.

Methods: Select acupoints along the Large Intestine, Spleen and Liver meridians to apply acupuncture, using the reducing manipulation.

Acupoints: *Quchi* (LI 11), *Hegu* (LI 4), *Xuehai* (SP 10), *Sanyinjiao* (SP 6), *Xingjian* (LR 2), *Qimen* (LR 14) and *Zhigou* (SJ 6).

Notes: *Quchi* and *Hegu* disperse heat accumulated in the Large Intestine and Stomach meridians; *Xuehai* and *Sanyinjiao* strengthen the spleen, eliminate dampness, regulate blood and disperse heat; puncturing at *Xingjian* and *Qimen* with reducing manipulation can help disperse fire and heat in the liver and gallbladder.

4) Reference materials

Applying acupuncture treatment to patients suffering herpes zoster (see *Clinical Experiences in Acupuncture and Moxibustion*)

The first method was as follows: *Ashi* points were selected. When treatment began, the patient was asked to lie on the back or side, with the affected part facing upward. According to the size of the affected area, three to five needles were inserted into the acupoints at an angle of 15 degrees towards the ribs and the depth of insertion was 1.0-1.5 *cun*. When the needles reached the required depth, they were kept in the skin for one to two hours and irradiated with infrared ray for 30-60 minutes. The treatment was given once a day.

The second method used *Ashi* points as main points, those near the vesicles as accessory ones. For example, *Yanglingquan* (GB 34) was used to treat vesicles on the chest, costa and the lateral side of abdomen; *Weizhong* (BL 40) for those on the lumbus and back. After routine sterilization, the skin surrounding the affected area was pricked with a three-edged needle until a little blood comes out. Moxibustion treatment was then given for 15-30 minutes. The needles were twisted quickly after being inserted into the accessory points. The treatment was given once a day until the patient recovered.

The first method was adopted to treat 17 patients who had lesions on the chest, lumbus and back, while the second method used to treat 13 patients with lesions on other parts of the body. All the patients regained their health after three to five treatments.

10. Mumps

Mumps is a contagious disease that causes painful swelling of the parotid gland in the neck and slight fever.

1) Etiology and pathogenesis

The retention of wind-warm pathogenic factors and phlegm-fire in the *Sanjiao* Meridian causes the obstruction of *qi* and blood circulation. As the *Sanjiao* and Liver meridians are related internally and externally to each other and the Liver Meridian goes round the genitals, the testis becomes swollen and painful when pathogenic factors are accumulated in the Liver Meridian.

2) Syndrome differentiation

The painful swelling of the parotid gland is the main symptom of the disease. If cases are mild, only parotitis appears which usually dies away within several days. When cases become serious, the parotid land gets more swollen and painful without any clear margins, which is accompanied by chilliness, fever, headache, vomiting, difficulty in chewing, thin white and yellowish tongue coating, or smooth and rapid pulse.

3) Treatment

Principles: To dispel wind and heat, remove toxins and relieve swelling.

Methods: Select acupoints along the *Sanjiao* Meridian to apply acupuncture, using the reducing manipulation.

Acupoints: *Yifeng* (SJ 17), *Waiguan* (SJ 5), *Jiache* (ST 6), *Hegu* (LI 4) and *Dazhui* (DU 14). *Taichong* (LR 3) can be used together to treat pain in the testis.

Notes: As the disease is caused by the accumulation of pathogenic factors in the *Sanjiao* Meridian, *Yifeng* and *Waiguan* are used to eliminate wind-heat and remove toxins. On the other hand, as the Large Intestine Meridian reaches the face, *Hegu* and *Jiache* are used to disperse heat and remove toxins. *Yifeng* and *Jiache* can also remove the stagnation of local *qi* and blood. *Dazhui*, the crossing point of *yang* meridians, can help to disperse heat and expel pathogenic factors. *Taichong* along the Liver Meridian can relieve swelling of the testis by way of reducing manipulation.

4) Other remedies

Moxibustion with burning Medulla Junci: First, have some of the hair growing round the *Jiaosun*

(SJ 20) point cut, and the skin sterilized. Next, burn a piece of oil-soaked rush (Medulla Junci) and put it on the acupoint before taking it away on hearing a sound of cracking. Repeat this procedure twice. Give the same treatment the next day unless swelling is relieved.

5) Reference materials

Applying acupuncture treatment to eight patients suffering serious mumps (see *Progress on Research in Acupuncture and Moxibustion*)

The method was as follows: *Yifeng* (SJ 17), *Jiache* (ST 6) and *Hegu* (LI 4) were punctured with the reducing manipulation, and the needles were kept in the skin for 20-30 minutes. This treatment was applied once every day. Fever diminished and the swelling of the parotid gland reduced after two or three days. After five to seven days, the temperature returned to normal and swelling disappeared.

11. Alopecia areata

Alopecia areata, known as *youfeng* in traditional Chinese medicine, is a disease which causes partial and sudden loss of hair.

1) Etiology and pathogenesis

a) The malnutrition of the upper part of the body by essence and blood due to deficiency of the liver and kidney opens the hair pores, exposing them to the effects of wind and resulting in loss of hair.

b) Blood stasis and *qi* retardation due to stagnation of *qi* in the liver causes the malnutrition of hair.

2) Syndrome differentiation

The hair suddenly falls out, leaving bald patches which appear different in form, as the loss of hair for each patch is not the same. There is no subjective symptom in most cases. In serious cases, most of or all of the hair, including the eyebrows, beard, armpit and pubic hair may fall out. The loss of hair is usually accompanied by dizziness, insomnia, thin tongue coating or thready and weak pulse if there is deficiency of blood. In cases of stagnation of blood, symptoms such as dark complexion, petechiae at the tip and margin of the tongue, and uneven pulse often appear.

3) Treatment

Principles: To nourish and moisturize blood, dispel wind or to promote blood circulation and remove blood-stasis.

Methods: Select acupoints along the *Du* and Bladder meridians to apply acupuncture, using the reinforcing manipulation in cases with deficiency of blood, and the reducing manipulation if there is blood-stasis. Tap certain areas as well as *Jiaji* (EX-B 2) on the nape and back with a plum-blossom needle. Moxibustion can also be used.

Acupoints: *Ashi* points, *Baihui* (DU 20), *Zusanli* (ST 36), *Sanyinjiao* (SP 6), *Shenshu* (BL 23), *Ganshu* (BL 18), *Geshu* (BL 17).

Notes: Hair nutrition comes from blood via the kidney. Puncturing at *Shenshu* and *Ganshu* may benefit essence and promote the growth of hair. The spleen and stomach are the source of *qi* and blood generation, so that *Sanyinjiao* and *Zusanli* help to invigorate the spleen and stomach and promote the generation of *qi* and blood. *Baihui* can help to disperse wind, benefit *qi* and activate blood circulation, while *Geshu* regulates the flow of blood and removes blood-stasis.

4) Reference materials

Applying acupuncture treatment to 395 patients suffering alopecia (see *A Selection of Clinical Experiences in Acupuncture and Moxibustion*)

The acupoints were *Waiguan* (SJ 5), *Tianjing* (SJ 10) and *Tianliao* (SJ 15) along the *Sanjiao* Meridian; *Feishu* (BL 13), *Pohu* (BL 42) and *Gaohuang* (BL 43) along the Bladder Meridian; *Zhongfu* (LU 1) and *Lieque* (LU 7) along the Lung Meridian. *Ashi* points near the affected area or 2 cm around the bald areas. Acupuncture treatment was given once every day or every other day, and 14-21 times would make up a whole course of treatment. Hair stopped falling out within six months and new hair started to grow in two or three more months in patients who had received two or three courses of treatment.

Of the 395 patients who received treatment, 351 cases achieved excellent results, 23 achieved good results, 14 felt better than before and only seven found the treatment ineffective against the loss of hair.

SECTION 4
DISEASES OF EYES, EARS, NOSE AND THROAT

1. Tinnitus and deafness

Tinnitus is a condition which causes a person to hear noises, while deafness refers to the partial or complete loss of hearing. Both conditions are similar in etiology, pathogenesis and the acupuncture treatment is similar for each condition.

1) Etiology and pathogenesis

a) The impairment of the liver by rage or emotional depression causes the stagnation of *qi* which gives rise to the production of fire in the liver and gallbladder and disturbance of the ear.

b) Eating too much impairs the function of the spleen which in turn causes the accumulation of dampness and phlegm and production of fire; phlegm-fire blocks up the passage of *qi* when it moves up inside the body.

c) Weak constitution or sexual indulgence causes the exhaustion of kidney-essence and malnutrition of the ear.

2) Syndrome differentiation

a) Excess syndrome: Tinnitus and deafness occur suddenly, with noises like ringing, chirping or rumbling. Tinnitus and deafness intensify when the patient flies into rage. The condition is usually accompanied by dizziness, headache, flushed face, thirst, yellow urine, constipation, reddened tongue with yellow coating, taut and rapid pulse if fire in the liver and gallbladder is hyperactive. If phlegm-heat is accumulated, the condition is accompanied by dizziness, heaviness in the head, chest upset, profuse expectoration, reddened tongue with yellow and greasy coating, taut and smooth pulse.

b) Deficiency syndrome: Tinnitus and deafness occur periodically over time, with a low noise ringing in the ear. Symptoms intensify at night or during exertion, and is accompanied by dizziness, insomnia, lumbago, weak knees, nocturnal emission of leukorrhagia, reddened tongue with scanty coating, thready pulse or thready and rapid pulse.

3) Treatment

Principles: To purge the liver fire and expel phlegm to induce resuscitation if there is excess syndrome but to invigorate the kidney and benefit essence if there is deficiency syndrome.

Methods: Select acupoints along the *Sanjiao* and Gallbladder meridians to apply acupuncture, using the reducing manipulation for excess syndrome and the reinforcing manipulation if there is deficiency syndrome.

Acupoints: *Tinghui* (GB 2), *Yifeng* (SJ 17) and *Zhongzhu* (SJ 3). *Taichong* (LR 3) is used together with the above points for hyperactivity of fire in the liver and gallbladder; *Fenglong* (ST 40) is used together for the accumulation of phlegm-heat; *Taixi* (KI 3) and *Shenshu* (BL 23) for kidney deficiency.

Notes: As the *Sanjiao* and Gallbladder meridians go round the ear, *Yifeng* and *Zhongzhu* along the *Sanjiao* Meridian and *Tinghui* along the Gallbladder Meridian are often used to activate the flow of *qi* and dredge the external acoustic meatus. *Taichong* purges the liver and gallbladder fire; *Fenglong* strengthens the spleen and stomach and eliminates phlegm-heat; *Taixi* and *Shenshu* invigorate the kidney essence to nourish the ear.

4) Other remedies

Acupoints injection: *Tinggong* (SI 19), *Tinghui* (GB 2), *Yifeng* (SJ 17), *Wangu* (GB 12) and *Shenshu* (BL 23) are used for injection. 5 mg of 654-2 or 0.2-0.5 ml of Vitamin B_{12} (100 ng) is injected into the above acupoints on either side, 0.5-1.0 *cun* deep.

2. Otopyorrhea

Otopyorrhea is a disease which causes pus to run out of the ear. It can be seen in acute and chronic suppurative otitis media.

1) Etiology and pathogenesis

a) Hyperactive fire in the liver and gallbladder or the effect of exogenous wind-heat on the ear can all lead to the production of pus.

b) Dysfunction of the spleen causes the retention of water in the body and further in the ear.

2) Syndrome differentiation

The main symptom is the outflow of pus from the ear. Syndrome of the excess type often exhibit chilliness, fever, distensive pain in the ear, tinnitus or hypoacusis, thick and yellow pus, bitter taste, dry throat, reddish urine, constipation, reddened tongue with yellow coating, taut and rapid pulse; while syndrome of the deficiency type exhibit scanty and thin pus from the ear, dizziness, tinnitus, hypoacusis, lassitude, poor appetite, sallow complexion, loose stools, pale tongue, retarded and weak pulse.

3) Treatment

Principles: To disperse wind and heat, eliminate toxins and induce resuscitation if there is excess syndrome, and to strengthen the spleen and eliminate dampness if there is deficiency syndrome.

Methods: Select acupoints along the *Sanjiao* and Gallbladder meridians to apply acupuncture, using the reducing manipulation for excess syndrome, and the reinforcing manipulation for deficiency syndrome.

Acupoints: *Tinggong* (SI 19), *Yifeng* (SJ 17) and *Hegu* (LI 4). *Fengchi* (GB 20) and *Waiguan* (SJ 5) can be added to treat excess syndrome; *Zusanli* (ST 36) and *Yinlingquan* (SP 9) can be added to treat deficiency syndrome.

Notes: *Yifeng* and *Waiguan* on the *Sanjiao* Meridian and *Fengchi* on the Gallbladder Meridian dredge the *Sanjiao* and Gallbladder meridians, purge heat and eliminate toxins; *Hegu* on the Large Intestine Meridian expels wind-heat; *Zusanli* and *Yinlingquan* strengthen the spleen and eliminate dampness.

4) Other remedies

Ear acupuncture: Select the auricular points for inner ear, kidney, tragic apex and occiput to apply acupuncture, giving a moderate stimulation. Keep the needles in the skin for 20 minutes. The treatment should be given once a day.

3. *Biyuan*

Biyuan is a disorder which causes turbid and fetid nasal discharge, nasal stuffiness and hyposmia or anosmia. It may be seen in chronic rhinitis and acute and chronic nasosinusitis.

1) Etiology and pathogenesis

a) The attack of wind-heat or wind-cold leads to the dysfunction of lung *qi* and accumulation of heat in the nasal passage.

b) The hyperactive fire in the liver and gallbladder attacks the nasal passage through the related meridians.

2) Syndrome differentiation

The main symptoms of the disease are nasal stuffiness, dysosmia, yellow and fetid nasal discharge. They are accompanied by chilliness, fever, productive cough, thin and white tongue coating, superficial and rapid pulse in cases of wind-heat; In cases with hyperactive heat in the liver and gallbladder, there appear symptoms of dizziness, headache, thirst, bitter taste in the mouth, red tongue with yellow coating, taut and rapid pulse.

3) Treatment

Principles: To disperse heat, facilitate the flow of lung *qi* and ventilate the nose, and to purge the hyperactive fire in the liver and gallbladder.

Methods: Select acupoints along the Lung and Large Intestine meridians to apply acupuncture, using the reducing manipulation.

Acupoints: *Yingxiang* (LI 20), *Yintang* (EX-HN 3), *Hegu* (LI 4) and *Lieque* (LU 7). *Taichong* (LR 3) and *Fengchi* (GB 20) can be added to treat hyperactive fire in the liver and gallbladder.

Notes: As the lung has its specific orifice in the nose, *Lieque* along the Lung Meridian is usually used to disperse heat, facilitate the flow of lung *qi* and ventilate the nose. On the other hand, as the lung and large intestine are interior-exteriorly related, *Yingxiang* and *Hegu* on the Large Intestine Meridian help disperse wind and heat. *Yingxiang* is also effective against nasal stuffiness and dysosmia. *Yintang* at the root of the nose helps ventilate the nose. *Yintang*, *Taichong* and *Fengchi* disperse wind and heat, and purge the hyperactive fire in the liver and gallbladder.

4) Other remedies

Ear acupuncture: Select the auricular points for internal nose, lung and forehead to give acupuncture with a strong stimulation, and keep the needles in the skin for 20-30 minutes. Needle embedment can also be used.

5) Reference materials

According to *Progress on Research in Acupuncture and Moxibustion*, acupuncture treatment is effective in treating chronic nasosinusitis. Points such as *Yingxiang* (LI 20), *Shangxing* (DU 23) and *Hegu* (LI 4), *Baihui* (DU 20), *Taiyang* (EX-HN 5), *Fengchi* (GB 20), *Touwei* (ST 8) and *Yintang* (EX-HN 3) were punctured to treat maspsomisotos. After three treatments, the osphresis resumed normal with a decrease in nasal discharge.

4. Conjunctivitis

This condition often occurs in pseudomenbranous conjunctivitis, acute catarrhal conjunctivitis or epidemic hemorrhagic conjunctivitis.

1) Etiology and pathogenesis

The attack on the eye by exogenous wind-heat or the disturbance of the upper body by fire in the liver and gallbladder can all lead to the obstruction of meridians and stagnation of *qi* and blood.

2) Syndrome differentiation

One eye is red, itchy, photophobic and painful at the onset of the condition. After a short period of time, the other eye becomes affected and secretions become mucopurulent. These symptoms are usually accompanied by chilliness, fever, headache, nasal stuffiness, and superficial pulse if the body is attacked by wind-heat. If fire in the liver is hyperactive, symptoms include bitter taste, thirst, irritability, reddened tongue, taut and rapid pulse.

3) Treatment

Principles: To disperse heat and wind, relieve swelling and alleviate pain.

Methods: Select acupoints along the Large Intestine and Bladder meridians to apply acupuncture, using the reducing manipulation.

Acupoints: *Jingming* (BL 1), *Hegu* (LI 4) and *Taiyang* (EX-HN 5). *Shaoshang* (LU 11) and *Fengchi* (GB 20) can be added to treat the effect of wind-heat; *Xingjian* (LR 2) can be added to treat hyperactive fire in the liver and gallbladder.

Notes: As the Large Intestine, Bladder and Gallbladder meridians encircle the eye region, *Hegu* along the Large Intestine Meridian is used to disperse wind-heat and dredge the meridian. *Jingming* dredges *qi* in the meridians, disperses heat and relieves swelling. Prompt prick at *Taiyang* to let out a little blood can help expel heat, relieve swelling and alleviate pain. *Shaoshang* and *Fengchi* disperse wind-heat; *Xingjian* can be used together to disperse fire in the liver and gallbladder.

4) Other remedies

a) Prompt prick: Sterilize the sensitive spots over the scapular region, or *Dazhui* (DU 14) and *Taiyang* (EX-HN 5) and then prick them with a three-edged needle or a sewing needle.

b) Ear acupuncture: Select the auricular points for the eyes, ear apex and liver to apply acupuncture, giving a strong stimulation. Keep the needles in the skin for 30 minutes. The bloodletting therapy can also be used on the ear apex.

5) Notes

a) Conjunctivitis is a common acute contagious disease in ophthalmology. Patients are required to keep the eye clean and avoid eating acrid and pungent food after contracting the disease.

b) Try to keep acupoints sterilized. Insert and withdraw the needles slowly if the acupoints are located within the orbit. Do not twist, twirl, lift or thrust the needle lest bleeding should occur.

6) Reference materials

Applying acupuncture treatment to 21 patients suffering conjunctivitis (see *A Selection of Clinical Experiences in Acupuncture and Moxibustion*)

Points: *Jingming* (BL 1) and the vessels behind the ear.

Methods: The doctor fixed the eyeball of the patient with the left hand, and then inserted the needle into *Jingming* about 0.2-0.3 *cun* deep. The needle was withdrawn after puncturing softly several times. After that, a visible vessel at the back of the ear was located, sterilized and pricked with a three-edged needle to let out a little blood. Most of the patients recovered their health after two treatments.

5. Hordeolum

Hordeolum refers to acute pyogenic inflammation of hair follicle and cortical gland of the eyelid.

1) Etiology and pathogenesis

The attack on the eyelid by exogenous wind-heat or the accumulation of heat in the spleen and stomach due to overeating leads to the stagnation of *qi* and blood and the retention of heat.

2) Syndrome differentiation

At the onset of the disease the patient feels itchy in the eyelid with a callous and painful wheat-like swelling at the skin round the hair follicle of the affected part. If the condition is mild or treated early, the disease disappears away before pus appears. In more severe cases, pustulation and rupture will occur. The condition is accompanied by chilliness, fever and headache if the body is attacked by wind-heat; by thirst, bitter taste in the mouth, restlessness, constipation and yellow tongue coating if the heat is accumulated in the spleen and stomach.

3) Treatment

Principles: To disperse wind-heat and eliminate toxins.

Methods: Select acupoints along the Large Intestine, Stomach and Bladder meridians to apply acupuncture, using the reducing manipulation.

Acupoints: *Jingming* (BL 1), *Taiyang* (EX-HN 5), *Hegu* (LI 4) and *Chengqi* (ST 1). *Yinlingquan* (SP 9) can be used together to treat the accumulation of heat in the spleen and stomach.

Notes: *Hegu* disperses wind and heat and dredges the meridians. *Chengqi* and *Jingming* in the eye region regulate *qi* in the local meridians, disperse heat and reduce swelling. Applying bloodletting therapy with prompt prick at *Taiyang* can disperse heat, relieve swelling and alleviate pain. *Yinlingquan*, the *he* point on the Spleen Meridian, disperses heat in the spleen and stomach.

4) Other remedies

a) Pricking therapy: Prick with a three-edged needle or a sewing needle to break the subcutaneous tissue under the sensitive points in the scapular region.

b) Ear acupuncture: Select the auricular points for eye, liver, spleen and ear apex to apply acupuncture, giving a strong stimulation. Keep the needles in the skin for 20 minutes once a day. Bloodletting therapy can be applied to the ear apex.

5) Notes

Aseptic hordeolum can be relieved with acupuncture treatment; if suppurative, it should be treated with the help of an ophthalmologist. Applying pressure is not advised due to the local risk of infection.

6) Reference materials

Applying acupuncture treatment to 35 patients suffering hordeolum (see *Progress on Research in Acupuncture and Moxibustion*)

Taiyang (EX-HN 5) point on the affected side was punctured with the reducing manipulation. After a needling sensation was obtained, the needle was kept in the skin for 15 minutes. A little blood was squeezed out after the needle was withdrawn. Of the total patients, 31 recovered after one treatment, two felt better after two treatments and two found the treatment effective with the help of incision and drainage of pus.

6. Myopia

Myopia refers to an abnormal condition of the eye in which, because of a refractive error, only objects close to the eye can be seen clearly.

1) Etiology and pathogenesis

This condition occurs when people read, write or work in poor light, with an awkward posture or for too long a time.

2) Syndrome differentiation

The main symptoms of the disease are blurred vision and loss of sight. They are usually accompanied by headache, asthenopia or other symptoms.

3) Treatment

Principles: To invigorate the liver and kidney and improve visual acuity.

Methods: Select acupoints around the eyes to apply acupuncture with mild reinforcement and reduction.

Acupoints: *Jingming* (BL 1), *Chengqi* (ST 1), *Cuanzhu* (BL 2) *Guangming* (GB 37), *Fengchi* (GB 20), *Shenshu* (BL 23) and *Zusanli* (ST 36).

Notes: *Jingming*, *Chengqi* and *Guangming* help to disperse *qi* in the local meridians. *Guangming* and *Fengchi* along the Gallbladder Meridian which starts from the eye region can dredge the meridians and improve visual acuity. Puncturing at *Shenshu* with the reinforcing manipulation can help invigorate the kidney essence and at *Zusanli* can invigorate the spleen and stomach. As the *zang* and *fu* organs are rich in *qi* and blood, the eye is nourished and visual acuity improved.

4) Other remedies

a) Plum-blossom needle therapy: The eye region as well as the nape and back along both sides of the spinal column are pricked once every day.

b) Ear acupuncture: Select the auricular points for the eye, liver and kidney to apply acupuncture, giving a strong stimulation. Keep the needles in the skin for 20-30 minutes once a day or every other day. Ten applications are required for a treatment.

5) Notes

To achieve better results, the patient is required to do eye exercises during treatment.

6) Reference materials

Applying plum-blossom needle therapy to treat 711 young people suffering myopia (see *Progress on Research in Acupuncture and Moxibustion*)

Points in the eye region and nape as well as *Fengchi* (GB 20), *Dazhui* (DU 14) and *Neiguan* (PC 6) were tapped with a plum-blossom needle, 20 to 30 taps each time. The treatment was given once a day with moderate stimulation. Fifteen days were sufficient for a whole course of treatment. Of the 1383 eyes in 711 cases, 821 eyes were treated by tapping the eye region and nape. As a result, in 93 cases eyesight was restored to normal, and in 656 cases patients reported an improvement in the condition. The treatment was not effective in 72 cases.

7. Toothache

This condition often occurs with dental caries, pulpitis, peridental abscess or pericoronitis.

1) Etiology and pathogenesis

a) Exogenous wind attacks the meridians and stagnates in the Large Intestine and Stomach meridians. Or exuberant stomach-fire attacks the upper part of the body along the meridians.

b) The kidney controls the bone, and the teeth are the surplus of the bone. If kidney *yin* is deficient, deficiency-fire disturbs the upper part of the body.

2) Syndrome differentiation

Cases with wind-fire exhibit toothache, gingival swelling, chilliness, fever, thin tongue coating, superficial and rapid pulse; cases with stomach-fire exhibit thirst, bitter taste, foul breath, constipation, yellow tongue coating, taut and rapid pulse; cases with asthenic fire show loose teeth, lumbago, sore knees, red tongue without coating, thready and rapid pulse.

3) Treatment

Principles: To disperse heat and alleviate pain.

Methods: Select acupoints on the Large Intestine and Stomach meridians to apply acupuncture, using the reducing manipulation.

Acupoints: *Xiaguan* (ST 7), *Jiache* (ST 6) and *Hegu* (LI 4). *Waiguan* (SJ 5) and *Fengchi* (GB 20) can be added for cases with wind-fire; *Neiting* (ST 44) for stomach-fire; *Taixi* (KI 3) and *Xingjian* (LR 2) for asthenic fire.

Notes: Since the Stomach and Large Intestine meridians reach the upper and lower gums, *Xiaguan*, *Jiache* and *Hegu* on these meridians help to disperse heat, promote the flow of *qi* in the meridians and relieve pain. *Waiguan* and *Fengchi* disperse wind and heat; *Neiting* purges stomach-fire. Puncturing at *Xingjian* (the *ying* point of the Liver Meridian) with the reducing manipulation helps purge fire. Puncturing at *Taixi* with the reinforcing manipulation promotes the production of fluid and nourishes *yin*.

4) Other remedies

Ear acupuncture: Select two or three auricular points for the upper and lower jaws, ear-*Shenmen* and tragic apex to apply acupuncture, giving a strong stimulation. Keep the needles in the skin for 20-30 minutes. Needle embedment can also be used.

5) Reference materials

Applying acupuncture treatment to 11 patients feeling acute pain due to the inflammation of the dental pulp (see *A Selection of Clinical Experiences in Acupuncture and Moxibustion*)

Acupuncture treatment was especially effective when local anesthesia could not help relieve the pain. When pain was relieved, other methods were adopted for treatment. Two to three points among *Xiaguan* (ST 7) and *Jiache* (ST 6) on the affected side and *Hegu* (LI 4), *Dicang* (ST 4) and *Daying* (ST 5) on both sides were chosen. *Neiting* (ST 44) was added when necessary. Toothache was relieved when the patient felt a sensation of soreness, numbness and distention. The needles were kept in the skin for 10-15 minutes. Six patients found the pain relieved; three patients felt much better; and two patients felt a little better.

8. Sore throat

Sore throat usually occurs with acute and chronic tonsillitis, acute pharyngitis, simple laryngitis or peritonsillar abscess.

1) Etiology and pathogenesis

a) Exogenous pathogenic wind-heat attacks the throat and lung, or overeating causes the attack on the throat.

b) *Yin* fluid fails to moisten the throat due to the deficiency of kidney *yin* and deficiency-fire disturbs the upper part of the body.

2) Syndrome differentiation

The main symptoms of the disease are redness, swelling and pain in the throat. If there is wind-heat, the main symptoms are chilliness, fever, productive cough, dysphagia, thin tongue coating, superficial and rapid pulse; if there is heat in the lung and stomach, the main symptoms are high fever, thirst, cough with thick and yellow sputum, foul breath, constipation, red tongue with thick and yellow coating, bounding and rapid pulse; if there is deficiency-fire, the main symptoms are mild pain, thirst, dry tongue, dry cough, feverish sensation in the palms and soles, red and uncoated tongue, thready and rapid pulse.

3) Treatment

a) Excess-heat syndrome

Principles: To disperse wind and heat or purge fire and ease the throat.

Methods: Select acupoints along the Lung and Large Intestine meridians to apply acupuncture, using the reducing manipulation.

Acupoints: *Shaoshang* (LU 11), *Chize* (LU 5), *Hegu* (LI 4) and *Quchi* (LI 11). *Neiting* (ST 44) can be added to treat stomach-fire.

Notes: *Shaoshang*, the *jiing* point along the Lung Meridian, can be pricked to induce a little blood so as to purge lung-heat. *Chize*, the *he* point of the Lung Meridian, can help disperse lung-heat and ease the throat if punctured with the reducing manipulation. *Hegu*, *Quchi* and *Neiting* are used to eliminate heat in the Stomach Meridian.

b) Deficiency-heat syndrome

Principles: To nourish *yin* and suppress fire.

Methods: Select acupoints along the Lung and Spleen meridians to apply acupuncture, using the reducing manipulation.

Acupoints: *Yuji* (LU 10), *Taixi* (KI 3) and *Zhaohai* (KI 6).

Notes: *Taixi* (the *yuan* point along the Kidney Meridian) and *Zhaohai* (one of the eight confluent points connecting with the *Yinqiao* Meridian and effective against disorders of the throat) can be used to nourish kidney-water and conduct the deficiency-fire downward. *Yuji*, the *ying* point along the Lung Meridian can be used to disperse lung-heat and ease the throat if punctured with the reducing manipulation.

4) Other remedies

Ear acupuncture: Select the auricular points for throat, tonsil, helix 1-6 to apply acupuncture, giving a moderate stimulation for two to three minutes. Keep the needles in the skin for 60 minutes once a day.

5) Reference materials

Applying acupuncture treatment to 24 children suffering acute tonsillitis (see *A Selection of Clinical Experiences in Acupuncture and Moxibustion*)

The auricle of the affected side was rubbed slightly to induce local congestion. After routine sterilization, a one-*cun*-long needle was inserted into the venule visible on the posterior aspect of the auricle to induce three to five drops of blood. The needle hole was then pressed with an alcoholic cotton ball. The treatment, which was given once a day, proved extremely effective for 21 of the 24 patients and less effective for the other three. Of the 21 patients, 11 regained their health after one course of treatment, seven after two courses and three after three courses.

Section 5
EMERGENCY TREATMENT

1. High fever

High fever refers to a condition in which the body temperature is higher than 39°C. This part of the book refers to fever caused by exogenous wind, heat, dampness, summer-heat and pestilence.

1) Etiology and pathogenesis

a) The attack of exogenous pathogenic wind: Exogenous pathogenic wind-cold or wind-heat attacks the body through the mouth, nose or skin and causes the impediment of the functional activities of the lung. As a result, it is impossible for heat to be dispersed from the skin.

b) The retention of pathogenic warm-heat in the interior: Exogenous pathogenic warm-heat attacks *qi*, *ying* and *xue* systems, which gives rise to the retention of heat in the interior.

c) The attack on the heart by summer-heat: Summer-heat, a pathogenic factor of *yang*, is liable to consume body fluid and then cause high fever.

d) The attack of pestilential agent: Pestilential agent, a potent infectious pathogenic factor, attacks the *zang-fu* organs, muscles and skin and causes many diseases.

2) Syndrome differentiation

a) The attack of exogenous pathogenic wind: Cough, running nose, nasal stuffiness and sneezing may occur. If there is wind-cold, symptoms are accompanied by anhidrosis, headache, general aching, thin and white tongue coating, superficial and tense pulse; if there is wind-heat, symptoms are accompanied by fever, mild chilliness, sore throat, thin and yellow tongue coating, superficial and rapid pulse.

b) Lung-heat syndrome: Fever, dyspneic cough, thick and yellow expectoration, thirst, dry throat, reddened tongue with yellow coating, smooth and rapid pulse.

c) The retention of pathogenic warm-heat in the interior: If the *qi* system is attacked by pathogenic warm-heat, there will be high fever, flushed face, thirst and preference for cold drink, constipation, abdominal distention, pain and tenderness, reddened tongue with dry and yellow coating, bounding and rapid pulse; if the *ying* and *xue* systems are attacked by heat, there will be high fever at night, irritability, coma, delirium, skin rashes or epistaxis, dry mouth with no desire to drink, dry and crimson tongue, thready and rapid pulse.

d) The attack on the heart by summer-heat: High fever, restlessness, thirst, poor sleep or sleepiness, delirium or even coma and convulsion, crimson tongue, rapid and large or taut and thready pulse.

e) The attack of pestilential agent: High fever, swelling, redness and pain in the head and face, painful swelling or even erosion of throat, and skin rashes.

3) Treatment

Principles: To disperse heat and eliminate pathogenic factors.

Methods: Select acupoints along the Large Intestine Meridian and the *jiing* points to apply acupuncture, using the reducing manipulation or prompt prick to let out a little blood.

Acupoints: *Dazhui* (DU 14), *Quchi* (LI 11), *Hegu* (LI 4), *Shaoshang* (LU 11), *Shangyang* (LI 1) and *Guanchong* (SJ 1). Prompt prick at the twelve *jiing* points to let out a little blood can help treat wind-heat syndrome. *Fengmen* (BL 12) can be added to treat lung-heat syndrome; *Neiting* (ST 44) for stomach-heat syndrome; *Shaochong* (HT 9), *Zhongchong* (PC 9), *Daling* (PC 7) and *Sanyinjiao* (SP 6) for the attack on the *ying* and *xue* systems by heat.

Notes: The main purpose of the above acupoints is to disperse wind and heat and calm the heart. *Dazhui* (on the *Du* Meridian), the crossing point of *yang* meridians, is used to disperse heat from the exterior and *qi* system. *Quchi* and *Hegu* along the Large Intestine Meridian are used to relieve exterior syndrome and reduce fever. Applying prompt prick to let out a little blood at *Shaoshang* helps eliminate lung-heat, at *Shangyang* helps disperse heat from the Large Intestine and Stomach meridians. *Guanchong* disperses heat from the *Sanjiao* Meridian.

4) Other remedies

Ear acupuncture: Select the auricular points for ear-*Shenmen*, infratragic apex (adrenal) and ear apex to apply acupuncture, giving a strong stimulation. Keep the needles in the skin for 15-20 minutes.

5) Reference materials

Applying acupuncture treatment to 188 patients who had a high fever at the onset of influenza (see *A Selection of Clinical Experiences in Acupuncture and Moxibustion*)

Dazhui (DU 14) was punctured with twisting manipulation for five to ten minutes till the patient felt cool in the lumbosacral region. Fever began to subside an hour later and the body temperature resumed normal six to eight hours later. All patients recovered within six to 20 hours.

2. Syncope

Syncope refers to a temporary loss of consciousness caused by cerebral ischemia and anoxia, orthostatic hypotension or hypoglycemia as a result of weak physique, hunger, fatigue or postpartum hemorrhage.

1) Etiology and pathogenesis

a) Deficiency of *qi* and blood: The consumption of *qi* and blood due to protracted illness, blood loss or the fact that *qi* and blood cannot be produced because of the dysfunctioning of the spleen and stomach causes the deficiency of *qi* and blood. Also, deficiency of *qi* disturbs lucid *yang* and makes the limbs quite cold. On the other hand, the weakening of defensive *yang* causes profuse sweating. These factors affect the supply of enough blood to the brain and result in the loss of consciousness.

b) Insufficiency of kidney-essence: The kidney is the origin of congenital constitution. It stores essence and produces marrow. Congenital defect, kidney-*yin* insufficiency, senility or strain may cause the deficiency of kidney-essence. Brain is the sea of marrow, and insufficiency of kidney-essence may make the sea of marrow empty. Thus, *yin* and *yang* fail to connect with each other and syncope occurs.

2) Syndrome differentiation

Sudden loss of consciousness, cold limbs, spontaneous sweating, pale complexion and indistinct and feeble pulse.

3) Treatment

Principles: To restore consciousness.

Methods: Select acupoints along the *Ren* and *Du* meridians to apply acupuncture, using the reinforcing manipulation. Moxibustion is recommended.

Acupoints: *Shuigou* (DU 26) and *Baihui* (DU 20). *Zusanli* (ST 36) and *Neiguan* (PC 6) can be used if necessary.

Notes: Applying moxibustion treatment to *Baihui* can elevate *yang* and promote resuscitation. Acupuncture treatment at *Shuigou* helps restore consciousness, and at *Neiguan* and *Zusanli* helps regulate *qi* in the middle *jiao*.

4) Notes

a) The main symptoms of the disease are temporary loss of consciousness, pale complexion and cold sweat. These factors can be used to tell syncope from shock, coma or apoplexy.

b) A good care of the patient can help him regain his health. The method is to have the patient lie down flat with the head lower than the body and feed him hot or sugar water. The patient must be kept warm.

c) Moxibustion treatment is more effective for patients with weak physique.

3. Coma

Coma is a state of unconsciousness caused by epidemic febrile diseases, apoplexy, *jue*-syndrome, epilepsy, phlegm-syndrome, fulminant dysentery, malignant malaria, diabetes or anuria.

1) Etiology and pathogenesis

a) Retention of pathogenic heat: Seasonal pathogenic factors turn into heat which then spreads into the body. The heat accumulates in the gastrointestines, lung or the *ying* and *xue* systems to disturb the pericardium and the mind. Summer-heat attacks the body and retains inside. The unhealthy *qi* thus produced blocks the upper orifices and coma occurs.

b) The hyperactivity of liver-*yang*: The deficiency of liver-*yin* and kidney-*yin* and preponderance of liver-*yang*, coupled with the disorder of the five emotions, result in the production of fire. This hyperactive fire disturbs the upper orifices and causes coma.

c) The attack on the heart by phlegm: Improper eating damages the spleen and stomach. The dysfunction of spleen leads to dampness which turns into phlegm. The phlegm and dampness turn into heat, blocking the upper orifices and resulting in coma.

d) Deficiency of *yin* and hyperactivity of *yang*: Prolonged illness due to hyperactivity of pathogenic factors consumes primordial *qi* and disturbs the mind, or prolonged retention of pathogenic heat causes the exhaustion of *yin* and *yang*, resulting in coma.

2) Syndrome differentiation

Coma is divided into *bi*-syndrome and prostration syndrome. *Bi*-syndrome belongs to the excess type, while the prostration syndrome belongs to the deficiency type.

a) *Bi*-syndrome: Coma is accompanied by lockjaw, clenched fists, flushed face, noisy breathing or rattling in the throat. If coma is caused by heat, fever, flushed face, irritability, constipation, abdominal distention or even convulsion will occur; if it is caused by phlegm, profuse expectoration, rattling in the throat, dark face, yellow or white and greasy tongue coating, smooth and rapid or deep and retarded pulse will occur.

b) Prostration syndrome: Coma is accompanied by cold limbs, perspiration, closed eyes, unclenched fist or incontinence of urine.

3) Treatment

a) *Bi*-syndrome

Principles: To restore consciousness.

Methods: Select acupoints along the *Du* and Large Intestine meridians to apply acupuncture, using the reducing manipulation.

Acupoints: *Shuigou* (DU 26), *Shixuan* (EX-UE 11), *Hegu* (LI 4) and *Taichong* (LR 3). *Dazhui* (DU 14) can be added for excessive heat, *Quze* (PC 3) for the invasion of the pericardium by heat,

Yongquan (KI 1) for hyperactive liver-*yang*, *Fenglong* (ST 40) and *Neiguan* (PC 6) for the attack on the heart by phlegm.

Notes: *Shuigou* is used to restore consciousness. Applying prompt prick to *Shixuan* to let out a little blood helps purge heat. *Hegu* disperses heat; *Taichong* calms liver-wind and relieves convulsion; *Dazhui* disperses heat from the *yang* meridians. Prompt prick at *Quze* to let out a little blood helps eliminate heat in the pericardium. *Yongquan* nourishes the liver and kidney; *Fenglong* eliminates phlegm; *Neiguan* regulates *qi* and the middle *jiao* and promotes resuscitation.

b) Prostration syndrome

Principles: To recuperate *yang* and relieve collapse.

Methods: Select acupoints along the *Ren* Meridian to apply moxibustion treatment.

Acupoints: *Baihui* (DU 20), *Qihai* (RN 6), *Guanyuan* (RN 4) and *Zusanli* (ST 36).

Notes: Applying moxibustion treatment to *Baihui* along the *Du* Meridian at the vertex can recuperate depleted *yang*, relieve collapse and promote resuscitation. *Guanyuan*, the crossing point of the *Ren* Meridian and three *yin* meridians of foot, is the root of primordial *qi*. *Qihai*, an important point for replenishment, is the sea of primordial *qi*. Applying moxibustion to *Guanyuan* and *Qihai* invigorate primordial *qi*, recuperate depleted *yang* and relieve collapse. *Zusanli* can help benefit *qi*, recuperate depleted *yang* and relieve collapse.

4) Other remedies

Ear acupuncture: Each time choose two or three points from ear-*Shenmen*, end of inferior antihelix crus and auricular points for the heart and brain to apply acupuncture, giving a strong stimulation. Keep the needles in the skin for 30 minutes. Rotate the needle every five minutes during needle retention period.

5) Notes

a) Coma is a common symptom for a number of conditions that have developed into a serious stage. To treat coma, the root cause must be found and a comprehensive treatment be given to the patient.

b) *A Handbook of Prescriptions for Emergencies* says *Shuigou* (DU 26) can be pressed to treat unconsciousness. According to *Miraculous Classic*, *Zhongzhu* (SJ 3), *Zusanli* (ST 36) and *Dadun* (LR 1) can be used to treat unconsciousness. *Epitome of Acupuncture and Moxibustion* states that *Shuigou* (DU 26), *Zulinqi* (GB 41) and *Hegu* (LI 4) are indicated for unconsciousness.

6) Reference materials

a) Applying acupuncture treatment to a boy of eight named Zhang who suddenly lost consciousness after breakfast (see *Clinical Experiences in Acupuncture and Moxibustion*)

The above symptom was accompanied by delirium, rigid neck, opisthotonos, lockjaw and convulsion. A physical exam showed petechiae on the chest and back, cyanotic lips, crimson tongue, taut and thready pulse. In addition, the body temperature was 40°C and Brudzineki's sign positive. To treat the disease, *Yintang* (EX-HN 3), *Weizhong* (BL 40), *Chize* (LU 5), the twelve *jing* points and the tips of ten toes were pricked to let out a little blood. *Baihui* (DU 20), *Shuigou* (DU 26), *Dazhui* (DU 14), *Neiguan* (PC 6), *Houxi* (SI 3) and *Yongquan* (KI 1) were punctured for two hours. The patient recovered consciousness, and other symptoms were relieved. The body temperature dropped to 39.1°C and the boy fell asleep for seven hours. After the boy woke up, his mind resumed normal and convulsion disappeared. Then *Quchi* (LI 11), *Dazhui* (DU 14), *Hegu* (LI 4) and *Neiguan* (PC 6) were punctured and the patient recovered completely.

b) Applying acupuncture treatment to a 27-year-old woman named He who suffered coma (see *Chen Yinglong's Medical Records of Acupuncture and Moxibustion*)

The coma was accompanied by a high fever and convulsion for a few days. Her disease had been diagnosed as encephalitis but the treatment had not been effective. In addition to a temperature of 39-40°C, coma and convulsion, she had also developed rigid neck, irritability, delirium, reddened tongue with yellow coating, taut and rapid pulse. After differentiation, she was diagnosed as suffering from summer-heat syndrome complicated by endogenous wind. Acupuncture treatment was given to the patient according to the principles of dispersing summer-heat, promoting resuscitation and relieving convulsion. *Shuigou* (DU 26), *Quchi* (LI 11) and *Hegu* (LI 4) were punctured with the reducing manipulation, and *Shaoshang* (LU 11) was pricked to let out a little blood. Afterward, her temperature dropped to 38°C. Then *Baihui* (DU 20), *Lieque* (LU 7) and *Zusanli* (ST 36) were punctured with the reducing manipulation according to *Ziwuliuzhu* (see Annex 2), and the temperature dropped to 37.5°C. After that, *Zhongwan* (RN 12) and *Taiyuan* (LU 9) were punctured, and prompt prick was applied to *Shixuan* (EX-UE 11) to let out a little blood. Her temperature returned to normal after the treatment. After five courses of treatment, the patient recovered consciousness completely and other symptoms disappeared.

4. Convulsion

Convulsion is a disorder which causes voluntary muscles to contract involuntarily and violently. Its symptoms include rigid neck and back, cramp in the limbs or even opisthotonos.

1) Etiology and pathogenesis

a) The accumulation of pathogenic factors in the meridians: Pathogenic wind, cold and dampness accumulate in the meridians, impede the flow of *qi* and blood circulation, attack the muscles and tendons and cause spasm.

b) Excessive heat: High fever consumes body fluid, and the lack of body fluid causes the undernourishment of tendons and muscles. Also, pathogenic heat attacks the *ying* and *xue* systems and disturbs the endogenous wind.

c) Deficiency of *qi* and blood: Blood loss or profuse sweating causes *qi* and blood deficiency, resulting in the undernourishment of the tendons and muscles.

d) Obstruction due to blood-stasis: Protracted illness enters the collaterals and produces blood-stasis. As a result, blood can not flow smoothly, leaving the tendons and muscles ill-nourished and causing convulsion.

2) Syndrome differentiation

There are two causes of convulsion. One is the attack on the *ying* and *xue* systems by pathogenic factors and the other the consumption of *yin* by excessive heat.

a) Pathogenic factors attacking the *ying* and *xue* systems: Dizziness, distensive headache, high fever, unconsciousness, lockjaw, convulsion, opisthotonos, crimson tongue with dry and yellow coating, taut and rapid pulse.

b) Excessive heat consuming *yin*: Persistent high fever, lockjaw, rigid neck and back, spasm of the hands and feet or even opisthotonos, thirst with a desire to drink, dry and reddened tongue with scanty coating, taut and thready pulse.

3) Treatment

Principles: To disperse heat, nourish *yin*, calm the liver and suppress wind.

Methods: Select acupoints along the *Du* and Liver meridians to apply acupuncture, using the reducing manipulation.

Acupoints: *Baihui* (DU 20), *Fengchi* (GB 20), *Fengfu* (DU 16), *Taichong* (LR 3) and *Hegu* (LI 4). *Zusanli* (ST 36) and *Yanglingquan* (GB 34) can be added to treat the accumulation of pathogenic factors in the meridians; *Dazhui* (DU 14) and *Shixuan* (EX-UE 11) for excessive heat; *Quze* (PC 3) and *Weizhong* (BL 40) for the attack on the *ying* and *xue* systems by heat; *Ququan* (LR 8) and *Sanyinjiao* (SP 6) for the consumption of *yin* by heat.

Notes: The above points are mainly used to disperse heat, nourish *yin*, calm the liver and suppress wind. *Baihui*, *Fengfu* and *Fengchi* suppress endogenous and exogenous wind; *Taichong* and *Hegu* suppress liver-wind; *Zusanli* strengthens the spleen and eliminates dampness; *Yanglingquan* relaxes the tendons and relieves spasm; *Dazhui* disperses heat; *Shixuan* purges heat and relieves spasm. Prompt prick at *Quze* (the *he* point of the Pericardium Meridian) and *Weizhong* (BL 40, the *he* point of the Gallbladder Meridian) to let out a little blood can help disperse heat from the *ying* and *xue* systems. *Ququan* and *Sanyinjiao* help benefit *yin* and relieve spasm.

4) Other remedies

Ear acupuncture: Select the auricular points such as ear-*Shenmen*, end of inferior antihelix crus, the liver, brain and brain stem to apply acupuncture, giving a strong stimulation. Keep the needles in the skin for 30-70 minutes.

5) Notes

Convulsion with high fever caused by epidemic meningitis, encephalitis B, toxic meningitis or other diseases can be treated with the above method.

6) Reference materials

a) Applying acupuncture treatment to 45 patients suffering toxic dysentery with convulsion (see *A Selection of Clinical Experiences in Acupuncture and Moxibustion*)

Hegu (LI 4), *Neiguan* (PC 6), *Yongquan* (KI 1), *Xiajuxu* (ST 39), *Baihui* (DU 20), *Yintang* (EX-HN 3), *Shuigou* (DU 26) and *Suliao* (DU 25) were punctured with the twisting manipulation for 2-3 minutes. The needles were kept in the skin for 20-50 minutes. Generally, convulsion was relieved two to five minutes after the treatment and no recurrence was found after two or three courses of acupuncture treatment. *Fengfu* (DU 16) was added when treating a patient to whom the above points showed no effect and his convulsion was relieved. Acupuncture treatment proved effective against fever, convulsion, respiratory and circulatory failure.

b) Prescriptions of acupoints for convulsion: *Verses for Acupuncture Manipulations*: *Fengfu* (DU 16) and *Baihui* (DU 20) for wind-syndrome. *Epitome of Acupuncture and Moxibustion*: *Yamen* (DU 15) and *Fengfu* for opisthotonos; *Yamen*, *Yanggu* (SI 5), *Wangu* (SI 4), *Daimai* (GB 26) and *Laogong* (PC 8) for clonic convulsion. *Verses of Acupoints for Miscellaneous Diseases*: *Shaoshang* (LU 11), *Shuigou* (DU 26) and *Yongquan* (KI 1) for infantile convulsion.

5. The hemorrhagic disease

The hemorrhagic disease refers to a disorder which causes blood to flow out of the mouth, nose, private parts or any other body orifice. What will be dealt with in this part of the book include epistaxis, hemoptysis, hematemesis, hematochezia and hematuria.

1) Etiology and pathogenesis

a) Exogenous wind, heat and dryness can impair the lung and cause hemoptysis or epistaxis.

b) Overeating pungent, dry or greasy food leads to the accumulation of dryness and heat in the stomach and intestines and impairs blood vessels. As a result, hematemesis, epistaxis or hematochezia occurs.

c) *Qi* stagnation causes fire, and fire in turn leads to hemoptysis and epistaxis. Anger damages the liver and stomach and causes hematemesis. Anxiety consumes heart-*yin* and the heat thus produced enters the small intestine and leads to hematuria.

d) If spleen *qi* is impaired, the spleen cannot control blood. As a result, hematemesis, epistaxis or hematochezia occurs.

e) Deficiency of *yin*, the consumption of *yin* by febrile diseases and sexual indulgence lead to the consumption of kidney *yin* and hyperactivity of ministerial fire. As a result, bleeding occurs.

2) Syndrome differentiation

a) Excess-heat syndrome: If the syndrome is caused by lung-heat, symptoms include thirst, dry throat, fever, itching in the throat, cough with bloody sputum, dry nose with epistaxis, reddened tongue, taut and rapid pulse; if it is caused by liver-heat, symptoms include pain in the chest and hypochondrium, irritability, dizziness, blurred vision, hemoptysis, epistaxis, hematemesis, reddened tongue, superficial and rapid pulse; if it is caused by stomach-fire, symptoms include thirst with a desire to drink, distention and oppression in the chest and abdomen, foul breath, constipation, epistaxis, hematemesis, reddened tongue with yellow coating, and rapid pulse; if it is caused by heart-heat, symptoms include vexation, thirst, flushed face, aphthae, insomnia, a burning sensation in the urethra during urination, hematuria, reddened tip of the tongue and rapid pulse.

b) *Yin*-deficiency syndrome: If it is caused by deficiency of lung *yin*, symptoms include hectic fever, night sweating, flushed face, thirst, dry throat, cough with scanty and bloody sputum, reddened tongue, thready and rapid pulse; if it is caused by deficiency of kidney *yin*, symptoms include sore and weak loins and legs, flushed face, hectic fever, dizziness, tinnitus, oliguria with dark and bloody urine, reddened tongue, thready and rapid pulse.

c) *Qi*-deficiency syndrome: Pale complexion, lassitude, dizziness, epistaxis, hematochezia or hematuria, pale tongue, deep and thready pulse.

3) Treatment

a) Excess-heat syndrome

Principles: To disperse heat and purge fire.

Methods: Select acupoints along the Large Intestine and three *yin* meridians of foot, using the reducing manipulation.

Acupoints: *Quchi* (LI 11) and *Sanyinjiao* (SP 6). *Kongzui* (LU 6) and *Chize* (LU 5) can be added to treat lung-heat; *Neiting* (ST 44) and *Liangqiu* (ST 34) for stomach-heat; *Shaofu* (HT 8) for heart-fire; *Xingjian* (LR 2) for liver-fire.

Notes: Since bleeding is usually caused by pathogenic heat, the heat should be dispersed at once. *Quchi* can help disperse heat and stop bleeding; *Sanyinjiao*, the crossing point of three *yin* meridians of foot, helps keep blood in the vessels. *Chize* and *Kongzui*, the *he* and *xi* points along the Lung Meridian, help purge lung-heat and stop bleeding if there is lung-heat. *Neiting* and *Liangqiu*, the *ying* and *xi* points along the Stomach Meridian, help purge stomach-heat and stop bleeding. *Shaofu*, the *ying* point along the Heart Meridian, helps to purge heart-fire if there is heart-heat. *Xingjian*, the *ying* point along the Liver Meridian, helps purge liver-fire if there is liver-heat.

b) *Yin*-deficiency syndrome

Principles: To disperse heat and nourish *yin*.

Methods: Select acupoints along the Lung and Kidney meridians, using mild reinforcing and reducing manipulation.

Acupoints: *Taiyuan* (LU 9), *Zhaohai* (KI 6) and *Sanyinjiao* (SP 6). *Yuji* (LU 10), *Kongzui* (LU 6) and *Gaohuang* (BL 43) can be added to treat lung-*yin* deficiency; *Yongquan* (KI 1) and *Rangu* (KI 2) for kidney-*yin* deficiency.

Notes: *Zhaohai* along the Kidney Meridian which enters the lung helps balance *yin* and *yang* and disperse asthenic heat. *Sanyinjiao* regulates *yin-qi*, benefits *yin* and stops bleeding. *Yuji* can be punctured to disperse heat if there is lung-*yin* deficiency; *Yongquan* brings heat downward if there is kidney-*yin* deficiency; *Rangu* helps disperse the asthenic heat from the Kidney Meridian.

c) *Qi*-deficiency syndrome

Principles: To benefit *qi* and control blood flow.

Methods: Select acupoints along the Stomach and Spleen meridians, using the reinforcing manipulation. Moxibustion can also be used.

Acupoints: *Zusanli* (ST 36) and *Taibai* (SP 3). *Hegu* (LI 4) and *Shangxing* (DU 23) can be added to treat epistaxis and gingival bleeding; *Pishu* (BL 20) and *Weishu* (BL 21) for hematohidrosis; *Guanyuan* (RN 4) and *Shenshu* (BL 23) for hematuria.

Notes: The spleen and stomach are the foundation of life and source of growth and development. *Zusanli* (along the Stomach Meridian) and *Taibai* (the *yuan* point along the Spleen Meridian) invigorate the spleen and stomach so as to benefit *qi* and control the flow of blood if there is spleen-*qi* deficiency. *Hegu* helps treat epistaxis and gingival bleeding for the Large Intestine Meridian enters the lower gum and ends in the nose. *Shangxing* along the *Du* Meridian is an effective point for epistaxis. *Pishu* can be used for hematohidrosis for it helps strengthen the spleen and benefit *qi*. *Guanyuan* and *Shenshu* can be used to treat hematuria for they help invigorate the kidney.

4) Other remedies

Ear acupuncture: Select auricular points such as ear-*Shenmen*, end of inferior antihelix crus, infratragic apex and heart to apply acupuncture, giving a moderate stimulation. Keep the needles in the skin for over 60 minutes. This therapy can be used as auxiliary treatment for the hemorrhagic disease.

5) Reference materials

a) According to *Acupuncture and Moxibustion Classic for Saving Life*, *Guanyuan* (RN 4) can be used to treat hematuria. Burning three cones (moxibustion treatment) at *Dadun* (LR 1) can treat hematuria. *Xialiao* (BL 34) is indicated for hematochezia, *Laogong* (PC 8) for hematochezia and hematuria, *Shangwan* (RN 13), *Burong* (ST 19) and *Daling* (PC 7) for hematemesis. *Epitome of Acupuncture and Moxibustion* says that *Hegu* (LI 4), *Shangxing* (DU 23) and *Fengfu* (DU 16) are indicated for lingering epistaxis, and *Feishu* (BL 13), *Zhongwan* (RN 12) and *Zusanli* (ST 36) for cough with bloody sputum.

b) Applying acupuncture treatment to 17 patients suffering pulmonary tuberculosis with hemoptysis (see a *A Selection of Clinical Experiences in Acupuncture and Moxibustion*)

Eight patients received acupuncture treatment at *Chize* (LU 5) on both sides, five patients on one side, and four patients on one side together with *Jugu* (LI 16). The needles were kept in the skin for 30-40 minutes after a needling sensation was obtained. The treatment was effective for 16 patients but ineffective for one.

c) Applying moxibustion treatment to a 52-year-old man named Zhu suffering hemafecia (see *A Selection of Clinical Experiences in Acupuncture and Moxibustion*)

The patient reported that he found blood spurting out from the anus every time he relieved the bowels. This condition had lasted over one month and the rectum prolapse during defecation could resume the normal position on pressure. There was neither constipation, local pain nor piles. The patient looked listless and anemic. Vitamin C, K, and Herba Agrimoniae had been taken but in vain. After burning seven moxa cones at *Mingmen* (DU 4), the the prolapse of rectum improved but blood still came out. Then moxibustion was applied to *Baihui* (DU 20) during which seven cones were burned. After four treatment, there was no more bleeding.

6. Shock

Shock refers to an acute circulatory insufficiency caused by the derangement of nervous, endocrine, metabolic and circulatory activities.

Microcirculatory disturbances cause the insufficiency of blood entering the organs and tissues. Symptoms include pale complexion, cold skin, thready and weak pulse, hypotension, oliguria and unconsciousness. Shock may be induced by infection, hemorrhage, fluid loss, allergy, trauma or cardiac disease, etc. It can be treated as *jue*-syndrome (syncope) and the exhaustion of *yang* and *yin*.

1) Etiology and pathogenesis

a) The abnormal flow of *qi* and blood: Exogenous pathogenic factors cause the adverse flow of *qi* which brings blood and phlegm to block the upper orifices. The insufficiency of *qi* prevents lucid *yang* from going upward. When lucid *yang* fails to go upward, *qi* collapses and blood does not go to the head. The result is unconsciousness and cold limbs. Generally, the retention of pathogenic heat may induce *jue*-syndrome of the heat type, while the sustained attack of pathogenic heat may cause the exhaustion of *yang-qi* and then *jue*-syndrome of the cold type.

b) The exhaustion of *yang* and *yin*: Blood and sweat, which have the same origin, are *yin* fluids. Since *yin* and *yang* are interdependent, *yang* perishes when *yin* is exhausted, and vice versa. It is for this reason that symptoms such as profuse sweating, severe vomiting and diarrhea and blood loss, are likely to cause the exhaustion of *yin* and *yang*.

2) Syndrome differentiation

Pallor, apathy, cold limbs, cyanosis, sweating, short breath, and weak, thready, rapid or impalpable pulse.

3) Treatment

Principles: To regulate the *qi* activity, restore depleted *yang* or *yin* and recover consciousness.

Methods: Select acupoints along the *Ren* and *Du* meridians to apply acupuncture, using the reinforcing manipulation. Moxibustion can also be used during treatment.

Acupoints: *Yongquan* (KI 1), *Zusanli* (ST 36), *Baihui* (DU 20), *Guanyuan* (RN 4), *Qihai* (RN 6), *Shuigou* (DU 26), *Suliao* (DU 25), *Shenque* (RN 8) and *Neiguan* (PC 6).

Notes: *Baihui* is used to elevate *yang* and restore consciousness, *Yongquan* to increase body fluid, suppress fire and relieve collapse, *Guanyuan* to invigorate healthy *qi*, *Qihai* to strengthen body resistance and replenish primordial *qi*, *Zusanli* to regulate middle *jiao* and *qi*, consolidate superficial resistance and arrest perspiration, *Shuigou* to induce resuscitation, *Suliao* to refresh the spirit, *Neiguan* to strengthen the heart and *Shenque* to restore depleted *yang* and recover consciousness.

4) Other remedies

a) Ear acupuncture: Select the auricular points such as infratragic apex, end of inferior antihelix crus and occiput and points for the brain and heart to apply acupuncture. Insert the needles intermittently and keep them in the skin for 60-120 minutes.

b) Electroacupuncture: Connect the needle with an electroacupuncture apparatus and insert the needle into *Shuigou* (DU 26), *Suliao* (DU 25), *Yongquan* (KI 1) and *Zusanli* (ST 36), applying intermittent wave. Keep the needles in the skin for 60-120 minutes. Adjust the intensity and frequency of stimulation according to the conditions of the patient.

5) Reference materials

a) *Progress on Research in Acupuncture and Moxibustion* says that acupuncture alone can hardly put shock under complete control, though it can help prevent and treat it. That means that it should be used together with other methods in treating shock.

b) Applying acupuncture treatment to 160 patients suffering shock (see *A Selection of Clinical Experiences in Acupuncture and Moxibustion*)

A physical exam showed that 130 of them suffered from infectious/toxic shock, seven from hemorrhagic shock, three from anaphylactic shock, eight from shock due to drug poisoning, six from shock due to chronic prostration and four from shock for some unknown reason. Besides causative treatment and general anti-shock measures, acupuncture was also used to raise blood pressure. When acupuncture did not serve the purpose, hypertensors were put into use.

The main points *Suliao* (DU 25) and *Neiguan* (PC 6) were used together with accessory points *Shaochong* (HT 9), *Shaoze* (SI 1), *Zhongchong* (PC 9), *Shaoze* (SI 1), *Zhongchong* (PC 9), *Shuigou*

(DU 26), *Yongquan* (KI 1), and points on the ear such as tragic notch and point for raising blood pressure. The main points were punctured first and one to two accessory points were added if the treatment did not produce good results in 30 minutes or if the systolic pressure was still lower than 80 millimeters Hg in 60 minutes. The above points were punctured with moderate or strong stimulation. During the needle retention period, the needles were twisted continuously or intermittently for three hours until the systolic pressure was above 80 mm Hg. The treatment proved extremely effective for 122 patients (76.3% of the total), effective for 18 patients (11.2% of the total) and ineffective for 20 patients (1.25% of the total).

c) Applying acupuncture treatment to 50 patients suffering infectious/toxic shock (see *A Selection of Clinical Experiences in Acupuncture and Moxibustion*)

Yongquan (KI 1) and *Zusanli* (ST 36) as well as the ear points for the brain, infratragic apex and intertragus were punctured with a strong stimulation. When the blood pressure rose, the needles were twisted at longer intervals and withdrawn after blood pressure became stable for a few hours. This treatment was effective for 48 patients (two died of serious infection and heart disease). Of the 48 patients, 41 were treated with acupuncture alone and the rest with acupuncture and medicine.

d) Applying moxibustion treatment to 30 patients suffering shock (see *Abstracts of Theses for the Second National Symposium on Acupuncture-Moxibustion and Acupuncture Anesthesia*)

Of the 30 cases of shock, seven were infectious shock and 23 hemorrhagic shock. Moxibustion treatment was given to *Guanyuan* (RN 4). It proved very effective for nine patients, effective for 16 and ineffective for eight.

After moxibustion, the systolic pressure increased greatly and the diastolic one increased slightly. The temperature of the fingertip rose notably and the difference in temperature between the anus and the fingertip decreased remarkably. The heart rate, respiratory frequency and anal temperature remained unchanged. It showed that giving moxibustion to *Guanyuan* could not only increase blood pressure but also improve the perfusion of peripheral capillaries.

Moxibustion, as evidenced in experiments, was considered effective against shock. Giving moxibustion to *Guanyuan* could promote the compensation of the body, improve the hemodynamic status and enhance the function of oxygen transportation. That is why applying moxibustion treatment to *Guanyuan* can be used as a comprehensive measure to treat shock.

7. Acute pain

It refers to pain which accompanies diseases and appears in different parts of the human body. This part of the book will deal with certain kinds of acute pain in the internal organs.

1) Etiology and pathogenesis

a) The attack of exogenous pathogenic cold: Cold is a pathogenic factor of the *yin* type. When cold attacks the meridians, *qi* and blood become stagnant and the meridians are blocked, giving rise to pain.

b) The impediment in the functional activities of *qi*: Emotional upset may impede the functional activities of *qi*, and the stagnation of *qi* may bring about blood-stasis which in turn blocks the meridians. Immoderate eating impairs the spleen and stomach and disturbs their transporting and digestive functions, thus causing the production of dampness-heat. The accumulation of dampness produces phlegm which impedes the functional activities of *qi* and causes pain.

c) The obstruction of meridians by blood-stasis: The irregular flow of blood caused by trauma, improper use of hemostatics or prolonged illness leads to blood-stasis which blocks the meridians and leads to pain.

d) General debility: Debility due to old-age or protracted illness gives rise to the deficiency of *qi* and blood, and the malnutrition of *zang-fu* organs. The hyperactivity of *yang* and deficiency of *yin* or exuberant *yin* or *yang* may impede the functional activities of *qi* and lead to pain.

2) Syndrome differentiation

a) Angina pectoris: Precordial pain which gnaws the back and spreads to the left shoulder and arm, chest distress, palpitation, short breath, spontaneous perspiration, dyspnea, pale complexion, cold limbs, dark purple tongue, deep and thready pulse.

b) Biliary colic: Paroxysms of pain in the right part of the hypochondria, chilliness, fever, bitter taste, thirst, jaundice, poor appetite, constipation, oliguria with dark urine, reddened tongue with yellow coating, taut and rapid pulse.

c) Renal colic: Paroxysms of lumbago which gnaw the middle and lower abdomen accompanied by discontinuous urination, hematuria, dysuria blended of turbid liquid or stone, chilliness, fever, nausea, thin and white or yellow and greasy tongue coating, taut and rapid pulse.

d) Epigastric pain: Distensive pain in the epigastric region which gnaws the hypochondria, predilection for warmth but aversion to cold, belching, acid regurgitation, white tongue coating, and taut pulse.

e) Intestinal colic: Paroxysms of abdominal pain which is accompanied by gurgling sounds, abdominal distention, nausea, diarrhea, constipation, pale complexion with cold sweat running down the cheek, yellow urine, white or yellow tongue coating, deep and taut pulse.

3) Treatment

a) Angina pectoris

Principles: To promote the flow of *qi* and blood, and warm the meridians to ensure the flow of *yang-qi*.

Methods: Select acupoints along the *Ren* and Pericardium meridians to apply acupuncture, using the reducing manipulation.

Acupoints: *Danzhong* (RN 17), *Neiguan* (PC 6), *Ximen* (PC 4) and *Zusanli* (ST 36).

Notes: Angina pectoris is usually caused by the obstruction of *yang-qi* in the chest due to the stagnation of *qi* and blood and cold-phlegm. *Danzhong*, the influential point of *qi*, promotes the flow of *qi*, removes blood-stasis, soothes the chest and alleviates pain; *Neiguan* soothes the diaphragm and heart; *Ximen*, the *xi* point of the Pericardium Meridian, calms the mind and alleviates pain; *Zusanli* regulates *qi* and activates *yang*. These four points, if used in combination, can help remove the obstruction and relieve pain.

b) Biliary colic

Principles: To purge liver-fire, promote bile secretion, activate *qi* and alleviate pain.

Methods: Select acupoints along the Gallbladder and Liver meridians to apply acupuncture, using the reducing manipulation.

Acupoints: *Riyue* (GB 24), *Qimen* (LR 14), *Yanglingquan* (GB 34), *Taichong* (LR 3) and *Xiaxi* (GB 43).

Notes: *Qimen* and *Riyue*, the front *mu* points of the liver and gallbladder respectively, help to regulate the functional activities of *qi* in the *zang-fu* organs. *Yanglingquan*, the *he* point of the Gallbladder Meridian, if used with *Xiaxi* (a *ying* point) can promote bile secretion and disperse dampness-heat. *Taichong* helps to purge liver-fire, regulate *qi* and alleviate pain.

c) Renal colic

Principles: To activate *qi*, alleviate pain, promote diuresis and relieve stranguria.

Methods: Select acupoints along the Bladder, Kidney and *Ren* meridians to apply acupuncture, using the reducing manipulation.

Acupoints: *Shenshu* (BL 23), *Zhongji* (RN 3), *Jingmen* (GB 25), *Weizhong* (BL 40) and *Sanyinjiao* (SP 6).

Notes: The back *shu* point *Shenshu* and the front *mu* point *Jingmen*, if used in combination, can help regulate the flow of *qi* and blood and alleviate pain. *Zhongji* helps regulate the functional activity of *qi* in the urinary bladder and disperse dampness-heat from the lower *jiao*. *Weizhong*, the *he* point along the Gallbladder Meridian, helps to relieve lumbago and backache as the *he* points are effective for disorders in the six *fu* organs. *Sanyinjiao* helps relieve dysuria.

d) Epigastric pain

Principles: To regulate the function of the stomach, sends the unhealthy *qi* downward, regulate the flow of *qi* and alleviate pain.

Methods: Select the back *shu* and front *mu* points along the Stomach Meridian to apply acupuncture, using the reducing manipulation. The reinforcing manipulation can also be used if necessary.

Acupoints: *Zhongwan* (RN 12), *Weishu* (BL 21), *Zusanli* (ST 36) and *Hegu* (LI 4).

Notes: The front *mu* point *Zhongwan* and the back *shu* point *Weishu* can help to regulate *qi* and alleviate pain if used together. *Zusanli*, the lower confluent point of the Stomach Meridian, helps regulate the function of the stomach and send the unhealthy *qi* downward; *Hegu* helps to regulate the flow of *qi* and alleviate pain.

e) Intestinal colic

Principles: To promote the functional activity of *qi* in the *fu* organs, relieve spasm and alleviate pain.

Methods: Select acupoints along the Large Intestine, Stomach and *Ren* meridians to apply acupuncture, using the reducing manipulation. Moxibustion can also be used.

Acupoints: *Zusanli* (ST 36), *Zhongwan* (RN 12), *Tianshu* (ST 25), *Neiting* (ST 44) and *Shangjuxu* (ST 37).

Notes: *Zusanli* and *Zhongwan* regulate the function of the intestine and stomach; *Tianshu*, the front *mu* point along the Large Intestine Meridian, helps regulate the functional activity of *qi* in the intestine; *Shangjuxu*, the lower confluent point, relieves spasm and alleviates pain; *Neiting* relieves pain.

4) Other remedies

a) Ear acupuncture: Select two or three positive points on the auricle and the auricular points such as ear-*Shenmen*, end of inferior antihelix crus, points for the heart, gallbladder, liver, stomach, kidney, lower portion of rectum and brain to apply acupuncture, giving a strong stimulation. Twist the needles every five minutes and keep them in the skin for 30-60 minutes.

b) Electroacupuncture: Choose acupoints in the same way as above. After a needling sensation is obtained, connect the needles with micropulse current to give a strong stimulation, using the intermittent wave or sparse-dense wave. Keep the needles in the skin for 30-60 minutes or even longer if necessary. Take care when treating patients with heart disease.

5) Notes

a) Acupuncture treatment can help relieve acute pain. But to cure pain, the cause must be established and treated.

b) According to *Illustrated Supplementary to the Classified Canon*, periumbilical pain is a disease of the large intestine, *Shuifen* (RN 9), *Tianshu* (ST 25), *Yinjiao* (RN 7) and *Zusanli* (ST 36) should be used to treat the disease.

6) Reference materials

a) Applying electroacupuncture treatment together with magnesium sulfate to 522 people suffering cholelithiasis (see *Abstracts of Theses for the National Symposium on Acupuncture-Moxibustion and Acupuncture Anesthesia*)

Qimen (LR 14) and *Riyue* (GB 24) on the right side were chosen as main points. If cholelithiasis was accompanied by acute pain and enlarged gallbladder, *Danshu* (BL 19) on the right side and the midpoint between *Juque* (RN 14) and *Fuai* (SP 16) on the right side could be added. After insertion, an electroacupuncture apparatus was connected with *Qimen* and *Riyue* and the sparse-dense wave was used with an intensity kept within the limit of the patient. After 60 minutes, the apparatus was removed and 40 ml of 50% magnesium sulfate were taken orally. The treatment was given once a day, and a course of treatment included ten sessions.

The patients who received electroacupuncture treatment were divided into three groups. Those whose condition remained unchanged were in the stable group, those affected spasmodically in the acute-attack group and those in a state of shock in the shock group. The percentage of the stone discharge was 35% in the stable group, 89.7% in the acute-attack group and 50% in the shock group.

b) Applying acupoint injection treatment to 50 patients suffering acute ileus (see *A Selection of Clinical Experiences in Acupuncture and Moxibustion*)

The patients' symptoms had developed for periods of between six hours to nine days before being brought to hospital. The reasons for the attack of the disease included postoperative intestinal adhesion, functional ileus, simple ileus, volvulus and intestinal intersusception. After a needling sensation was obtained, 0.25-0.50 ml procaine HCl was injected into *Zusanli* (ST 36), *Tianshu* (ST 25), *Shangwan* (RN 13), *Xiawan* (RN 10), *Hegu* (LI 4), *Qihai* (RN 6) and *Dachangshu* (BL 25). *Guanyuan* (RN 4) can be added if abdominal pain was severe. Deep injection was not advisable for points at the abdomen. As a result of this treatment, obstruction was removed for most of the patients within 48 hours after injection. Only six patients who did not show any progress required surgical operation. The treatment in this book is mainly effective against mild cases with mechanical ileus.

c) According to *A Selection of Clinical Experiences in Acupuncture and Moxibustion*, 631 patients suffering coronary heart disease and angina pectoris were divided into five groups. The first group had symptoms attributed to a deficiency of *yin*, the second group to a deficiency of *yang*, the third group to a deficiency of *qi*, the fourth group to phlegm accumulation and the fifth group to blood-stasis. *Xinshu* (BL 15), *Juque* (RN 14), *Xinping* (2 *cun* below *Shaohai*, HT 3), *Qihai* (RN 6) and *Zusanli* (ST 36) for the first group; *Jueyinshu* (BL 14), *Danzhong* (RN 17) and *Neiguan* (PC 6) for the second one; *Fenglong* (ST 40) and *Feishu* (BL 13) for the fourth group; *Geshu* (BL 17) and *Xuehai* (SP 10) for the fifth group. The needle was kept in the skin for 20 minutes after a needling sensation was obtained. The treatment was given once a day or every other day, and a whole course of treatment included ten sessions. Another course was given after a rest of three to five days. At least three sessions of treatment were given to the patients and more was offered if necessary.

Of the 506 patients suffering angina pectoris, 219 (43.3% of the total) patients felt much better; 242 (47.81% of the total) found some progress; 45 (8.89% of the total) found the treatment ineffective. Most of the patients suffering from angina pectoris began to feel better after the first or second course of treatment.

APPENDIX

ANNEX 1
ACUPUNCTURE ANESTHESIA

Acupuncture anesthesia is a new method of anesthesia which induces analgesia by puncturing at acupoints on the human body.

1. Characteristics

a) A wide range of indications: Extensive practice has proved that acupuncture anesthesia is effective for 20-30 surgical operations, and is especially useful for goiter, sinus maxillaris, glaucoma and ligation of Fallopian tubes. Acupuncture anesthesia is now used for surgical operation for over 100 medical conditions.

b) Less interference with physiological functions: As acupuncture can help to regulate the functions of the human body, the blood pressure, pulse and respiration of a patient remain relatively stable during an operation using acupuncture anesthesia. Recovery is faster than under other forms of anesthesia.

c) Easy and safe to use: Acupuncture analgesia is simple and can be used without sophisticated equipment. Acupuncture has the least affect on the physiological functions of the patient, and can be used even when the patient is in shock, or is unable to fully use the functions of *zang* and *fu* organs.

2. Methods

a) Preparations: Acupuncture anesthesia demands full preparation before operation. Most of the preparation is the same as for other kinds of anesthesia. The practitioner should determine the patient's response and endurance to acupuncture sensation prior to administration. In addition, to ensure that the patient is relaxed during the operation, the practitioner should explain the anesthesia procedure.

b) Principles of acupoint selection: The principles of acupoint selection for acupuncture anesthesia are almost the same as those for acupuncture and moxibustion treatment. Listed here are two common methods of acupuncture anesthesia: body acupuncture and ear acupuncture.

Acupoint selection for body acupuncture: Give priority to acupoints near the region of incision or along the meridians and pick those points which can produce a strong needling sensation or good analgesic effect on the patient. For example, *Hegu* (LI 4) along the Large Intestine Meridian can be used for operations on the head, face, neck or nape; *Zusanli* (ST 36) along the Stomach Meridian for gastrectomy. Suitable points near the affected part may also be selected, such as *Jiache* (ST 6) and *Quanliao* (SI 18) for upper-gum operation; and *Daimai* (GB 26) for cesarean section. Moreover, painful spots as well as back *shu* and front *mu* points and *Jiaji* (EX-B 2) can be used for operations on the corresponding organs. There are times acupoints are picked according to innervation. Those acupoints usually play a supportive part in operation. For instance, *Futu* (LI 18) is used for operations on thyroid gland, while the third and fourth lumbar nerves, femoral nerve and sciatic nerve are suitable for operations on lower limbs.

The above three principles can be used singularly or in combination.

Acupoint selection for ear acupuncture: The viscera-state doctrine usually serves as a guiding principle of selecting acupoints for ear acupuncture. The kidney point is used for orthopedic operations because the kidney controls the bone; the liver point for ophthalmic operations because the liver opens into the eyes; the lung point can help relieve pain when an incision is made in the skin for the lung controls the skin and hair. A second principle for ear acupuncture is related to an area for operation. For example, the appendix point is used for appendectomy and the neck point for thyroidectomy. In addition, tenderness, electric resistance and discoloration of the auricle may also help in the selection of ear points. For example, reactive spots may be found at the digestive tract of the auricle as stimulating points for gastrectomy and duodenectomy. Neurophysiology can also help in the selection of ear points. For example, the auricular points for mouth and root of auricular vagus nerve are used for abdominal operation since they are controlled by vagus nerve; for better anesthesia and less reaction from the internal organs, the auricular points for brain and end of inferior antihelix crus are selected.

Generally, acupoints and ear points on the affected side or two sides of the body can be used, if the procedure does not interfere with the operation.

Table 23 Commonly Used Points for Acupuncture Anesthesia

Name of Operation	Body Acupuncture	Ear Acupuncture
Correction of strabismus	*Hegu* (LI 4), *Sibai* (ST 2) towards *Chengqi* (ST 1), *Yangbai* (GB 14) towards *Yuyao* (EX-HN 4)	Auricular points for eye and liver
Glaucoma operation	*Hegu* (LI 4), *Zhigou* (SJ 6), *Sibai* (ST 2), *Chengqi* (ST 1), *Yangbai* (GB 14) towards *Yuyao* (EX-HN 4)	Auricular points for eye and liver
Dental extraction	For upper teeth: *Hegu* (LI 4), *Jiache* (ST 6), *Quanliao* (SI 18); for lower teeth: *Hegu* (LI 4), *Daying* (ST 5)	Upper and lower points for tooth-extracting anesthesia
Maxillary sinus operation	*Hegu* (LI 4), *Zhigou* (SJ 6), *Quanliao* (SI 18), *Sibai* (ST 2), *Yangbai* (GB 14) towards *Yuyao* (EX-HN 4), *Sibai* (ST 2) towards *Chengqi* (ST 1)	Infratragic apex towards internal nose, upper jaw towards forehead
Tonsillectomy	*Hegu* (LI 4), *Zhigou* (SJ 6), *Futu* (LI 18)	Auricular points for throat and tonsil
Prosocoele operation	*Quanliao* (SI 18), *Taichong* (LR 3), *Zulinqi* (GB 41), *Jinmen* (BL 63)	Ear-*Shenmen* towards kidney, end of inferior antihelix crus, lung
Pulmonary lobectomy	*Ximen* (PC 4), *Neiguan* (PC 6) towards *Sanyangluo* (SJ 8)	Ear-*Shenmen*, lung
Separation of mitral valve	*Hegu* (LI 4), *Neiguan* (PC 6), *Zhigou* (SJ 6)	Ear-*Shenmen*, lung, chest
Esophageal operation	*Hegu* (LI 4), *Neiguan* (PC 6)	
Resection of mammary tumor	*Hegu* (LI 4), *Neiguan* (PC 6)	Ear-*Shenmen*, end of inferior antihelix crus, intertragus, chest, lung
Gastrectomy	*Zusanli* (ST 36), *Shangjuxu* (ST 37)	Auricular points for stomach, ear-*Shenmen*, end of inferior antihelix crus, lung
Thyroid operation	*Hegu* (LI 4), *Neiguan* (PC 6), *Futu* (LI 18)	Ear-*Shenmen*, lung, neck, intertragus
Cystectomy	*Zusanli* (ST 36), *Sanyinjiao* (SP 6), *Dannang* (EX-LE 6)	Gallbladder, abdomen, ear-*Shenmen*, end of inferior antihelix crus, lung, brain
Splenotomy	*Zusanli* (ST 36), *Sanyinjiao* (SP 6), *Taichong* (LR 3)	
Appendectomy	*Shangjuxu* (ST 37), *Taichong* (LR 3), *Lanwei* (EX-LE 7)	Appendix, mouth
Herniorrhaphy	*Yinlingquan* (SP 9), *Sanyinjiao* (SP 6), *Henggu* (KI 11), *Weidao* (GB 28)	Ear-*Shenmen*, external genitalia, brain
Laparotomy	*Zusanli* (ST 36), *Sanyinjiao* (SP 6), *Daimai* (GB 26) and the area near the incision	Ear-*Shenmen*, uterus, abdomen, lung
Tubal ligation	*Sanyinjiao* (SP 6)	Lung, brain, uterus
Cystolithotomy, cystostomy	*Sanyinjiao* (SP 6), *Zhongji* (RN 3), *Guanyuan* (RN 4)	Auricular points for bladder, abdomen, ear-*Shenmen*, lung

Closed reduction of fracture of limbs	Upper limbs: *Jiquan* (HT 1), *Quchi* (LI 11), *Hegu* (LI 4); lower limbs: *Yanglingquan* (GB 34), *Xuanzhong* (GB 39), *Taichong* (LR 3), *Waiqiu* (GB 36) and one or two sensitive points on both ends of the fracture	Auricular points for the upper limbs: wrist, elbow, shoulder; lower limbs: knee, hip, ankle, ear-*Shenmen*, kidney, the corresponding area of fracture

c) Needling techniques: It is very important for a doctor to help the patient get a needling sensation, and to assist in the smooth progress of the operation.

Preoperative induction: The method is to give stimulation through needling before the operation begins to help the patient regulate the body's function, and mentally prepare for the operation. The stimulation usually lasts about 15-20 minutes.

Methods: When using body puncture to cause anesthesia, the needle is usually rotated, lifted and thrust. Generally, it is rotated 120-200 times every minute at an angle of 90-360 degrees, and the amplitude of lifting and thrusting is within 10 mm. For ear acupuncture, the amplitude of rotation should be small lest the auricle should be injured.

Electric stimulation: An electroacupuncture apparatus is connected with the needle after a needling sensation is obtained, to achieve a better analgesic effect. The method of giving electric stimulation is the same as that of giving routine electroacupuncture treatment.

Other stimulating methods such as acupoint injection and finger pressure are also adopted in anesthesia.

The practitioner should note that the intensity of stimulation in acupuncture anesthesia should not be too strong, or the patient will feel a pain somewhere in the body. Usually, soreness, numbness, distention and heaviness are adequate indications.

3. Adjuvants

As with other kinds of anesthesia, acupuncture anesthesia should not be used alone. Acupuncture is much more effective if used with some adjuvants. There are many kinds of adjuvants, and the most common ones are sedatives, analgesics and anticholinergics.

The sedatives include phenobarbital, acetylpromazine, holoperidol and diazepam. Typical analgesics are dolantin, morphine and fentanyl, with the final two being used carefully for their toxic and side effects. As for the anticholinergics, atropine and scopolamine can be often used during surgical operations.

Adjuvants should be used at the right time and in proper doses to avoid drowsiness and the loss of an opportunity to cooperate with the doctor. Generally, an adult patient should be injected subcutaneously with 0.5 mg of atropine 60 minutes before an operation, using an intravenous dose of 50 mg dolantin 10-15 minutes in advance. Sedatives, analgesics, local anesthetics or muscle relaxants are administered as changes occur in the operation. Relaxants must be used with care, and effective measures should be taken immediately if the surgical procedure does not proceed as planned.

4. Requirements

It should be noted that the effectiveness of acupuncture anesthesia is usually determined by acupuncture and some other factors such as the use of adjuvants, the environment of the operation, the mental state of the patient, the typical reaction of each patient, and the skill of the surgeon. Doctors should therefore be flexible in their procedure during the operation.

There are some unresolved problems in acupuncture anesthesia, including incomplete analgesia, muscular tension and reaction due to the traction of the internal organs. Since the patient is clear-minded in the operation, everything should be done steadily, accurately, gently and rapidly to reduce pain and assist in early recovery. Care should be taken to ensure that the skin is not clamped with toothed forceps, the muscular layers are not separated bluntly, the internal organs are not pulled with force, and the skin is cut rapidly.

The combination of acupuncture anesthesia with drug anesthesia is very much in vogue at home and abroad. The use of this method not only improves the effect of acupuncture anesthesia but also reduces the dose and side effects of narcotics. It is believed that acupuncture anesthesia will eventually become the preferred method of anesthesia.

ANNEX 2
ZIWULIUZHU ACUPUNCTURE

1. Brief introduction

Ziwuliuzhu is a theory of acupuncture treatment that was developed in ancient China. *Ziwu* represents time, such as the time of a day and the lunar period, while *liuzhu* indicates the flow of *qi* and blood in the human body. More specifically, Zi refers to midnight and the 11th month of the lunar calendar, while *wu* stands for noon and the fifth month of the lunar calendar. Changes in light, temperature and climate during the times and seasons are closely related to the flow of *qi* and blood in the human body. It is after a long period of practice that the doctrine of *ziwuliuzhu* has established itself as a part of traditional Chinese medicine.

1) Heavenly stems and earthly branches standing for the years, months and days.

a) Heavenly stems: *Jia* (甲), *Yi* (乙), *Bing* (丙), *Ding* (丁), *Wu* (戊), *Ji* (己), *Geng* (庚), *Xin* (辛), *Ren* (壬) and *Gui* (癸).

b) Earthly branches: *Zi* (子), *Chou* (丑), *Yin* (寅), *Mao* (卯), *Chen* (辰), *Si* (巳), *Wu* (午), *Wei* (未), *Shen* (申), *You* (酉), *Xu* (戌) and *Hai* (亥).

A heavenly stem can be used with an earthly branch: *Jia-Zi, Yi-Chou, Bing-Yin, Ding-Mao* and *Wu-Chen*. Since there are ten heavenly stems and 12 earthly branches, when used together to indicate the years, months, days or hours, they must repeat from beginning to end five and six times respectively before one *Jia-Zi* meets another *Jia-Zi*. (See Table 24)

Table 24 Heavenly Stems in Combination with Earthly Branches

Jia-Zi	*Yi-Chou*	*Bing-Yin*	*Ding-Mao*	*Wu-Chen*	*Ji-Si*	*Geng-Wu*	*Xin-Wei*	*Ren-Shen*	*Gui-You*
Jia-Xu	*Yi-Hai*	*Bing-Zi*	*Ding-Chou*	*Wu-Yin*	*Ji-Mao*	*Geng-Chen*	*Xin-Si*	*Ren-Wu*	*Gui-Wei*
Jia-Shen	*Yi-You*	*Bing-Xu*	*Ding-Hai*	*Wu-Zi*	*Ji-Chou*	*Geng-Yin*	*Xin-Mao*	*Ren-Chen*	*Gui-Si*
Jia-Wu	*Yi-Wei*	*Bing-Shen*	*Ding-You*	*Wu-Xu*	*Ji-Hai*	*Geng-Zi*	*Xin-Chou*	*Ren-Yin*	*Gui-Mao*
Jia-Chen	*Yi-Si*	*Bing-Wu*	*Ding-Wei*	*Wu-Shen*	*Ji-You*	*Geng-Xu*	*Xin-Hai*	*Ren-Zi*	*Gui-Chou*
Jia-Yin	*Yi-Mao*	*Bing-Chen*	*Ding-Si*	*Wu-Wu*	*Ji-Wei*	*Geng-Shen*	*Xin-You*	*Ren-Xu*	*Gui-Hai*

c) The attributes of heavenly stems and earthly branches

Each heavenly stem or earthly branch has its own ordinal number with the odd number attributing to *yang* and the even number to *yin*. In other words, *Jia, Bing, Wu, Geng* and *Ren* are heavenly stems of the *yang* type, while *Chou, Mao, Si, Wei, You* and *Hai* are earthly branches of the *yin* type, see Table 25. The principles of *ziwuliuzhu* are to use acupoints along the *yang* meridians during *yang* periods on *yang* days but to use acupoints along the *yin* meridians during *yin* periods on *yin* days.

Table 25 The *Yin-Yang* Attribution of Heavenly Stems and Earthly Branches

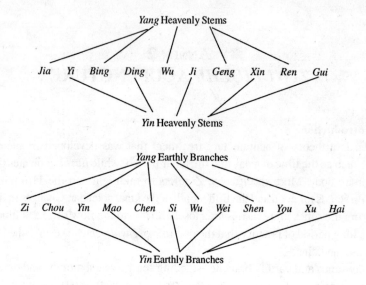

2) Two-hour periods

According to the timing method developed in ancient China, and using a 24-hour day, two hours stand for one *shichen*, and 24 hours are divided into 12 *shichen* (two-hour) periods, designated the 12 earthly branches. (See Table 26)

Table 26 Two-Hour Periods in Comparison with Time (Hour)

Two-Hour Periods	Zi	Chou	Yin	Mao	Chen	Si	Wu	Wei	Shen	You	Xu	Hai
Time (Hour)	23-1	1-3	3-5	5-7	7-9	9-11	11-13	13-15	15-17	17-19	19-21	21-23

3) Designating the years, months and days with heavenly stems and earthly branches

Heavenly stems and earthly branches stand for the year, month and day of the lunar calendar. To find the name of 1986 in the lunar calendar, one should know the name of present year in the lunar calendar. For example, this year is 1997 and it is called *Ding-Chou* in the lunar calendar. According to this method, the name of 1988 is *Wu-Chen*. To find the name of each month, start the first month with *Yin*, the second one with *Mao*, the third one with *Chen*, and so on. This book uses the same method as the above to find days.

Designating the days with the heavenly stems and earthly branches is important in *ziwuliuzhu*. Some prior knowledge is necessary to use acupuncture treatment correctly. To designate the days with the above method, one must first select the appropriate heavenly stem and earthly branch for the first day of a given year in the Gregorian calendar. Only then can one nominate a designated day. For example, if you know that *Yi-Si* fell on the first day of 1986, you can figure out that *Ji-Wei* fell on January 15 that year by referring to the sexagenary cycle. Care must be taken to select the correct days during the calculation. According to the Gregorian calendar, each month has either 30 or 31 days (except February which has 28 days in a non-leap year but 29 in a leap year), see Table 27.

Table 27 New Year's Day in the Stem-Branch System
(from 1984 to 2007)

Leap Year		Common Year					
Year	New Year's Day in Sexagenary Cycles	Year	New Year's Day in Sexagenary Cycles	Year	New Year's Day in Sexagenary Cycles	Year	New Year's Day in Sexagenary Cycles
1984	Jia-Wu	1985	Geng-Zi	1986	Yi-Si	1987	Geng-Xu
1988	Yi-Mao	1989	Xin-You	1990	Bing-Yin	1991	Xin-Wei
1992	Bing-Zi	1993	Ren-Wu	1994	Ding-Hai	1995	Ren-Chen
1996	Ding-You	1997	Gui-Mao	1998	Wu-Shen	1999	Gui-Chou
2000	Wu-Wu	2001	Jia-Zi	2002	Ji-Si	2003	Jia-Xu
2004	Ji-Mao	2005	Yi-You	2006	Geng-Yin	2007	Yi-Wei

4) Combining heavenly stems with twelve meridians

Heavenly stems are used together with meridians in traditional Chinese medicine. For example, the Gallbladder Meridian is used on *Jia* days and the Liver Meridian used on *Yi* days. (See Table 28)

Table 28 Heavenly Stems with the Twelve Meridians

Heavenly Stems	Twelve Meridians
Jia	Gallbladder Meridian
Yi	Liver Meridian
Bing	Small Intestine Meridian, *Sanjiao* Meridian
Ding	Heart Meridian, Pericardium Meridian
Wu	Stomach Meridian
Ji	Spleen Meridian
Geng	Large Intestine Meridian
Xin	Lung Meridian
Ren	Bladder Meridian
Gui	Kidney Meridian

This principle of combination is mainly used in *ziwuliuzhu*. For instance, *Zuqiaoyin* (GB 44), the *jiing* point of the Gallbladder Meridian, is used as the first point on *Jia* days and *Shaoze* (SI 1), the *jiing* point of the Small Intestine Meridian, is used as the first point on *Bing* days.

Ziwuliuzhu uses two types of points to find acupoints.

a) Five *shu* points

The five *shu* points near the elbow and knee have proved effective against diseases in acupuncture treatment. If used with the heavenly stems and earthly branches in the light of the flow of *qi* and blood, they can produce still better results. Following is a table in which you can find the relationship between five *shu* points and *yin-yang* as well as Five Elements. (See Table 29)

Table 29 The Five Shu Points in Combination with
Yin-Yang and the Five Elements

The Five *Shu* Points on the *Yang* Meridians

Name of Meridian	Points				
	Jiing (metal)	*Ying* (water)	*Shu* (wood)	*Jing* (fire)	*He* (earth)
Gallbladder Meridian (wood)	Zuqiaoyin (GB 44)	Xiaxi (GB 43)	Zulinqi (GB 41)	Yangfu (GB 38)	Yanglingquan (GB 34)
Small Intestine Meridian (fire)	Shaoze (SI 1)	Qiangu (SI 2)	Houxi (SI 3)	Yanggu (SI 5)	Xiaohai (SI 8)
Stomach Meridian (earth)	Lidui (ST 45)	Neiting (ST 44)	Xiangu (ST 43)	Jiexi (ST 41)	Zusanli (ST 36)
Large Intestine Meridian (metal)	Shangyang (LI 1)	Erjian (LI 2)	Sanjian (LI 3)	Yangxi (LI 5)	Quchi (LI 11)
Bladder Meridian (water)	Zhiyin (BL 67)	Tonggu (BL 66)	Shugu (BL 65)	Kunlun (BL 60)	Weizhong (BL 40)
Sanjiao Meridian (fire)	Guanchong (SJ 1)	Yemen (SJ 2)	Zhongzhu (SJ 3)	Zhigou (SJ 6)	Tianjing (SJ 10)

The Five *Shu* Points on the *Yin* Meridians

Name of Meridian	Points				
	Jiing (wood)	*Ying* (fire)	*Shu* (earth)	*Jing* (metal)	*He* (water)
Liver Meridian (wood)	Dadun (LR 1)	Xingjian (LR 2)	Taichong (LR 3)	Zhongfeng (LR 4)	Ququan (LR 8)
Heart Meridian (fire)	Shaochong (HT 9)	Shaofu (HT 8)	Shenmen (HT 7)	Lingdao (HT 4)	Shaohai (HT 3)
Spleen Meridian (earth)	Yinbai (SP 1)	Dadu (SP 2)	Taibai (SP 3)	Shangqiu (SP 5)	Yinlingquan (SP 9)
Lung Meridian (metal)	Shaoshang (LU 11)	Yuji (LU 10)	Taiyuan (LU 9)	Jingqu (LU 8)	Chize (LU 5)
Kidney Meridian (water)	Yongquan (KI 1)	Rangu (KI 2)	Taixi (KI 3)	Fuliu (KI 7)	Yingu (KI 10)
Pericardium Meridian (fire)	Zhongchong (PC 9)	Laogong (PC 8)	Daling (PC 7)	Jianshi (PC 5)	Quze (PC 3)

b) Twelve *yuan* points

The twelve *yuan* points are also essential points to be used in *ziwuliuzhu*. A *yuan* point should be selected with a *shu* point on the same day that both of their meridians are combined with a heavenly stem and earthly branch.

Table 30 The *Yuan* Points of the Twelve Meridians

Meridians	*Yuan* Points	Meridians	*Yuan* Points	Meridians	*Yuan* Points
Heart Meridian	Shenmen (HT 7)	Liver Meridian	Taichong (LR 3)	Spleen Meridian	Taibai (SP 3)
Lung Meridian	Taiyuan (LU 9)	Kidney Meridian	Taixi (KI 3)	Pericardium Meridian	Daling (PC 7)
Gallbladder Meridian	Qiuxu (GB 40)	Stomach Meridian	Chongyang (ST 42)	Large Intestine Meridian	Hegu (LI 4)
Small Intestine Meridian	Wangu (SI 4)	Bladder Meridian	Jinggu (BL 64)	Sanjiao Meridian	Yangchi (SJ 4)

In routine acupuncture treatment, the *yuan* points are used to treat the disorders of the 12 regular meridians and their corresponding *zang-fu* organs, which provides another effective treatment to *ziwuliuzhu*. (See Table 30)

2. Acupoint selection in the *ziwuliuzhu* doctrine

There are two ways of selecting acupoints according to the *ziwuliuzhu* doctrine.

1) *Nazi*

The meridians are selected in the order of *shichen*. For example, points along the Lung Meridian should be selected during the *Yin* period and those along the Large Intestine Meridian during the *Mao* period.

a) Matching the twelve *shichen* with the twelve regular meridians. (See Table 31)

Table 31 Twelve Two-Hour Periods with the Twelve Meridians

Meridians	Two-Hour Periods
Lung Meridian	*Yin* (3:00 am-5:00 am)
Large Intestine Meridian	*Mao* (5:00 am-7:00 am)
Stomach Meridian	*Chen* (7:00 am-9:00 am)
Spleen Meridian	*Si* (9:00 am-11:00 am)
Heart Meridian	*Wu* (11:00 am-1:00 pm)
Small Intestine Meridian	*Wei* (1:00 pm-3:00 pm)
Bladder Meridian	*Shen* (3:00 pm-5:00 pm)
Kidney Meridian	*You* (5:00 pm-7:00 pm)
Pericardium Meridian	*Xu* (7:00 pm-9:00 pm)
Sanjiao Meridian	*Hai* (9:00 pm-11:00 pm)
Gallbladder Meridian	*Zi* (11:00 pm-1:00 am)
Liver Meridian	*Chou* (1:00 am-3:00 am)

b) Selecting acupoints according to principle of reinforcing the mother and reducing the child.

On the principle of matching the 12 regular meridians with the stem-branch combination, something should be done to reduce the son or secondary point along a given meridian when its *qi* is effulgent, but to reinforce the mother or major point along it when its *qi* is less effulgent. (See Table 32)

2) *Najia*

Najia is the main method of *ziwuliuzhu* acupuncture. The principle is to select acupoints along a given meridian at a given time. In other words, acupoints along *yang* meridians should be selected during *yang* periods on *yang* days while those along *yin* meridians are picked during *yin* periods on *yin* days. The acupoints to be used should be in conformity with the mutual-generation relationship of meridians and acupoints which is subjected to the Five-Element attribution.

For instance, the Gallbladder Meridian controls *qi* on *Jia* days so that its *jiing* point Zuqiaoyin (GB 44) should be selected during the *Jia-Xu* period. In accordance with the principle of selecting acupoints along *yang* meridians during *yang* periods on *yang* days, the *yang* period after *Jia-Xu* is *Bing-Zi* on a *Yi* day. Since the gallbladder of the *Jia* type attributes to wood which promotes fire, Qiangu (SI 2), the *ying* point along the Small Intestine Meridian of the *Bing* type, is selected during the *Bing-Zi* period, because Zuqiaoyin (GB 44) selected during the *Jia-Xu* period attributes to metal which promotes water and Qiangu attributes to water. The *yang* period after *Bing-Zi* is *Wu-Yin*, since the Small Intestine Meridian and *Bing-Zi* attribute to fire which promotes earth, Xiangu (ST 43), the *shu* point along the Stomach

Table 32 Selecting Acupoints by the Principle of "Reinforcing the Mother and Reducing the Child"

Meridians	Qi Infusing Time	Reinforcing				Reducing		
		Mother Points	Five Elements of Acupoints	Time for Reinforcing	Child Points	Five Elements of Acupoints	Time for Reducing
Lung	*Yin* (3:00 am–5:00 am)	*Taiyuan* (LU 9)	Earth	*Mao* (5:00 am–7:00 am)	*Chize* (LU 5)	Water	*Yin* (3:00 am–5:00 am)
Large Intestine	*Mao* (5:00 am–7:00 am)	*Quchi* (LI 11)	Earth	*Chen* (7:00 am–9:00 am)	*Erjian* (LI 2)	Water	*Mao* (5:00 am–7:00 am)
Stomach	*Chen* (7:00 am–9:00 am)	*Jiexi* (ST 4)	Fire	*Si* (9:00 am–11:00 am)	*Lidui* (ST 45)	Metal	*Chen* (7:00 am–9:00 am)
Spleen	*Si* (9:00 am–11:00 am)	*Dadu* (SP 2)	Fire	*Wu* (11:00 am–1:00 pm)	*Shangqiu* (SP 5)	Metal	*Si* (9:00 am–11:00 am)
Heart	*Wu* (11:00 am–1:00 pm)	*Shaochong* (HT 9)	Wood	*Wei* (1:00 pm–3:00 pm)	*Shenmen* (HT 7)	Earth	*Wu* (11:00 am–1:00 pm)
Small Intestine	*Wei* (1:00 pm–3:00 pm)	*Houxi* (SI 3)	Wood	*Shen* (3:00 pm–5:00 pm)	*Xiaohai* (SI 8)	Earth	*Wei* (1:00 pm–3:00 pm)
Bladder	*Shen* (3:00 pm–5:00 pm)	*Zhiyin* (BL 67)	Metal	*You* (5:00 pm–7:00 pm)	*Shugu* (BL 65)	Wood	*Shen* (3:00 pm–5:00 pm)
Kidney	*You* (5:00 pm–7:00 pm)	*Fuliu* (KI 7)	Metal	*Xu* (7:00 pm–9:00 pm)	*Yongquan* (KI 1)	Wood	*You* (5:00 pm–7:00 pm)
Pericardium	*Xu* (7:00 pm–9:00 pm)	*Zhongchong* (PC 9)	Wood	*Hai* (9:00 pm–11:00 pm)	*Daling* (PC 7)	Earth	*Xu* (7:00 pm–9:00 pm)
Sanjiao	*Hai* (9:00 pm–11:00 pm)	*Zhongzhu* (SJ 3)	Wood	*Zi* (11:00 pm–1:00 am)	*Tianjing* (SJ 10)	Earth	*Hai* (9:00 pm–11:00 pm)
Gallbladder	*Zi* (11:00 pm–1:00 am)	*Xiaxi* (GB 43)	Water	*Chou* (1:00 am–3:00 am)	*Yangfu* (GB 38)	Fire	*Zi* (11:00 pm–1:00 am)
Liver	*Chou* (1:00 am–3:00 am)	*Ququan* (LR 8)	Water	*Yin* (3:00 am–5:00 am)	*Xingjian* (LR 2)	Fire	*Chou* (1:00 am–3:00 am)

(earth) Meridian, is selected during the *Wu-Yin* period. Because *Qiangu* attributes to water which promotes wood, *Xiangu* along the Stomach Meridian attributes to wood. *Geng-Chen* is the next *yang* period. *Wu* pertains to earth which generates metal, and *Yangxi* (LI 5) along the Large Intestine (metal) Meridian is selected during the *Geng-Chen* period. This is because *Xiangu* selected during the *Wu-Yin* period pertains to wood which generates fire and *Yangxi* (LI 5) along the Large Intestine Meridian pertains to fire. *Ren-Wu* is the next *yang* period. *Geng* pertains to metal which generates water, so *Weizhong* (BL 40), the *he* point along the Bladder (water) Meridian, is selected during the *Ren-Wu* period, for *Yangxi* (LI 5) selected during the *Geng-Chen* period pertains to fire which promotes earth, and *Weizhong* along the Bladder Meridian pertains to earth. *Jia-Shen* is a *yang* period after *Ren-Wu*. *Jia* appears once again to select acupoints. This is called a reappearance of heavenly stem day in *ziwuliuzhu*. If it is a *yang* day, an acupoint along the *Sanjiao* Meridian can be used, which is called the convergence of *qi* in *Sanjiao*. If it is a *yin* day, an acupoint along the Pericardium Meridian can be used, which is called the flow of blood back to the Pericardium Meridian. Therefore, acupoint along the *Sanjiao* Meridian is selected during the *Jia-Shen* period. In conformity with the principle of mutual generation in the Five Elements, *Yemen* (SJ 2), the *ying* point along the *Sanjiao* Meridian, is selected because *Yemen* pertains to water which generates wood on the premise that it is a *Jia* day when the Gallbladder (wood) Meridian controls *qi*. All these show that a *yuan* point along certain meridian on a given day should be used with a *shu* point.

After passing through the points and the meridians acting on a *Jia* day, *qi* and blood flow into the points and meridians acting on a *Yi* day. On a *Yi* day, since the Liver Meridian controls *qi*, *Dadun* (LR 1), the *jiing* point along the Liver Meridian, is selected during the *Yi-You* period. In accordance with the principle of selecting acupoints along *yin* meridians during *yin* periods on *yin* days, the *yin* period after *Yi-You* is *Ding-Hai*. Since *Yi* and the Liver Meridian attribute to wood which generates fire, *Shaofu* (HT 8), the *ying* point along the Heart (fire) Meridian, is selected during the *Ding-Hai* period. Because *Dadun* (LR 1) selected during the *Yi-You* period attributes to wood which promotes fire, the *ying* point along the Heart Meridian attributes to fire. *Ji-Chou* is the next *yin* period. As *Ding-Hai* attributes to fire which generates earth, *Taibai* (SP 3), the *shu* point along the Spleen Meridian, is selected during the *Ji-Chou* period. Because *Shaofu* (HT 8) selected during the *Ding-Hai* period attributes to fire which generates earth, and *Taibai*, the *shu* point along the Spleen Meridian, attributes to earth. The *yin* period following *Ji-Chou* is *Xin-Mao*. *Ji* attributes to earth which generates metal, and *Jingqu* (LU 8) along the Lung (metal) Meridian is selected during the *Xin-Mao* period because *Taibai* selected during the *Ji-Chou* period attributes to earth which generates metal, and *Jingqu* along the Lung Meridian pertains to metal. The *yin* period after *Xin-Mao* is *Gui-Si*. *Xin* attributes to metal which generates water, and *Yingu* (KI 10), the *he* point along the Kidney (water) Meridian, is selected during the *Gui-Si* period because *Jingqu* selected during the *Xin-Mao* period attributes to metal which generates water, and *Yingu*, the *he* point along the Kidney Meridian, attributes to water. The *yin* period following *Gui-Si* is *Yi-Wei* which meets another day of the *Yi* period, signifying the reappearance of a heavenly-stem day, and the Pericardium Meridian should be selected on the principle of sending blood back to the pericardium. In line with mutual generation in the Five Elements, *Laogong* (PC 8) along the Pericardium Meridian is selected. Since the Liver Meridian controls *qi* and attributes to wood which generates fire, *Laogong* attributes to fire. On a *Yi* day, *Taichong* (LR 3), the *yuan* point along the Liver Meridian which acts on that day, should be selected simultaneously. This is called a return to the original condition.

In short, the selection of acupoints should start with *Jia* in the heavenly stems. With the end of a ten-stem cycle, a new cycle starts for the second time with *Jia* and ends with *Gui*.

The following points should be noted when using the *najia* method:

1) Acupoints must be selected according to the above principle. For example, *Zuqiaoyin* (GB 44) is selected during the *Wu* period on a *Jia* day, and *Qiangu* (SI 2) selected during the *Zi* period on a *Yi* day.

At the same time, indications of each point should also be taken into account so that better results will be achieved in treatment.

2) An acupoint can still be selected when the best time is over, or the day is good for it but the time not, or vice versa. Usually, an acupoint is selected during a *yang* period on a *yang* day. If the current day is a *yin* period on a *yang* day or a *yang* period on a *yin* day, there is still a solution, because *Jia* matches with *Ji*, *Yi* with *Geng*, *Bing* with *Xin*, *Ding* with *Ren*, and *Wu* with *Gui*. So an acupoint for a *Jia* day can also be selected on a *Ji* day, and vice versa. This principle of acupoint selection may help a doctor to deal with emergency cases as more acupoints can be selected using the *ziwuliuzhu* doctrine.

3) Acupoints should be selected in the light of both the time and symptoms. Usually, the acupoints selected on the principle of time should be used before those chosen on the principle of symptoms.

4) In case of chronic diseases, when the time of consultation is not coincident with the day and period for acupoint selection, the treatment should be postponed to the expected period and day. (See Table 4-1)

Table 4-1 Selecting Acupoints with *Najia* Method in *Ziwuliuzhu*

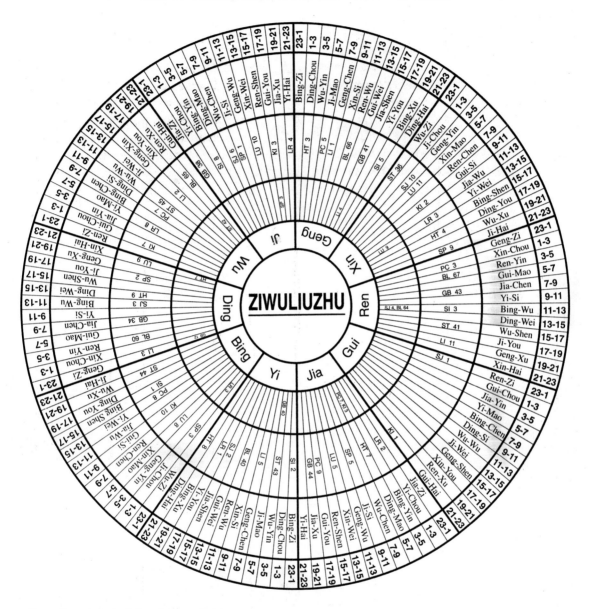

Notes: (from the inner circle to the outer circle)

The first ring is the name of the diagram;

The second ring is heavenly stems of days;

The third ring is the *yuan* points in *Najia* method;

The fourth ring is the points to be selected according to *Najia* method;

The fifth ring is the twelve *shichen*;

The sixth ring is the corresponding time (hour) to *shichen*.

图书在版编目(CIP) 数据

中医中药教材 第四卷：英文/国家中医药管理局编．
－北京：新世界出版社，1997.2
ISBN 7－80005－301－6
I. 中...
II. 国...
III. 中国医药学－教材－英文
IV.R2

中医中药教材（第四册）
国家中医药管理局 编

*

新世界出版社出版
(北京百万庄路 24 号)
北京外文印刷厂印刷
中国国际图书贸易总公司发行
(中国北京车公庄西路 35 号)
北京邮政信箱第 399 号 邮政编码 100044
1997 年(英文)第一版
ISBN 7－80005－301－6
05800
14－E－2838SD